The fact that I am so young
So immature
Seems unforgivable to
The decrepit
Perfect and faultless adults

BLEACH 53 The Deathberry Returns 2

STARS AND

Riruka Dokugamine

銀城空吾
Kugo Ginjo

Ichigo Kurosaki

★ plot

Ichigo Kurosaki meets Soul Reaper Rukia Kuchiki and ends up helping her eradicate Hollows. After developing his powers as a Soul Reaper, Ichigo enters battle against Aizen and his dark ambitions! Ichigo finally defeats Aizen in exchange for his powers as a Soul Reaper.

With the battle over, Ichigo regains his routine life. But his tranquil days end when he meets Ginjo, who offers to help Ichigo get his powers back. But it was all a dark plot by Ginjo and his partner Tsukishima! As Ichigo sinks into despair after his powers are robbed from him once again, a mysterious blade pierces him. At the other end of the blade is Rukia! A deafening roar and smoke then surrounds Ichigo and reveals...

BLEACH ALL

雪緒

Yukio

ジャッキー・トリスタン

Jackie Tristan

Giriko Kutsuzawa

沓澤ギリコ

STORIES

BLEACH53

The Deathberry Returns 2

Contents

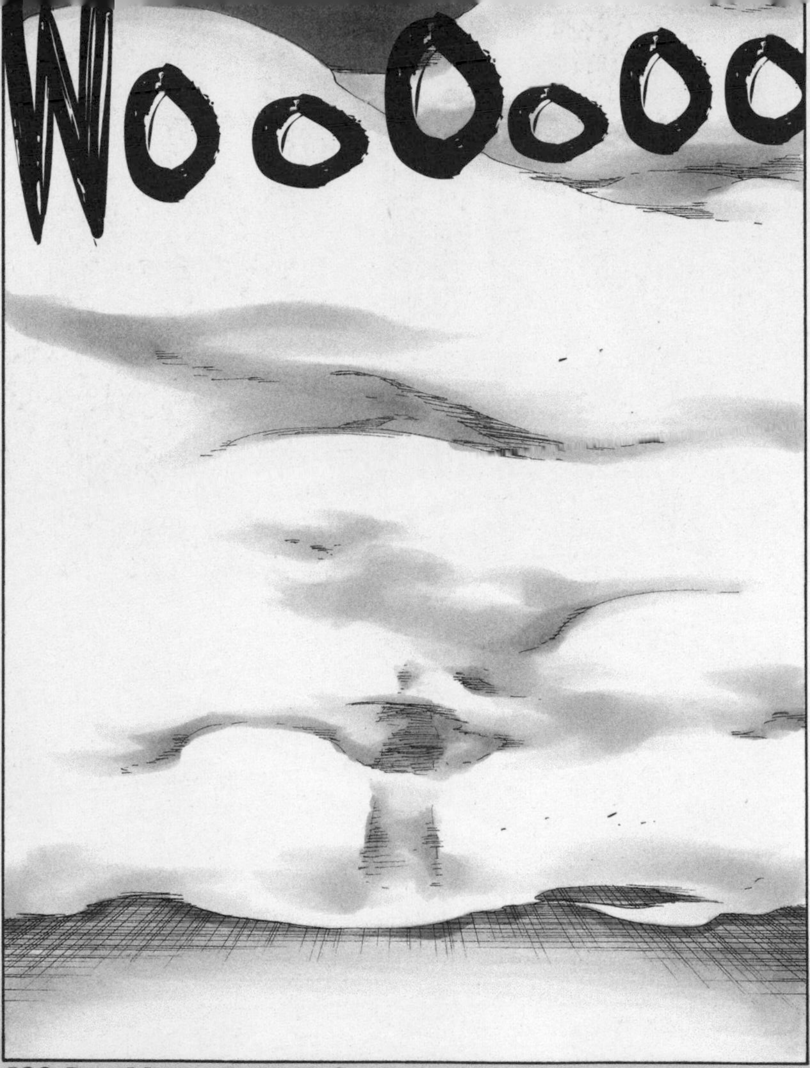
WOOOOOO

460. Deathberry Returns 2

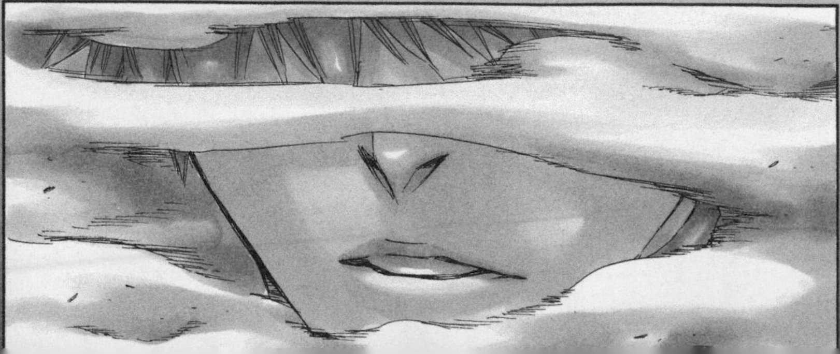

460. Returns 2

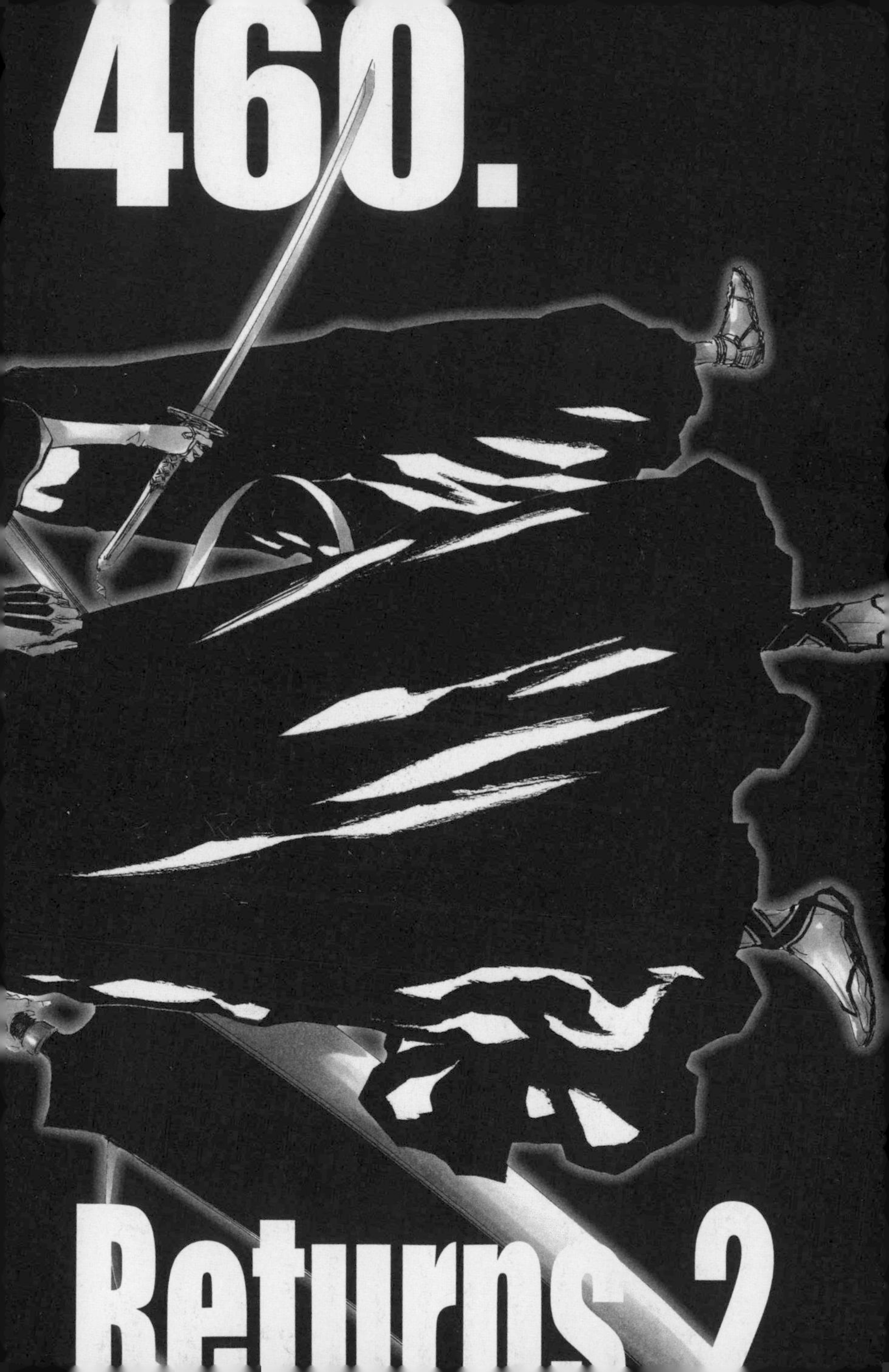

BLEACH

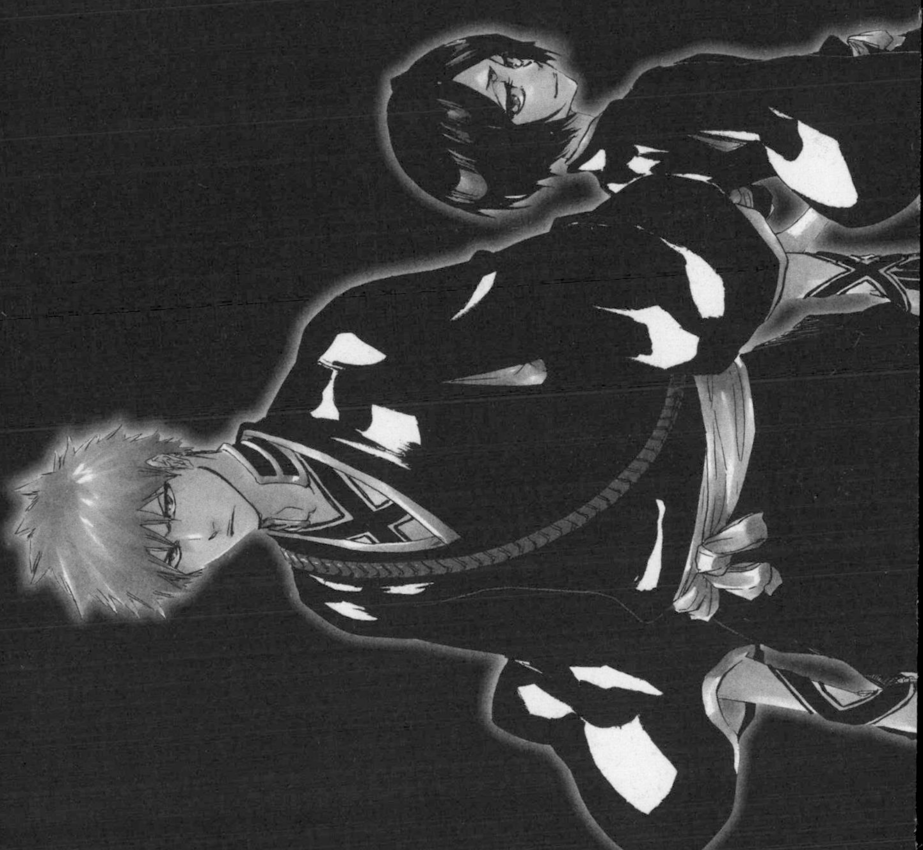

Deathberry

BLEACH
ブリーチ

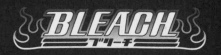

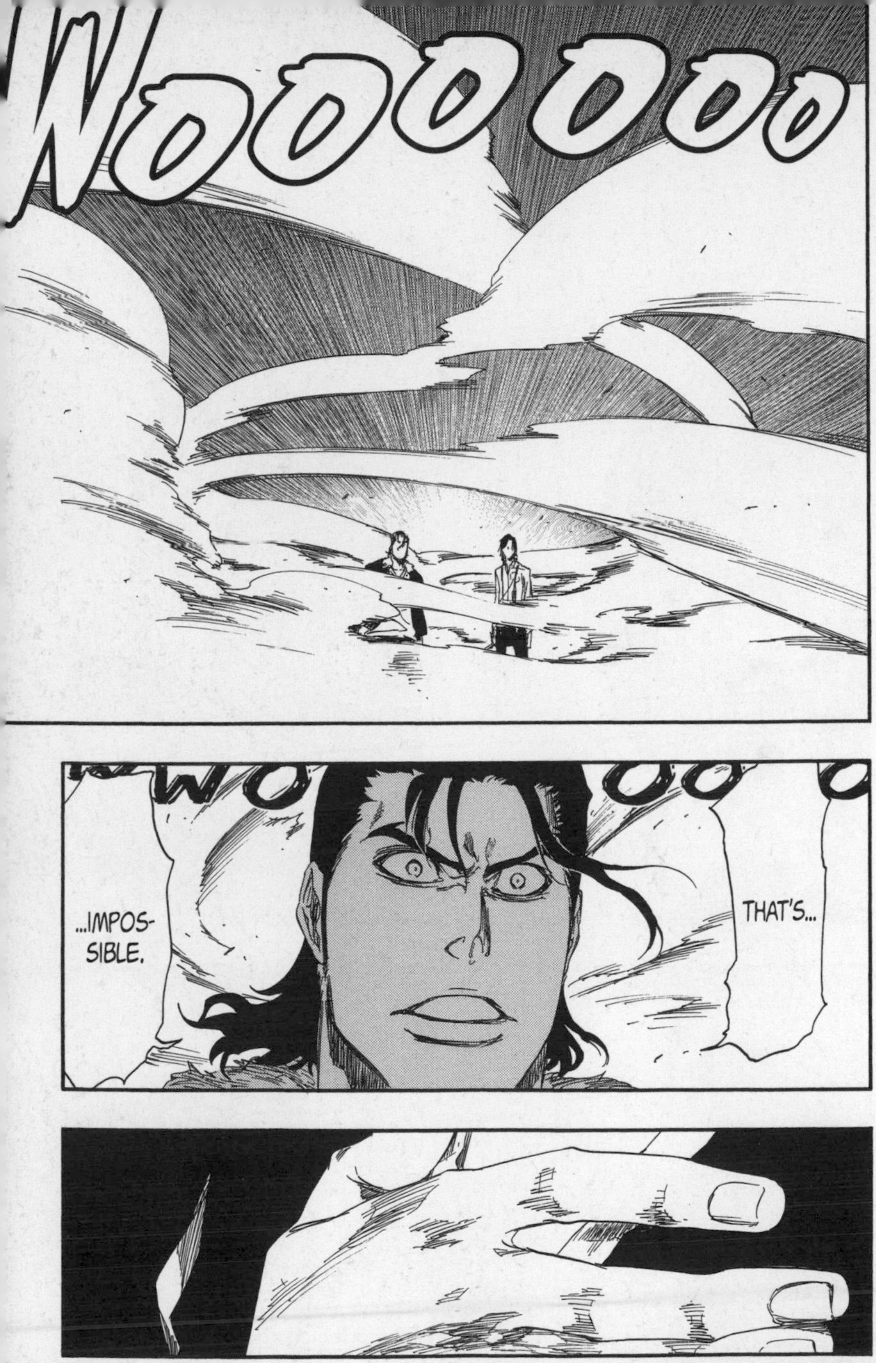
WOOOOOO
THAT'S...
...IMPOS-
SIBLE.

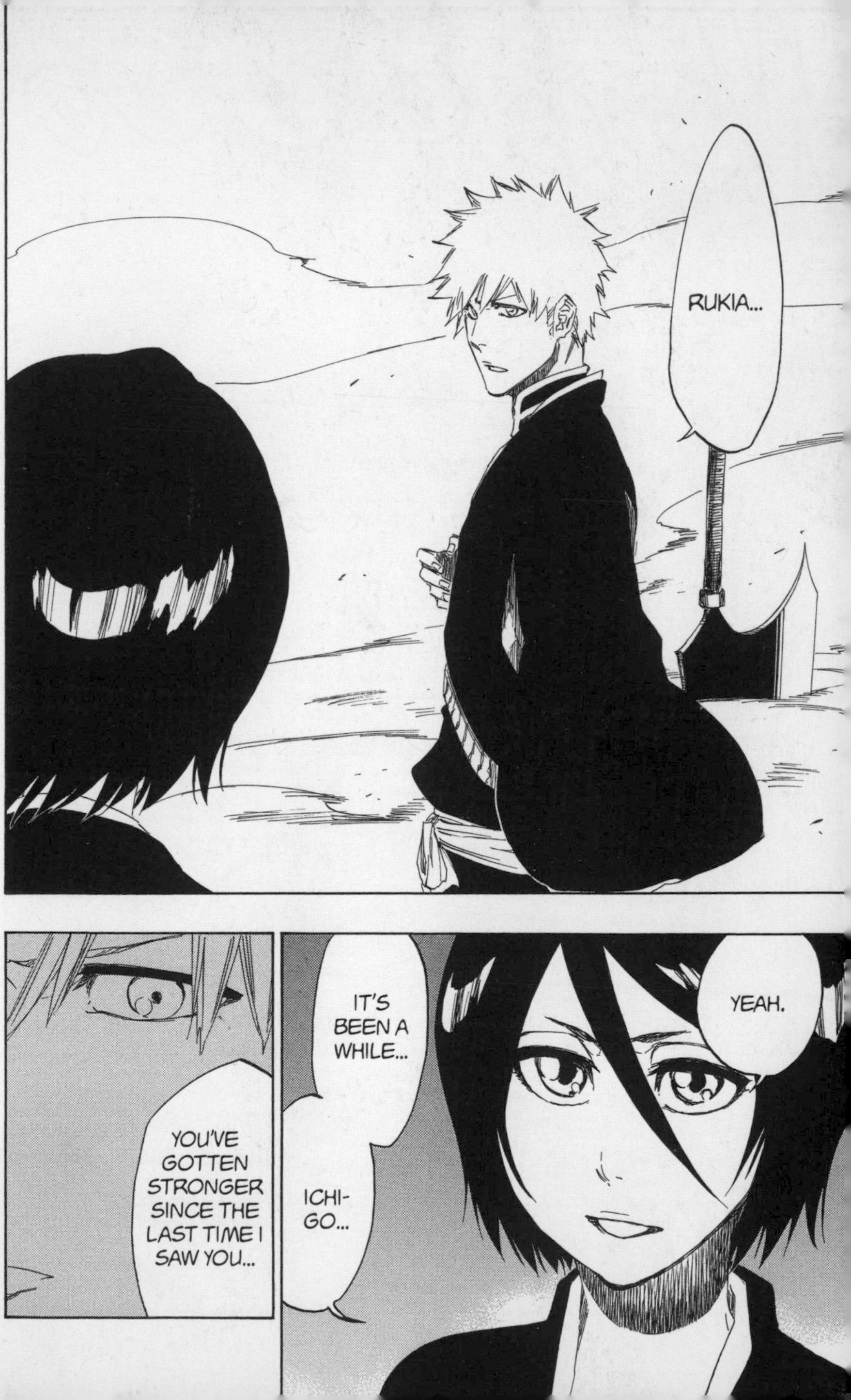
RUKIA...
YEAH.
IT'S BEEN A WHILE...
ICHI-GO...
YOU'VE GOTTEN STRONGER SINCE THE LAST TIME I SAW YOU...

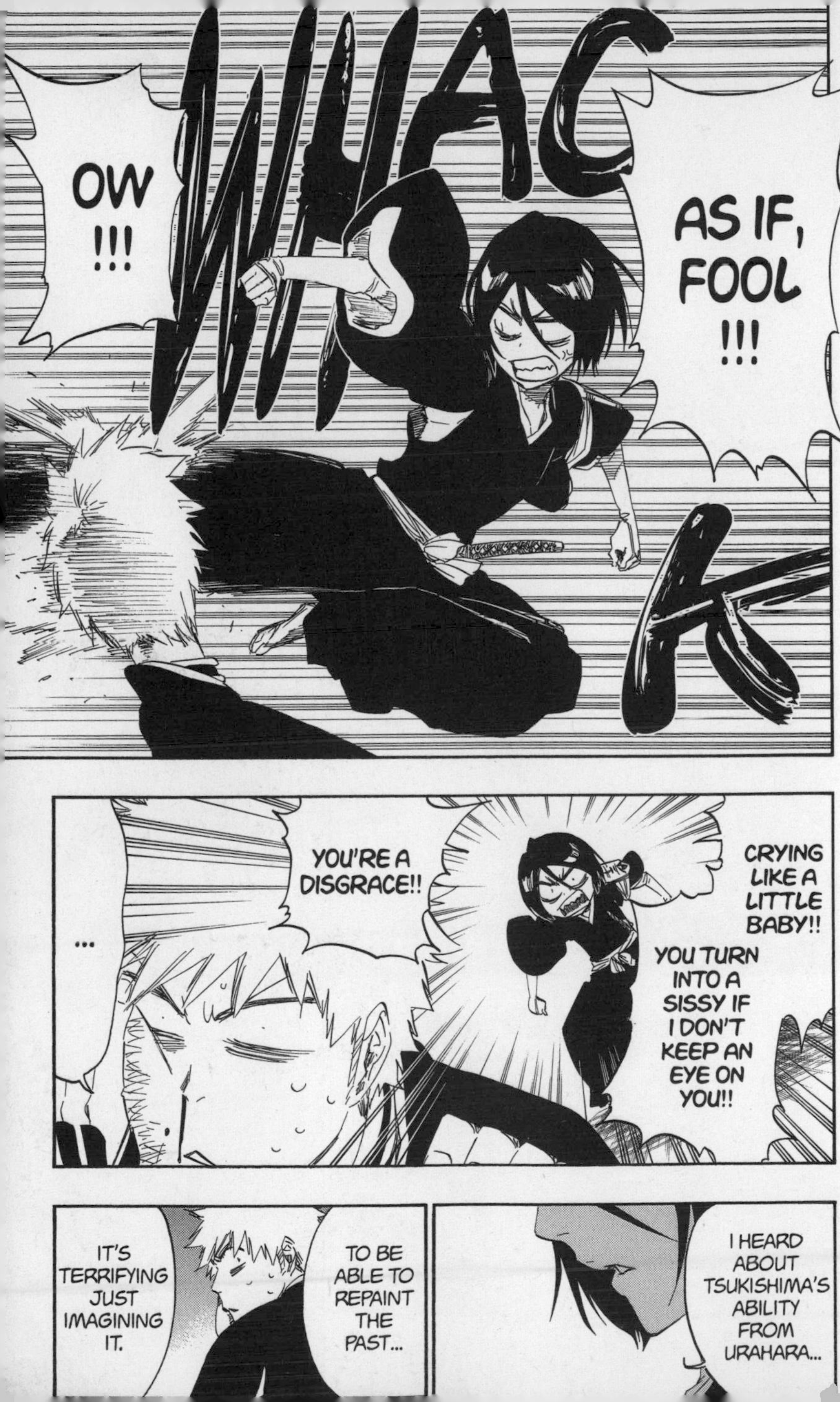
AS IF, FOOL !!!
WHACK
OW !!!
CRYING LIKE A LITTLE BABY!!
YOU TURN INTO A SISSY IF I DON'T KEEP AN EYE ON YOU!!
YOU'RE A DISGRACE!!
...
I HEARD ABOUT TSUKISHIMA'S ABILITY FROM URAHARA...
TO BE ABLE TO REPAINT THE PAST...
IT'S TERRIFYING JUST IMAGINING IT.

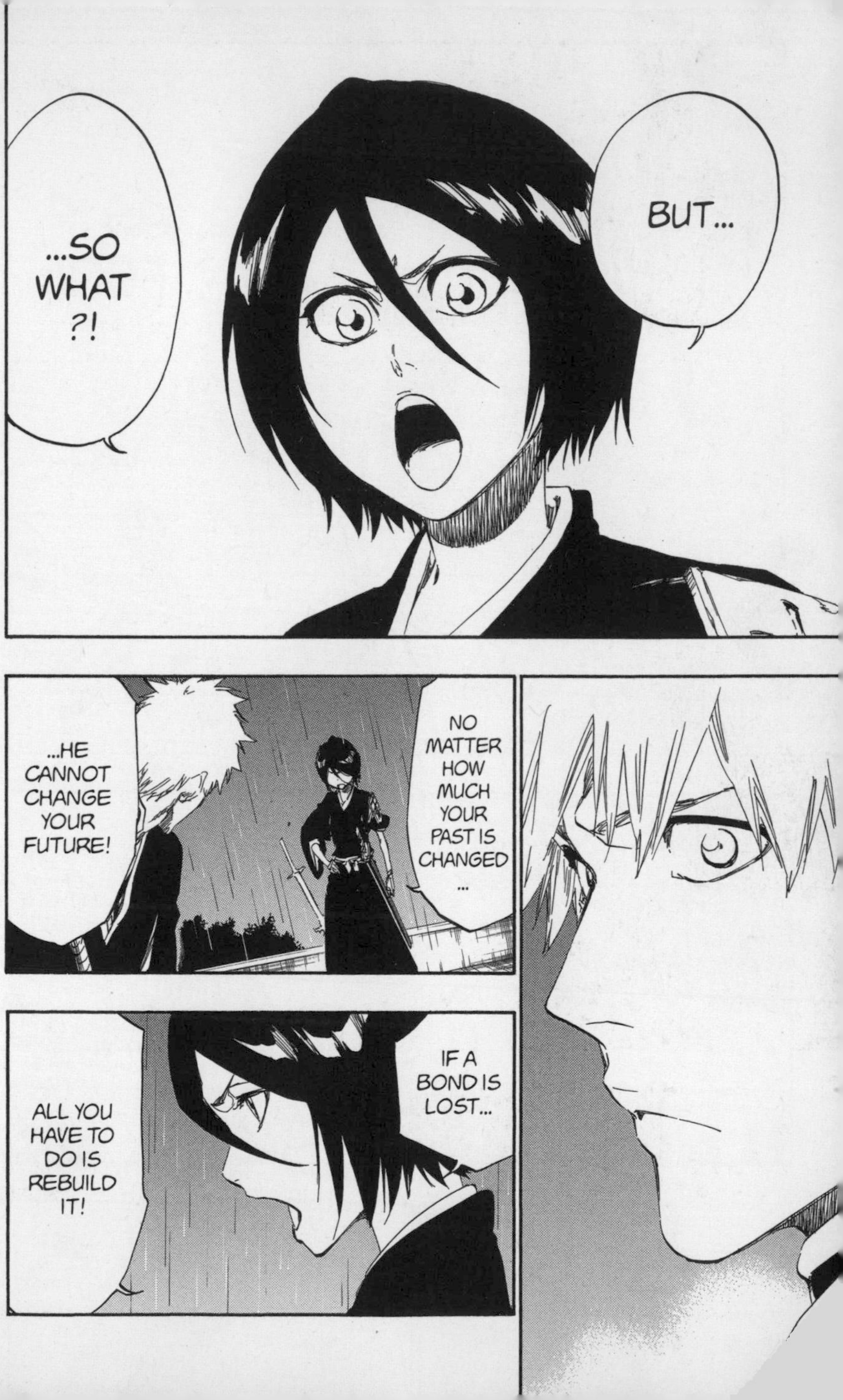
BUT...
...SO WHAT?!
NO MATTER HOW MUCH YOUR PAST IS CHANGED...
...HE CANNOT CHANGE YOUR FUTURE!
IF A BOND IS LOST...
ALL YOU HAVE TO DO IS REBUILD IT!

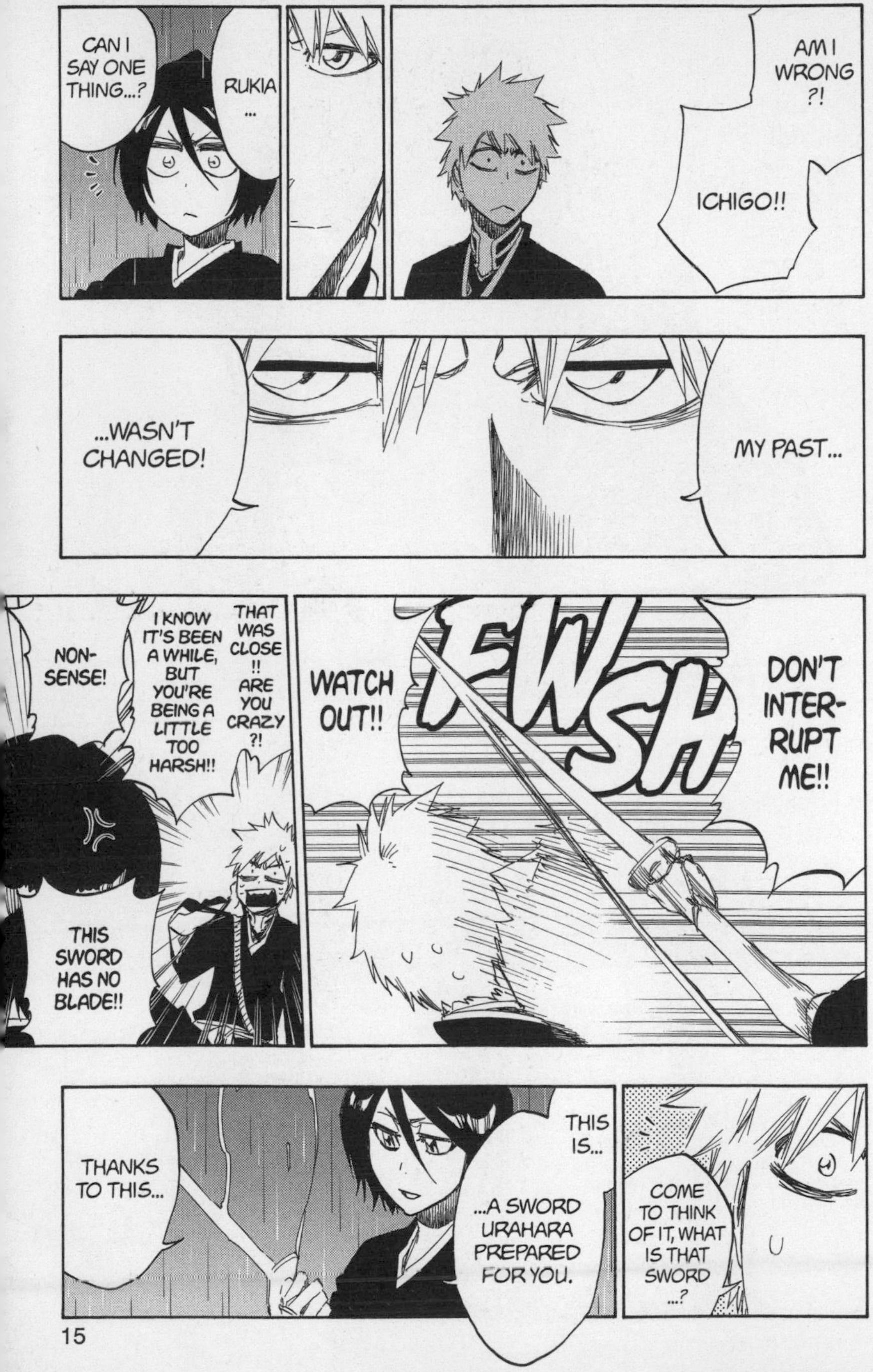
AM I WRONG ?!
ICHIGO!!
RUKIA ...
CAN I SAY ONE THING...?
MY PAST...
...WASN'T CHANGED!
DON'T INTER-RUPT ME!!
FWSH
WATCH OUT!!
THAT WAS CLOSE!! ARE YOU CRAZY ?!
I KNOW IT'S BEEN A WHILE, BUT YOU'RE BEING A LITTLE TOO HARSH!!
NON-SENSE!
THIS SWORD HAS NO BLADE!!
COME TO THINK OF IT, WHAT IS THAT SWORD ...?
THIS IS...
...A SWORD URAHARA PREPARED FOR YOU.
THANKS TO THIS...

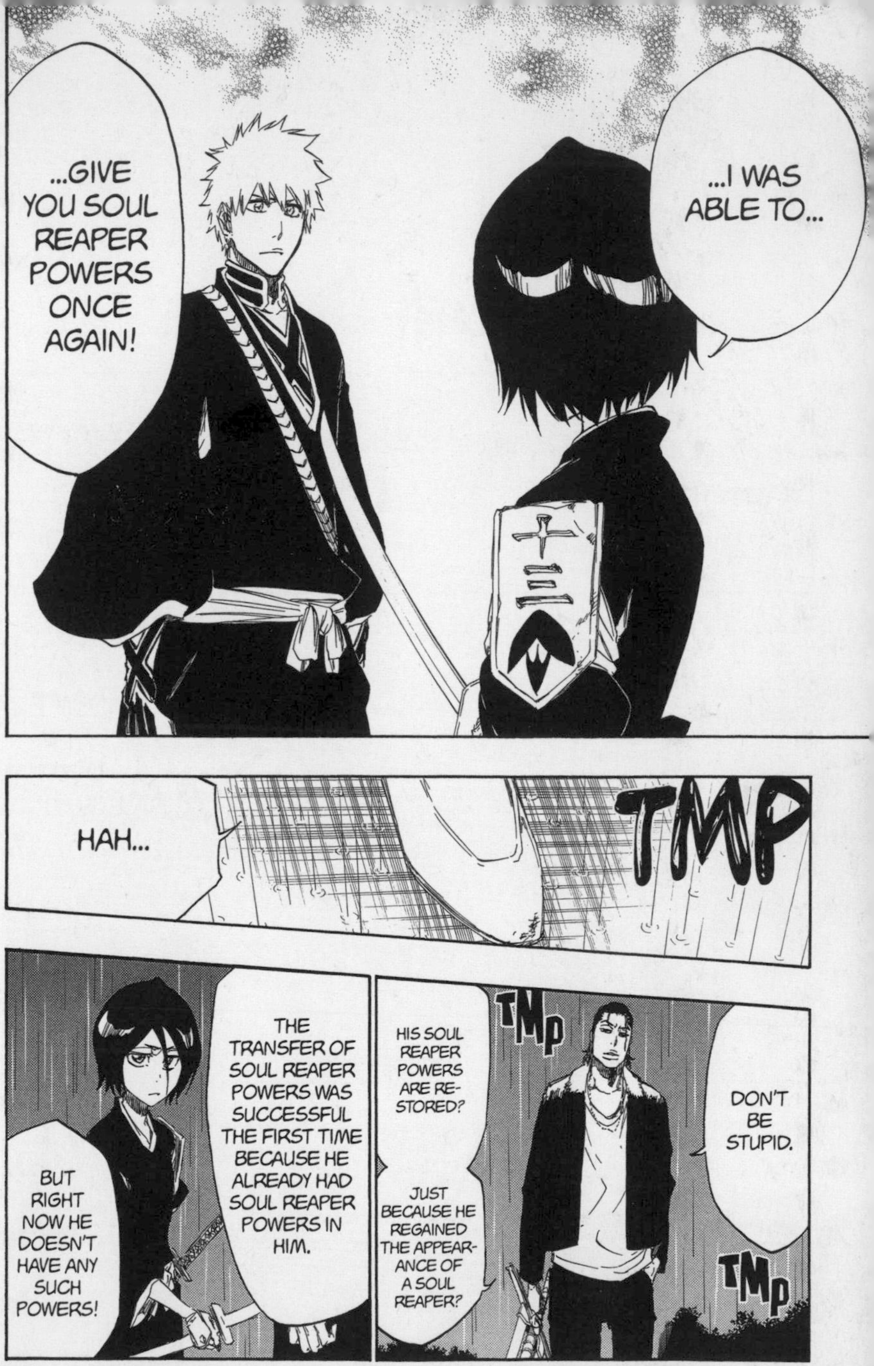
...I WAS ABLE TO...
...GIVE YOU SOUL REAPER POWERS ONCE AGAIN!
TMP
HAH...
TMP
DON'T BE STUPID.
HIS SOUL REAPER POWERS ARE RE-STORED?
JUST BECAUSE HE REGAINED THE APPEAR-ANCE OF A SOUL REAPER?
TMP
THE TRANSFER OF SOUL REAPER POWERS WAS SUCCESSFUL THE FIRST TIME BECAUSE HE ALREADY HAD SOUL REAPER POWERS IN HIM.
BUT RIGHT NOW HE DOESN'T HAVE ANY SUCH POWERS!

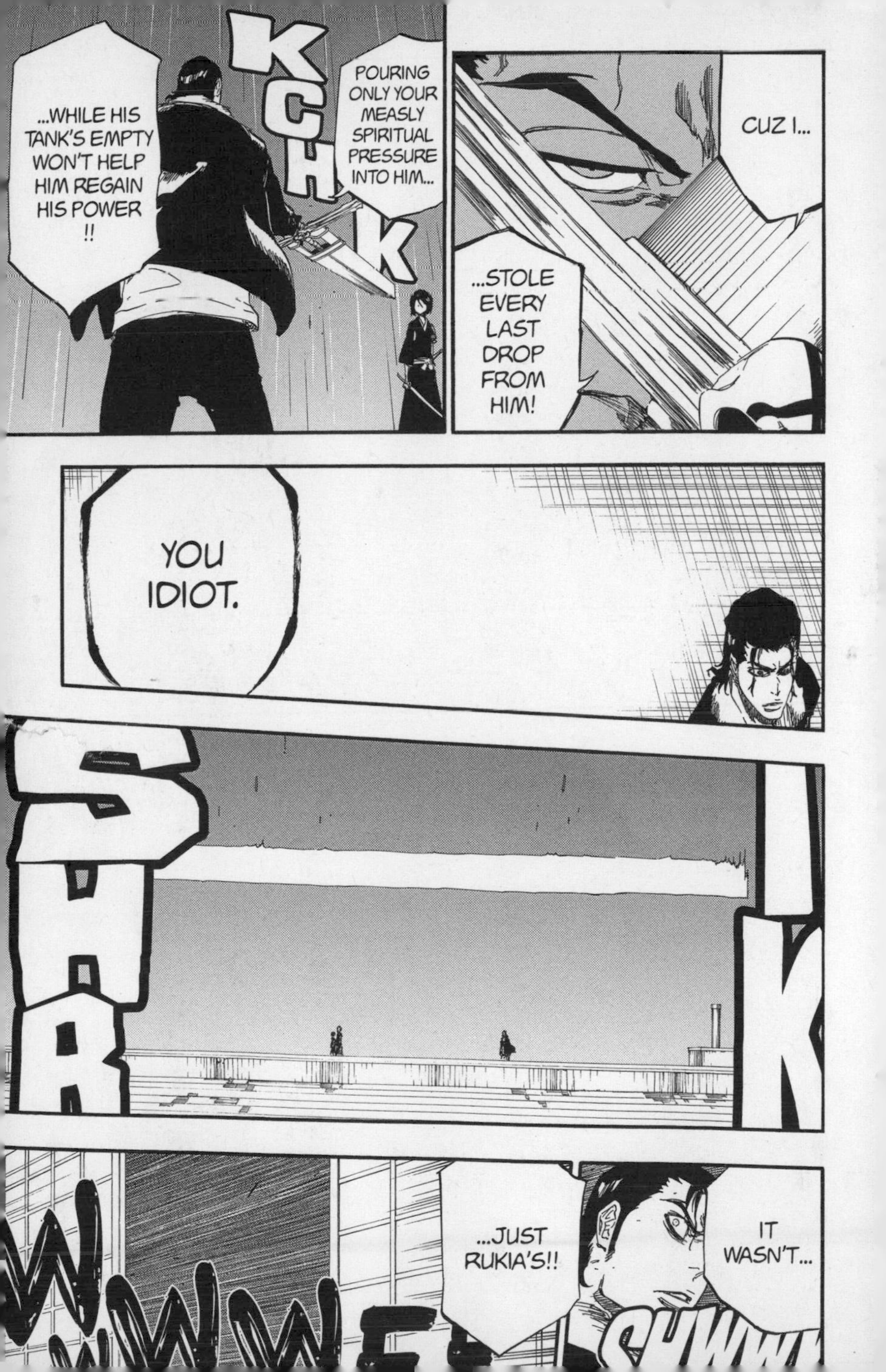
CUZ I...
...STOLE EVERY LAST DROP FROM HIM!
POURING ONLY YOUR MEASLY SPIRITUAL PRESSURE INTO HIM...
KCHK
...WHILE HIS TANK'S EMPTY WON'T HELP HIM REGAIN HIS POWER !!
YOU IDIOT.
SHRK
IT WASN'T...
...JUST RUKIA'S!!

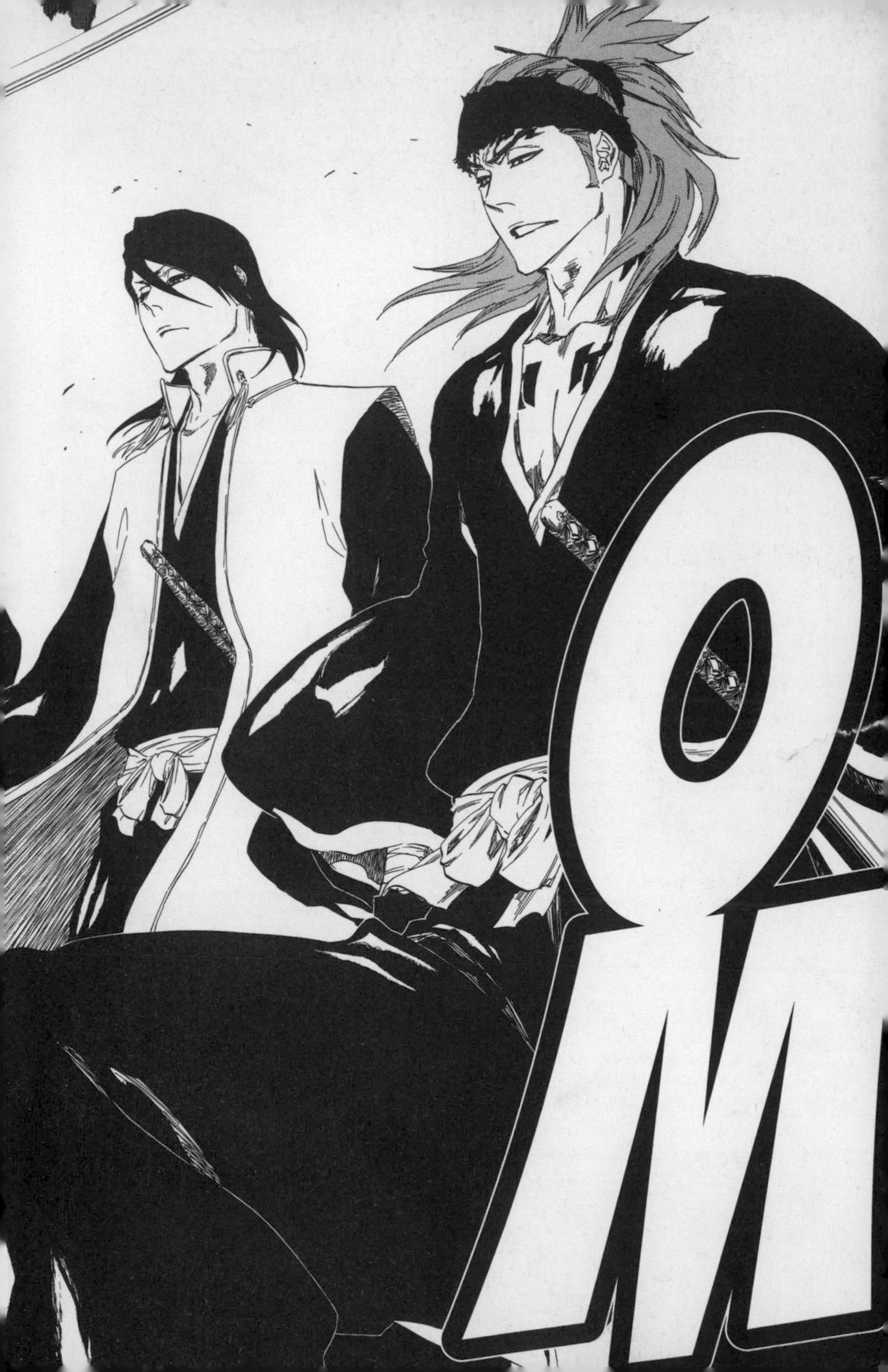
OM

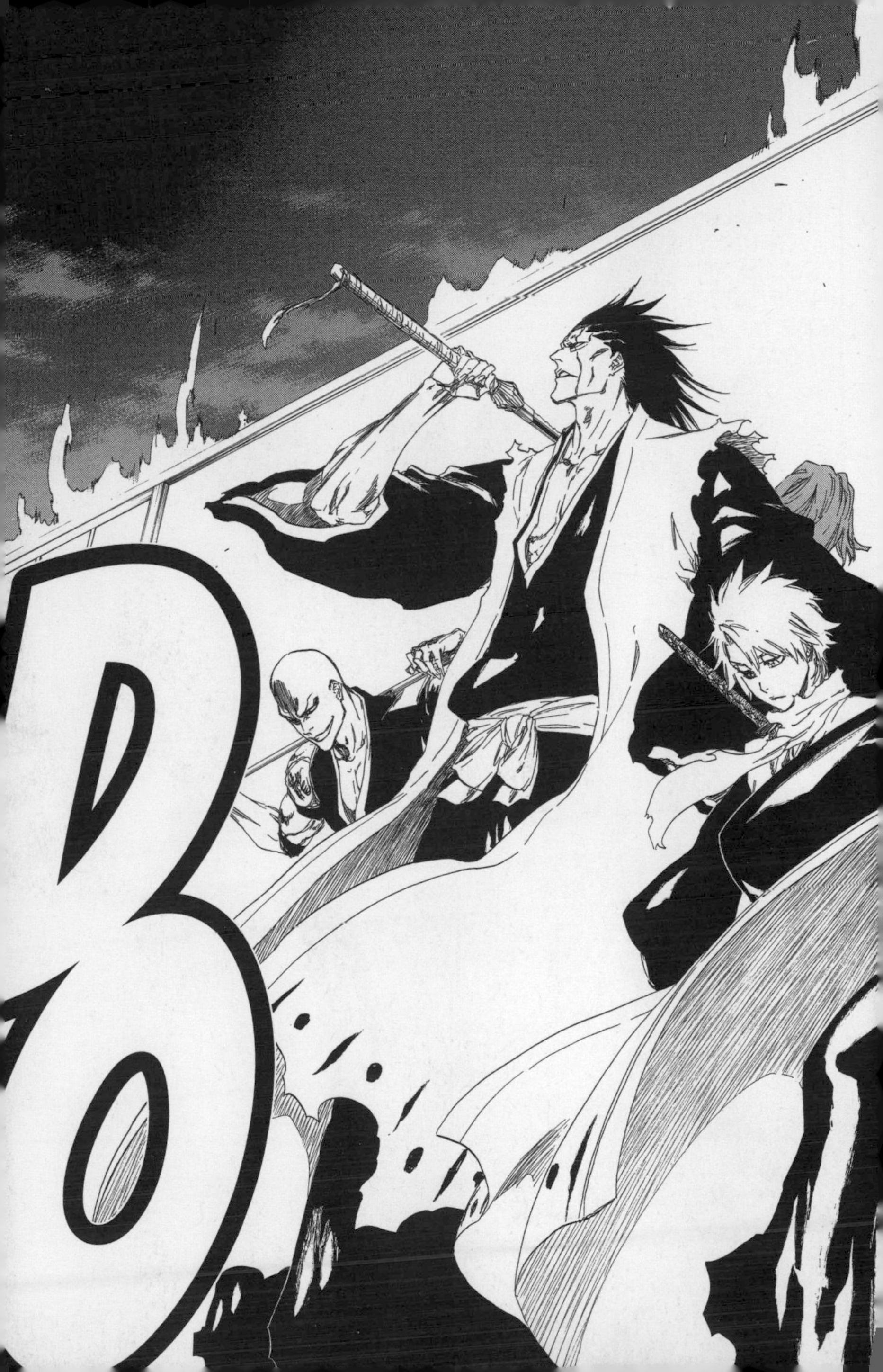
B

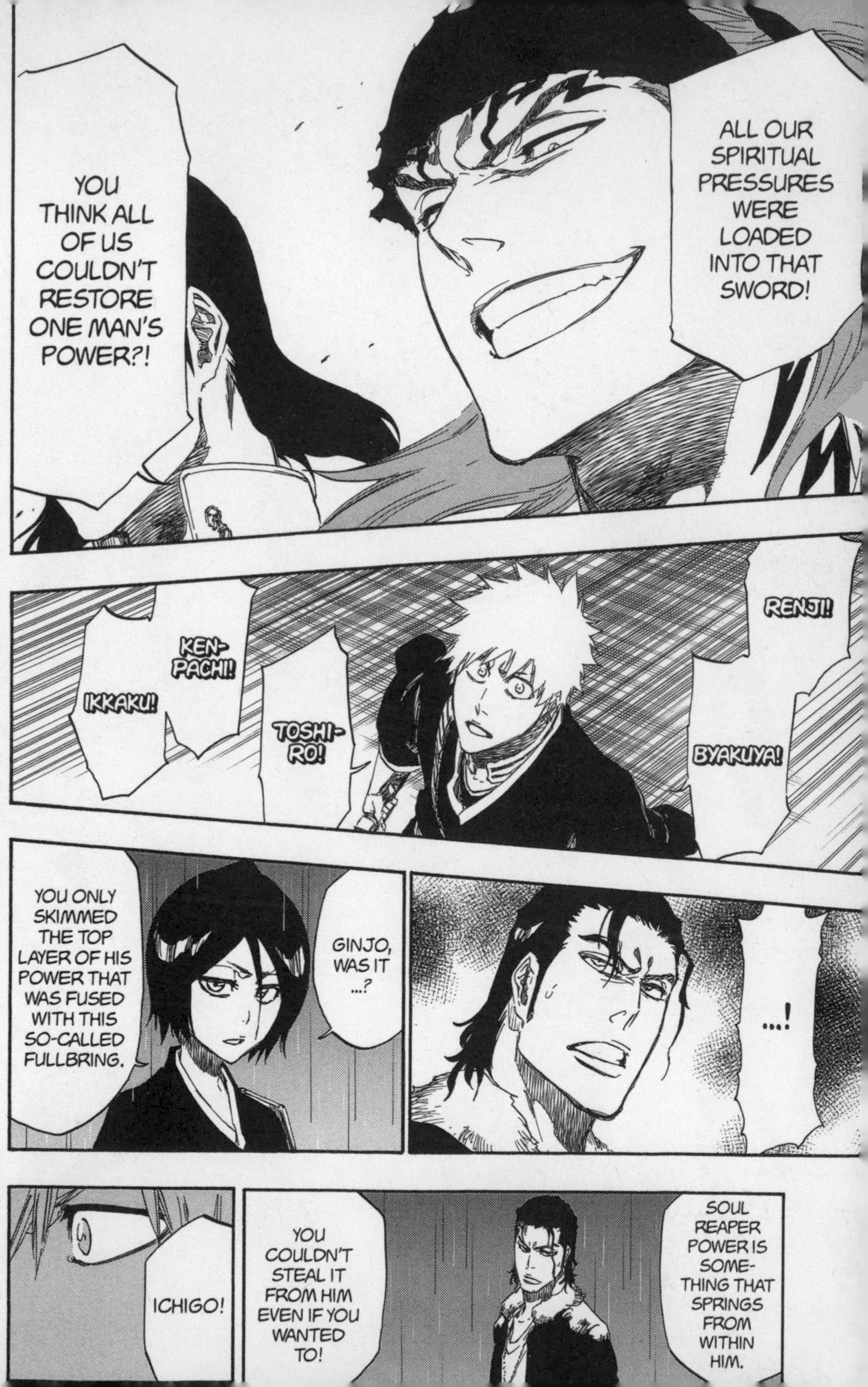
ALL OUR SPIRITUAL PRESSURES WERE LOADED INTO THAT SWORD!
YOU THINK ALL OF US COULDN'T RESTORE ONE MAN'S POWER?!
RENJI!
BYAKUYA!
KEN-PACHI!
TOSHI-RO!
IKKAKU!
...!
GINJO, WAS IT ...?
YOU ONLY SKIMMED THE TOP LAYER OF HIS POWER THAT WAS FUSED WITH THIS SO-CALLED FULLBRING.
SOUL REAPER POWER IS SOME-THING THAT SPRINGS FROM WITHIN HIM.
YOU COULDN'T STEAL IT FROM HIM EVEN IF YOU WANTED TO!
ICHIGO!

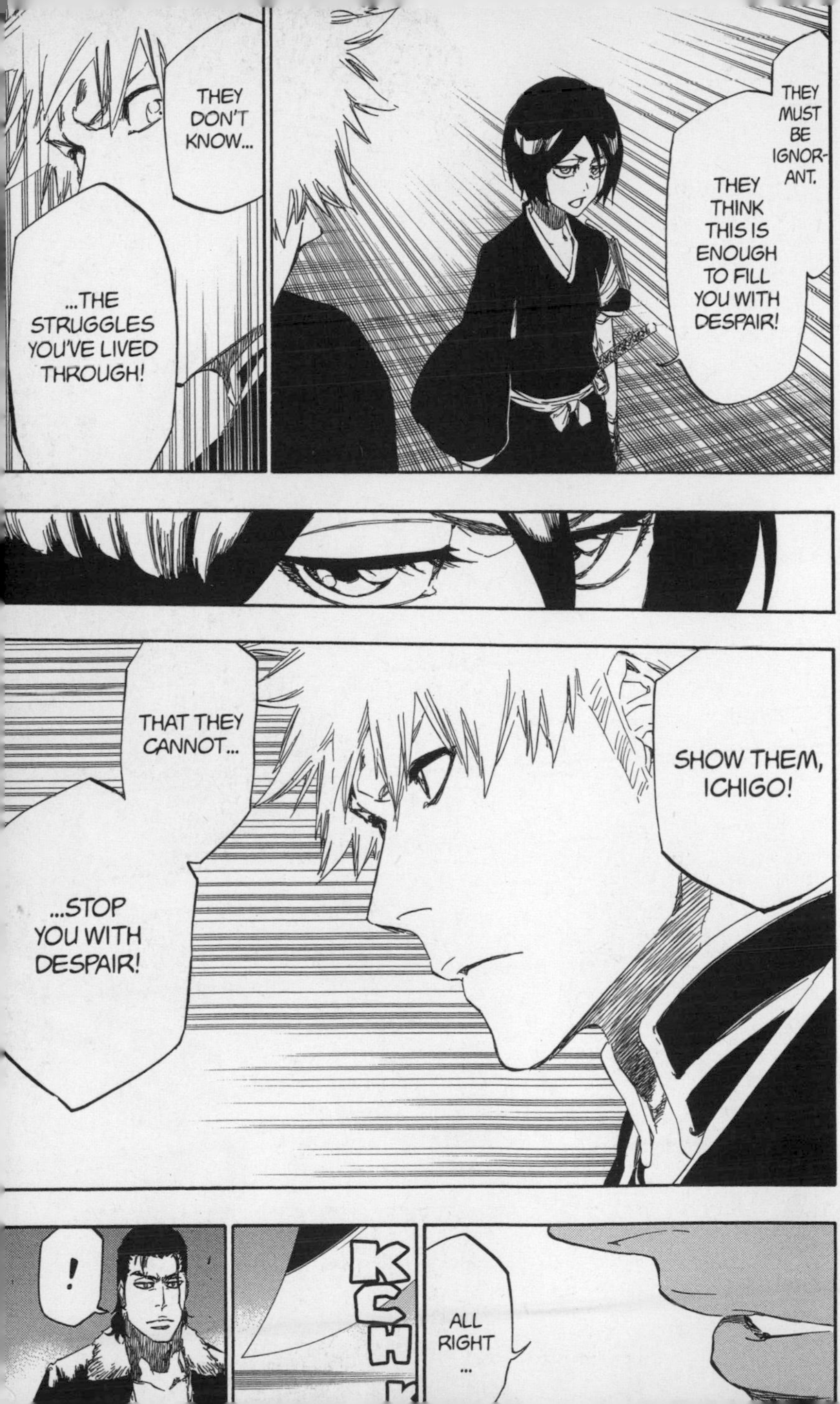
THEY MUST BE IGNORANT.
THEY THINK THIS IS ENOUGH TO FILL YOU WITH DESPAIR!
THEY DON'T KNOW...
...THE STRUGGLES YOU'VE LIVED THROUGH!
SHOW THEM, ICHIGO!
THAT THEY CANNOT...
...STOP YOU WITH DESPAIR!
ALL RIGHT ...
KCH
!

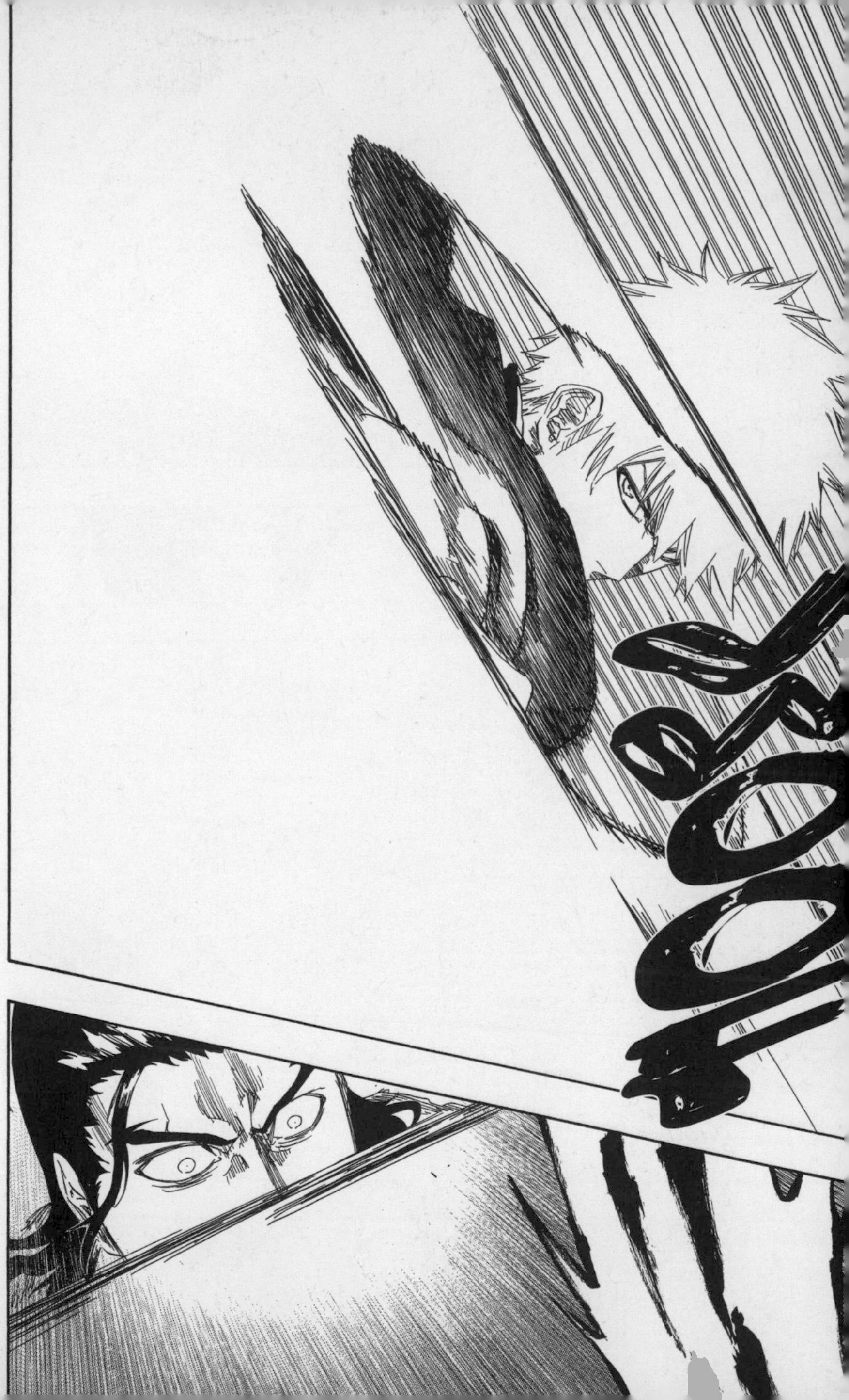

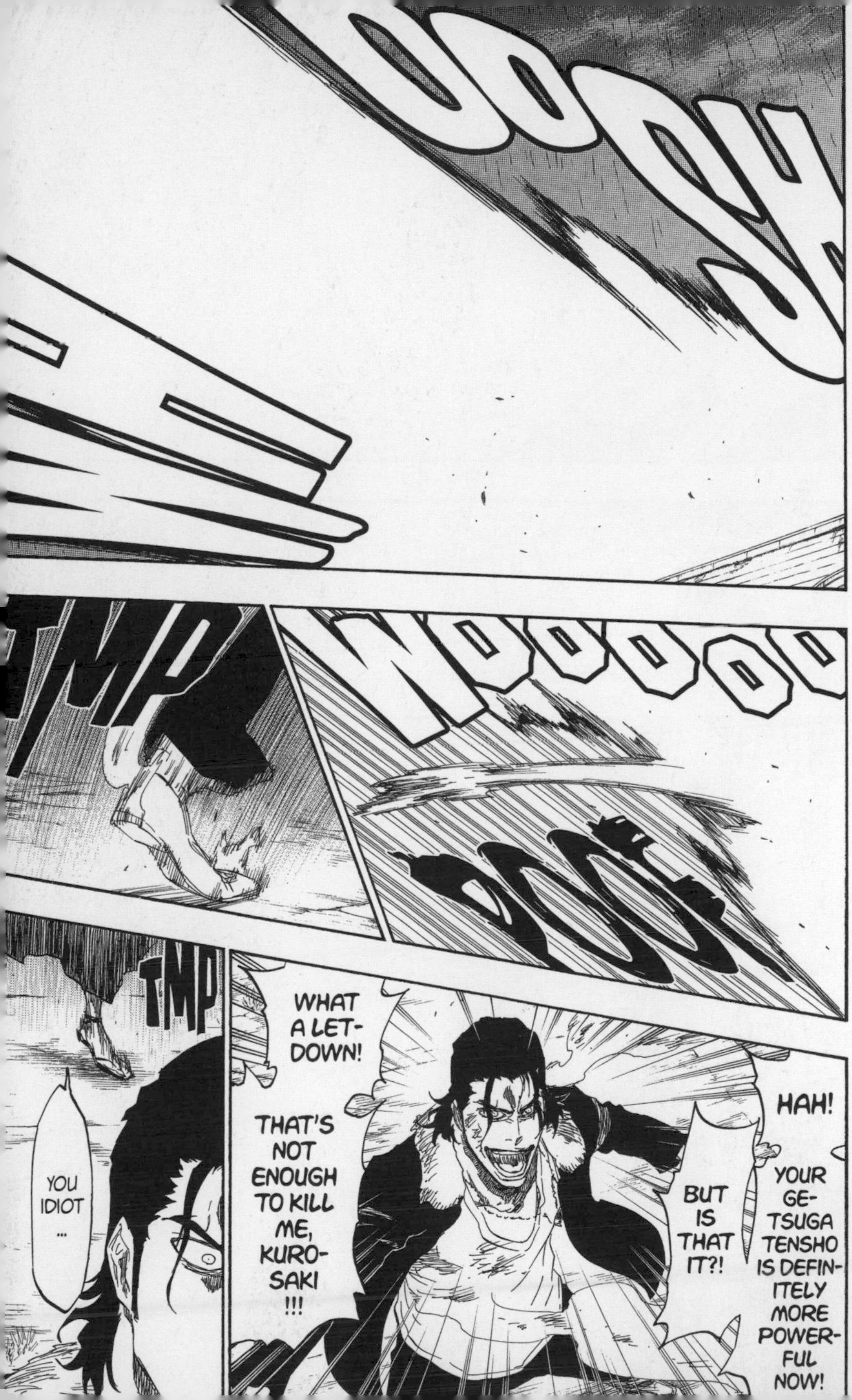
TMP
HAH!
YOUR GE-TSUGA TENSHO IS DEFINI-ITELY MORE POWER-FUL NOW!
BUT IS THAT IT?!
WHAT A LET-DOWN!
THAT'S NOT ENOUGH TO KILL ME, KURO-SAKI !!!
TMP
YOU IDIOT ...

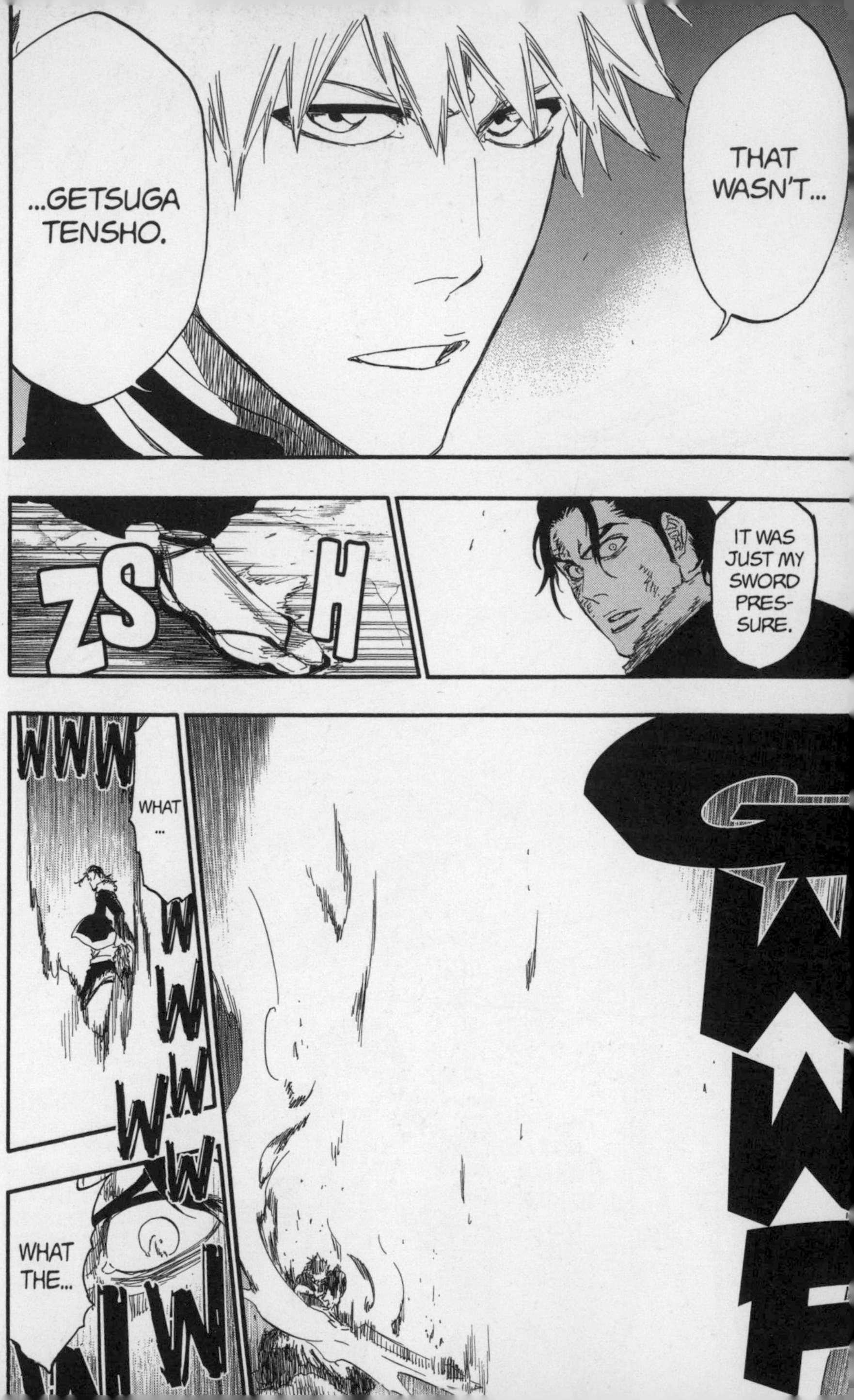

THAT WASN'T...
...GETSUGA TENSHO.
IT WAS JUST MY SWORD PRES-SURE.
ZSH
WHAT ...
WHAT THE...

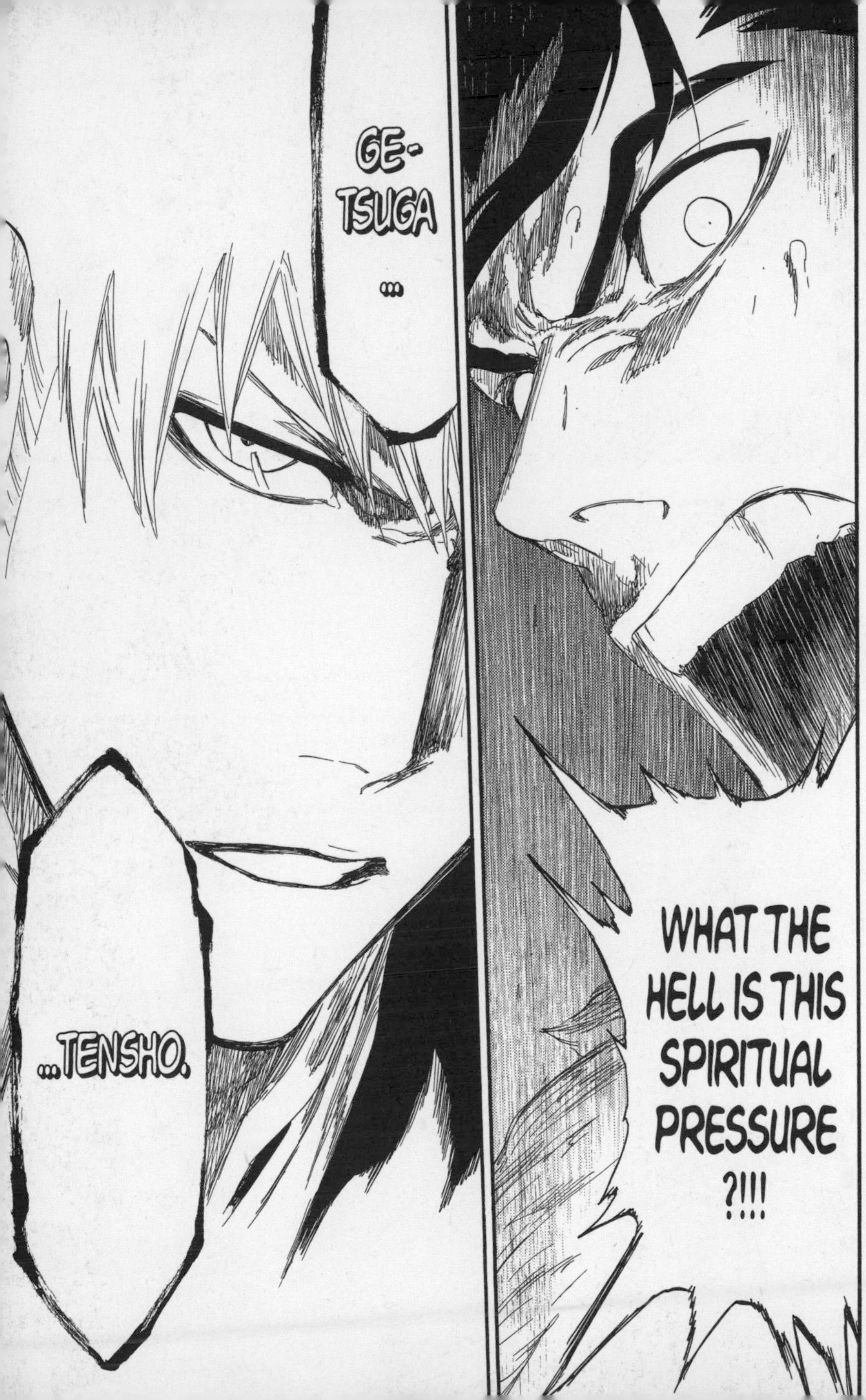
WHAT THE HELL IS THIS SPIRITUAL PRESSURE ?!!!
GE-TSUGA ...
...TENSHO.

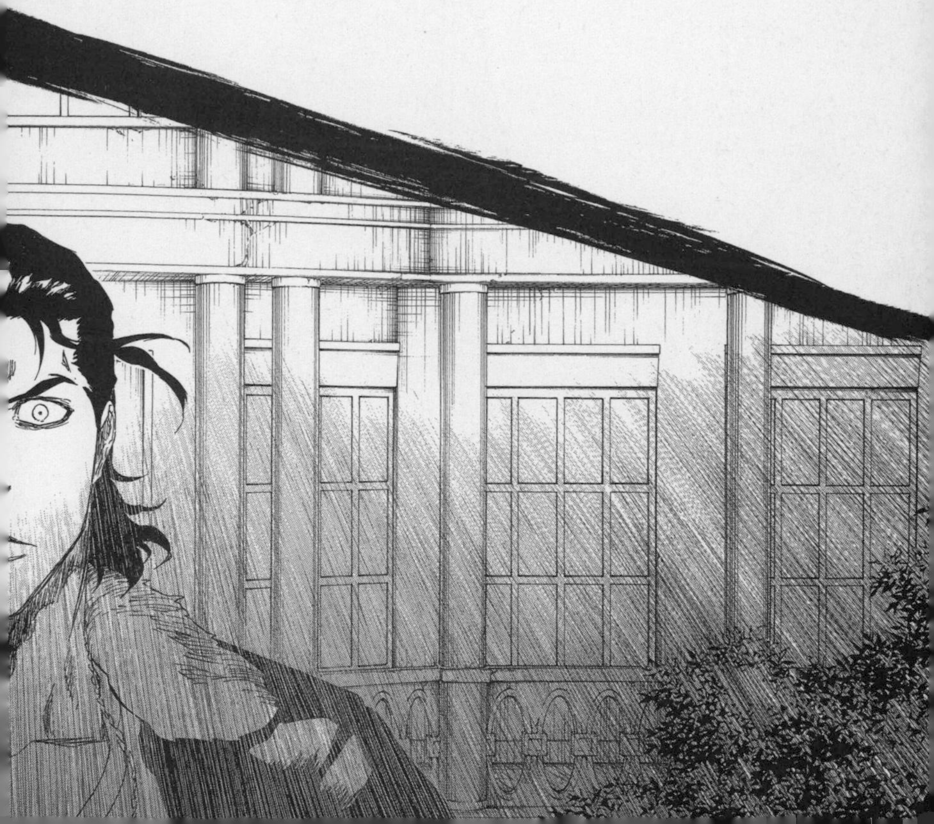

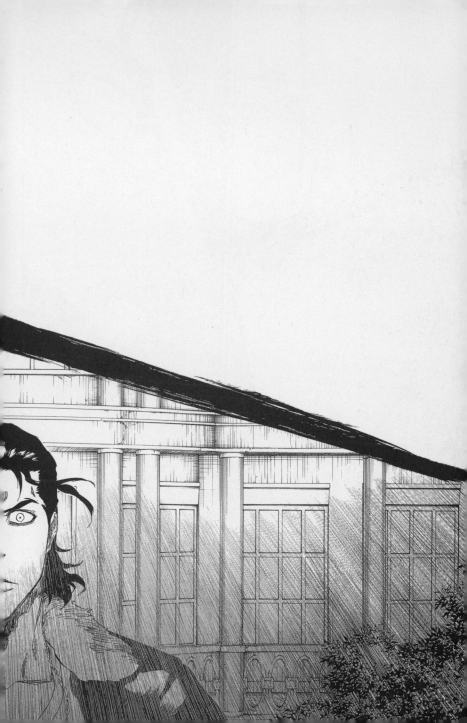

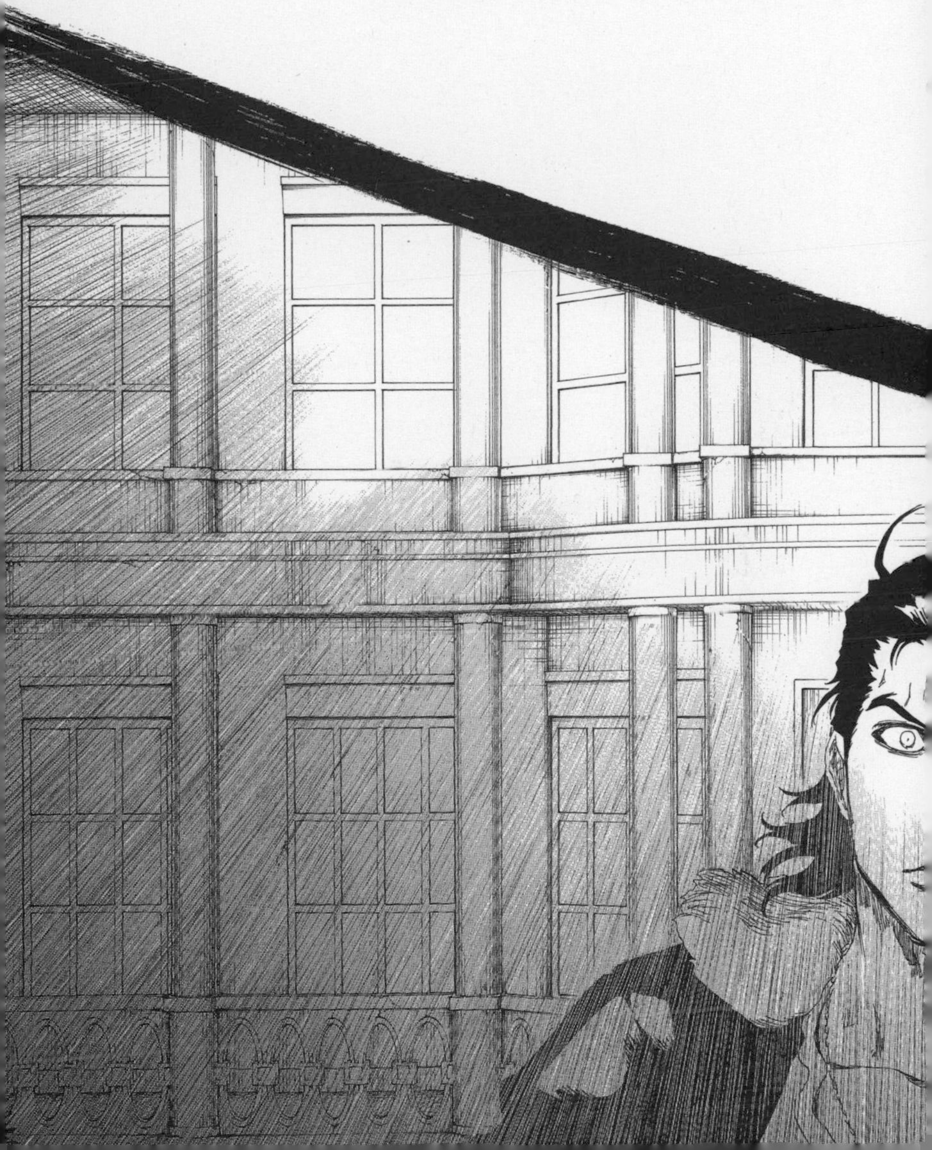

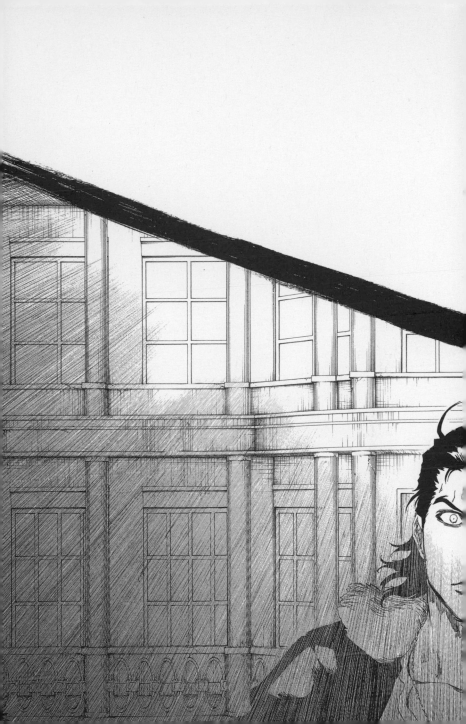

TUT,
TUT...

WHAT?
YOU WANNA
KNOW WHERE I
GOT THIS
ASSISTANT
CAPTAIN
BADGE...?

THAT'S A
SECRET...!

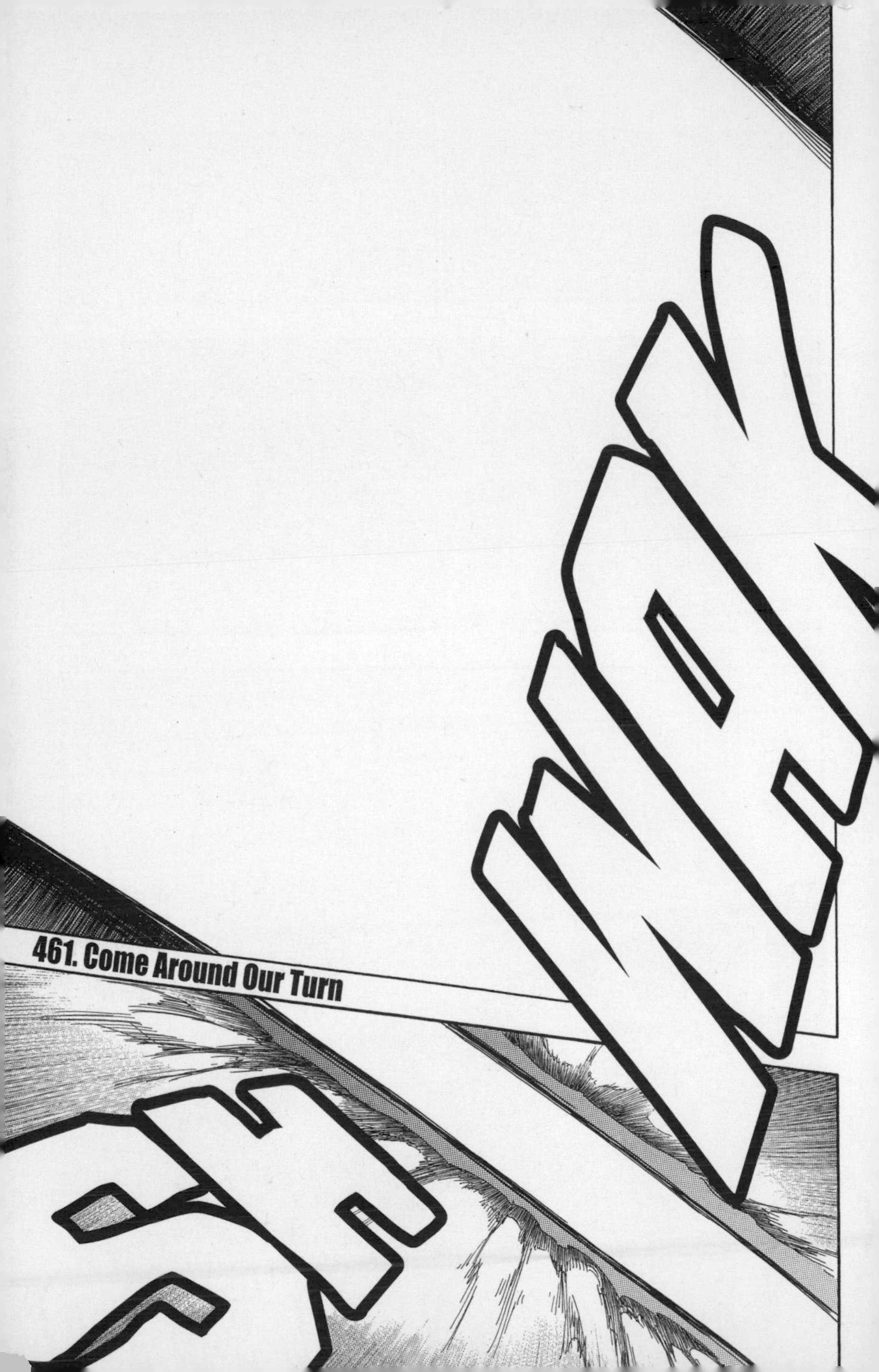
461. Come Around Our Turn

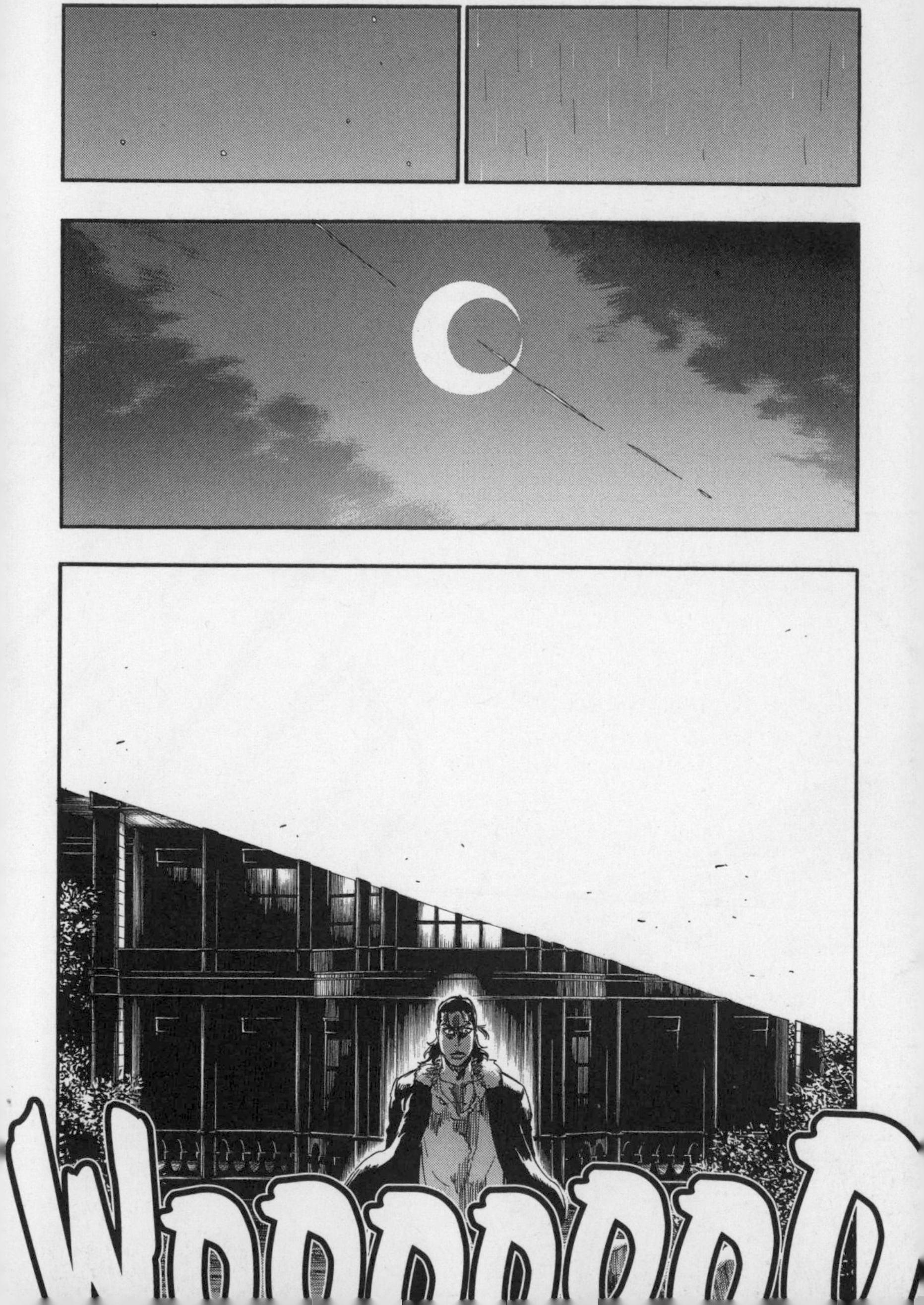
WOOOOOO

SORRY...

I MISSED.

NEXT TIME, I WON'T.

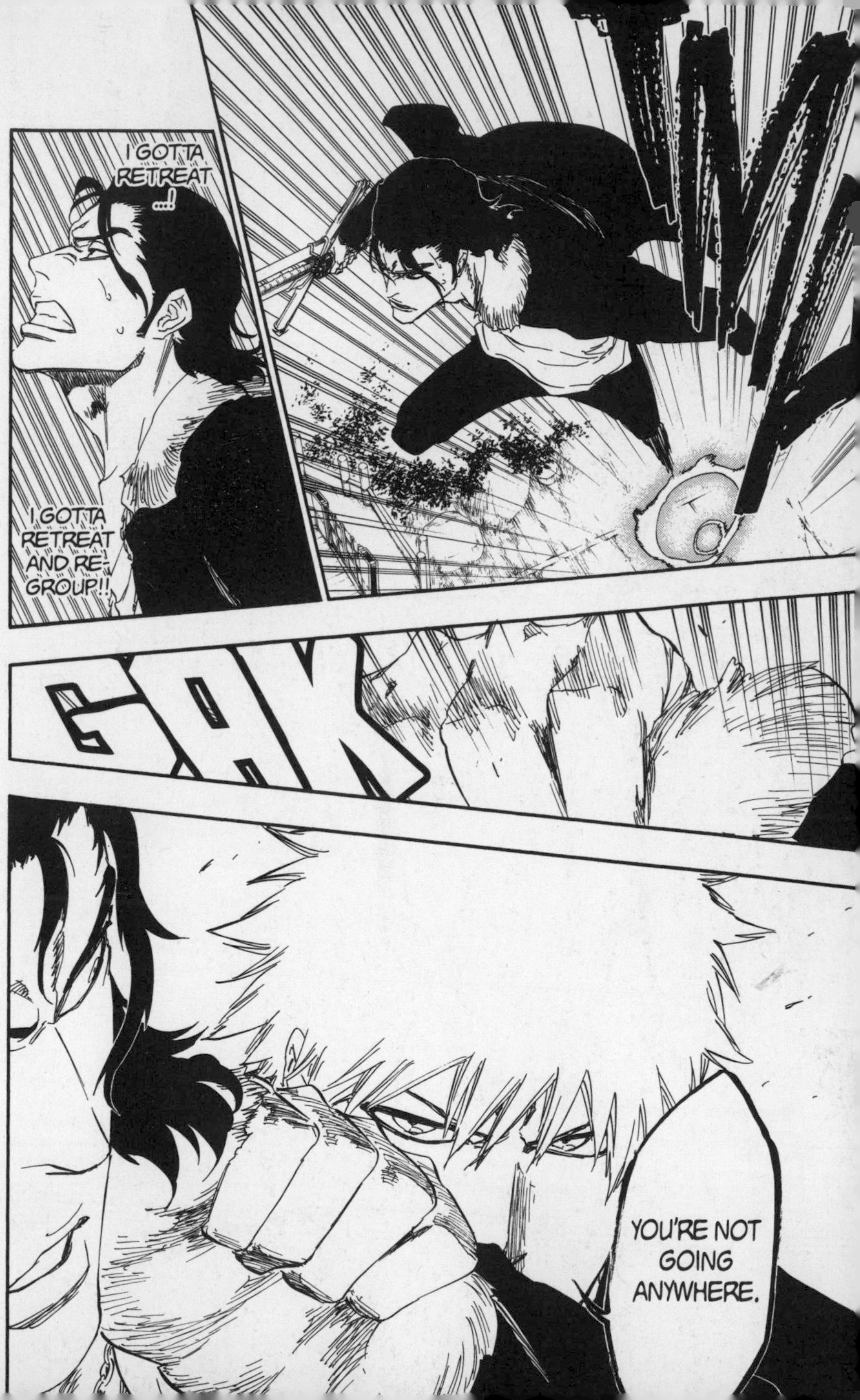
I GOTTA RETREAT ...!
I GOTTA RETREAT AND RE-GROUP!!
YOU'RE NOT GOING ANYWHERE.

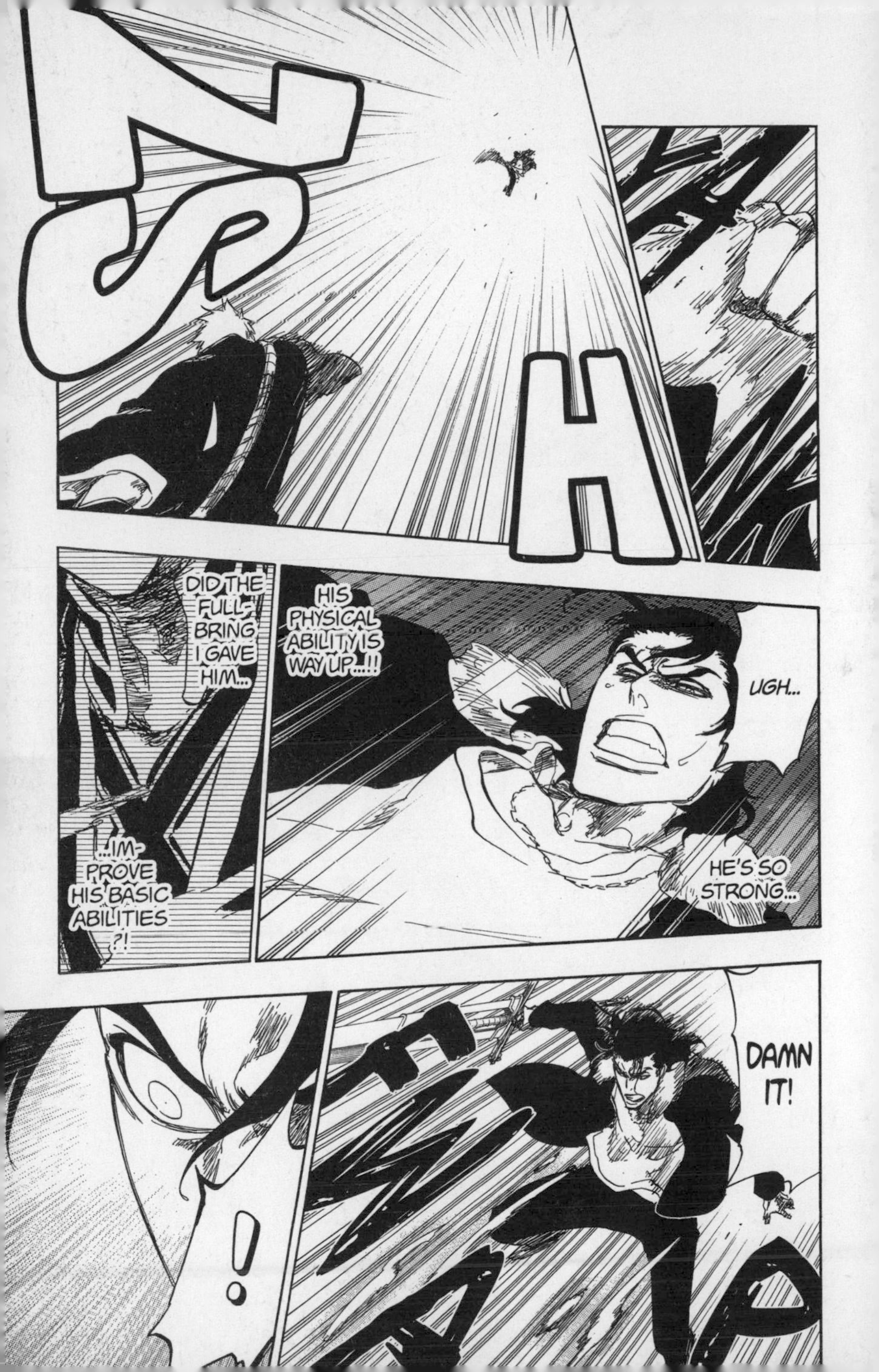
UGH...
HIS PHYSICAL ABILITY IS WAY UP...!!
HE'S SO STRONG...
DID THE FULLBRING I GAVE HIM...
...IMPROVE HIS BASIC ABILITIES?!
DAMN IT!
!

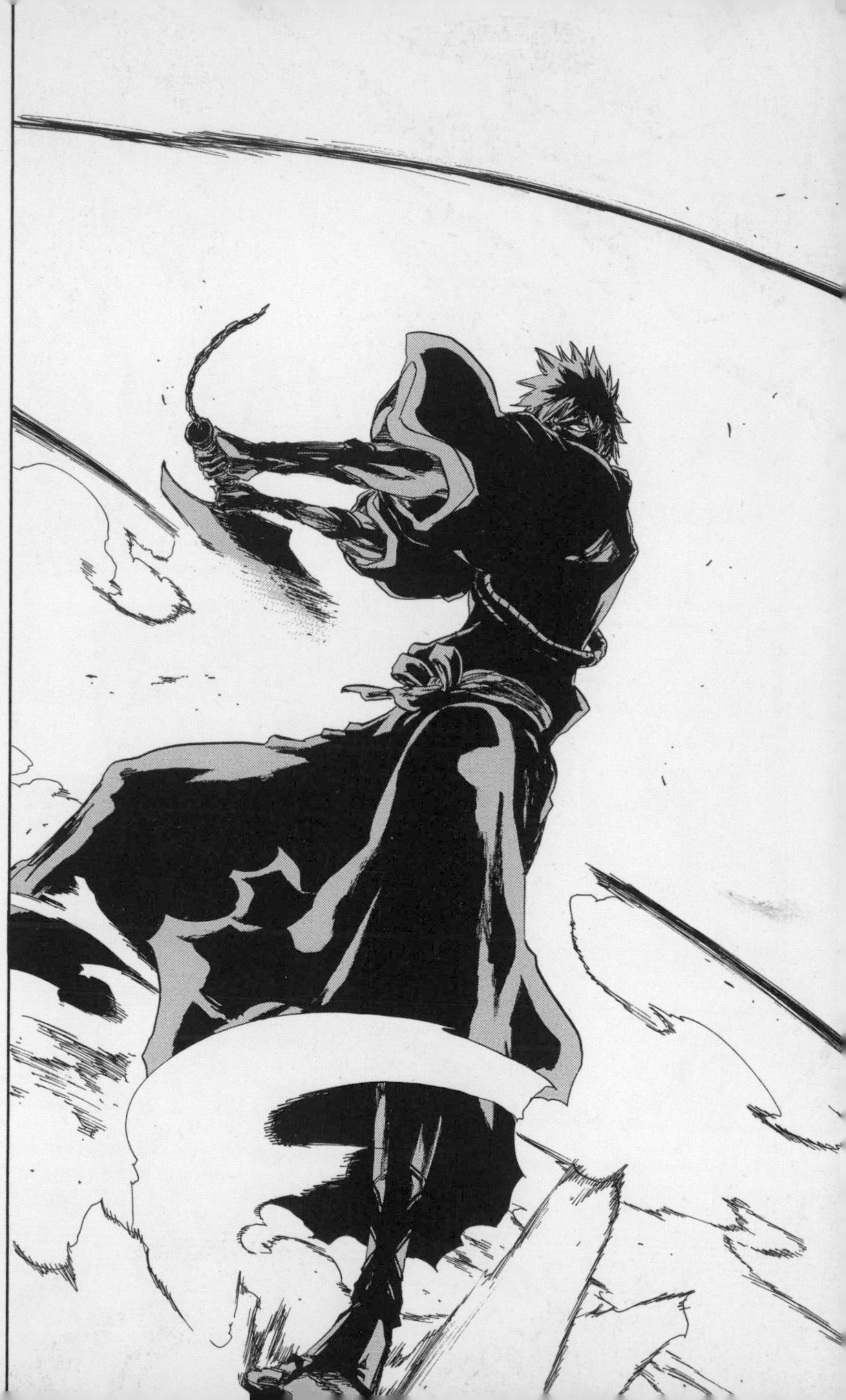

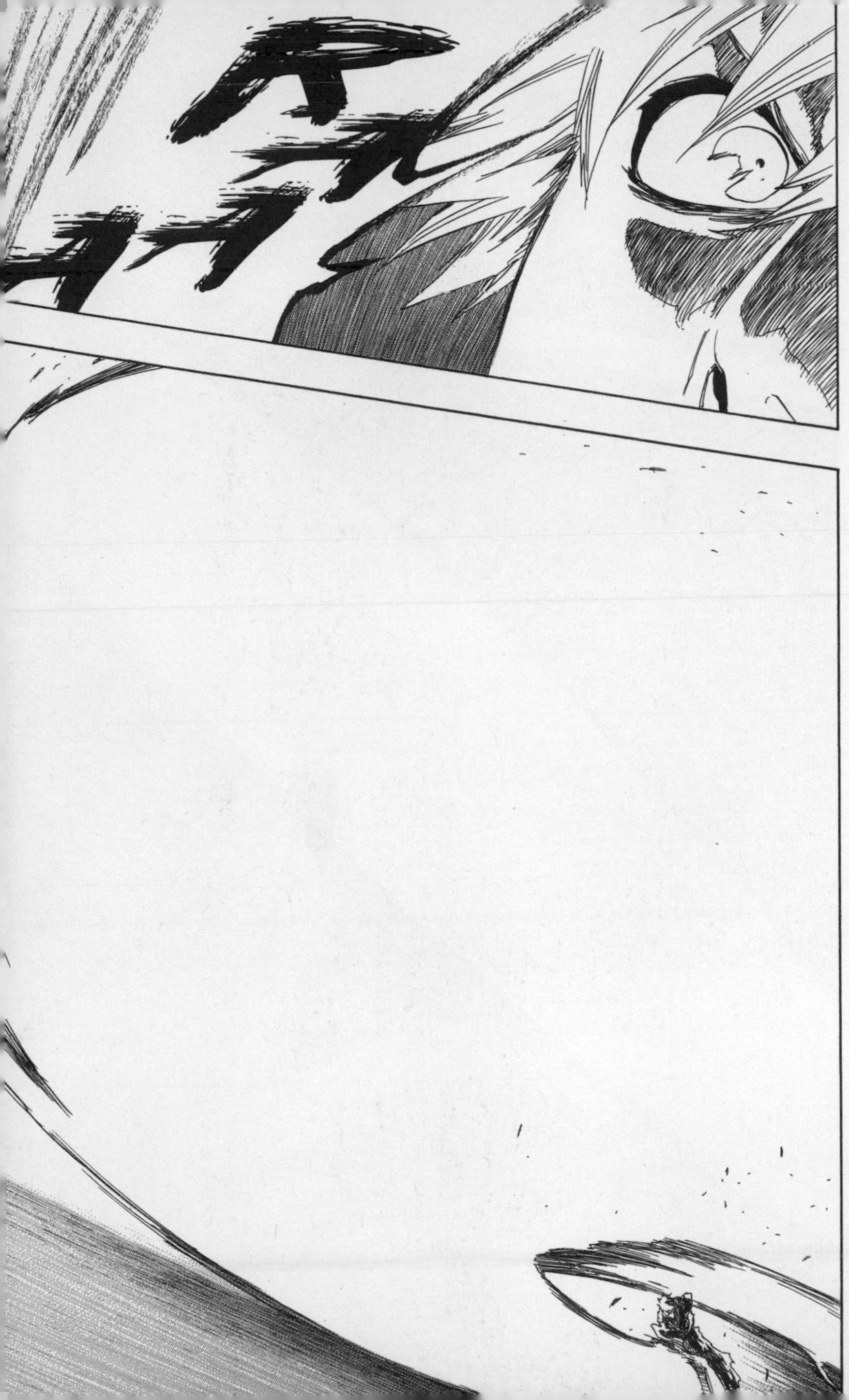

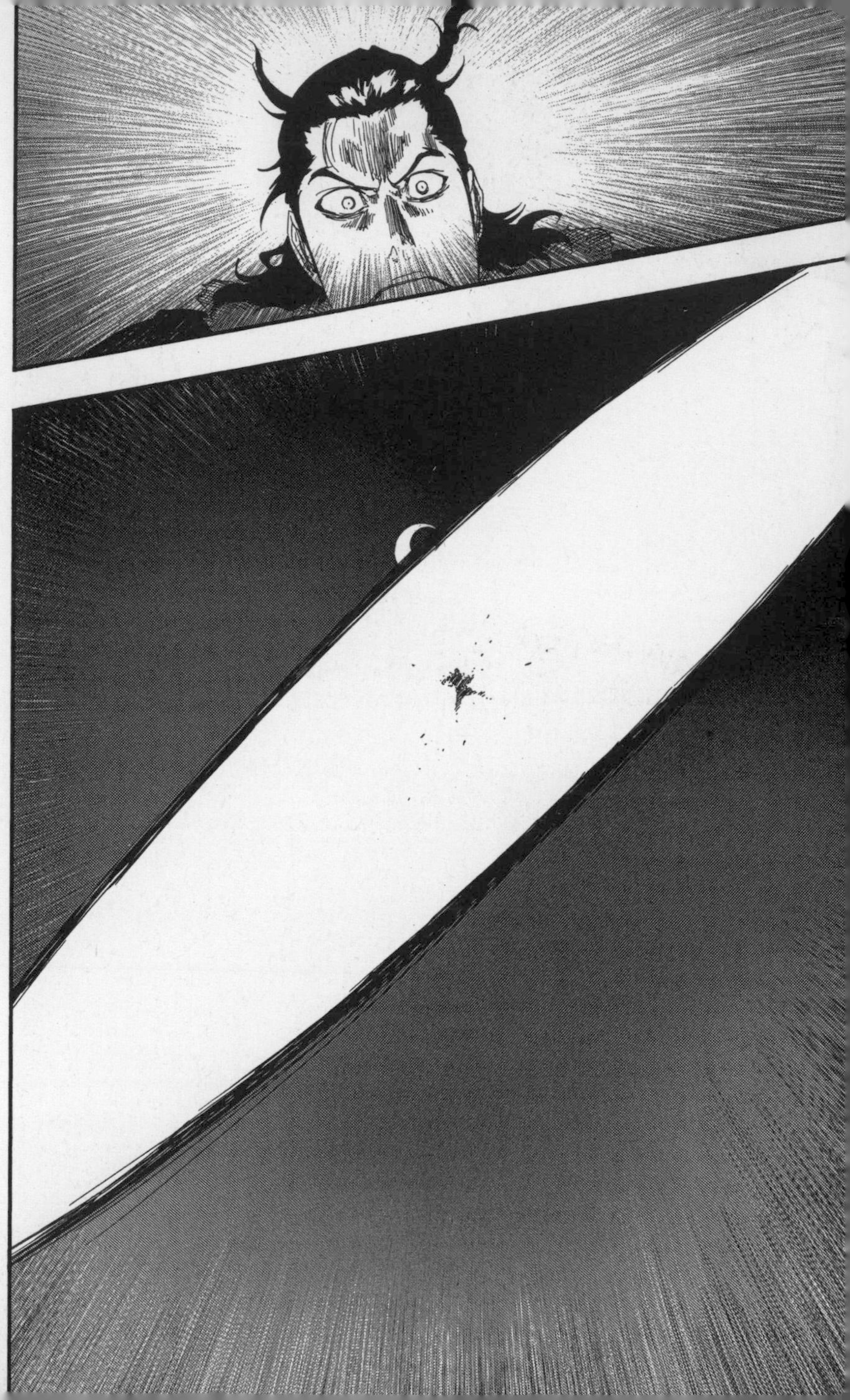

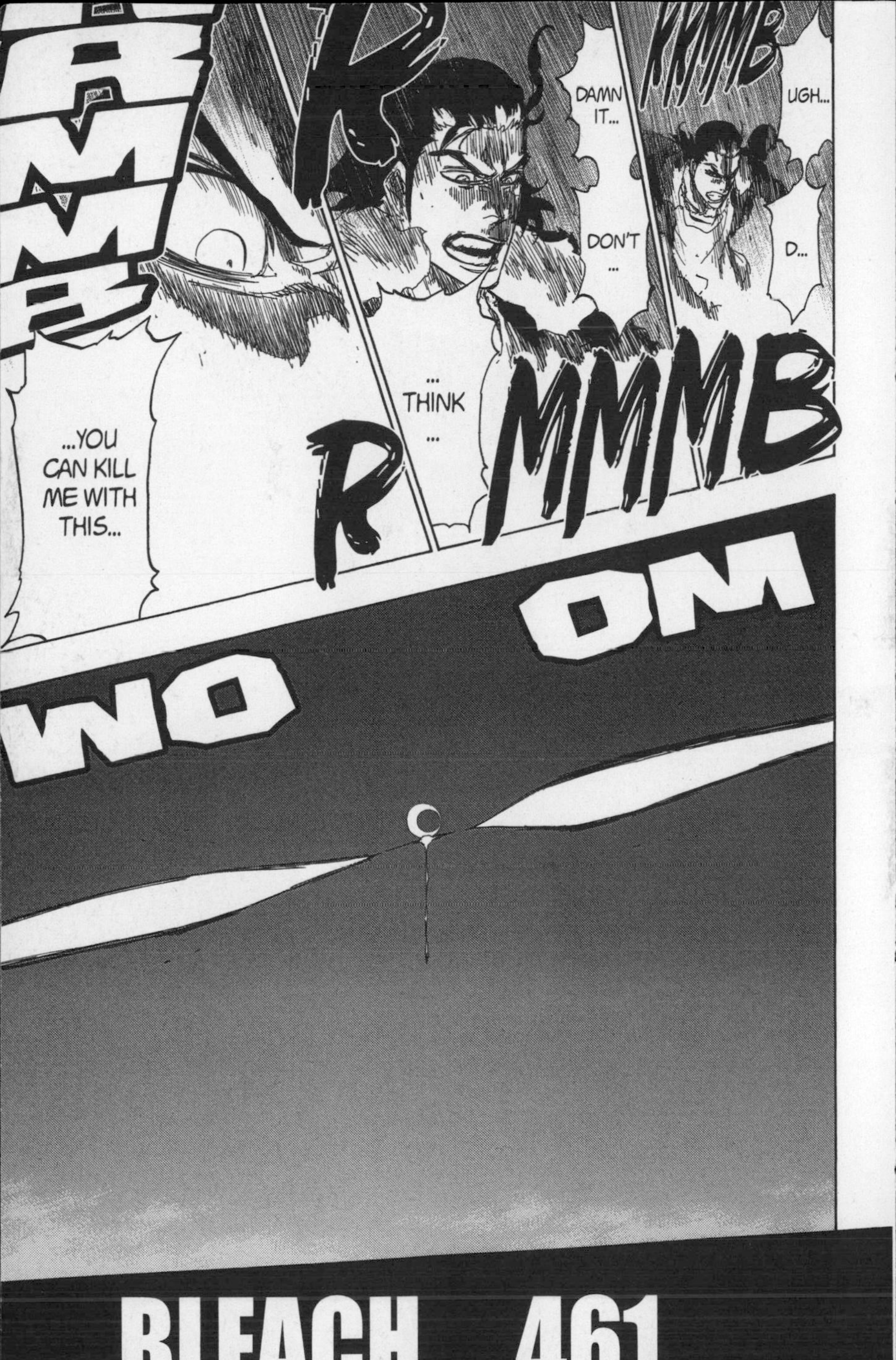
KRMMB
UGH...
D...
DAMN IT...
DON'T ...
... THINK ...
...YOU CAN KILL ME WITH THIS...
RMMMB
OM
WO

BLEACH 461.

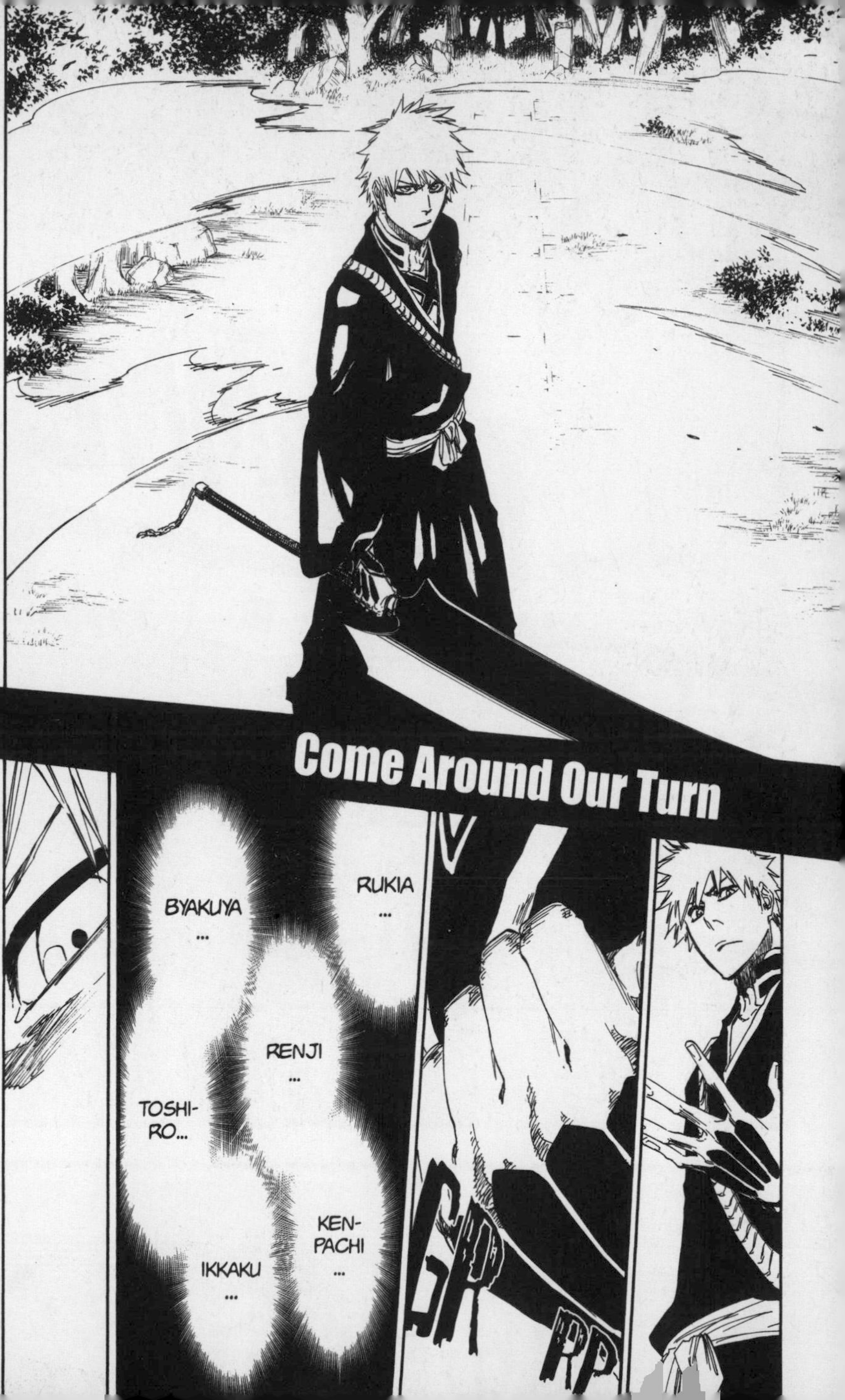
Come Around Our Turn
RUKIA ...
BYAKUYA ...
RENJI ...
TOSHI-RO...
KEN-PACHI ...
IKKAKU ...

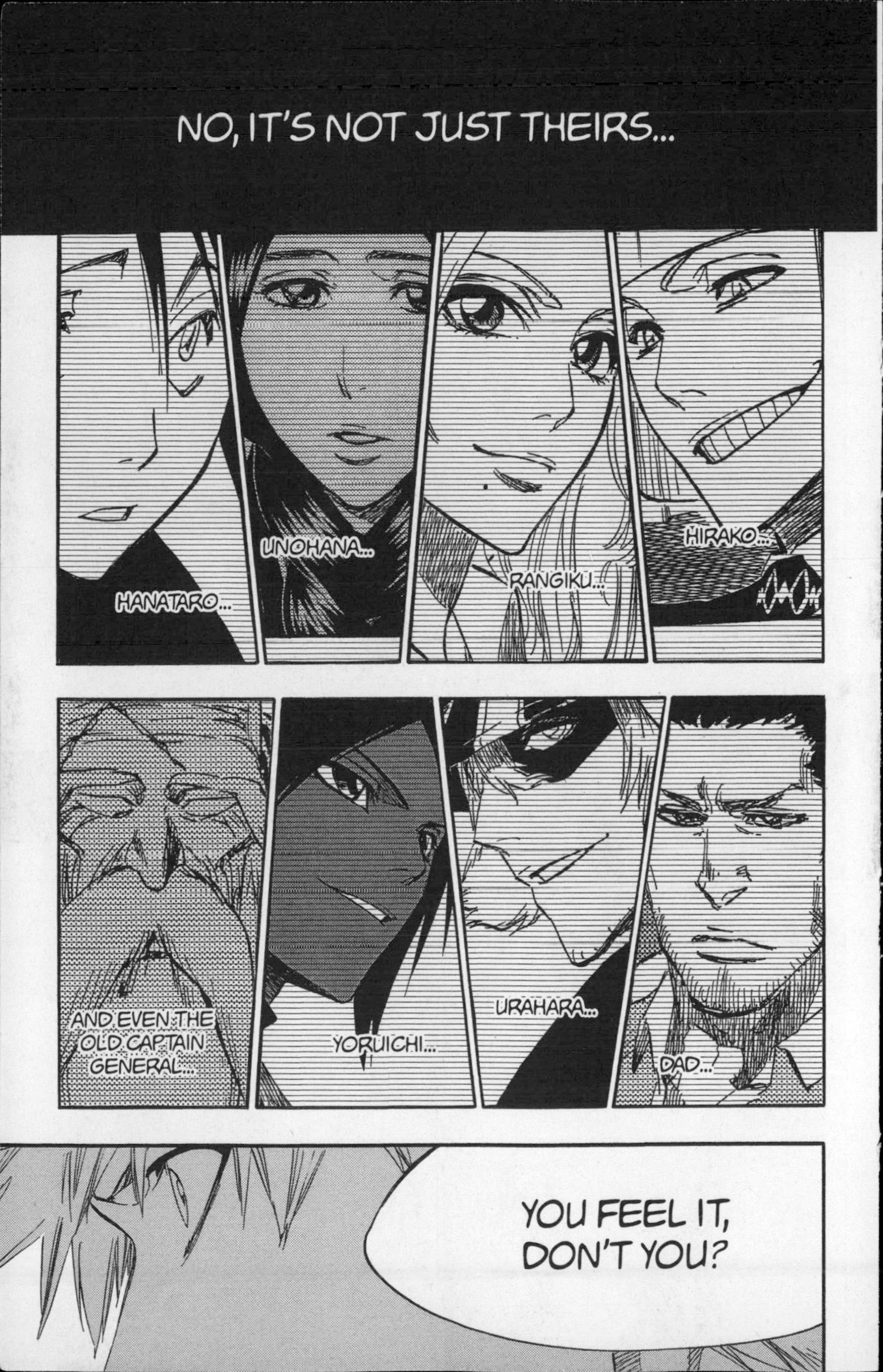
NO, IT'S NOT JUST THEIRS...
HIRAKO...
RANGIKU...
UNOHANA...
HANATARO...
DAD...
URAHARA...
YORUICHI...
AND EVEN THE OLD CAPTAIN GENERAL...
YOU FEEL IT, DON'T YOU?

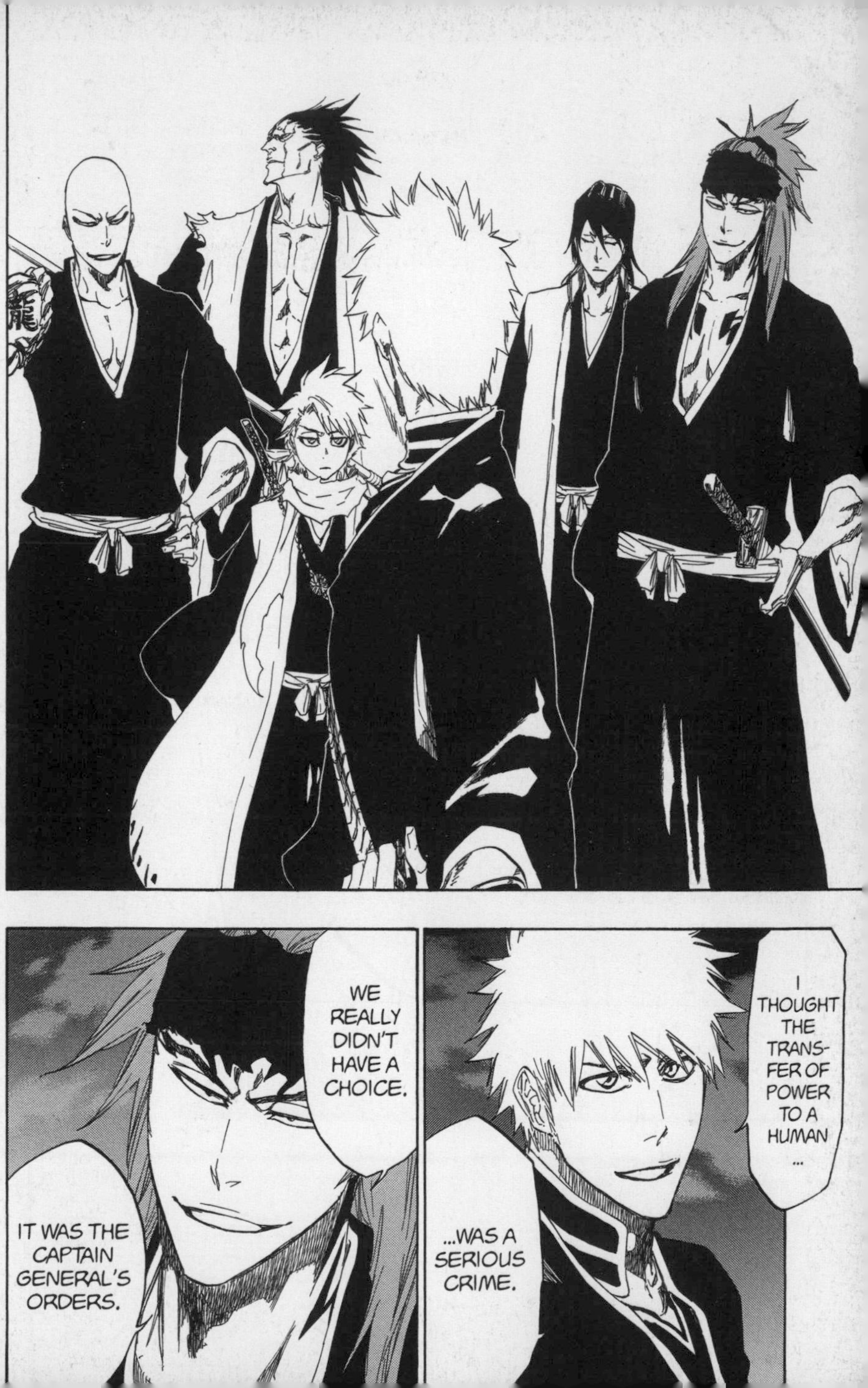
I THOUGHT THE TRANS-FER OF POWER TO A HUMAN ...
...WAS A SERIOUS CRIME.
WE REALLY DIDN'T HAVE A CHOICE.
IT WAS THE CAPTAIN GENERAL'S ORDERS.

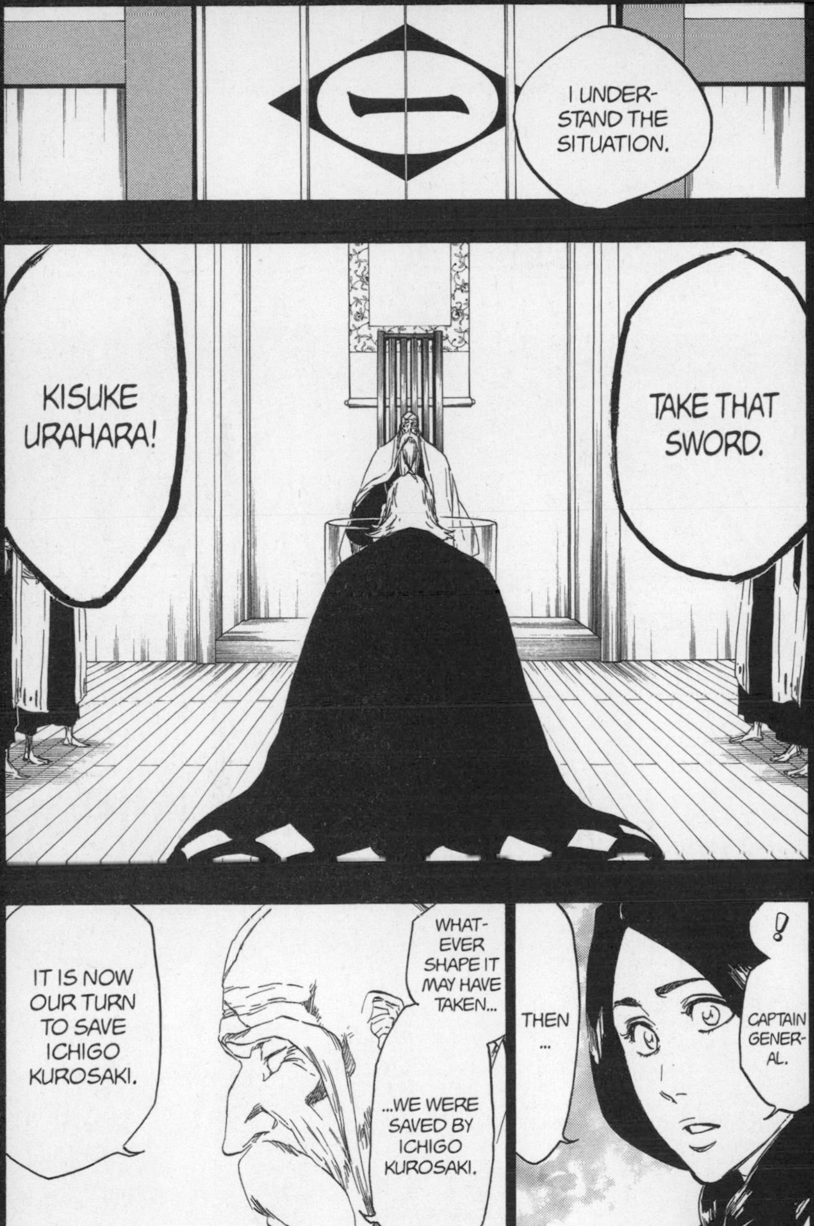
I UNDERSTAND THE SITUATION.
TAKE THAT SWORD.
KISUKE URAHARA!
!
CAPTAIN GENERAL.
THEN ...
WHATEVER SHAPE IT MAY HAVE TAKEN...
...WE WERE SAVED BY ICHIGO KUROSAKI.
IT IS NOW OUR TURN TO SAVE ICHIGO KUROSAKI.

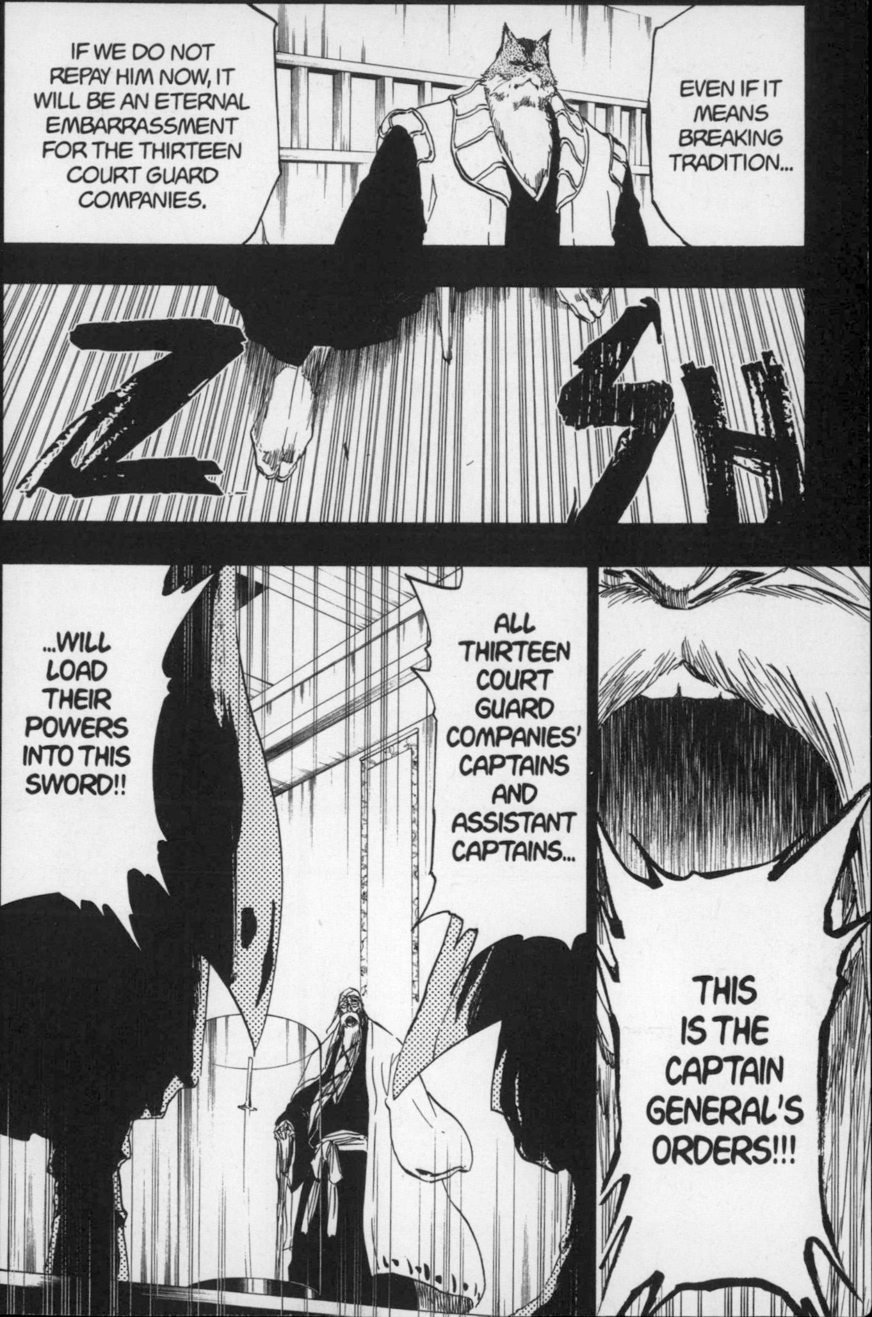
EVEN IF IT MEANS BREAKING TRADITION...
IF WE DO NOT REPAY HIM NOW, IT WILL BE AN ETERNAL EMBARRASSMENT FOR THE THIRTEEN COURT GUARD COMPANIES.
ZSH
THIS IS THE CAPTAIN GENERAL'S ORDERS!!!
ALL THIRTEEN COURT GUARD COMPANIES' CAPTAINS AND ASSISTANT CAPTAINS...
...WILL LOAD THEIR POWERS INTO THIS SWORD!!

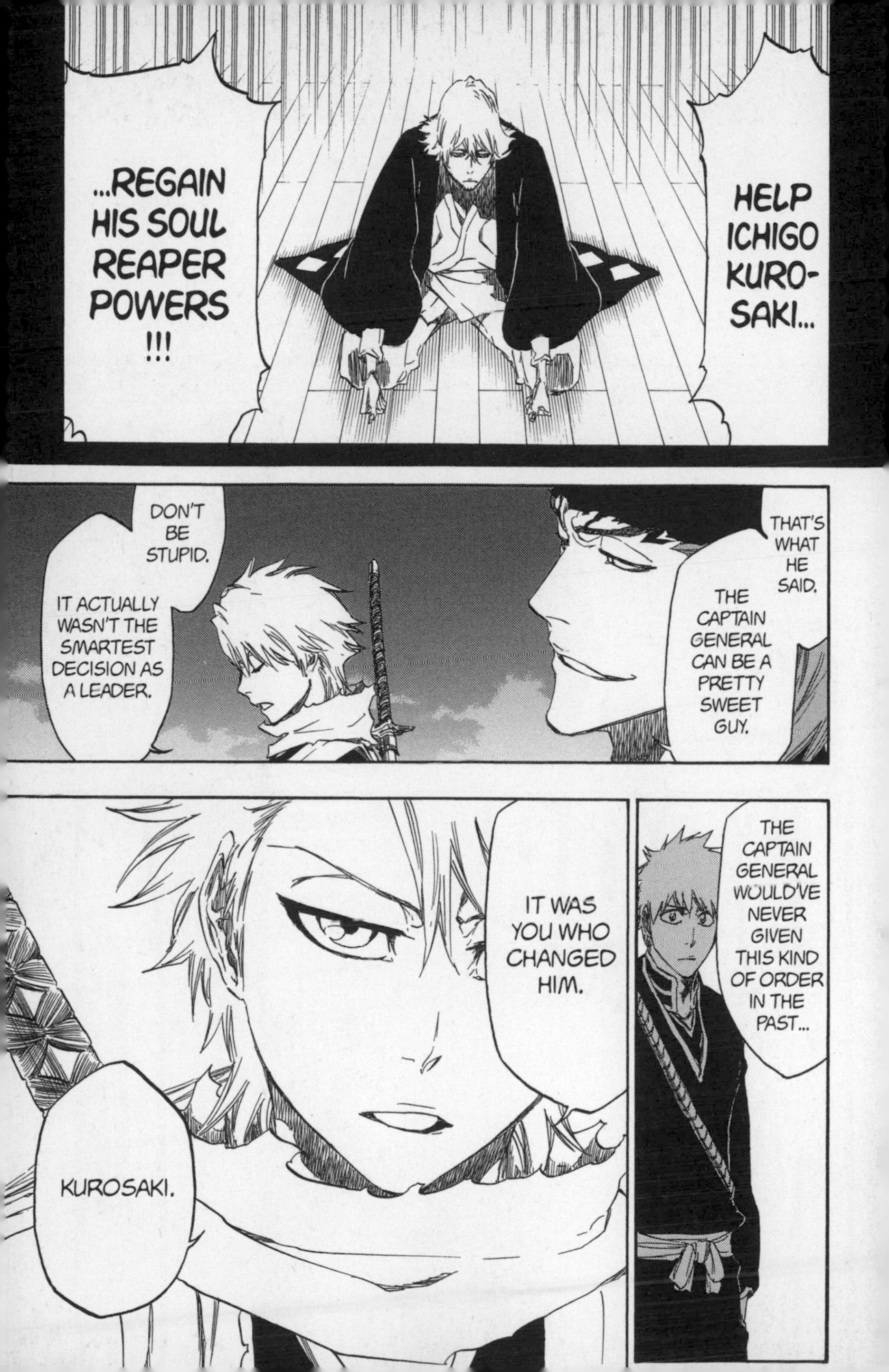
HELP ICHIGO KUROSAKI...
...REGAIN HIS SOUL REAPER POWERS!!!
THAT'S WHAT HE SAID.
THE CAPTAIN GENERAL CAN BE A PRETTY SWEET GUY.
DON'T BE STUPID.
IT ACTUALLY WASN'T THE SMARTEST DECISION AS A LEADER.
THE CAPTAIN GENERAL WOULD'VE NEVER GIVEN THIS KIND OF ORDER IN THE PAST...
IT WAS YOU WHO CHANGED HIM.
KUROSAKI.

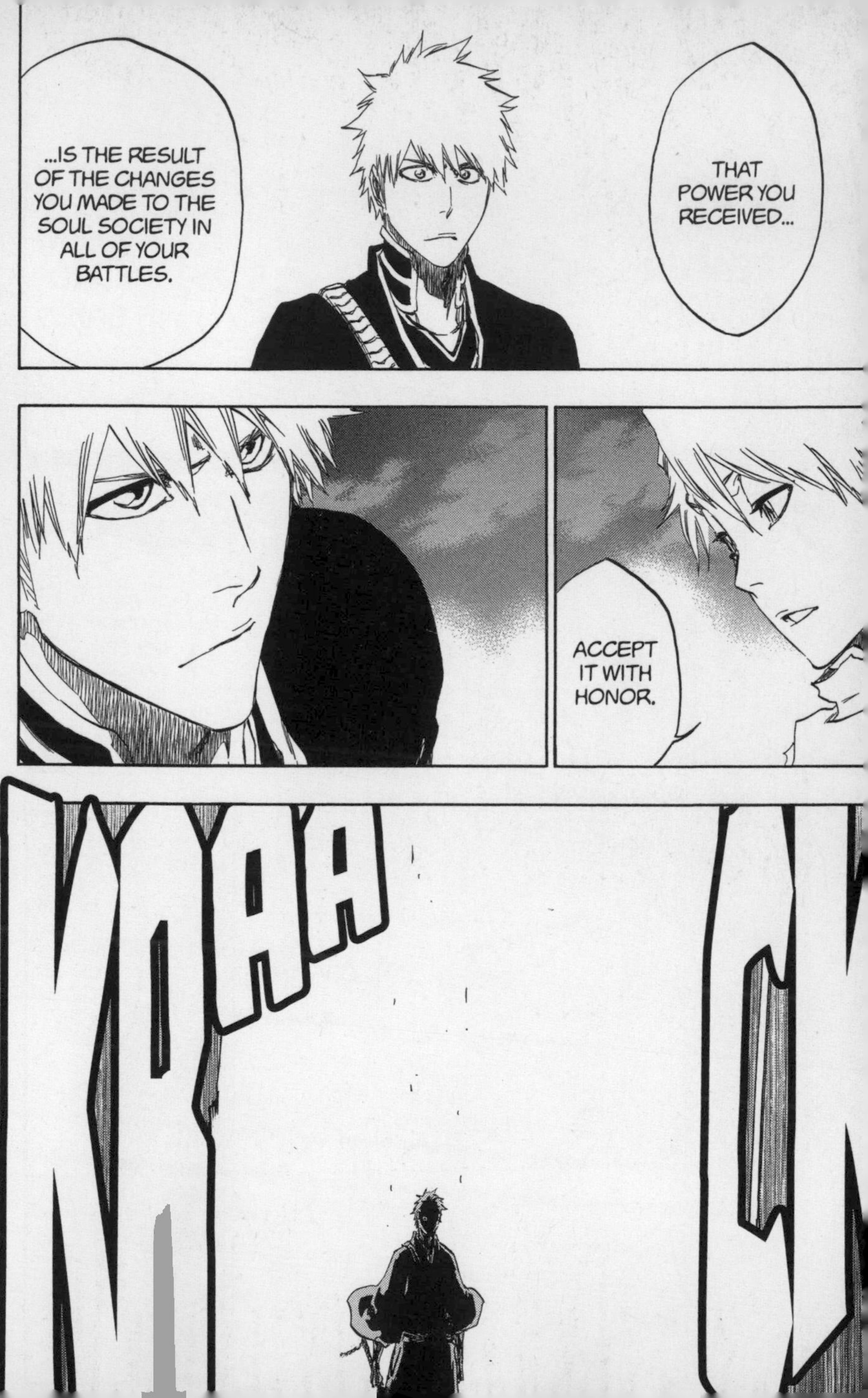
THAT POWER YOU RECEIVED...
...IS THE RESULT OF THE CHANGES YOU MADE TO THE SOUL SOCIETY IN ALL OF YOUR BATTLES.
ACCEPT IT WITH HONOR.
KRAA
CK

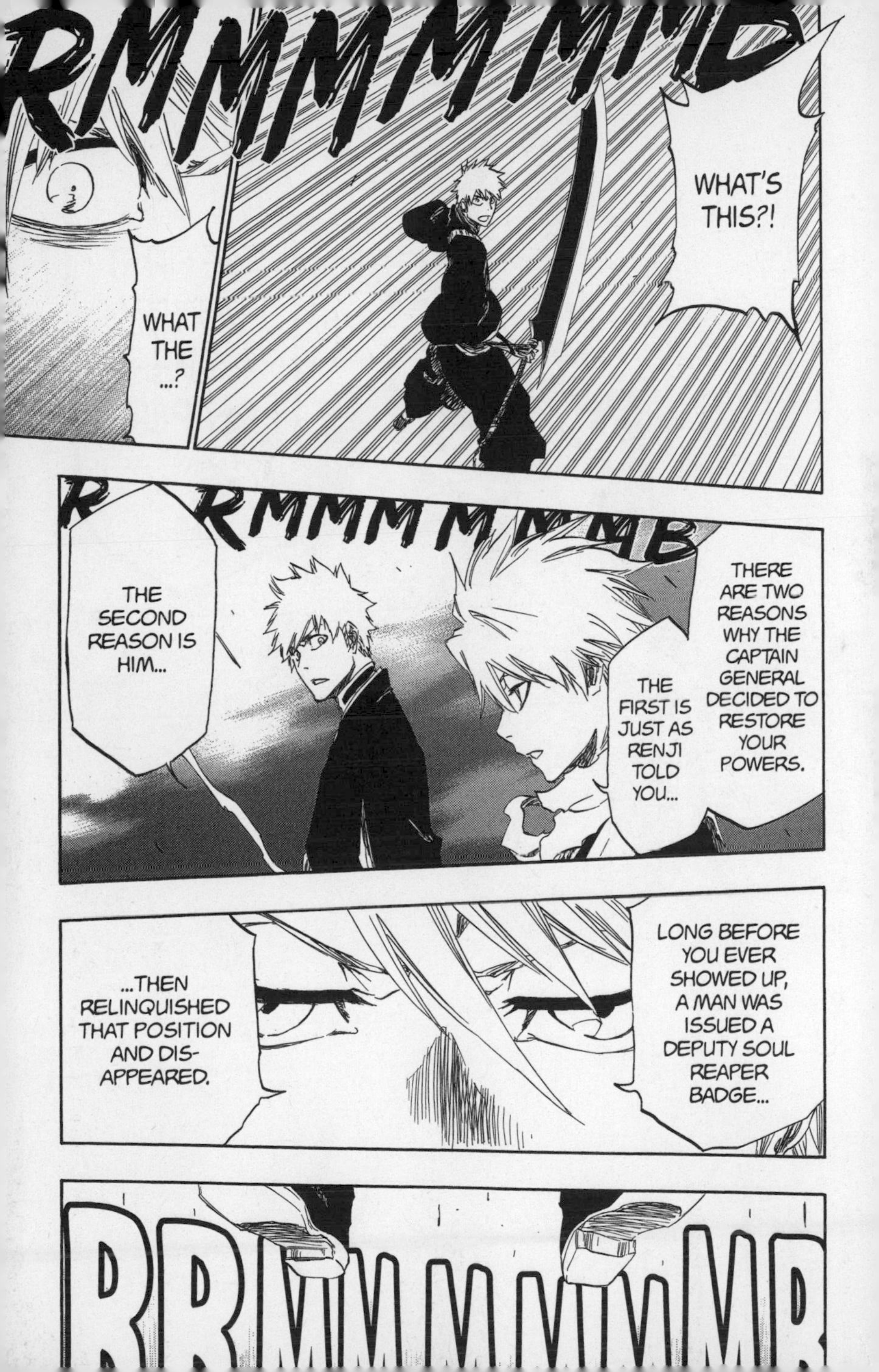
RMMMMMB
WHAT'S THIS?!
WHAT THE ...?
RMMMMMMB
THERE ARE TWO REASONS WHY THE CAPTAIN GENERAL DECIDED TO RESTORE YOUR POWERS.
THE FIRST IS JUST AS RENJI TOLD YOU...
THE SECOND REASON IS HIM...
LONG BEFORE YOU EVER SHOWED UP, A MAN WAS ISSUED A DEPUTY SOUL REAPER BADGE...
...THEN RELINQUISHED THAT POSITION AND DIS-APPEARED.
RRMMMMMB

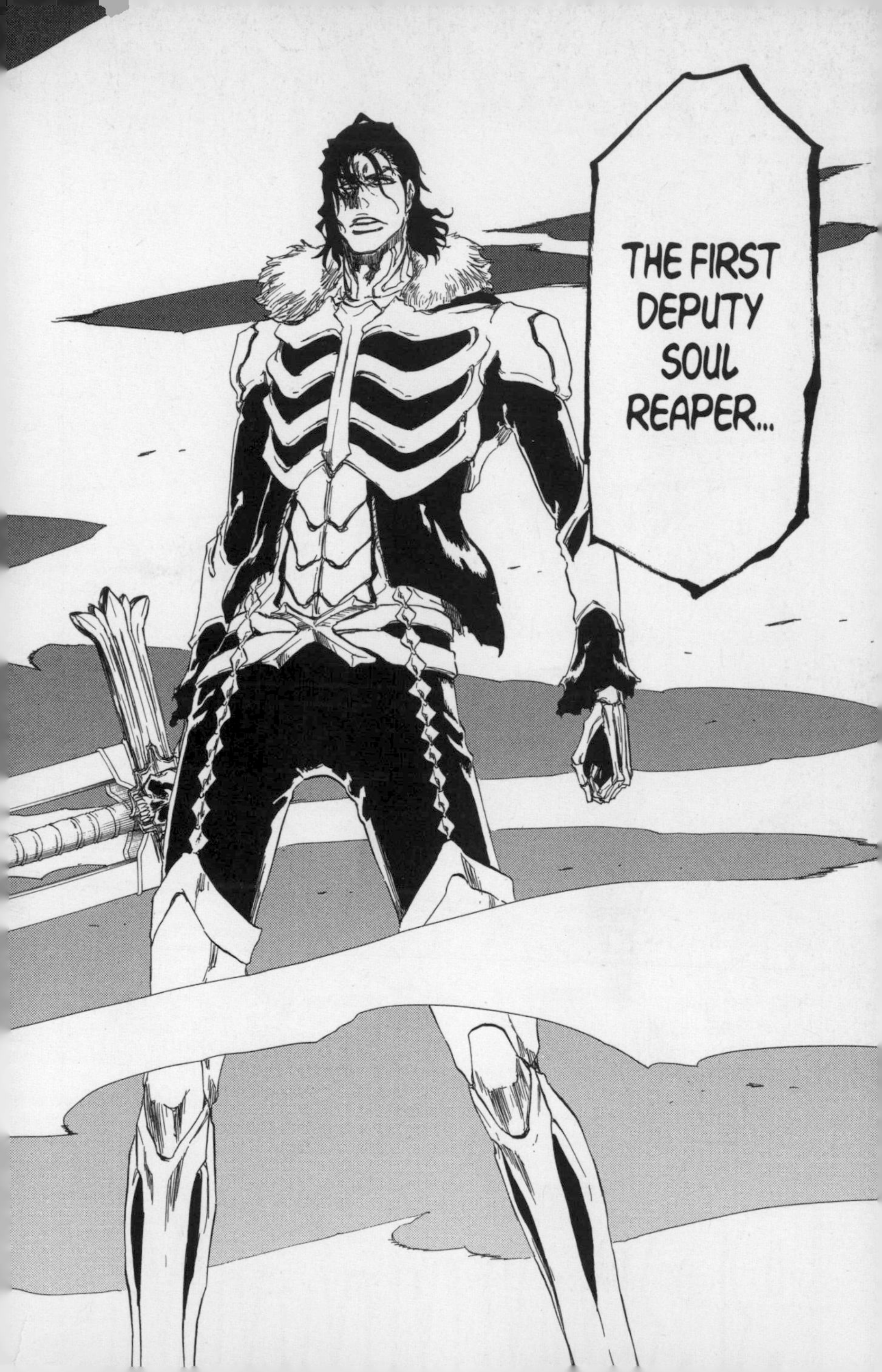
THE FIRST DEPUTY SOUL REAPER...

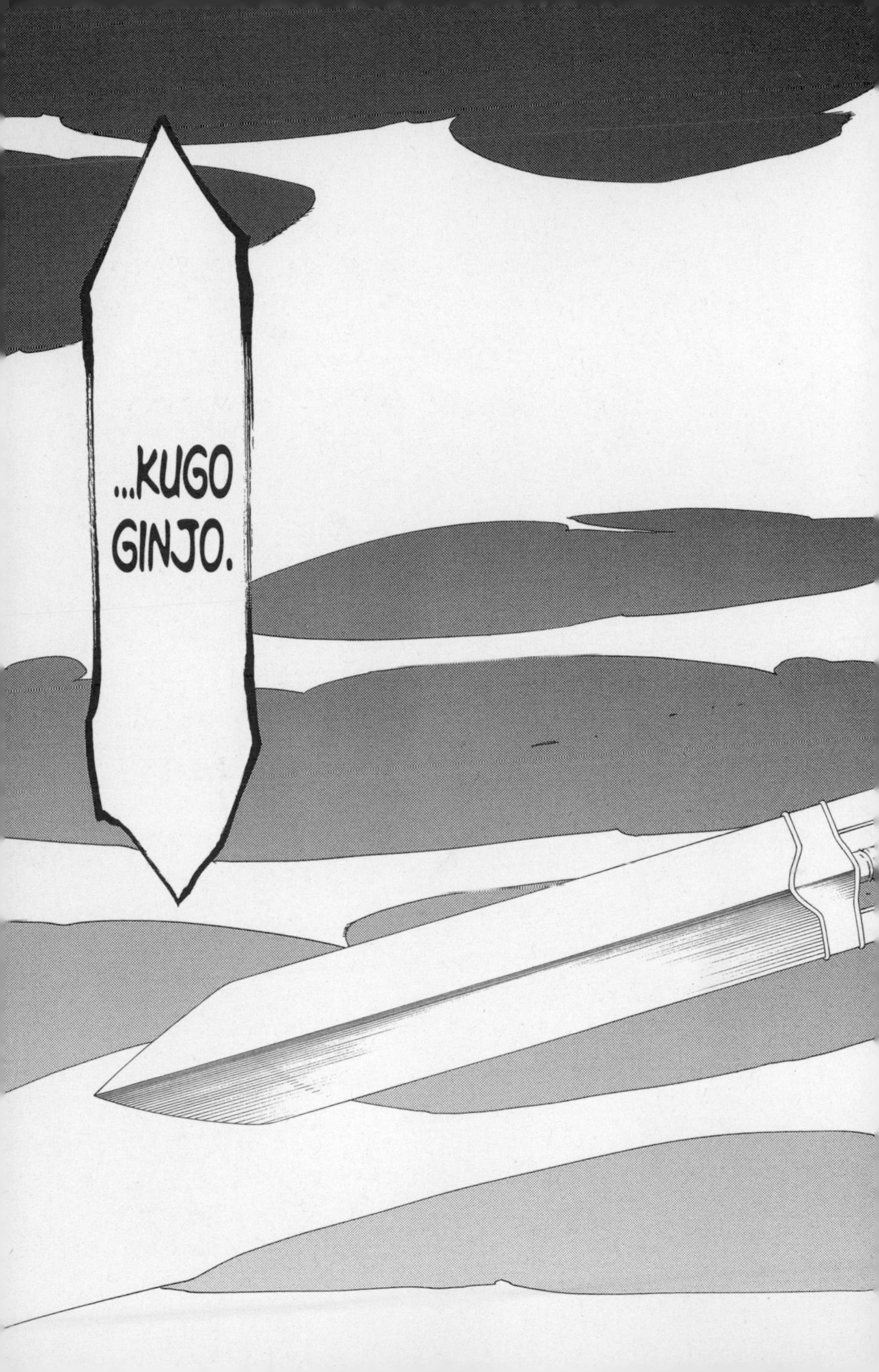
...KUGO GINJO.

IT'S
BEEN A
LONG
TIME.

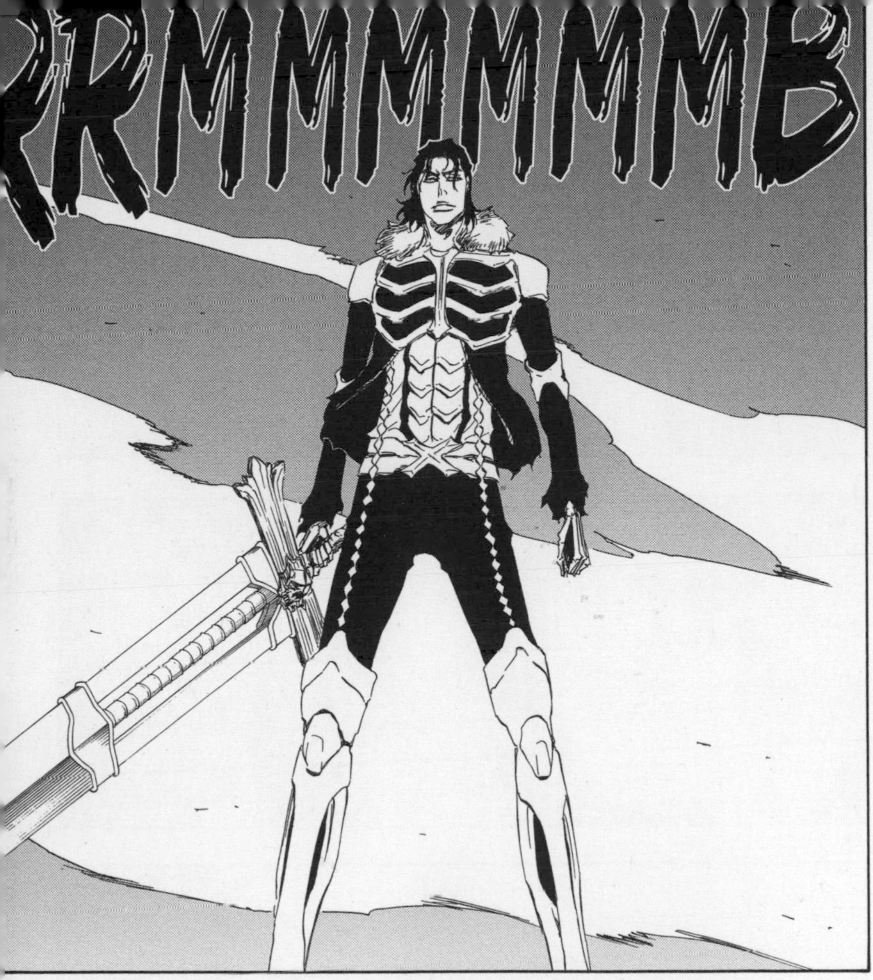
RMMMMMMB

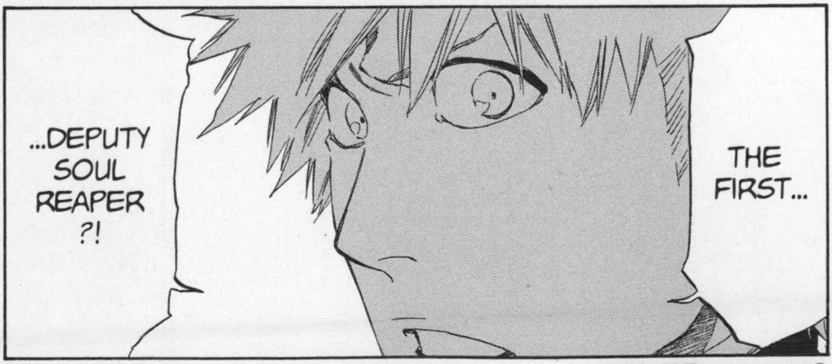
THE FIRST...
...DEPUTY SOUL REAPER ?!

462. Why me sad.

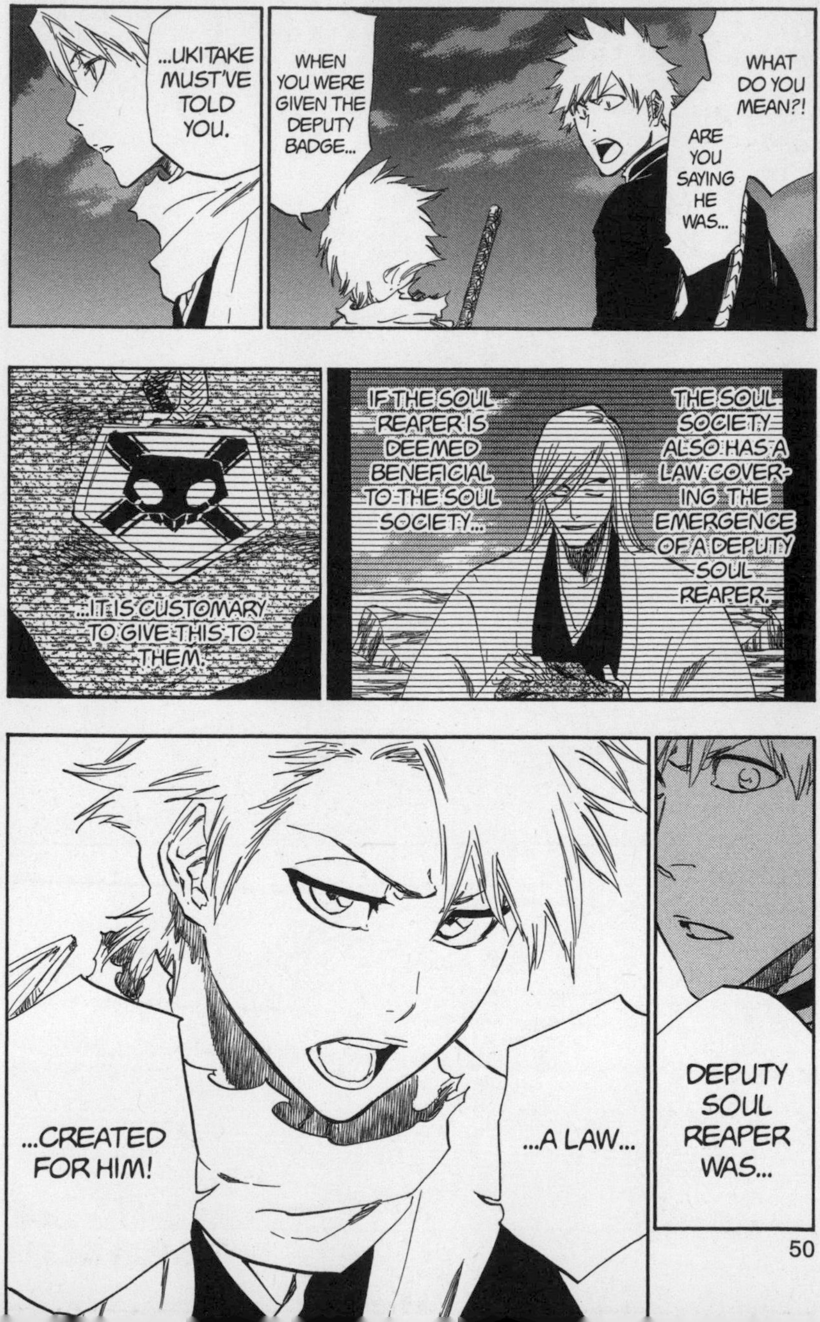
WHAT DO YOU MEAN?!
ARE YOU SAYING HE WAS...
WHEN YOU WERE GIVEN THE DEPUTY BADGE...
...UKITAKE MUST'VE TOLD YOU.
THE SOUL SOCIETY ALSO HAS A LAW COVERING THE EMERGENCE OF A DEPUTY SOUL REAPER.
IF THE SOUL REAPER IS DEEMED BENEFICIAL TO THE SOUL SOCIETY...
...IT IS CUSTOMARY TO GIVE THIS TO THEM.
DEPUTY SOUL REAPER WAS...
...A LAW...
...CREATED FOR HIM!

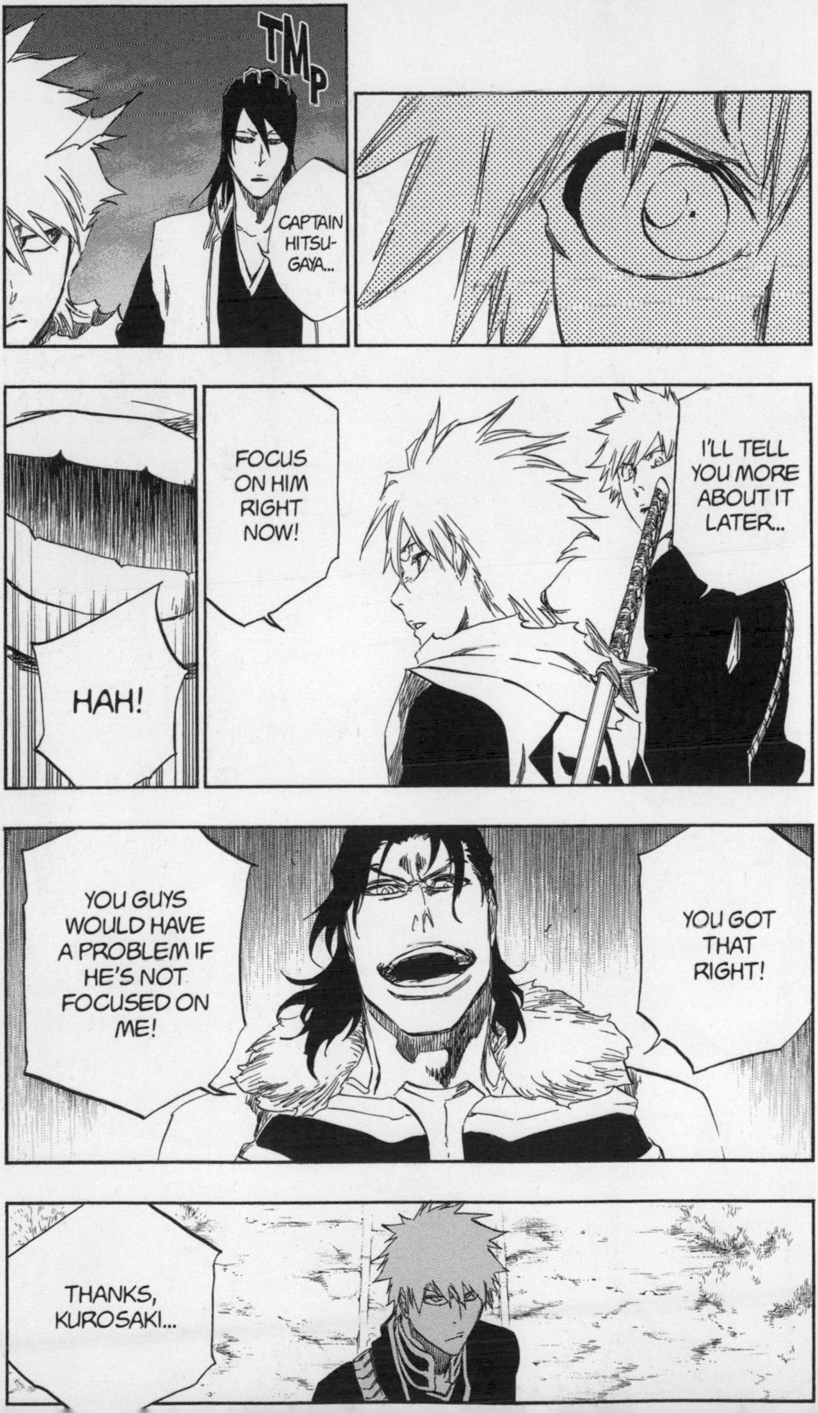
TMP
CAPTAIN HITSU-GAYA...
I'LL TELL YOU MORE ABOUT IT LATER...
FOCUS ON HIM RIGHT NOW!
HAH!
YOU GOT THAT RIGHT!
YOU GUYS WOULD HAVE A PROBLEM IF HE'S NOT FOCUSED ON ME!
THANKS, KUROSAKI...

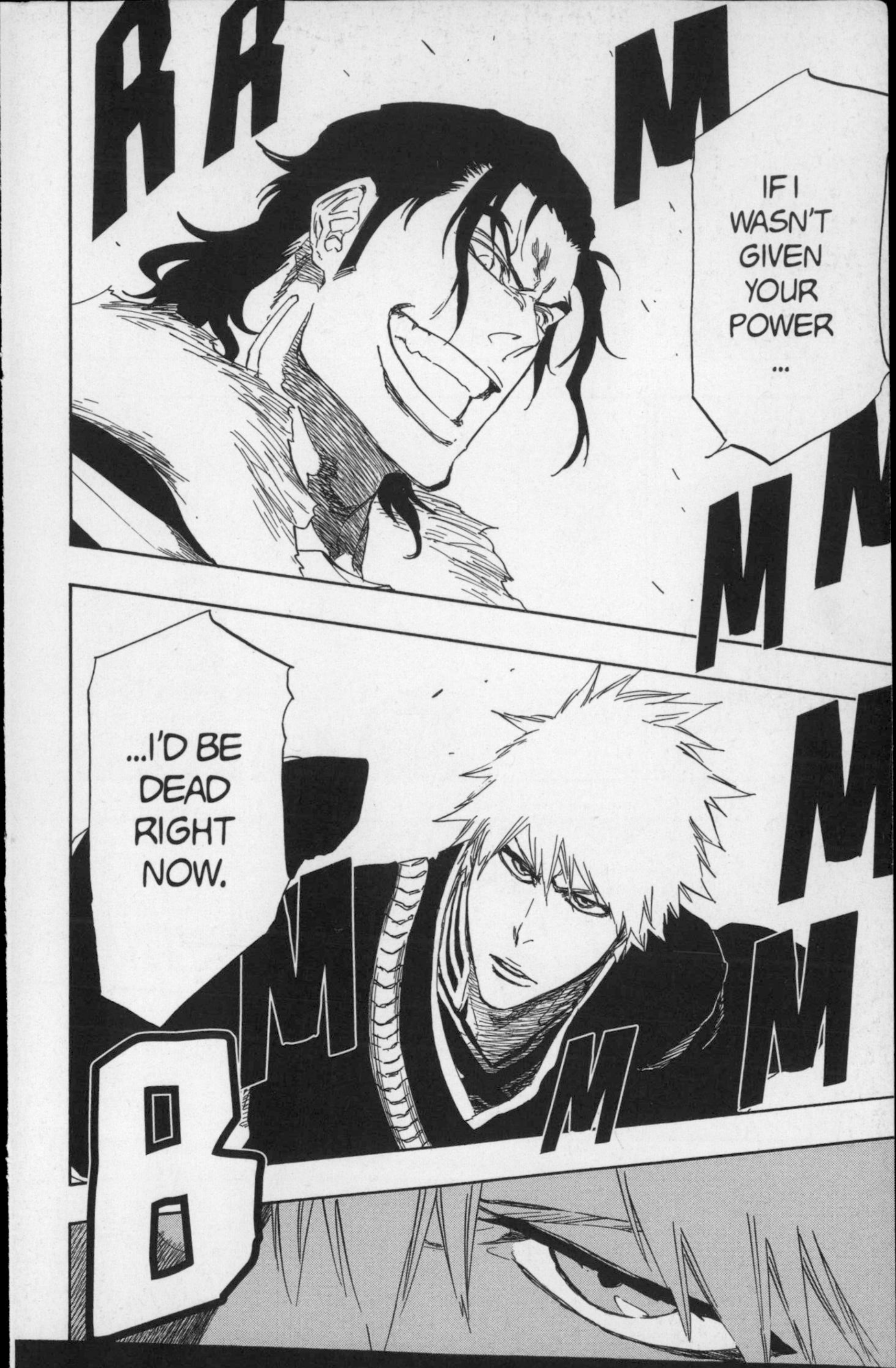
IF I WASN'T GIVEN YOUR POWER ...
...I'D BE DEAD RIGHT NOW.

BLEACH 462.

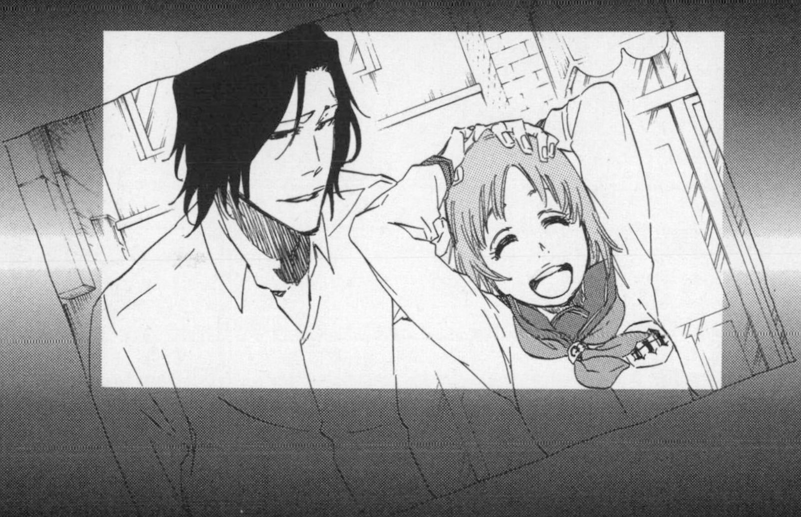

Why me sad.

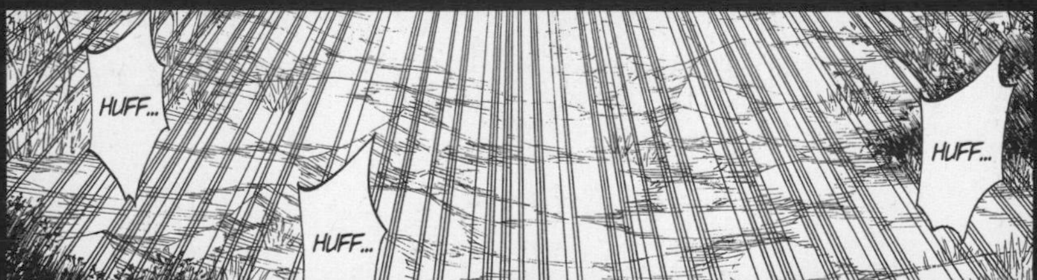
HUFF...
HUFF...
HUFF...

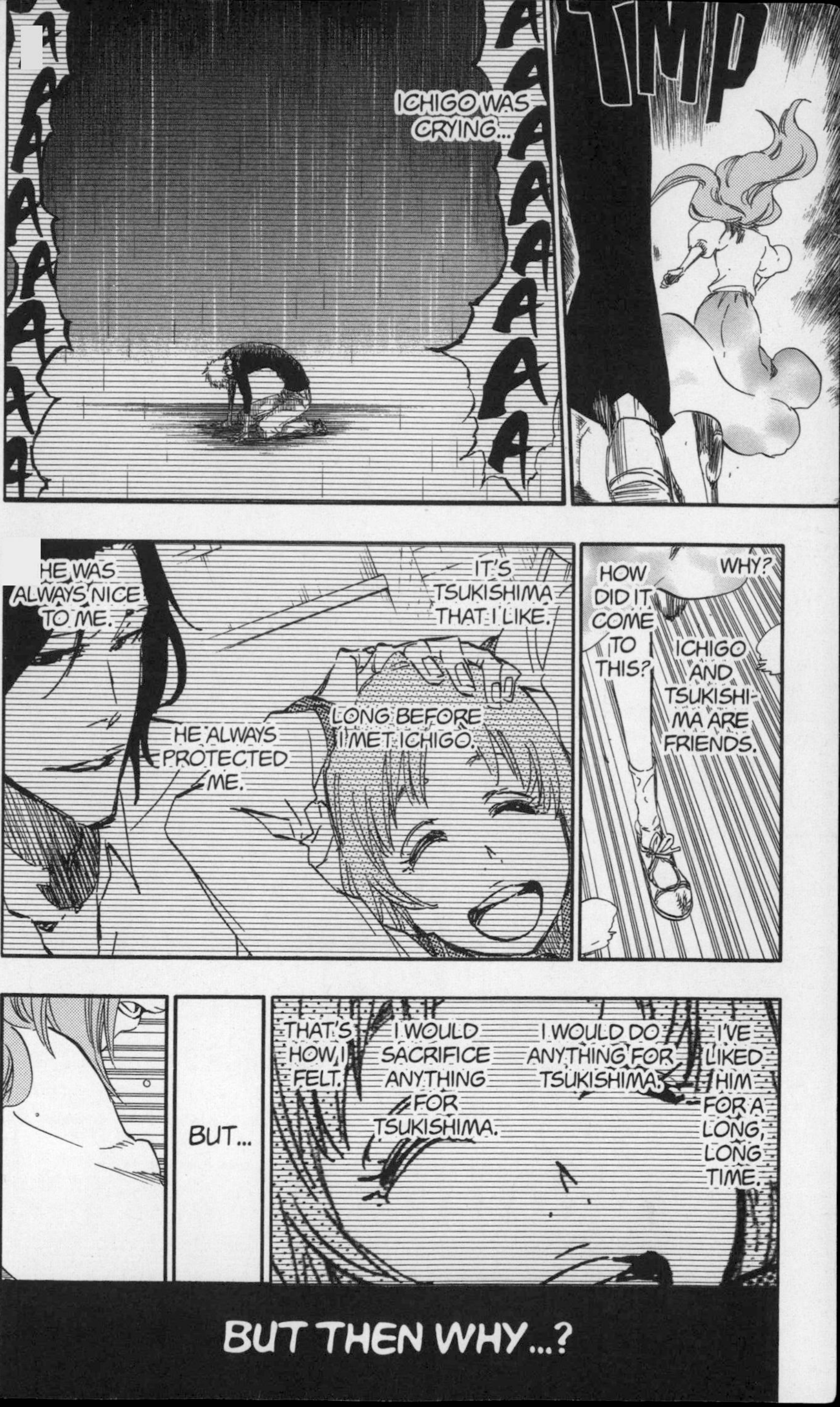
TMP
ICHIGO WAS CRYING...
AAAAAAAAAAA
WHY?
HOW DID IT COME TO THIS?
ICHIGO AND TSUKISHIMA ARE FRIENDS.
IT'S TSUKISHIMA THAT I LIKE.
HE WAS ALWAYS NICE TO ME.
LONG BEFORE I MET ICHIGO.
HE ALWAYS PROTECTED ME.
I'VE LIKED HIM FOR A LONG, LONG TIME.
I WOULD DO ANYTHING FOR TSUKISHIMA.
I WOULD SACRIFICE ANYTHING FOR TSUKISHIMA.
THAT'S HOW I FELT.
BUT...
BUT THEN WHY...?

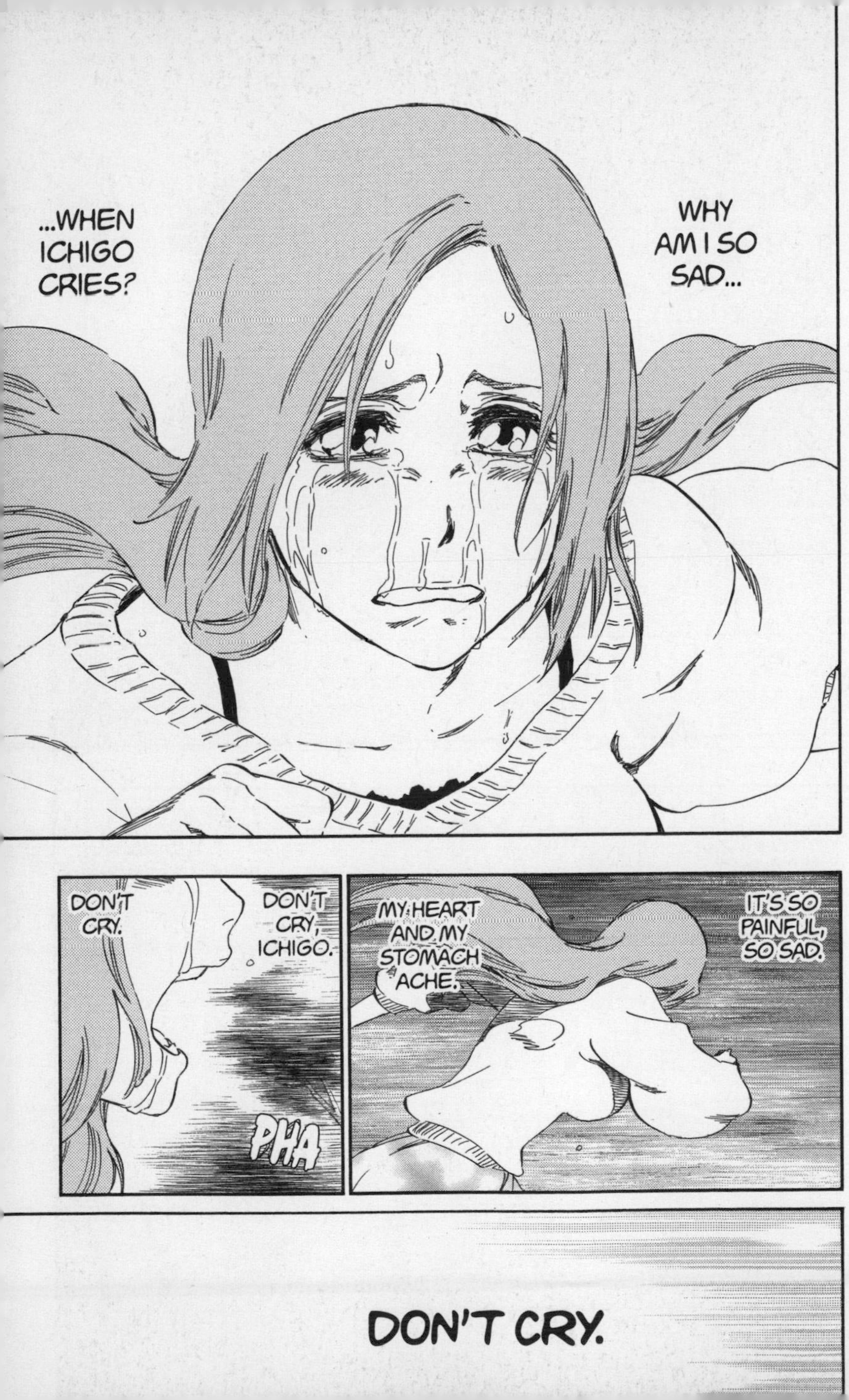
WHY AM I SO SAD...
...WHEN ICHIGO CRIES?
IT'S SO PAINFUL, SO SAD.
MY HEART AND MY STOMACH ACHE.
DON'T CRY, ICHIGO.
DON'T CRY.
PHA
DON'T CRY.

ICHI-
GO...

ICHIGO
ISN'T
CRYING...

GOOD...

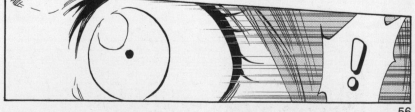

!

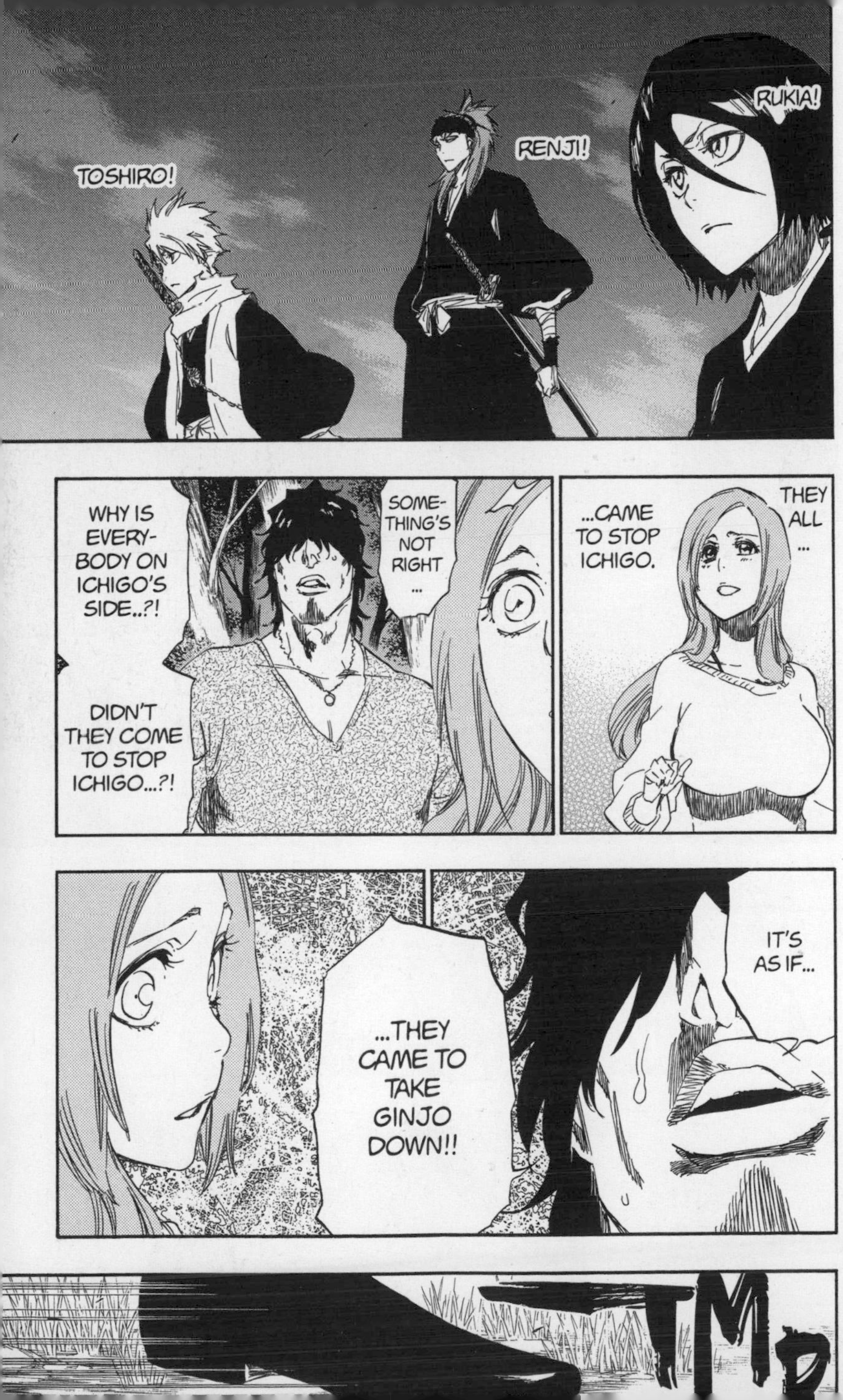
RUKIA!
RENJI!
TOSHIRO!
THEY ALL ...
...CAME TO STOP ICHIGO.
SOMETHING'S NOT RIGHT ...
WHY IS EVERYBODY ON ICHIGO'S SIDE..?!
DIDN'T THEY COME TO STOP ICHIGO...?!
IT'S AS IF...
...THEY CAME TO TAKE GINJO DOWN!!

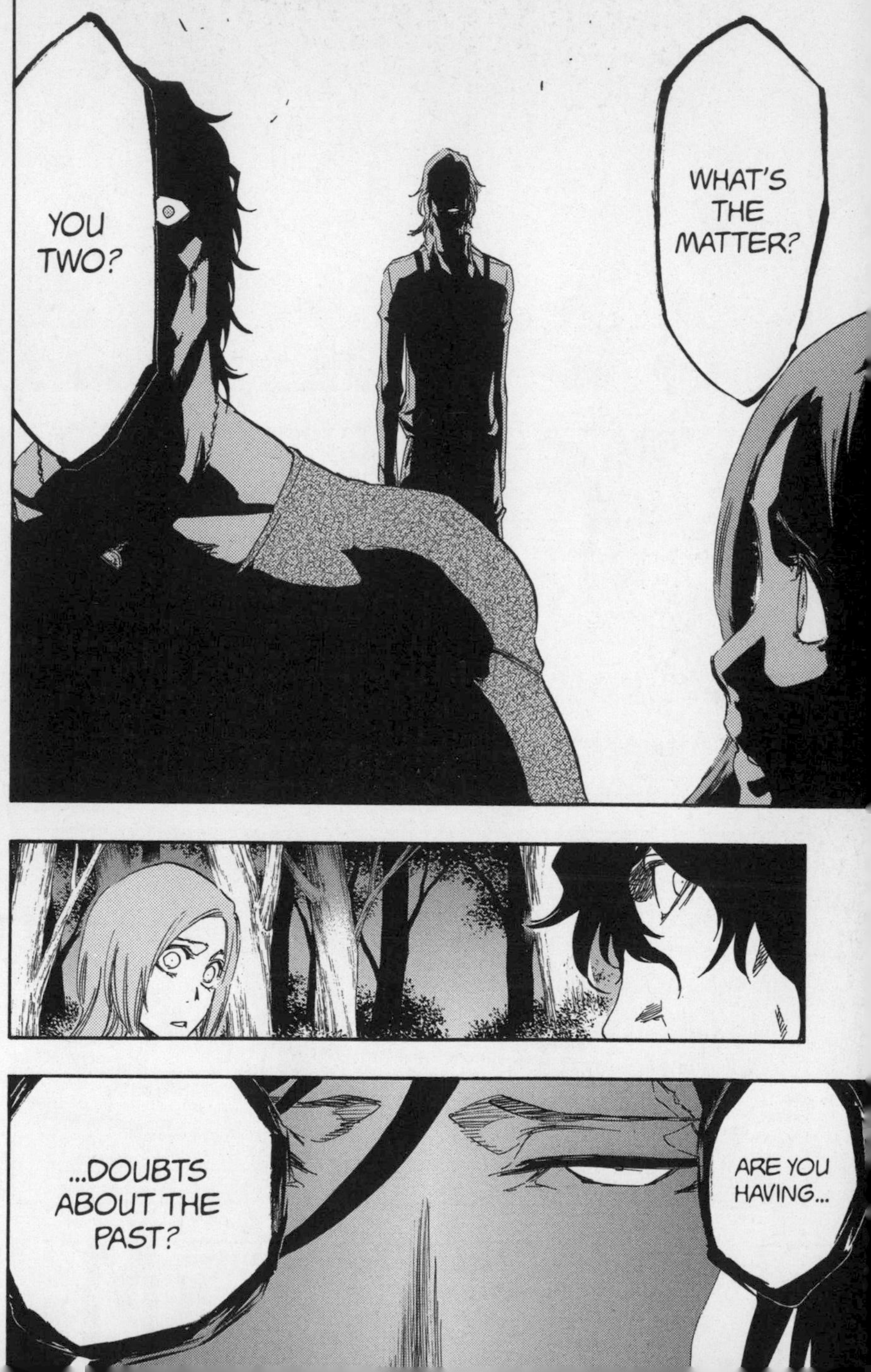
WHAT'S THE MATTER?
YOU TWO?
ARE YOU HAVING...
...DOUBTS ABOUT THE PAST?

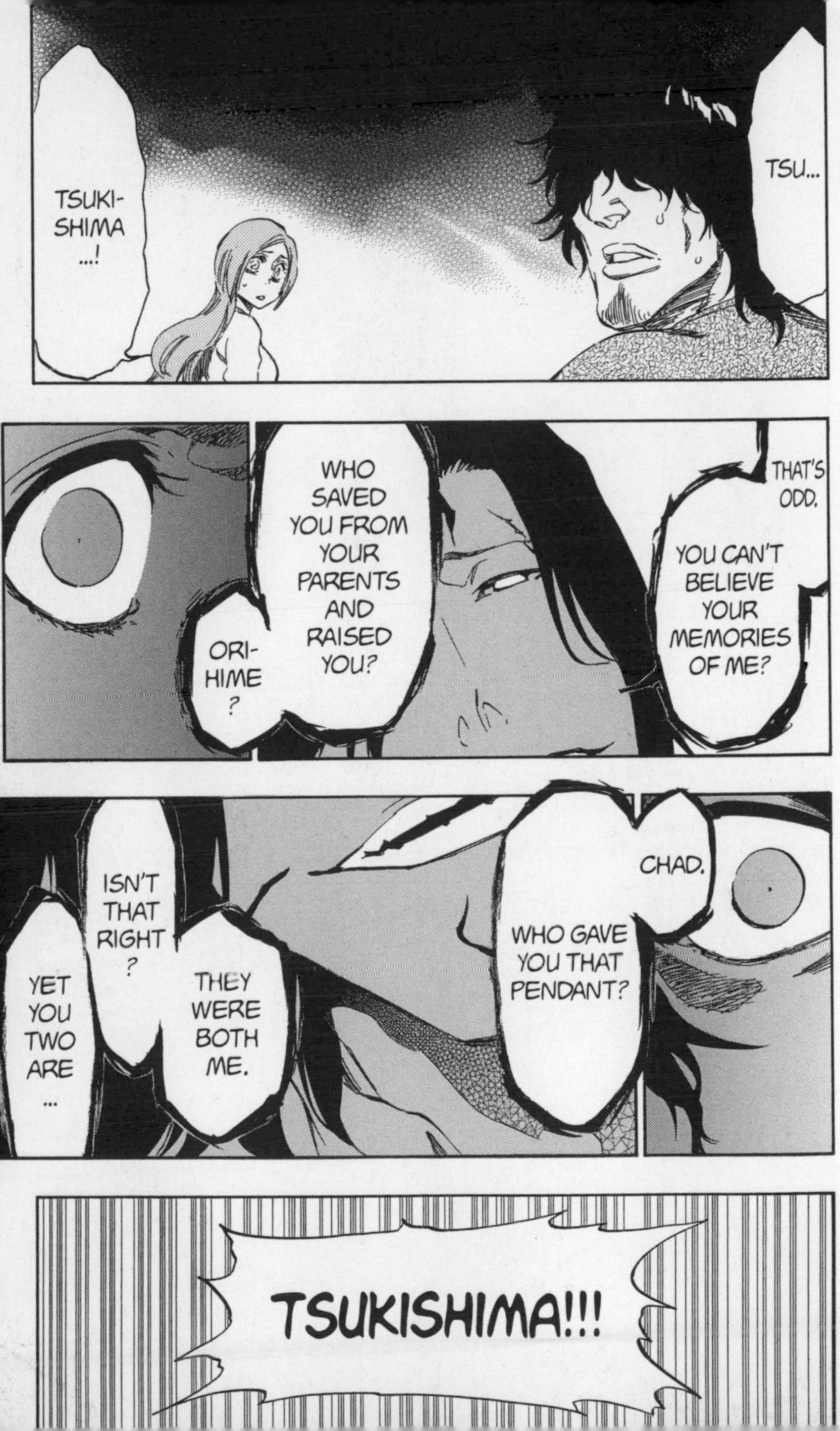
TSU...
TSUKI-SHIMA ...!
THAT'S ODD.
YOU CAN'T BELIEVE YOUR MEMORIES OF ME?
WHO SAVED YOU FROM YOUR PARENTS AND RAISED YOU?
ORI-HIME?
CHAD.
WHO GAVE YOU THAT PENDANT?
THEY WERE BOTH ME.
ISN'T THAT RIGHT?
YET YOU TWO ARE ...
TSUKISHIMA!!!

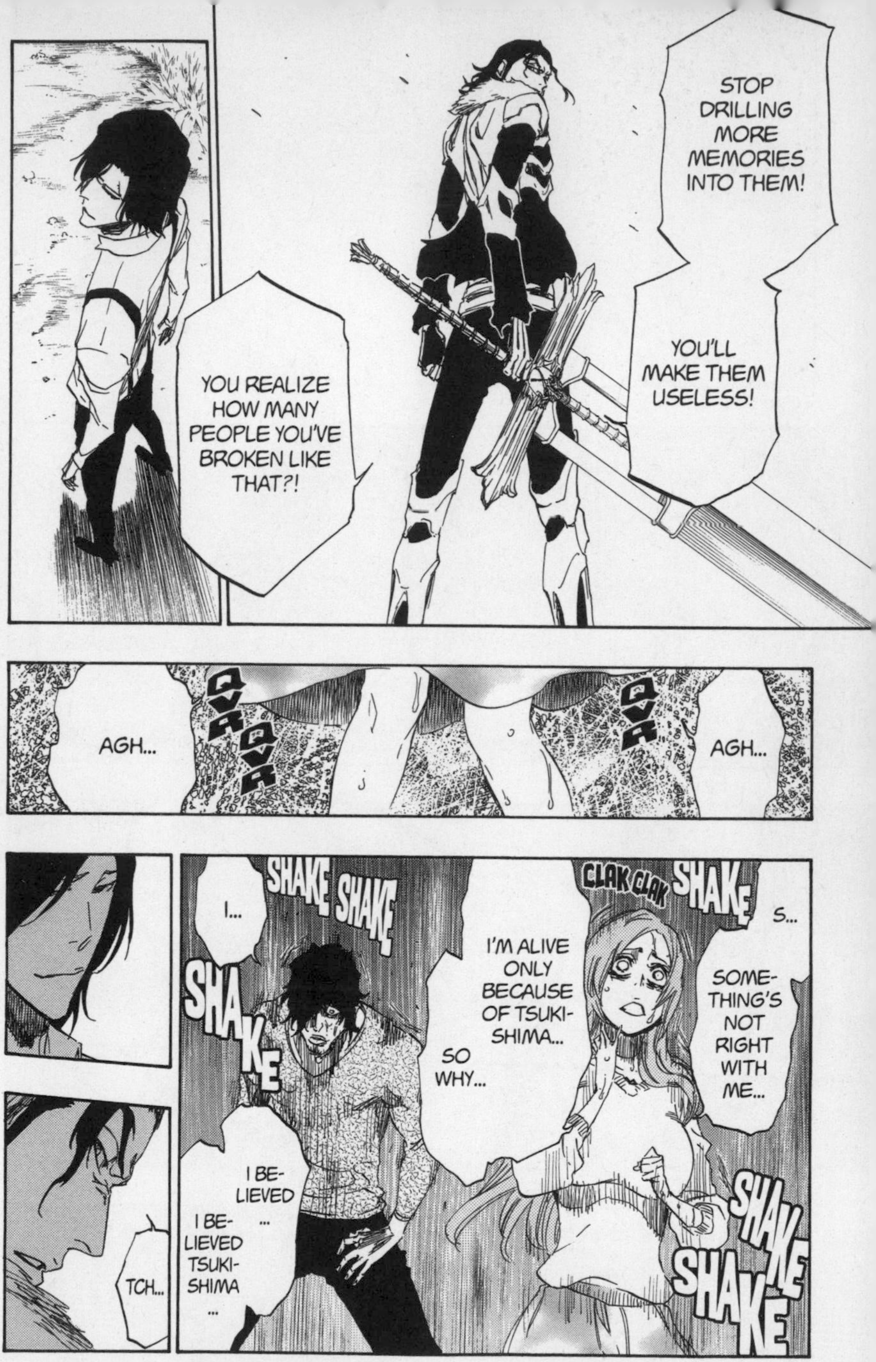
STOP DRILLING MORE MEMORIES INTO THEM!
YOU'LL MAKE THEM USELESS!
YOU REALIZE HOW MANY PEOPLE YOU'VE BROKEN LIKE THAT?!
AGH...
QVR
QVR QVR
AGH...
S...
SHAKE
CLAK CLAK
SOMETHING'S NOT RIGHT WITH ME...
I'M ALIVE ONLY BECAUSE OF TSUKISHIMA...
SO WHY...
SHAKE SHAKE
SHAKE SHAKE
I...
SHAKE SHAKE
SHAKE
I BELIEVED...
I BELIEVED TSUKISHIMA...
TCH...

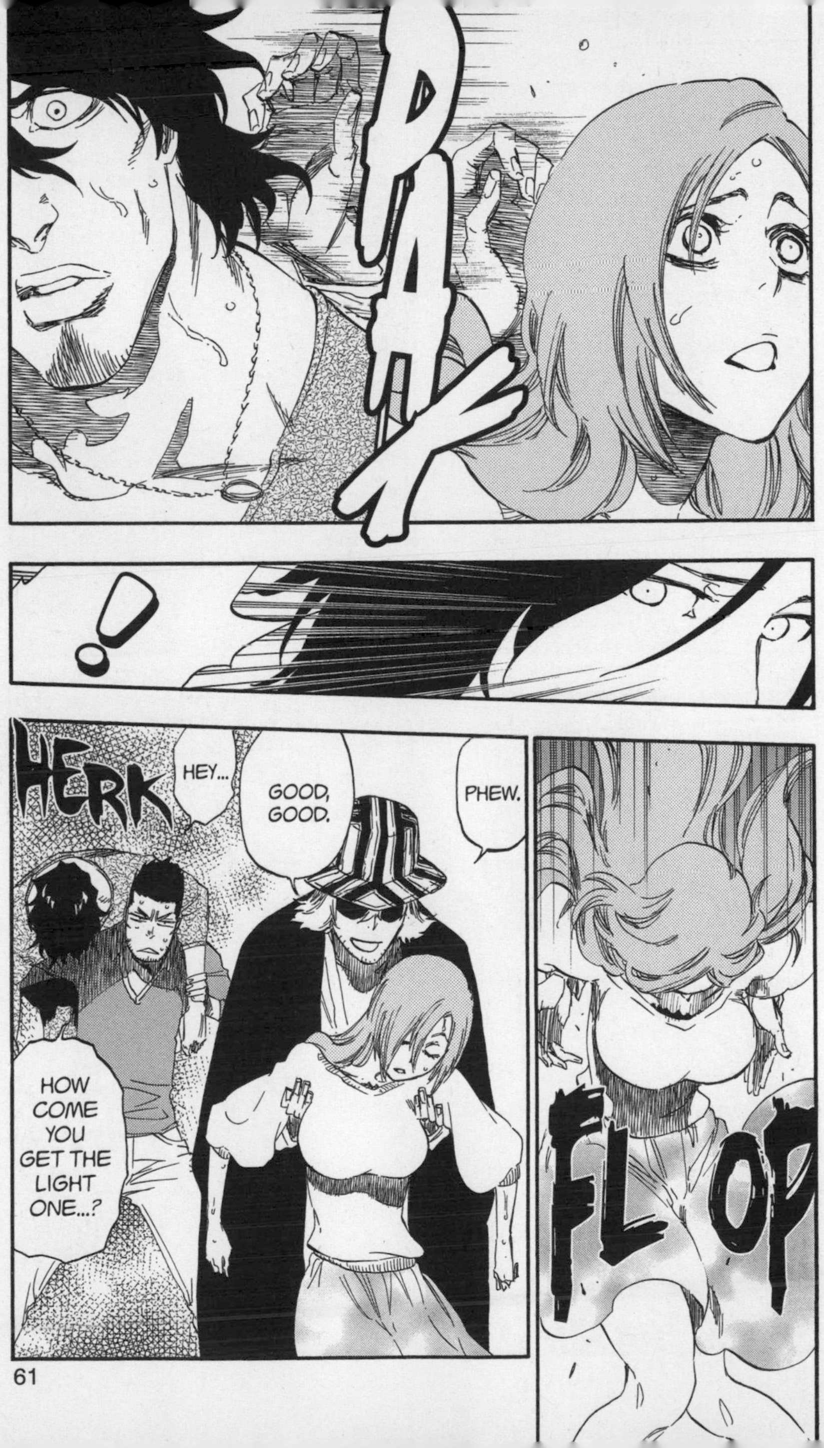
PAK
!
FLOP
PHEW.
GOOD, GOOD.
HEY...
HERK
HOW COME YOU GET THE LIGHT ONE...?

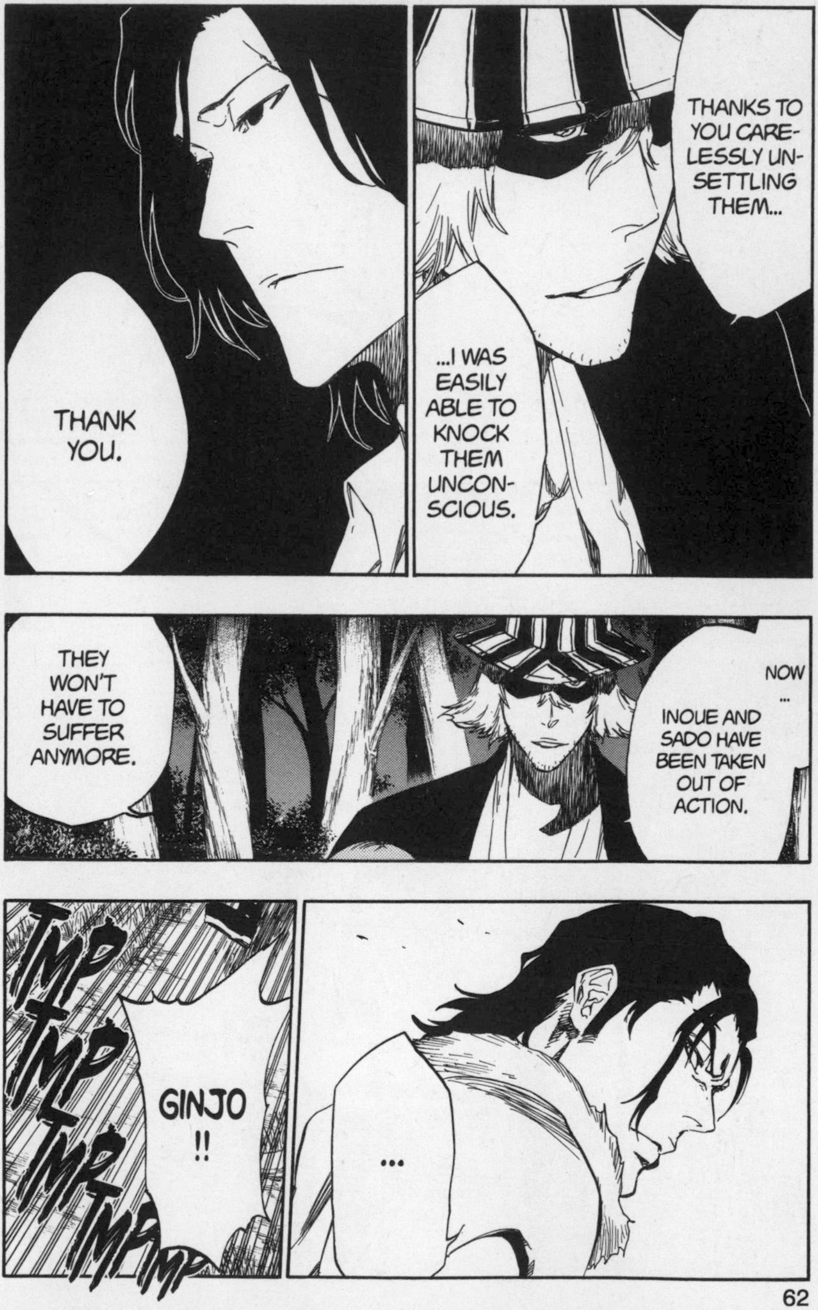
THANKS TO YOU CARE-LESSLY UN-SETTLING THEM...
...I WAS EASILY ABLE TO KNOCK THEM UNCON-SCIOUS.
THANK YOU.
NOW ... INOUE AND SADO HAVE BEEN TAKEN OUT OF ACTION.
THEY WON'T HAVE TO SUFFER ANYMORE.
...
GINJO !!
TMP TMP TMP TMP TMP TMP

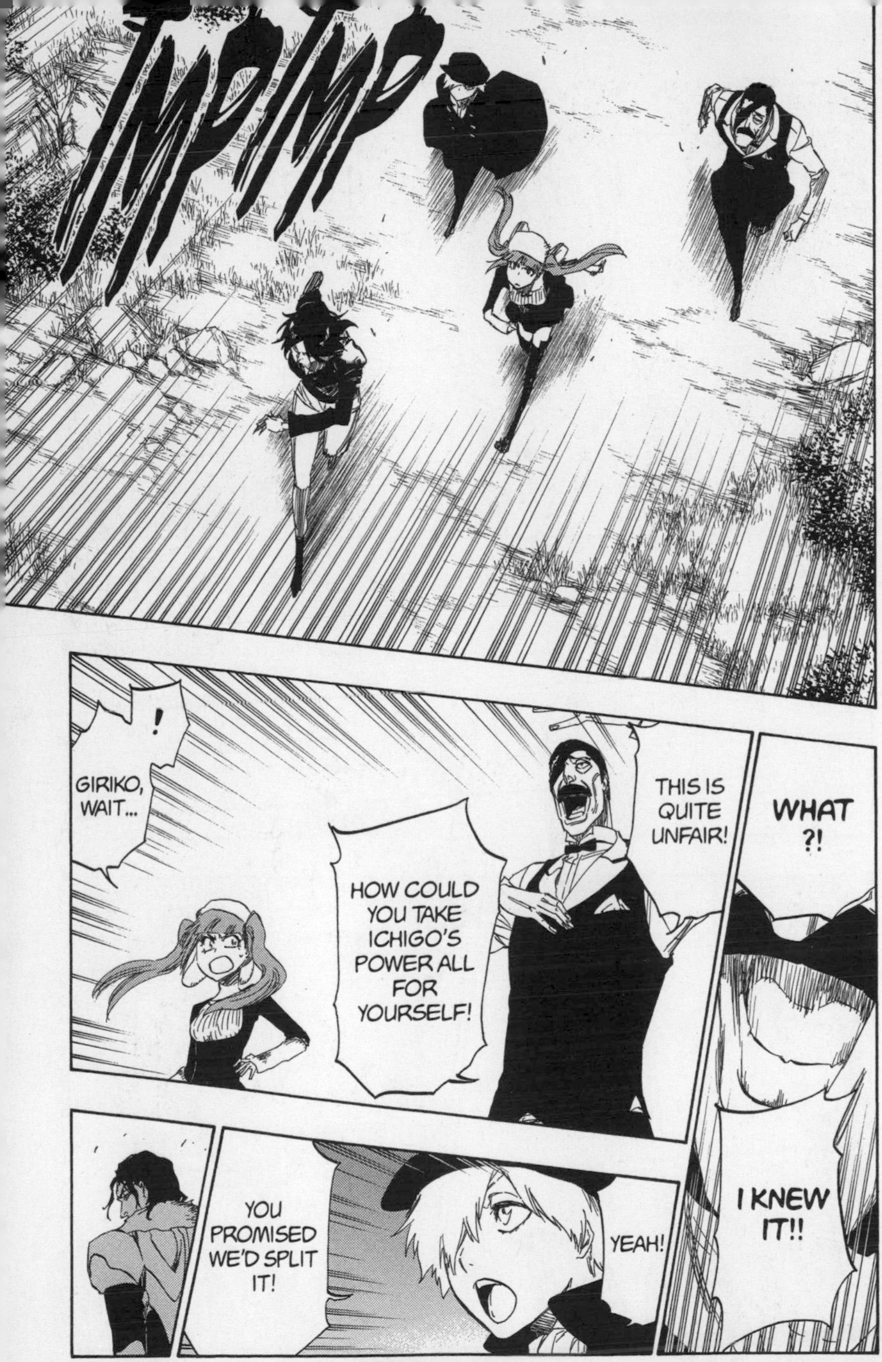
TMP TMP
WHAT ?!
I KNEW IT!!
THIS IS QUITE UNFAIR!
HOW COULD YOU TAKE ICHIGO'S POWER ALL FOR YOURSELF!
!
GIRIKO, WAIT...
YEAH!
YOU PROMISED WE'D SPLIT IT!

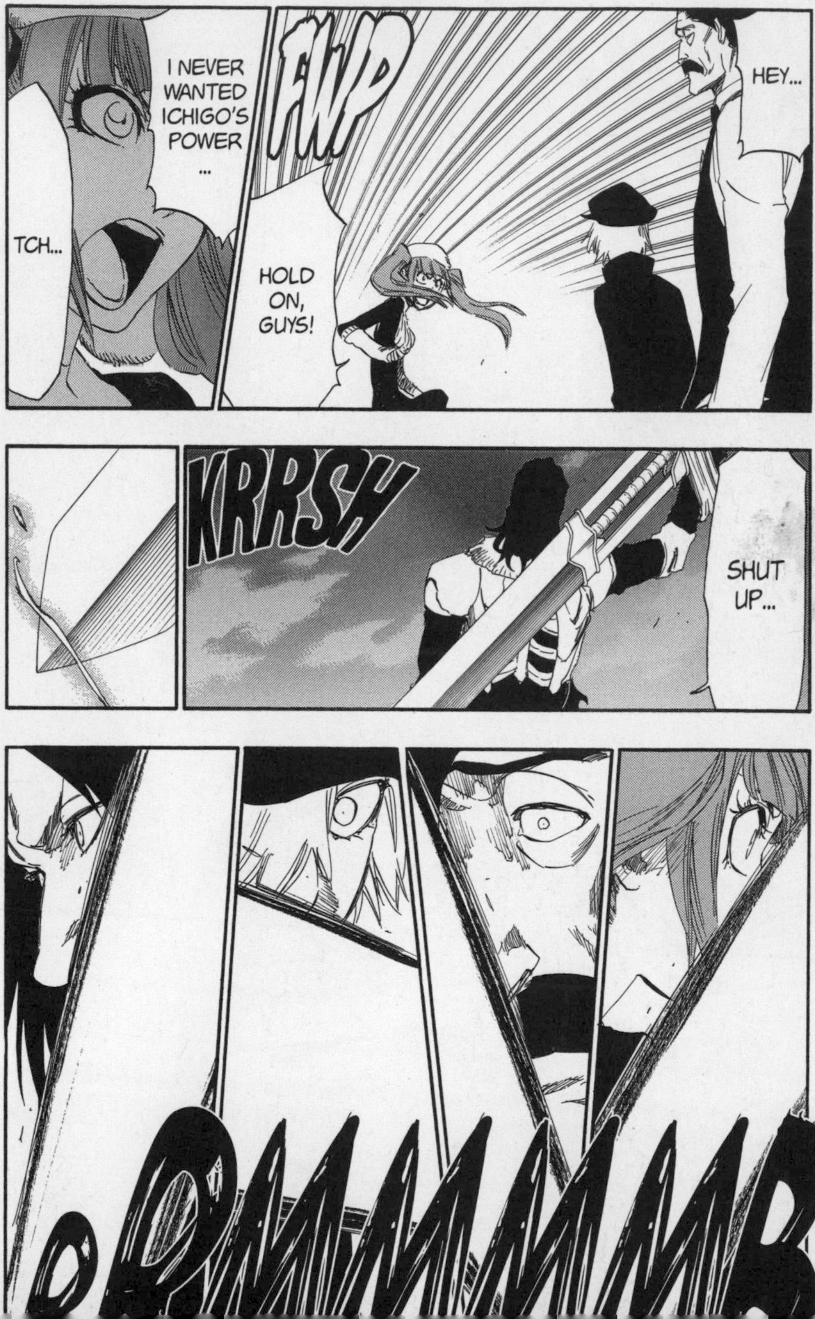
HEY...
FWP
HOLD ON, GUYS!
I NEVER WANTED ICHIGO'S POWER ...
TCH...
SHUT UP...
KRRSH
DMMMMB

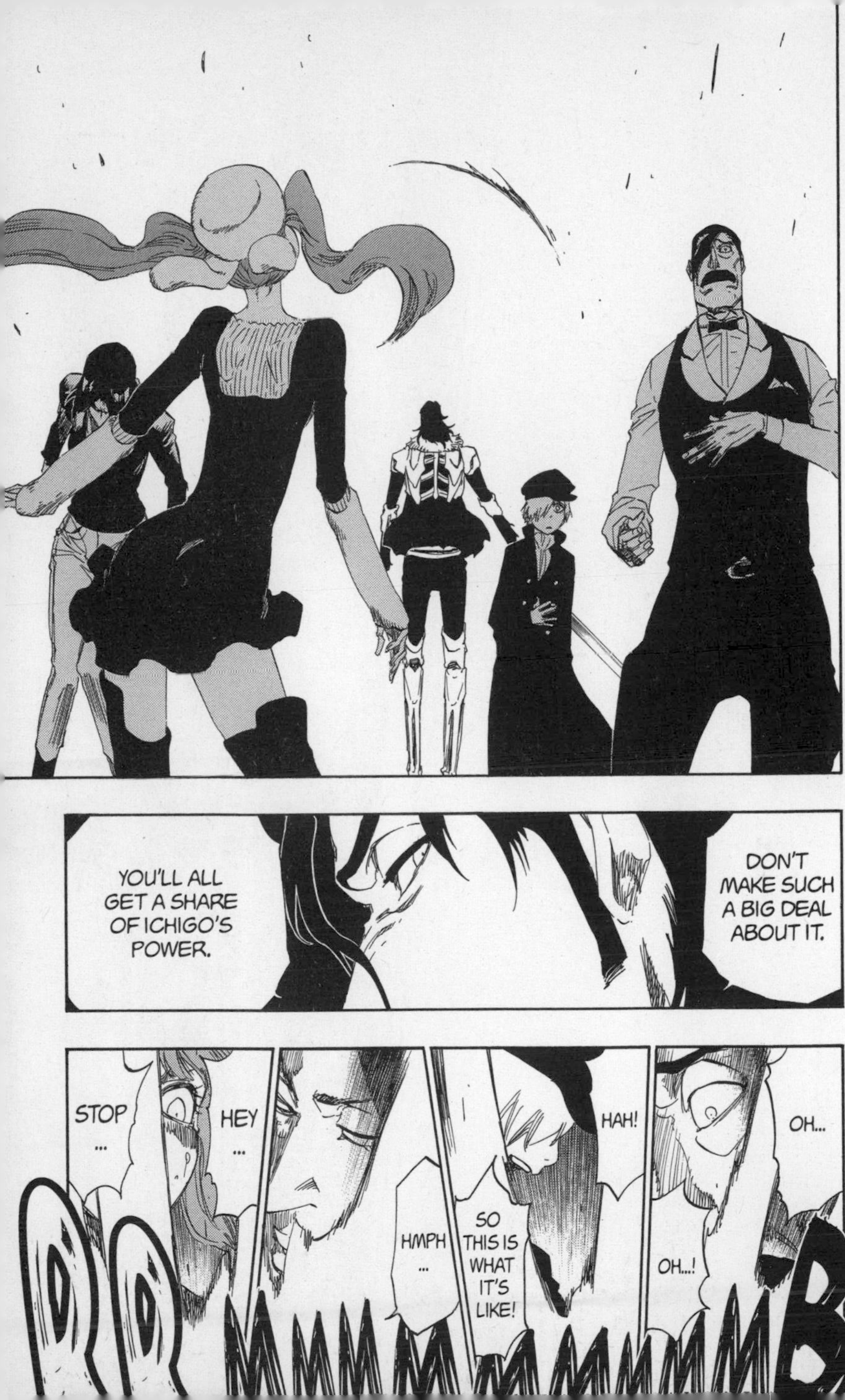
DON'T MAKE SUCH A BIG DEAL ABOUT IT.
YOU'LL ALL GET A SHARE OF ICHIGO'S POWER.
OH...
OH...!
HAH!
SO THIS IS WHAT IT'S LIKE!
HMPH ...
HEY ...
STOP ...
DDMMMMMMMMMB

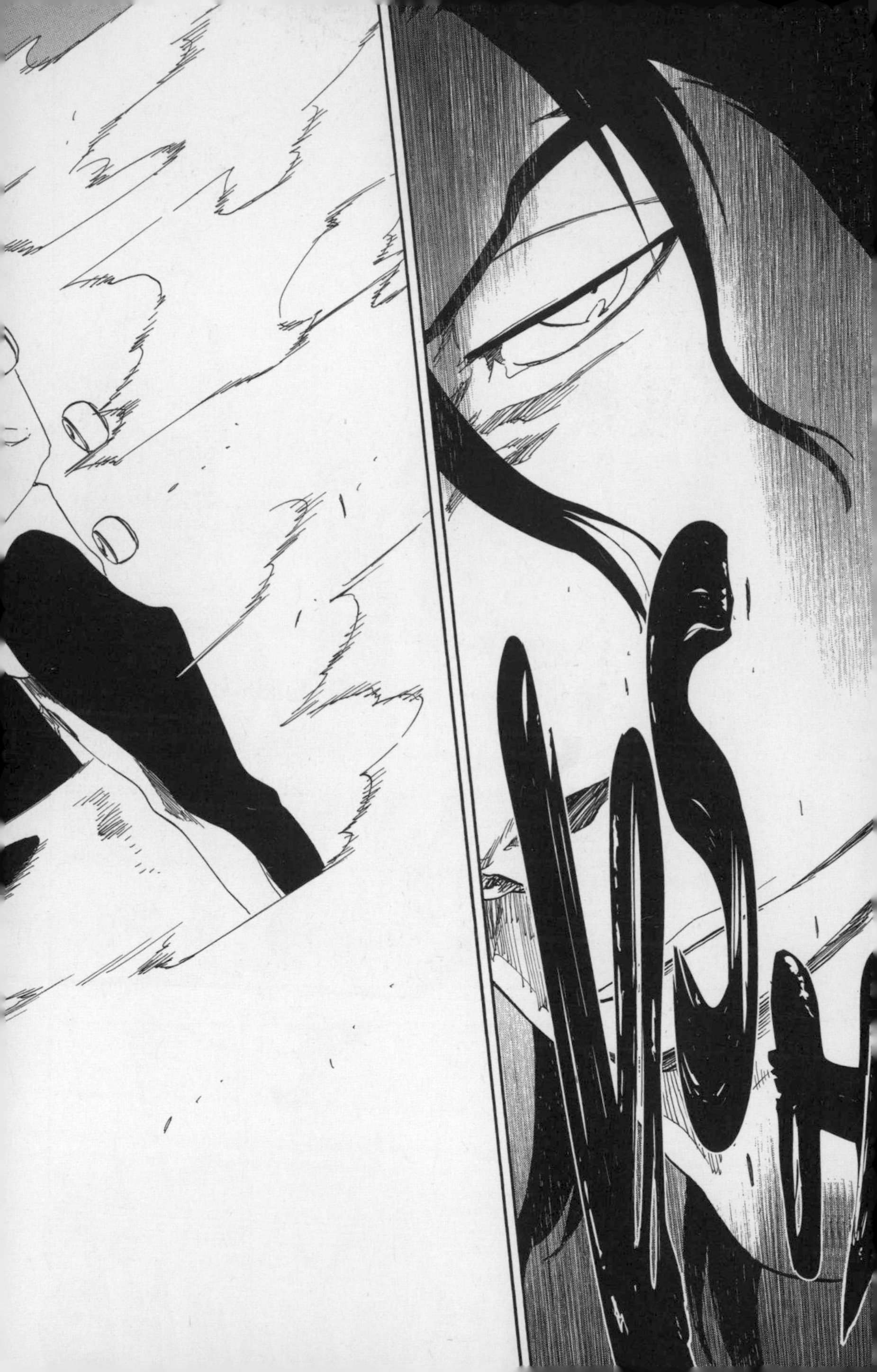

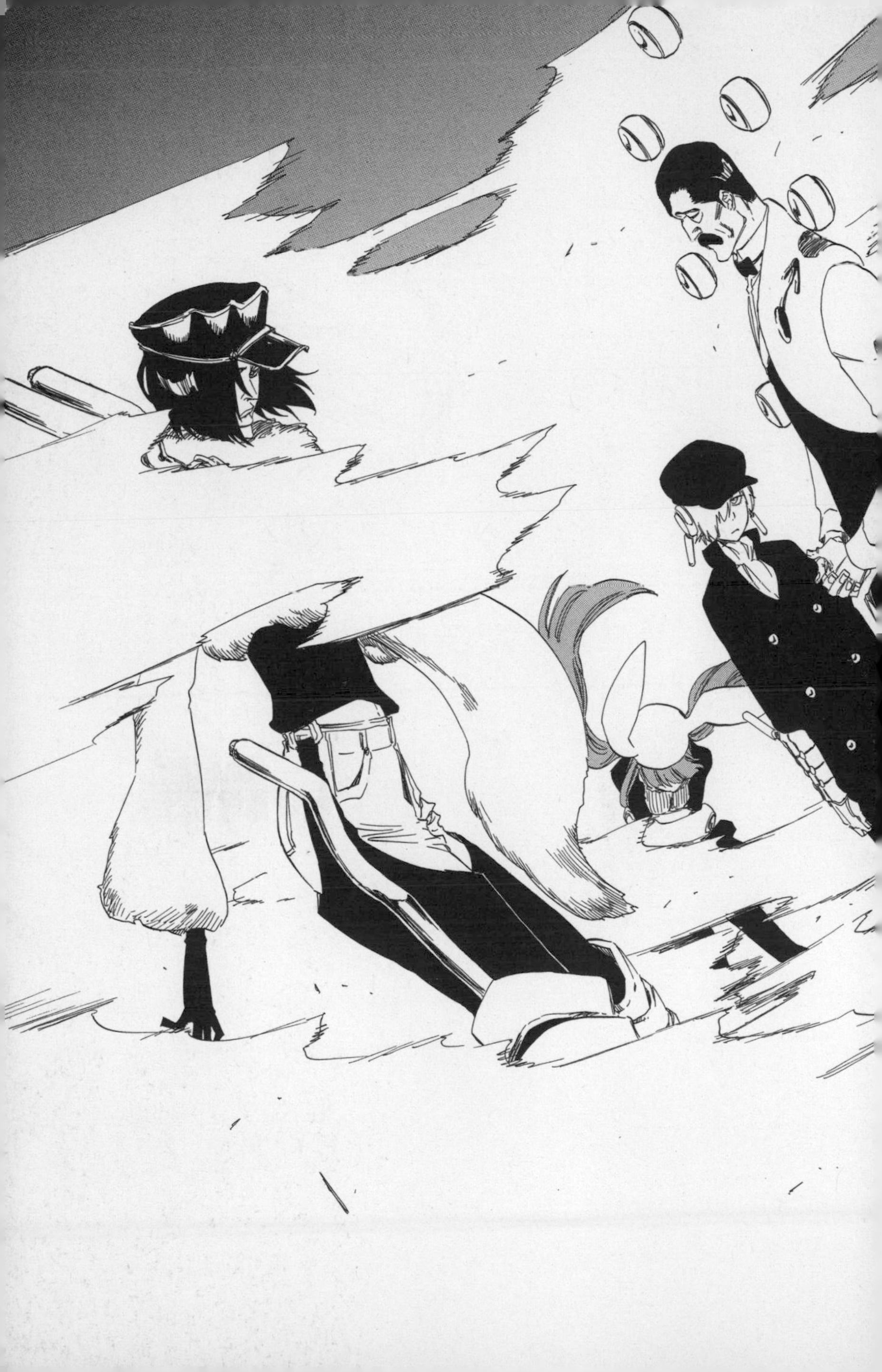

sometimes a
past is poisonous.

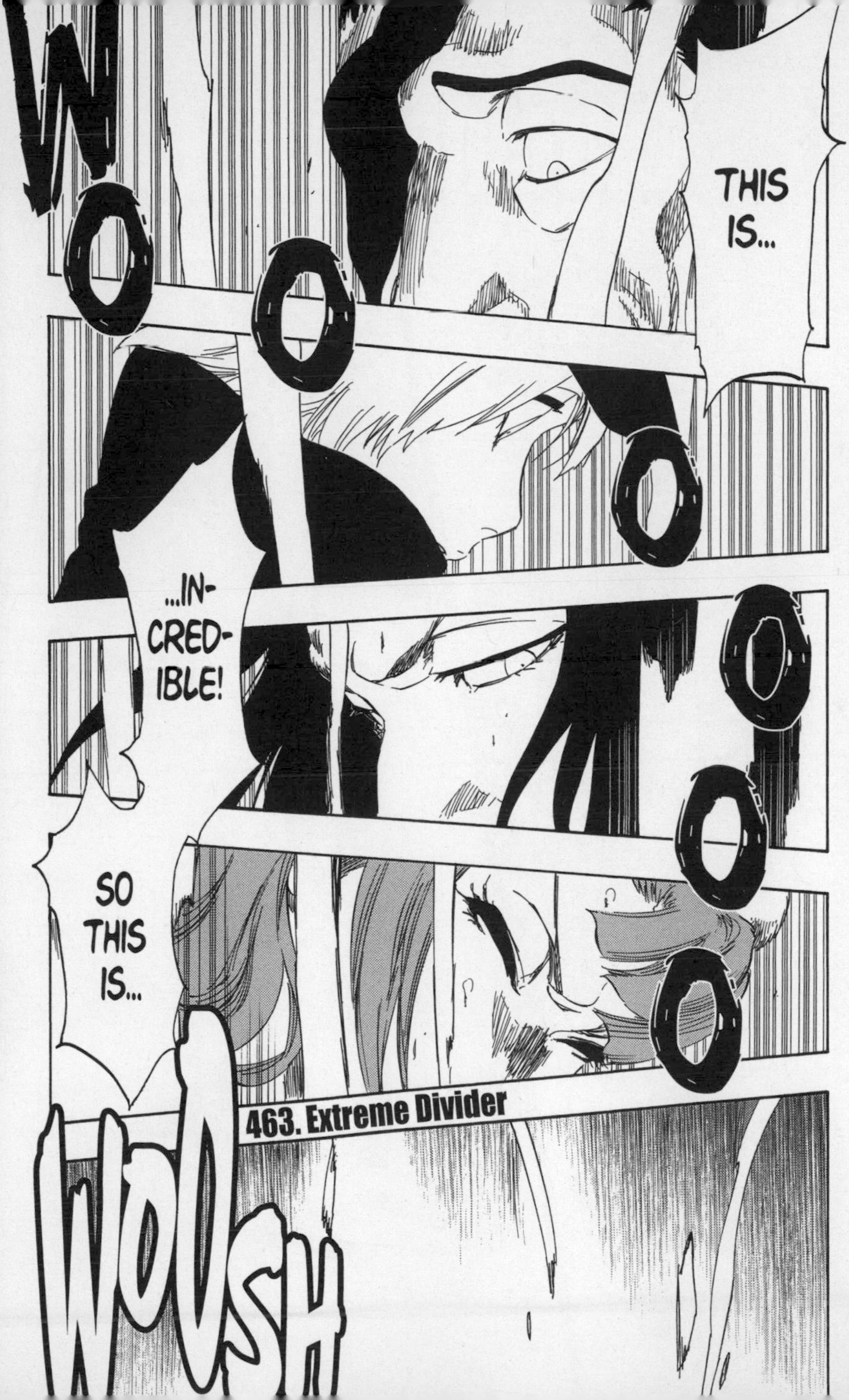
WOO
THIS IS...
...IN-CRED-IBLE!
SO THIS IS...
463. Extreme Divider
WOOSH

Extreme Divider

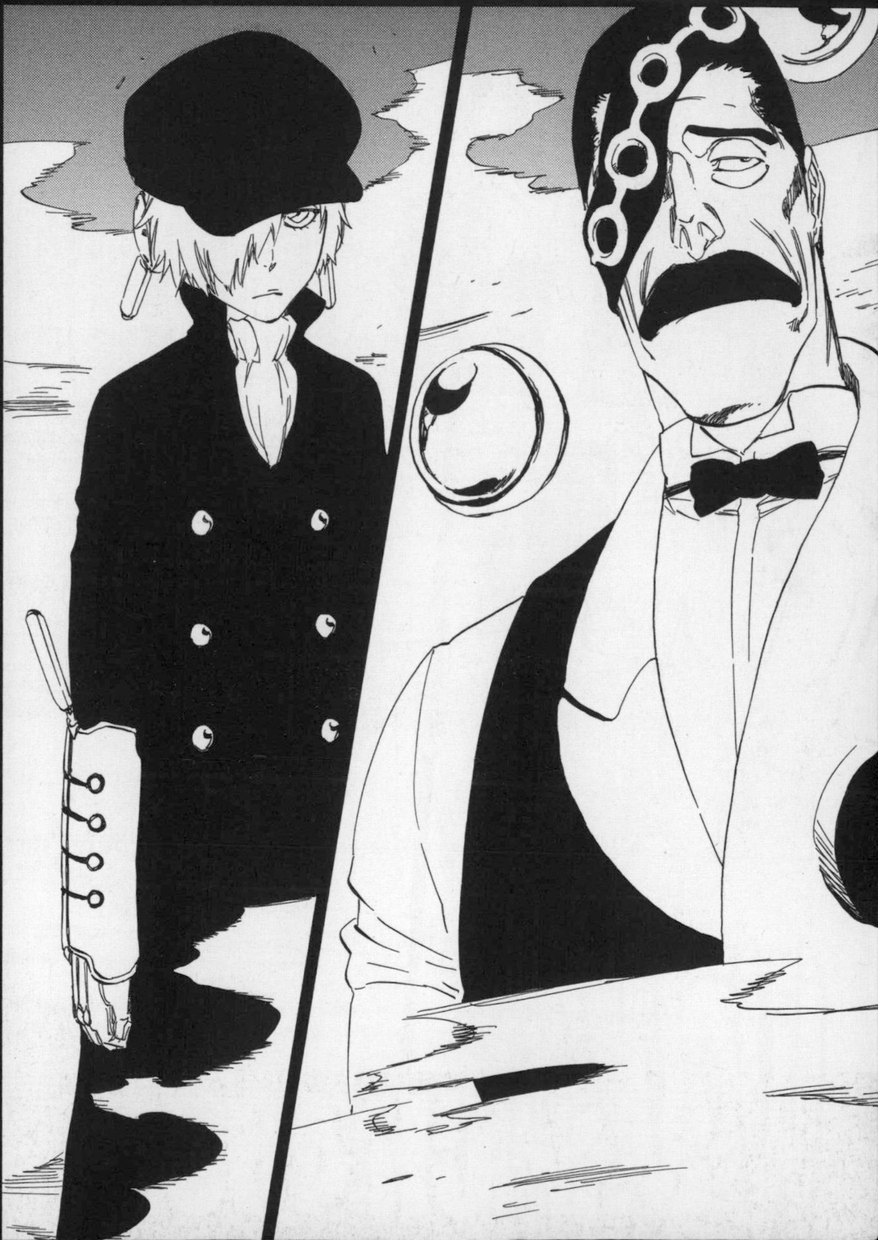

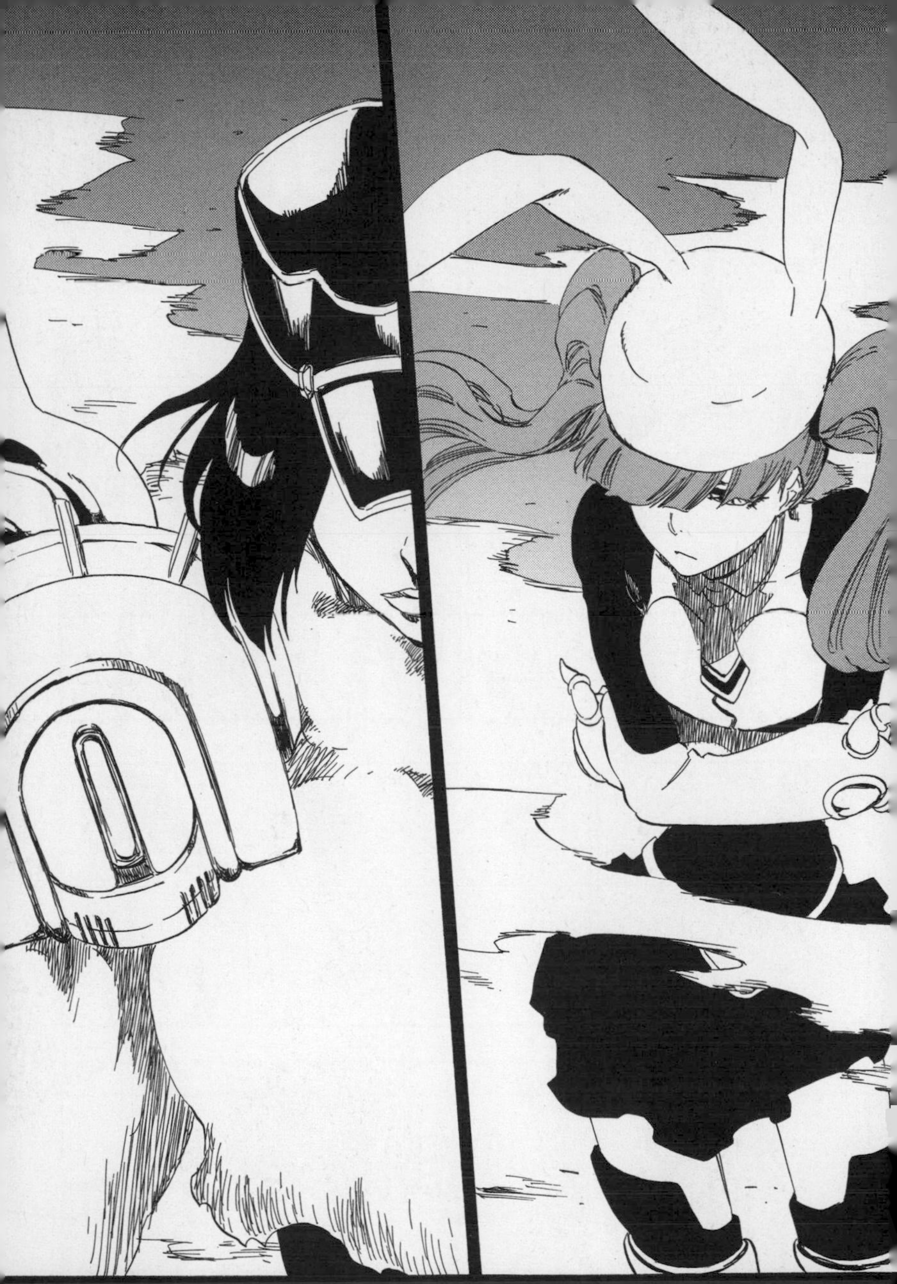

BLEACH 463.

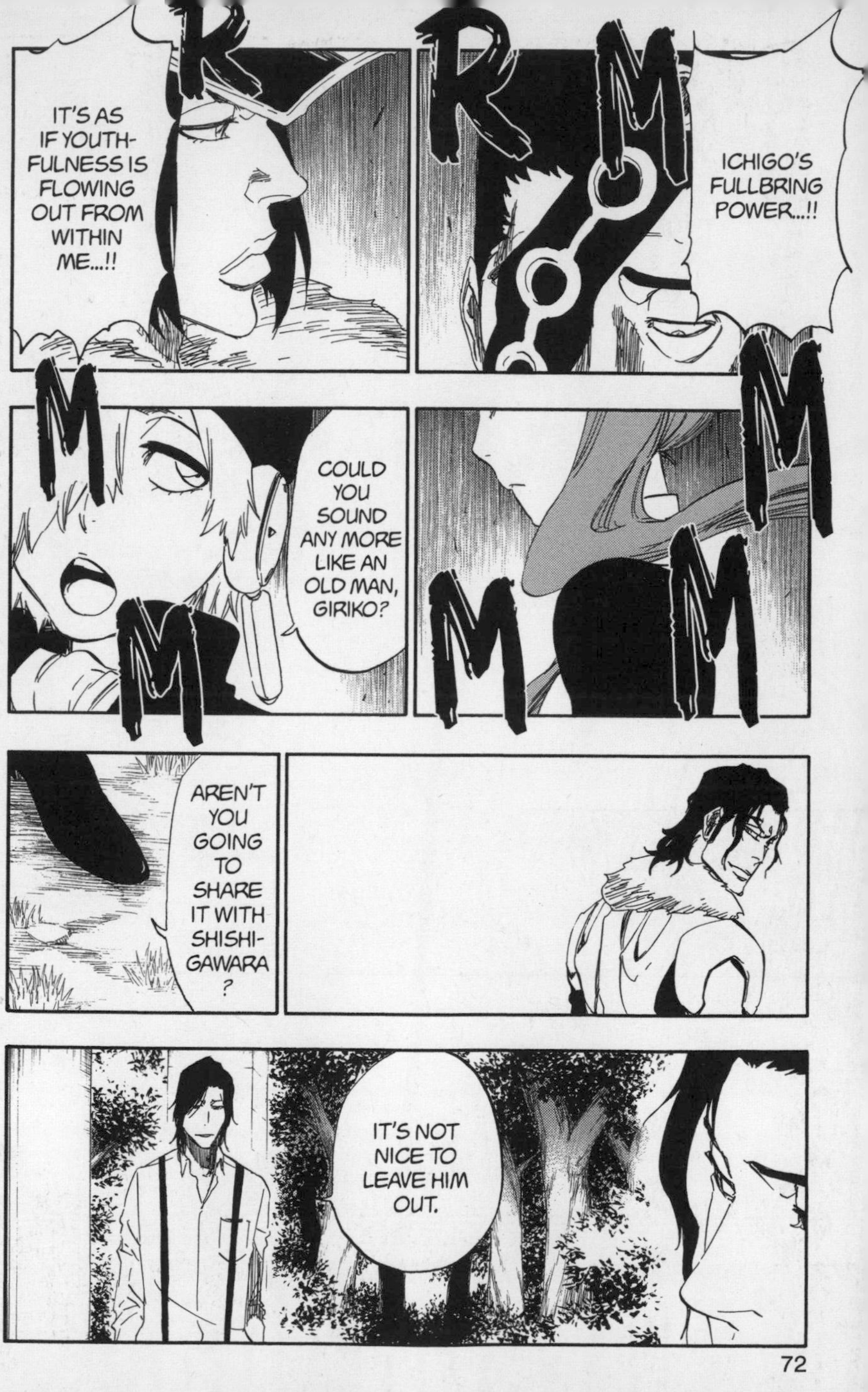
KRM
ICHIGO'S FULLBRING POWER...!!
IT'S AS IF YOUTH-FULNESS IS FLOWING OUT FROM WITHIN ME...!!
MMMMMM
COULD YOU SOUND ANY MORE LIKE AN OLD MAN, GIRIKO?
AREN'T YOU GOING TO SHARE IT WITH SHISHI-GAWARA?
IT'S NOT NICE TO LEAVE HIM OUT.

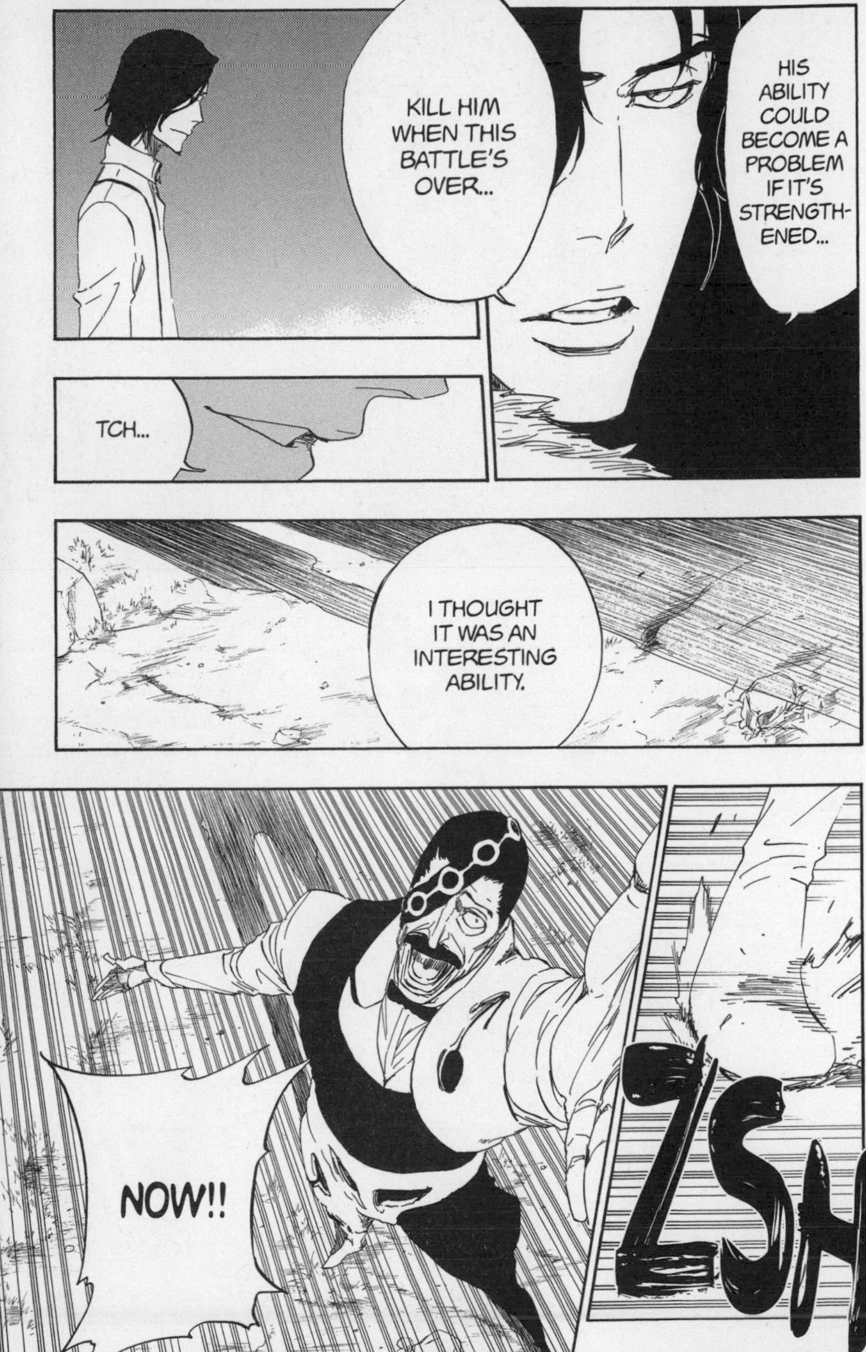
HIS ABILITY COULD BECOME A PROBLEM IF IT'S STRENGTH-ENED...
KILL HIM WHEN THIS BATTLE'S OVER...
TCH...
I THOUGHT IT WAS AN INTERESTING ABILITY.
ZSH
NOW!!

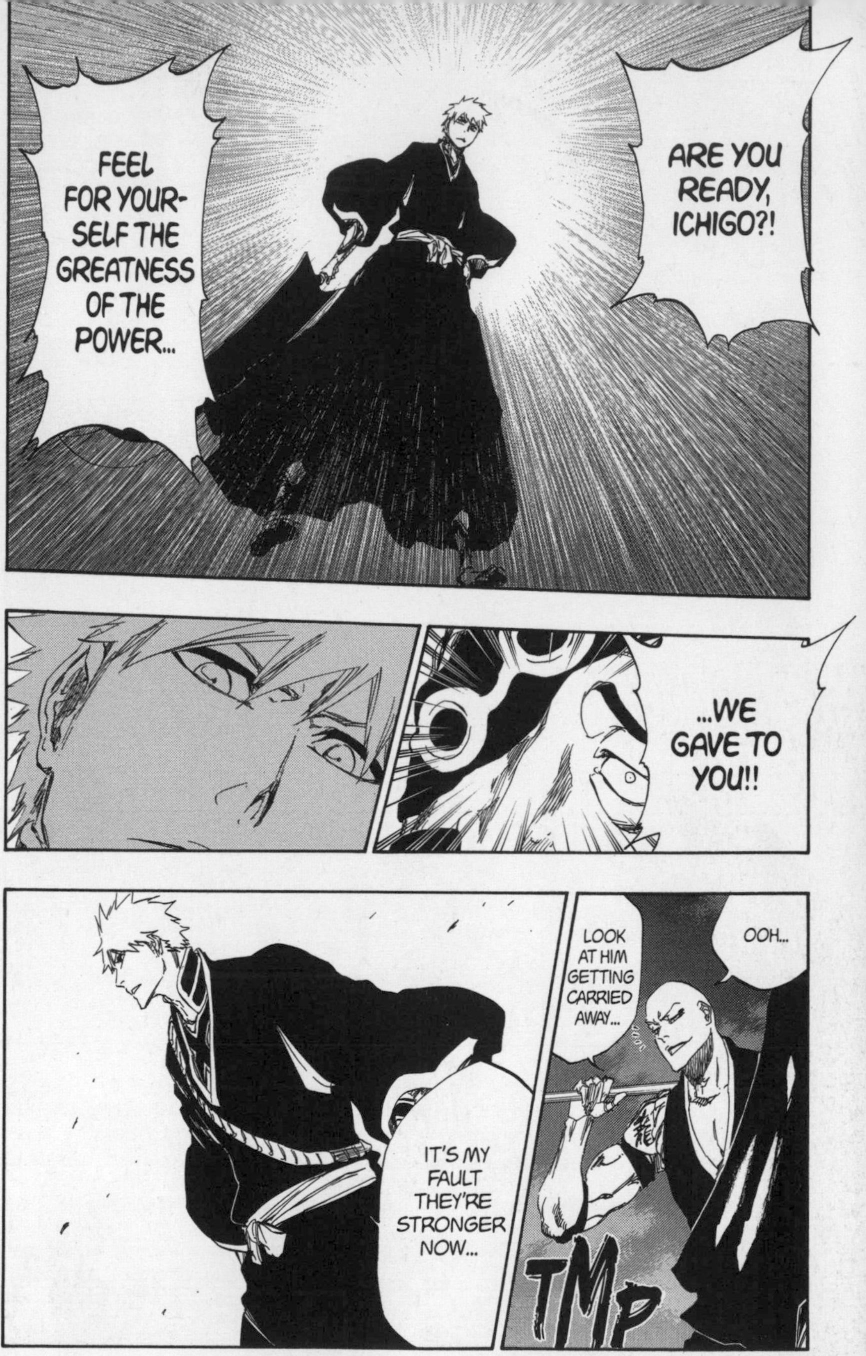
ARE YOU READY, ICHIGO?!
FEEL FOR YOUR-SELF THE GREATNESS OF THE POWER...
...WE GAVE TO YOU!!
OOH...
LOOK AT HIM GETTING CARRIED AWAY...
TMP
IT'S MY FAULT THEY'RE STRONGER NOW...

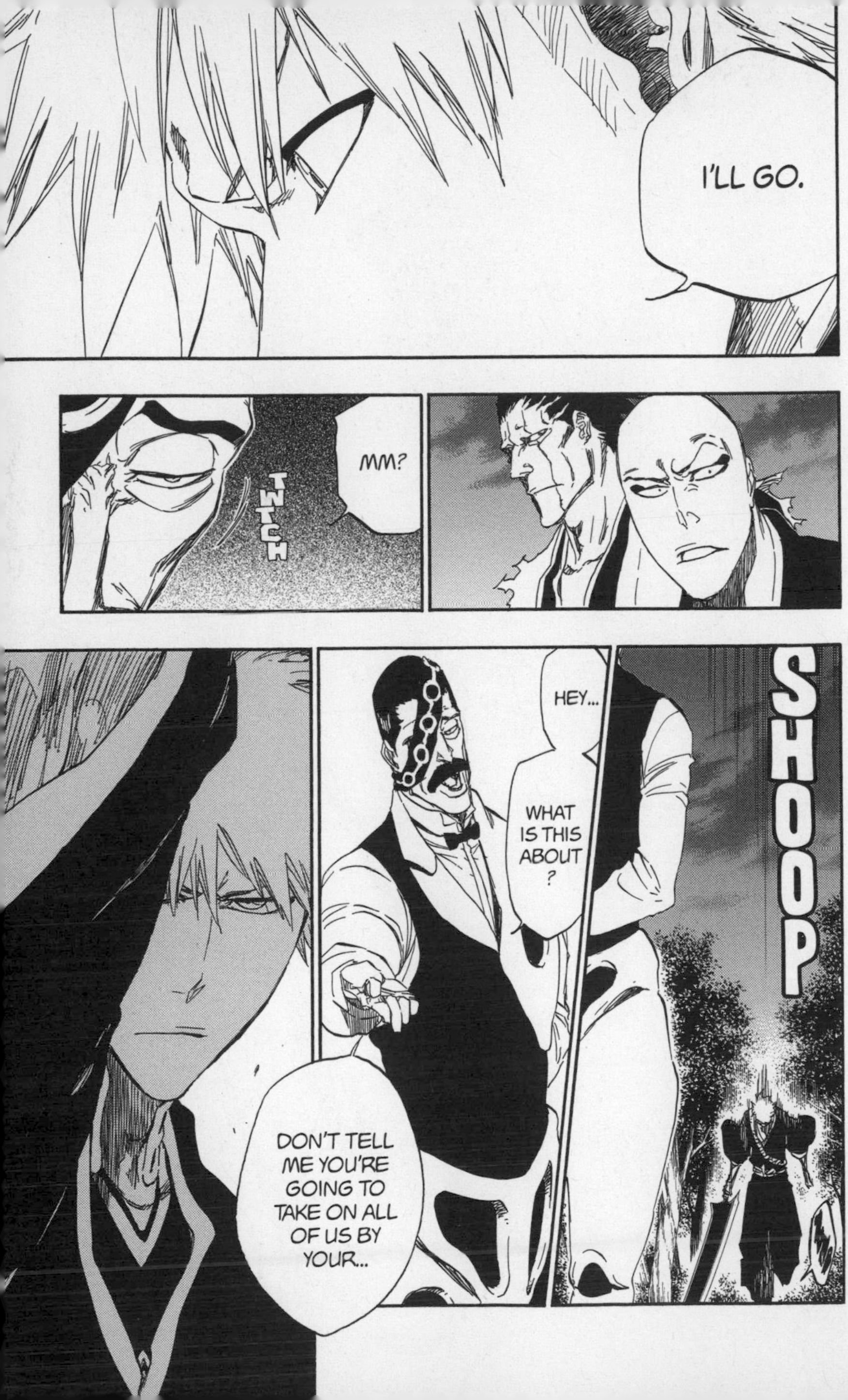
I'LL GO.
MM?
TWTCH
SHOOP
HEY...
WHAT IS THIS ABOUT?
DON'T TELL ME YOU'RE GOING TO TAKE ON ALL OF US BY YOUR...

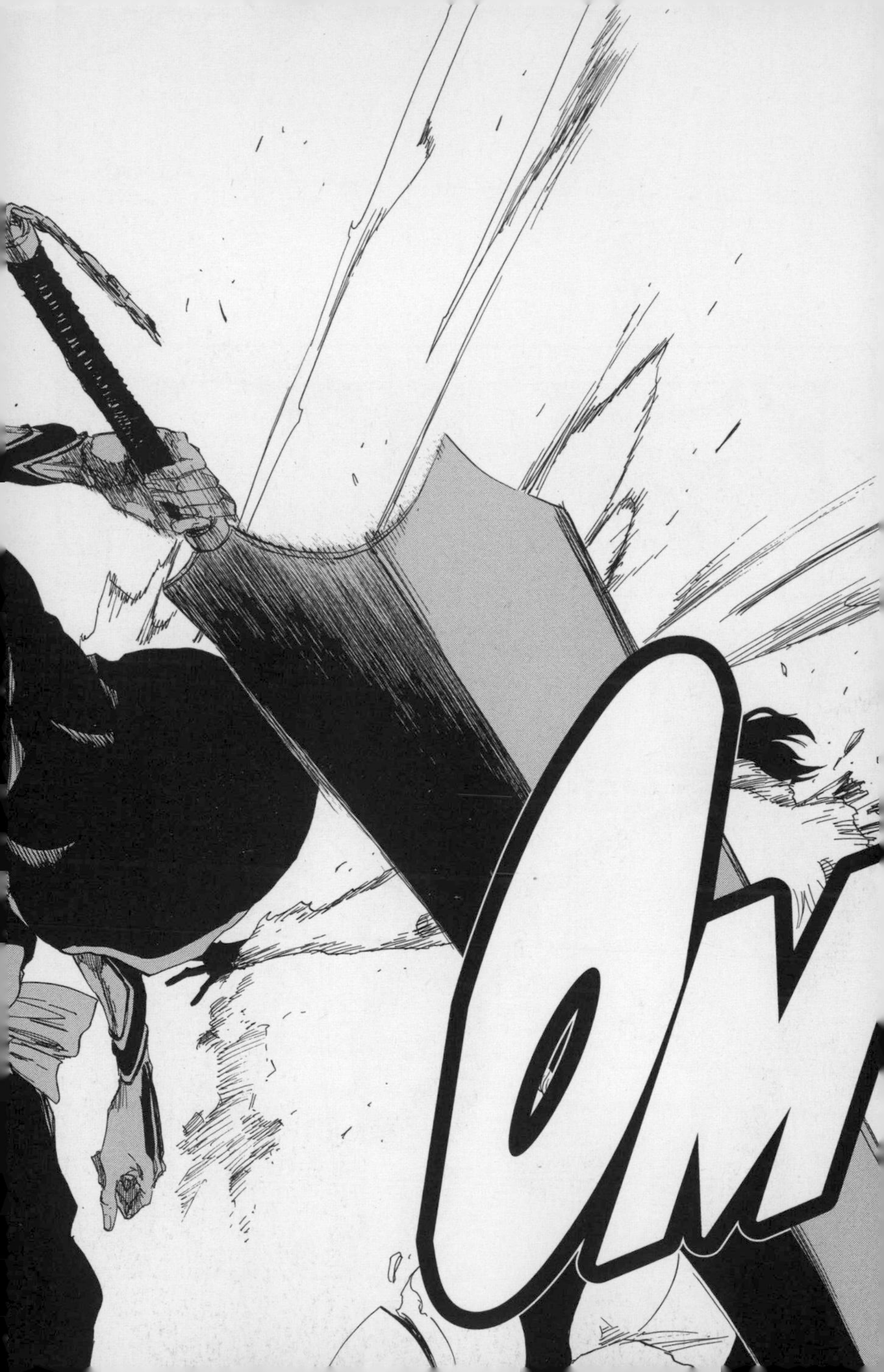

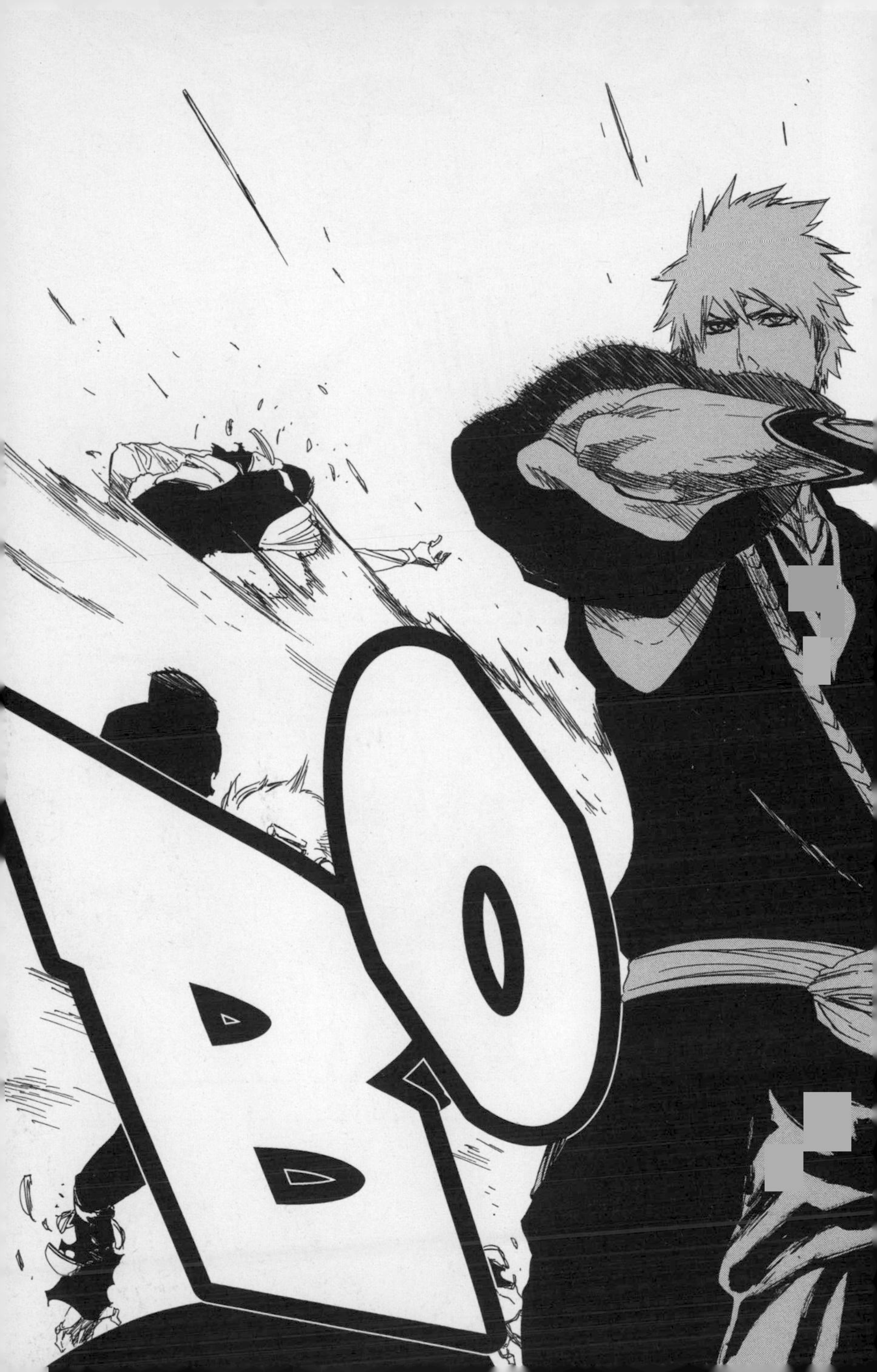
BO

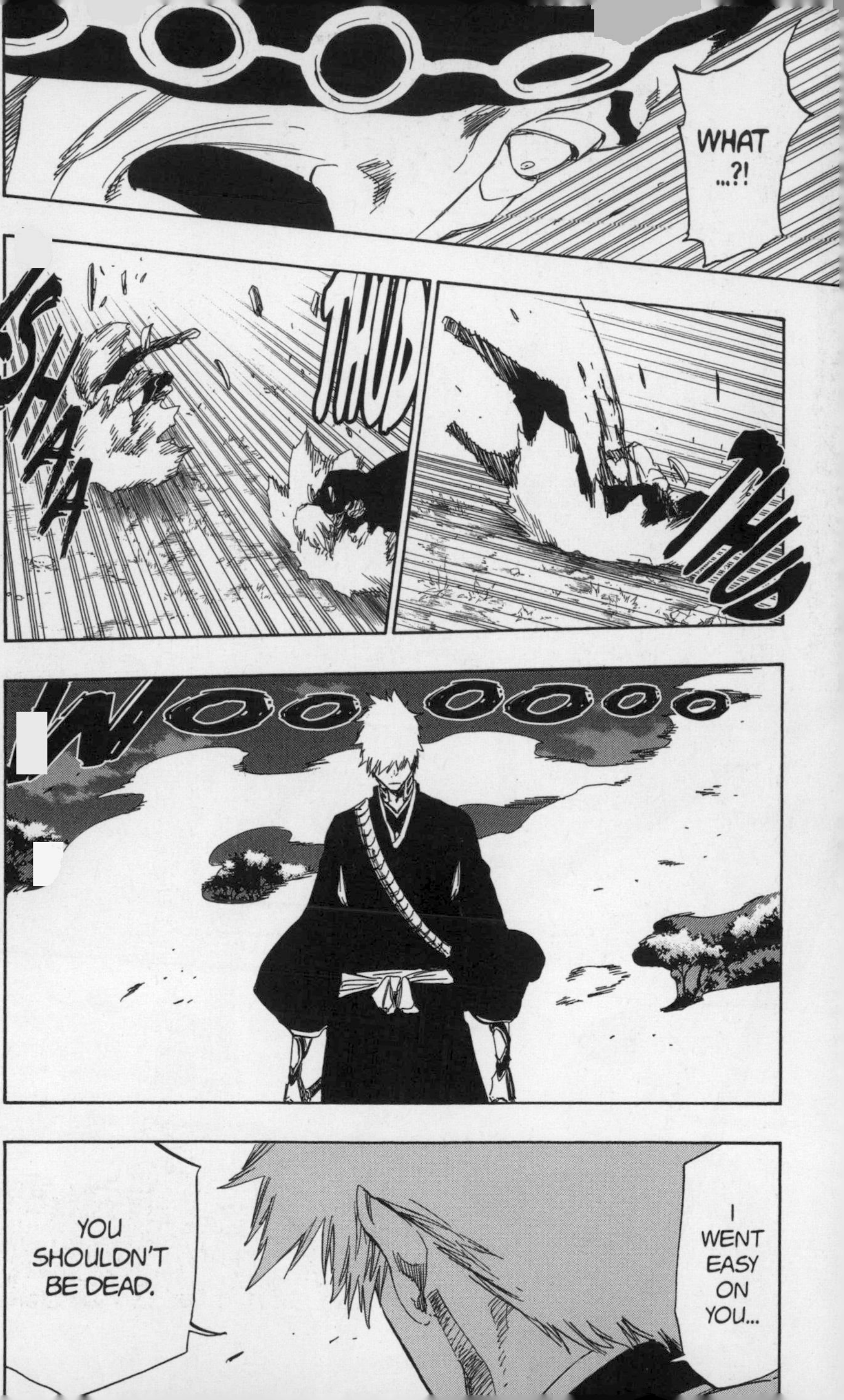
WHAT ...?!
THUD
THUD
SHAAA
WOOOOOO
I WENT EASY ON YOU...
YOU SHOULDN'T BE DEAD.

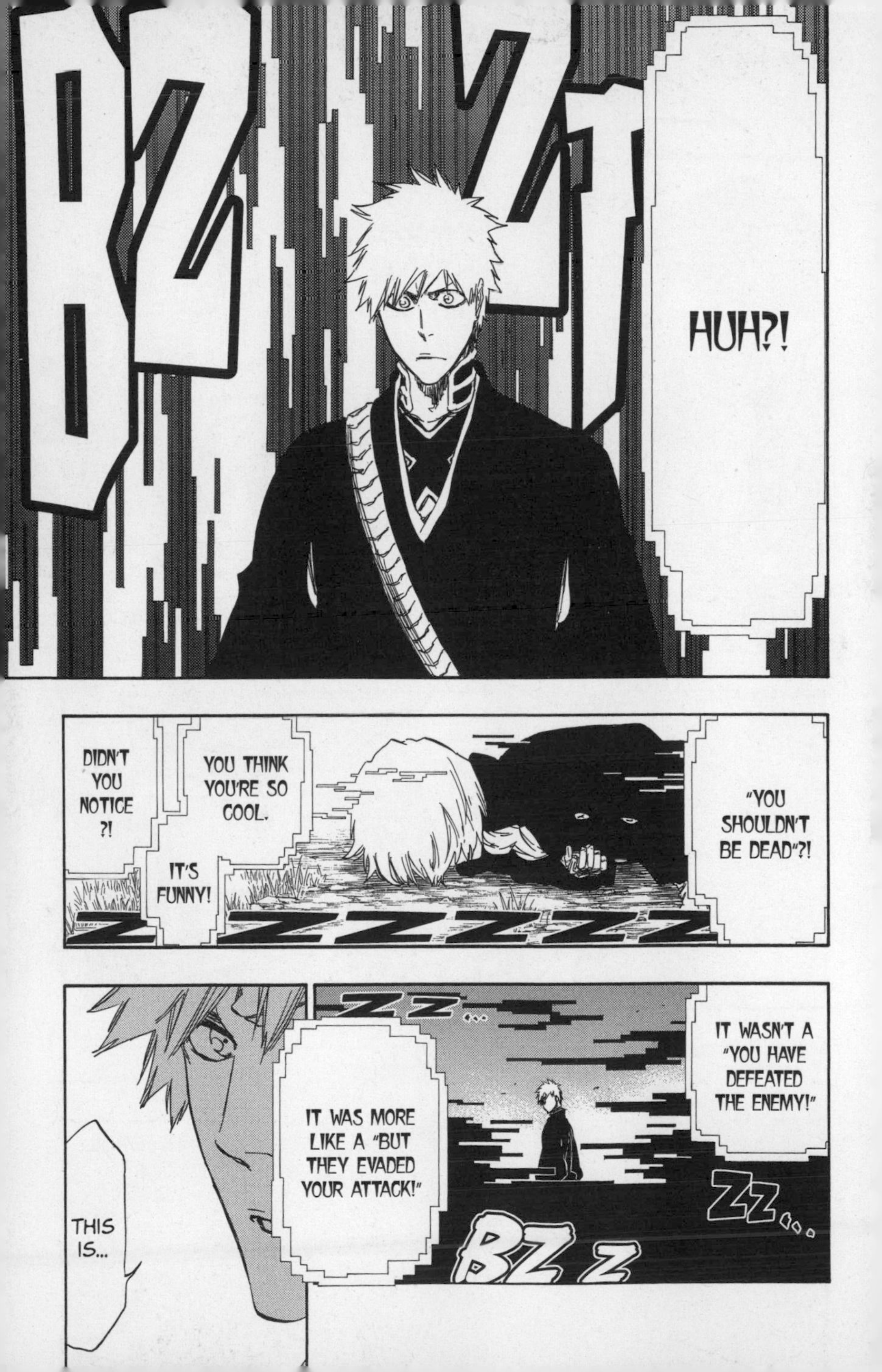
HUH?!
BZZT
"YOU SHOULDN'T BE DEAD"?!
YOU THINK YOU'RE SO COOL.
IT'S FUNNY!
DIDN'T YOU NOTICE ?!
IT WASN'T A "YOU HAVE DEFEATED THE ENEMY!"
ZZ...
IT WAS MORE LIKE A "BUT THEY EVADED YOUR ATTACK!"
ZZ...
BZZ
THIS IS...

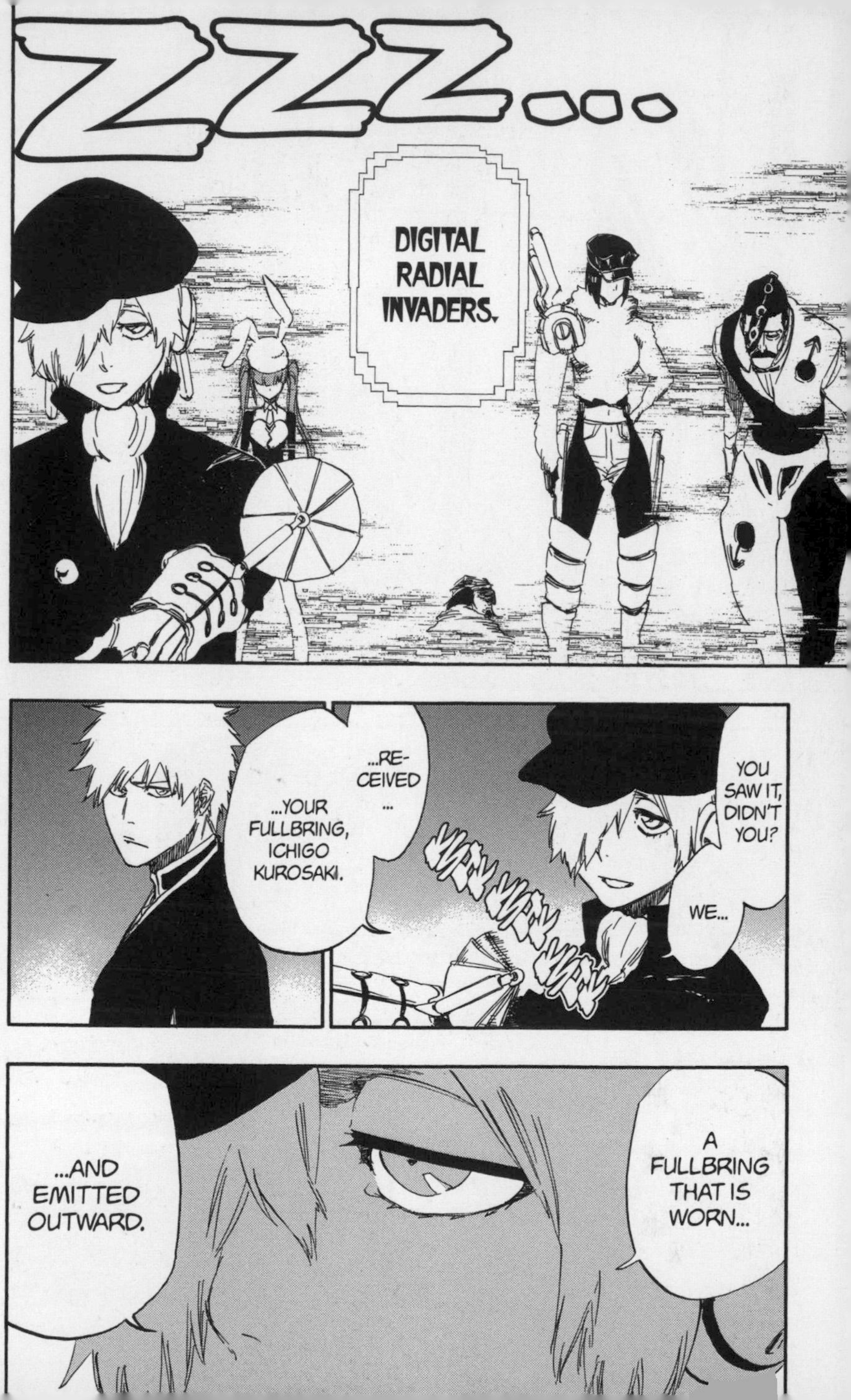
ZZZ...
DIGITAL RADIAL INVADERS.
YOU SAW IT, DIDN'T YOU?
WE...
...RE-CEIVED ...
...YOUR FULLBRING, ICHIGO KUROSAKI.
A FULLBRING THAT IS WORN...
...AND EMITTED OUTWARD.

READ THIS WAY

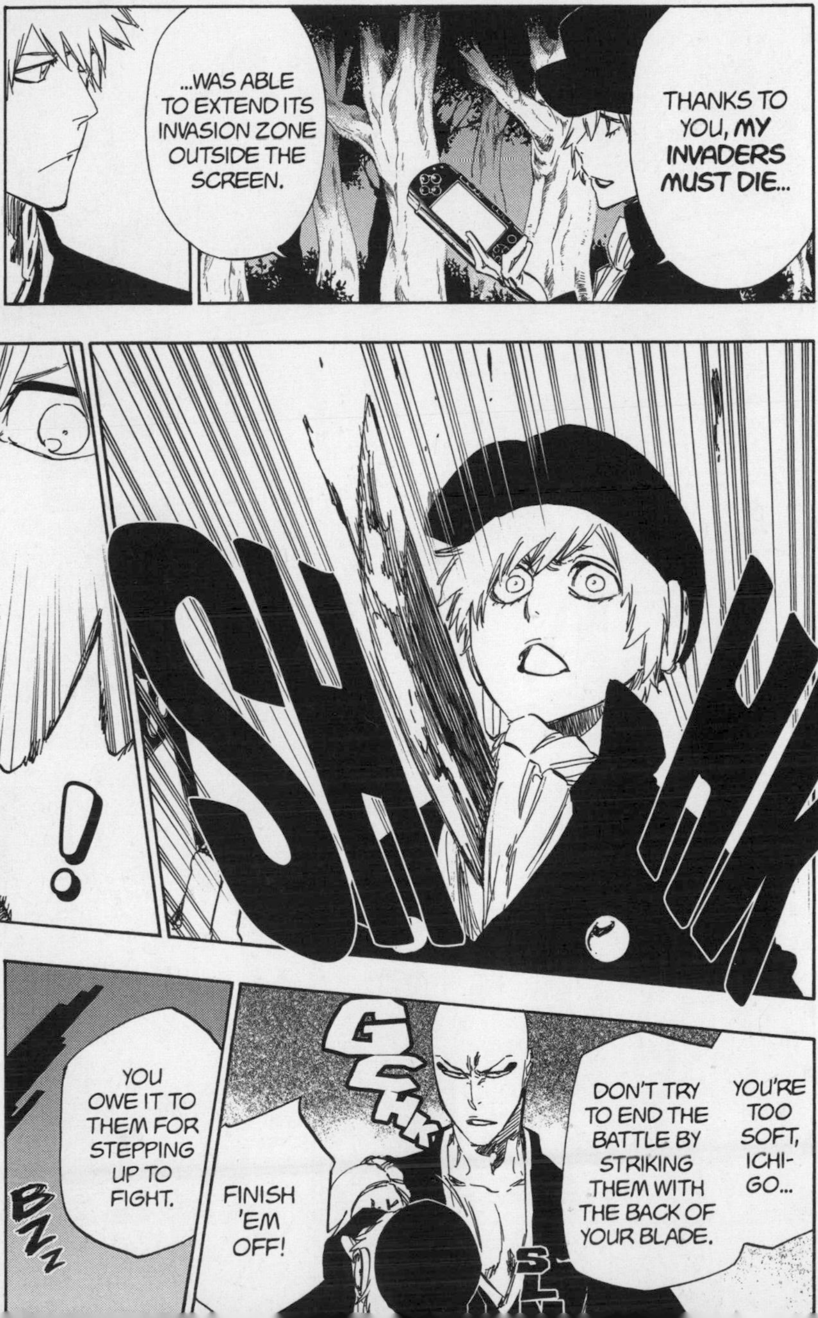
THANKS TO YOU, MY INVADERS MUST DIE...
...WAS ABLE TO EXTEND ITS INVASION ZONE OUTSIDE THE SCREEN.
!
!
YOU'RE TOO SOFT, ICHI-GO...
DON'T TRY TO END THE BATTLE BY STRIKING THEM WITH THE BACK OF YOUR BLADE.
GCHK
FINISH 'EM OFF!
YOU OWE IT TO THEM FOR STEPPING UP TO FIGHT.
BZZ

NOT BAD...

WANT SOME BONUS POINTS?

I'LL PASS.

KCHK

DON'T LET YOUR GUARD DOWN, MADA-RAME!

I'M SORRY...

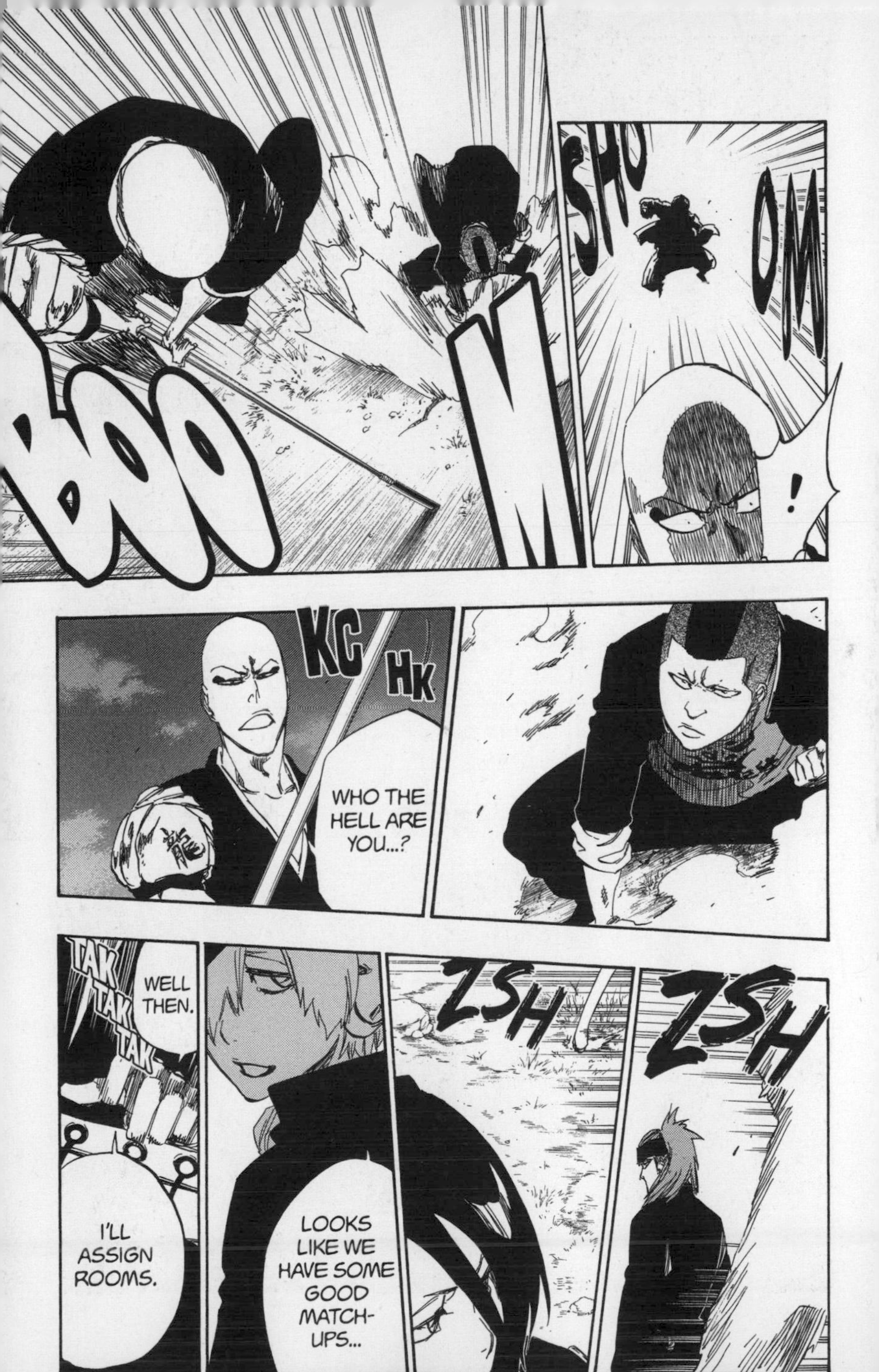
SHO
OM
!
BOO
M
KC
HK
WHO THE HELL ARE YOU...?
ZSH
ZSH
LOOKS LIKE WE HAVE SOME GOOD MATCH-UPS...
TAK
TAK
TAK
WELL THEN.
I'LL ASSIGN ROOMS.

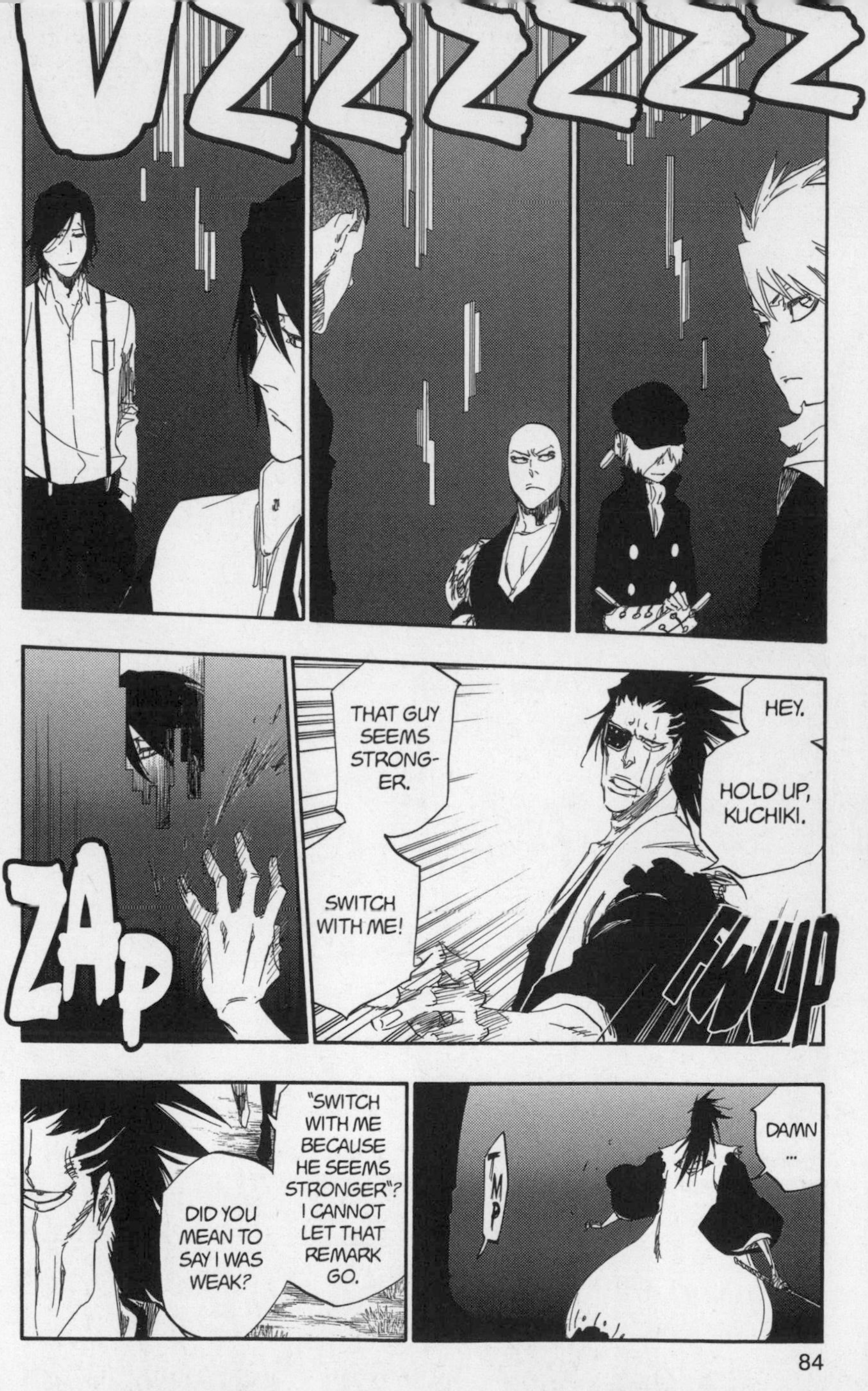
VZZZZZZ
HEY.
HOLD UP, KUCHIKI.
THAT GUY SEEMS STRONG-ER.
SWITCH WITH ME!
FWUP
ZAP
DAMN ...
TMP
"SWITCH WITH ME BECAUSE HE SEEMS STRONGER"? I CANNOT LET THAT REMARK GO.
DID YOU MEAN TO SAY I WAS WEAK?

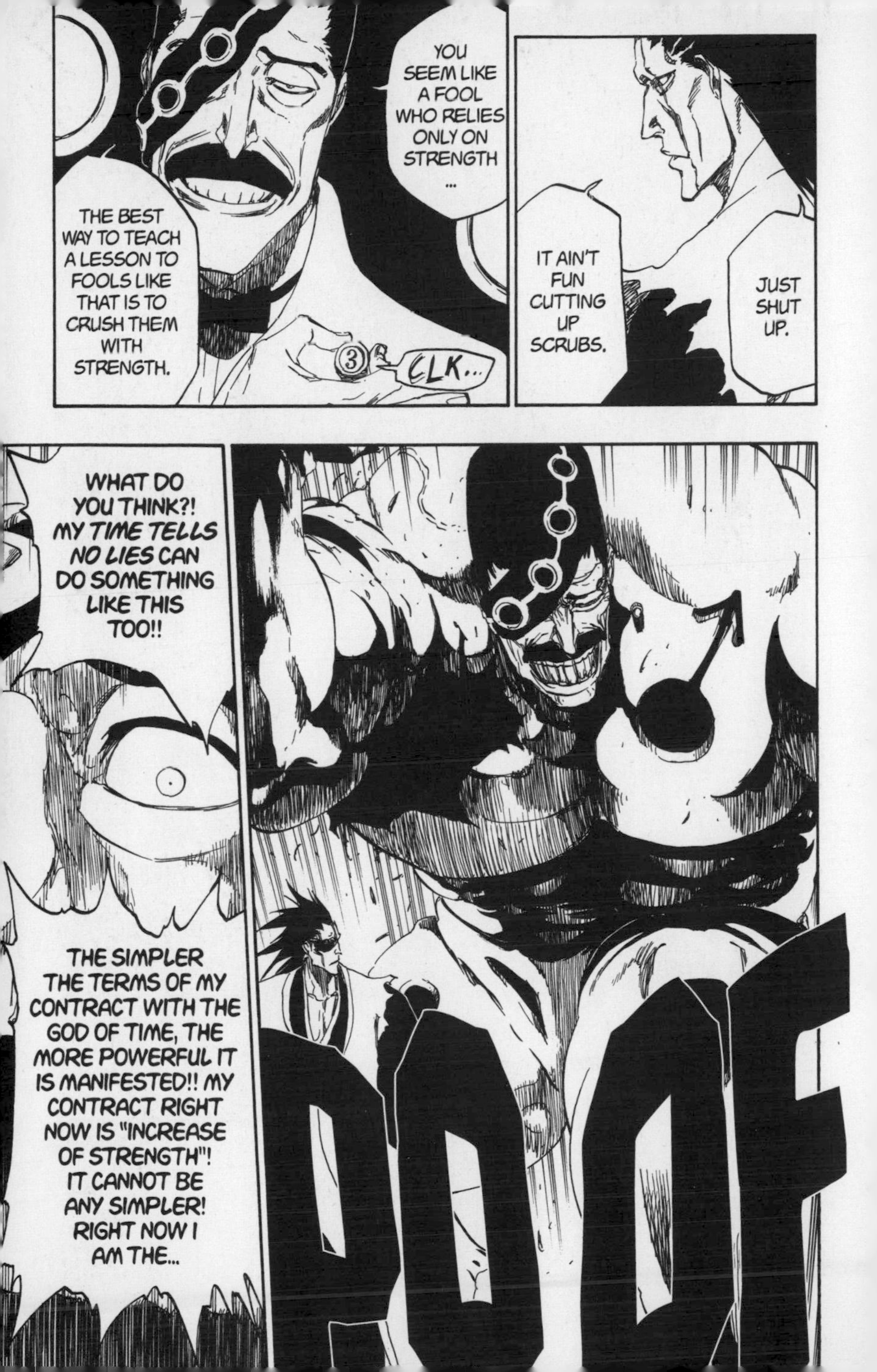
JUST SHUT UP.
IT AIN'T FUN CUTTING UP SCRUBS.
YOU SEEM LIKE A FOOL WHO RELIES ONLY ON STRENGTH ...
THE BEST WAY TO TEACH A LESSON TO FOOLS LIKE THAT IS TO CRUSH THEM WITH STRENGTH.
CLK...
POOF
WHAT DO YOU THINK?! MY *TIME TELLS NO LIES* CAN DO SOMETHING LIKE THIS TOO!!
THE SIMPLER THE TERMS OF MY CONTRACT WITH THE GOD OF TIME, THE MORE POWERFUL IT IS MANIFESTED!! MY CONTRACT RIGHT NOW IS "INCREASE OF STRENGTH"! IT CANNOT BE ANY SIMPLER! RIGHT NOW I AM THE...

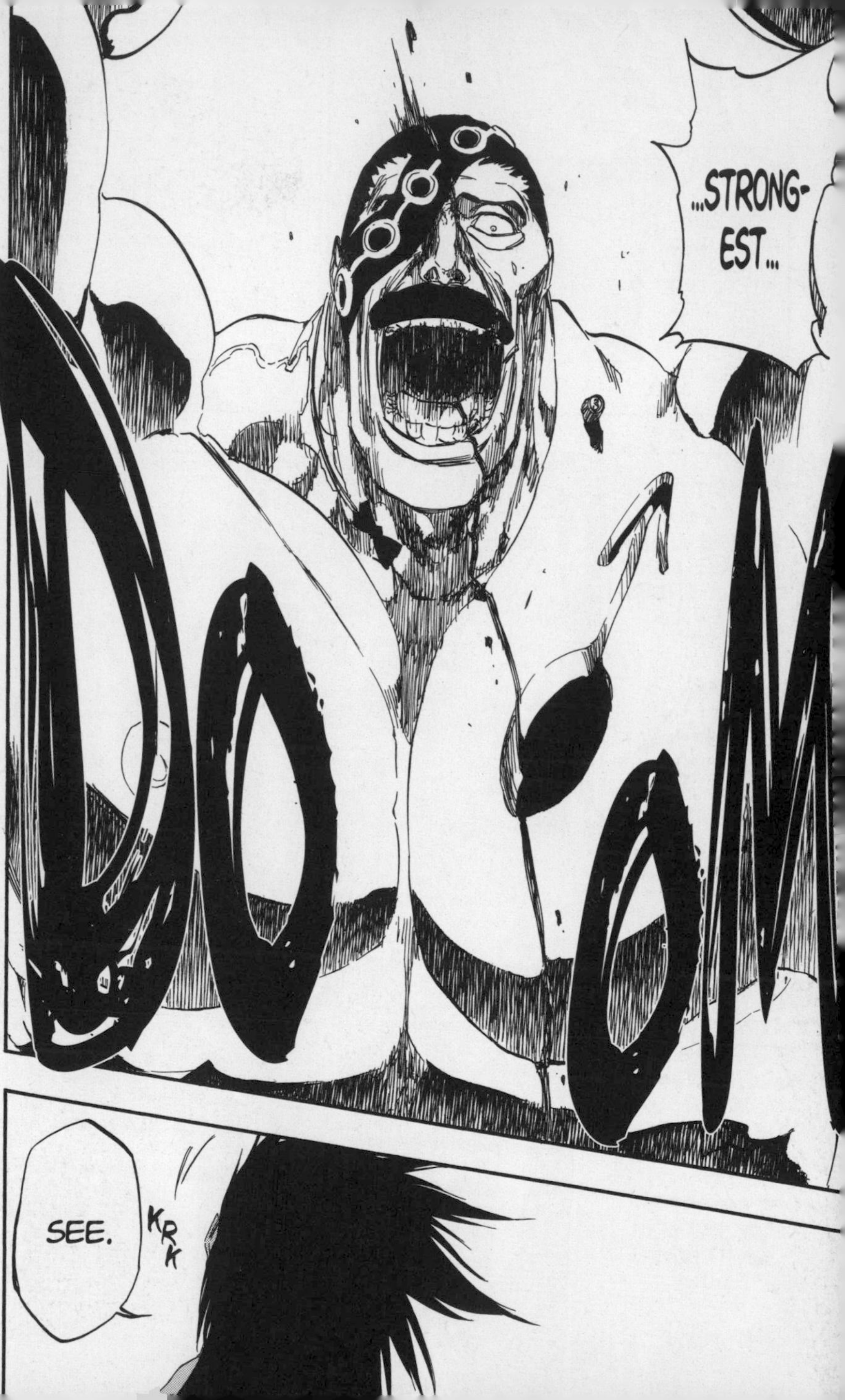
...STRONG-EST...
DOOOM
KRK
SEE.

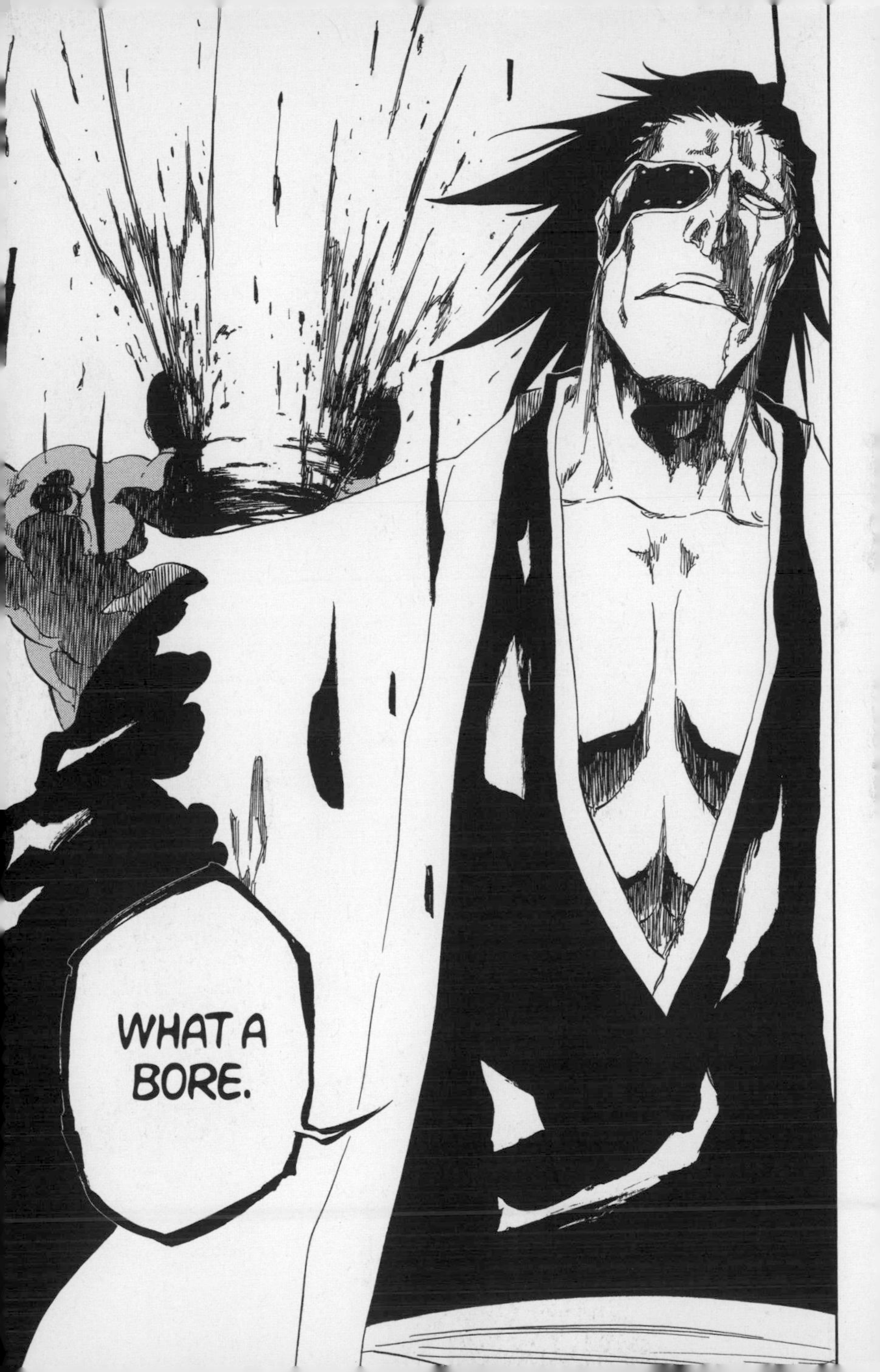
WHAT A BORE.

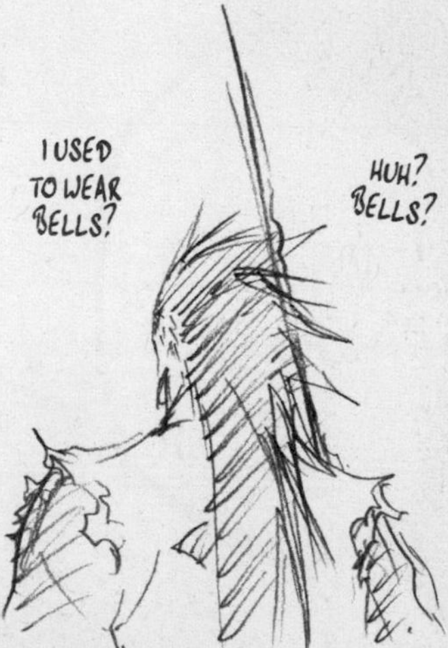
HUH? BELLS?
I USED TO WEAR BELLS?

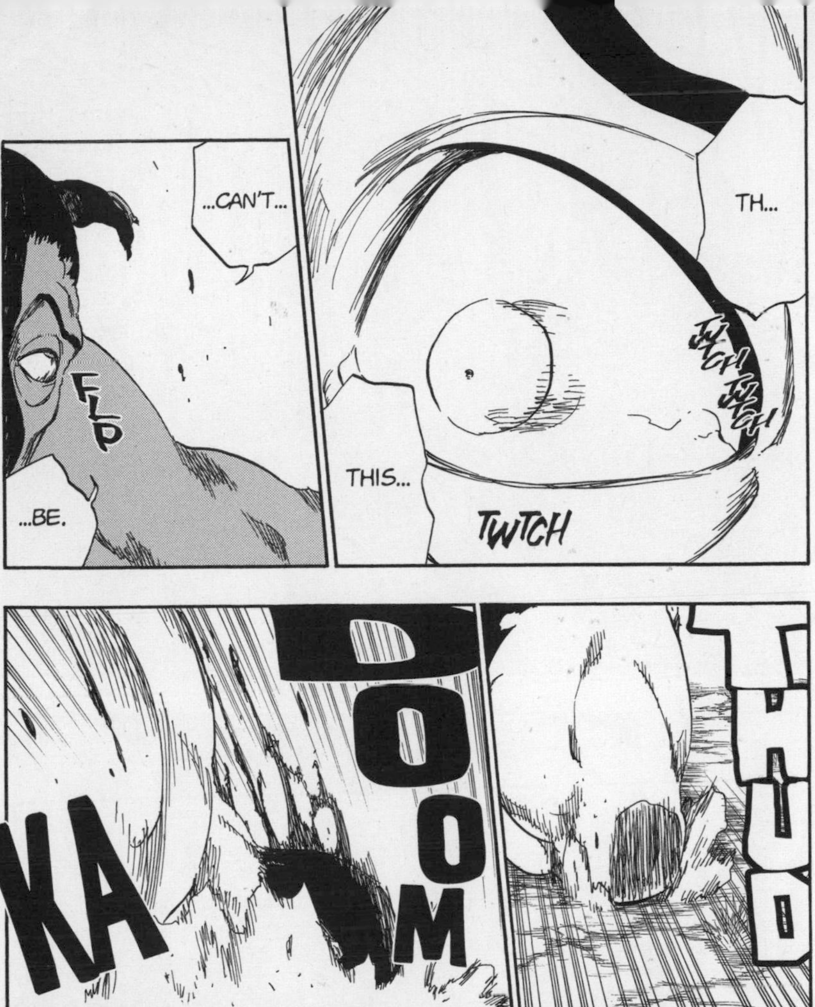
TH...
THIS...
TWITCH
...CAN'T...
FLP
...BE.
THUD
KA
DOOM

454. Quiet Chamber, Noisy Heart

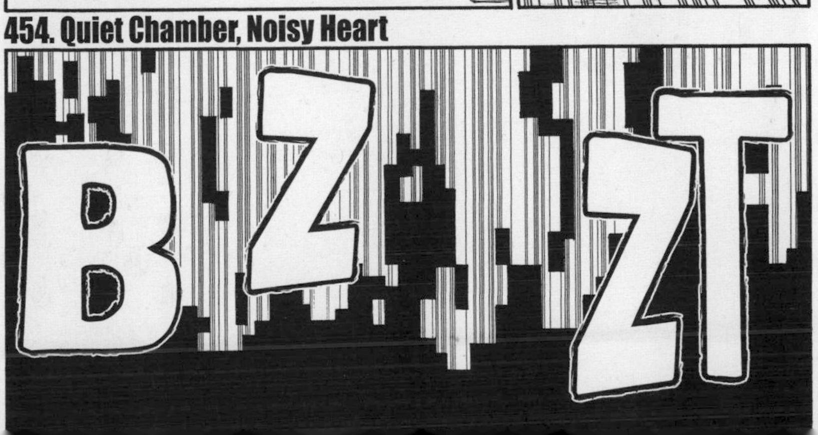
BZZT

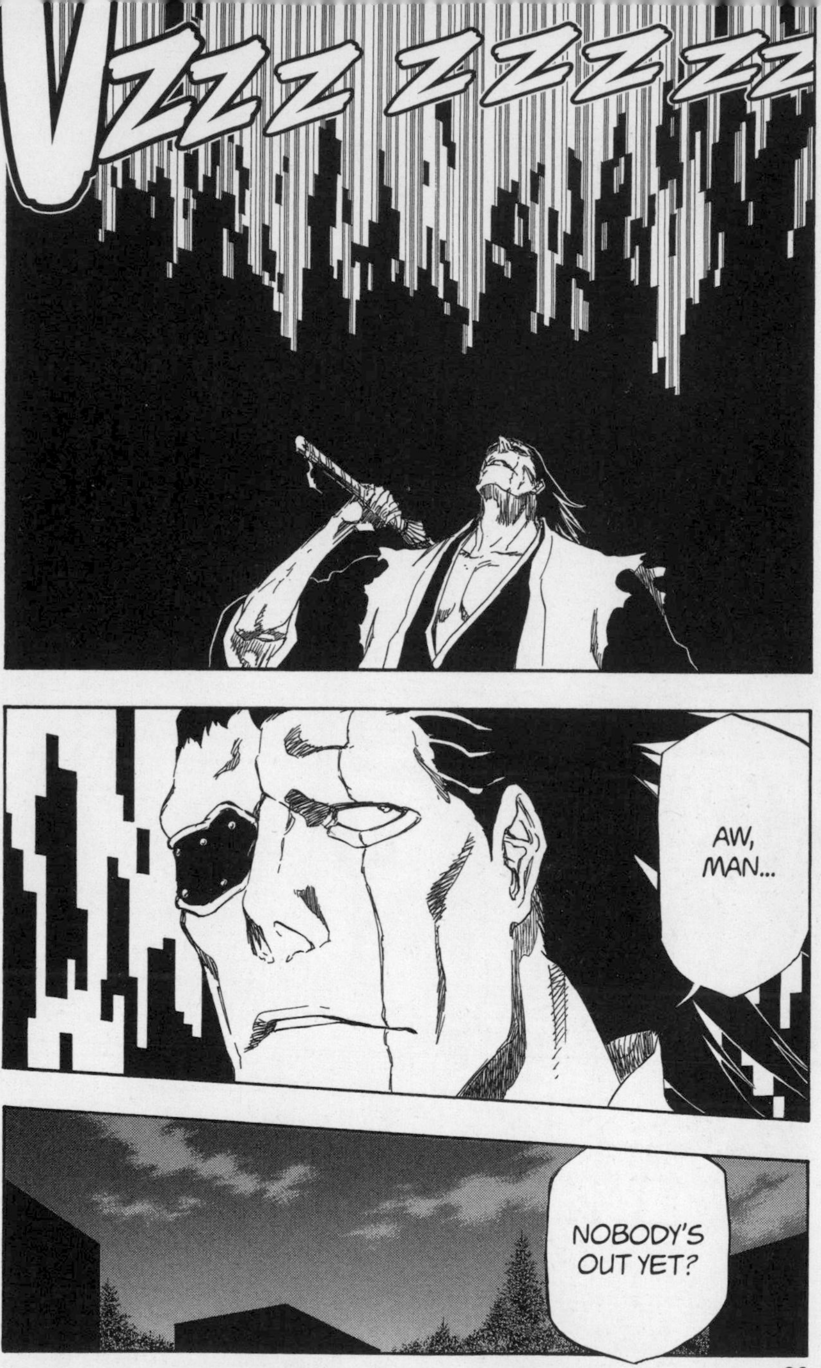
VZZZ ZZZZZZ
AW, MAN...
NOBODY'S OUT YET?

READ THIS WAY

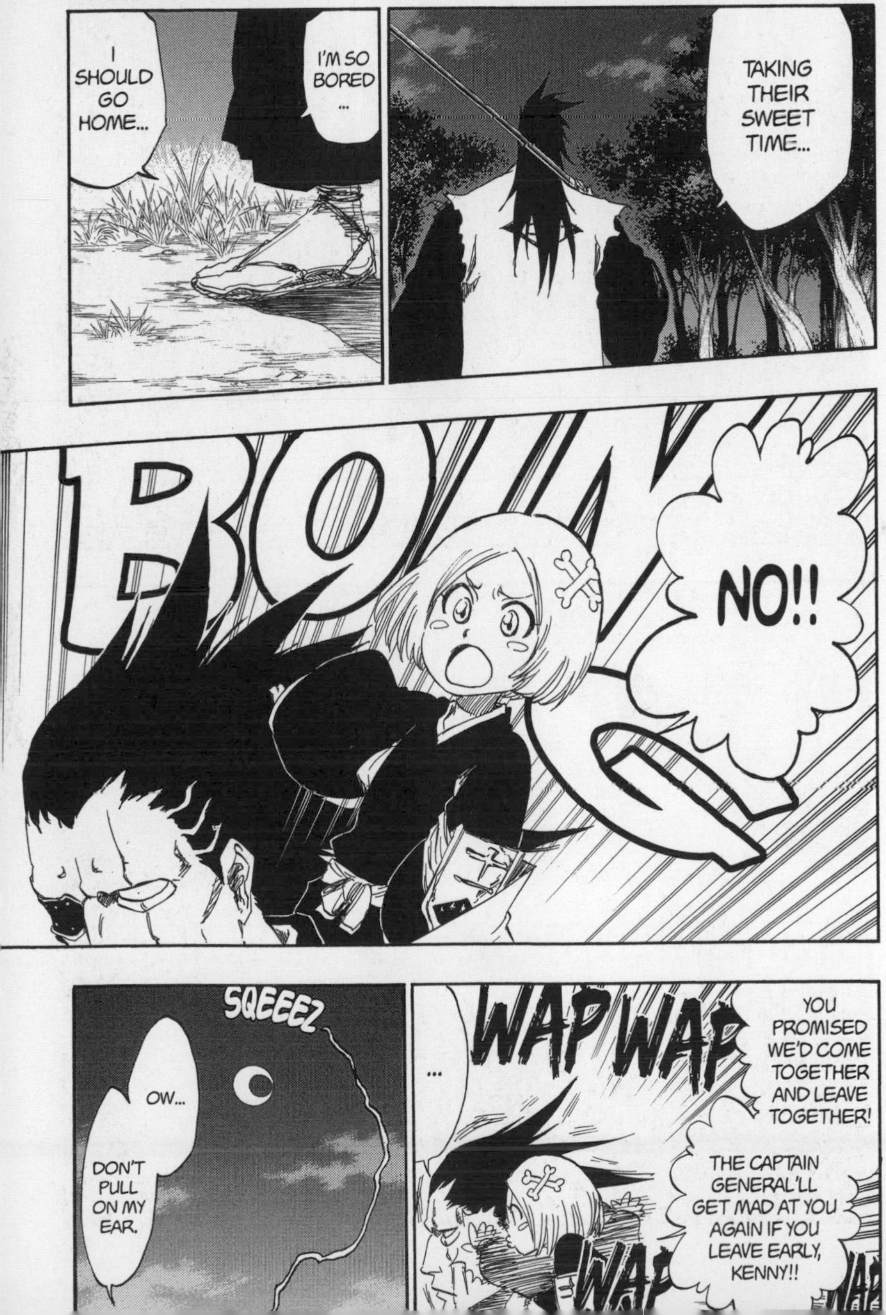
TAKING THEIR SWEET TIME...
I'M SO BORED ...
I SHOULD GO HOME...
NO!!
YOU PROMISED WE'D COME TOGETHER AND LEAVE TOGETHER!
WAP WAP
THE CAPTAIN GENERAL'LL GET MAD AT YOU AGAIN IF YOU LEAVE EARLY, KENNY!!
...
SQEEEZ
OW...
DON'T PULL ON MY EAR.

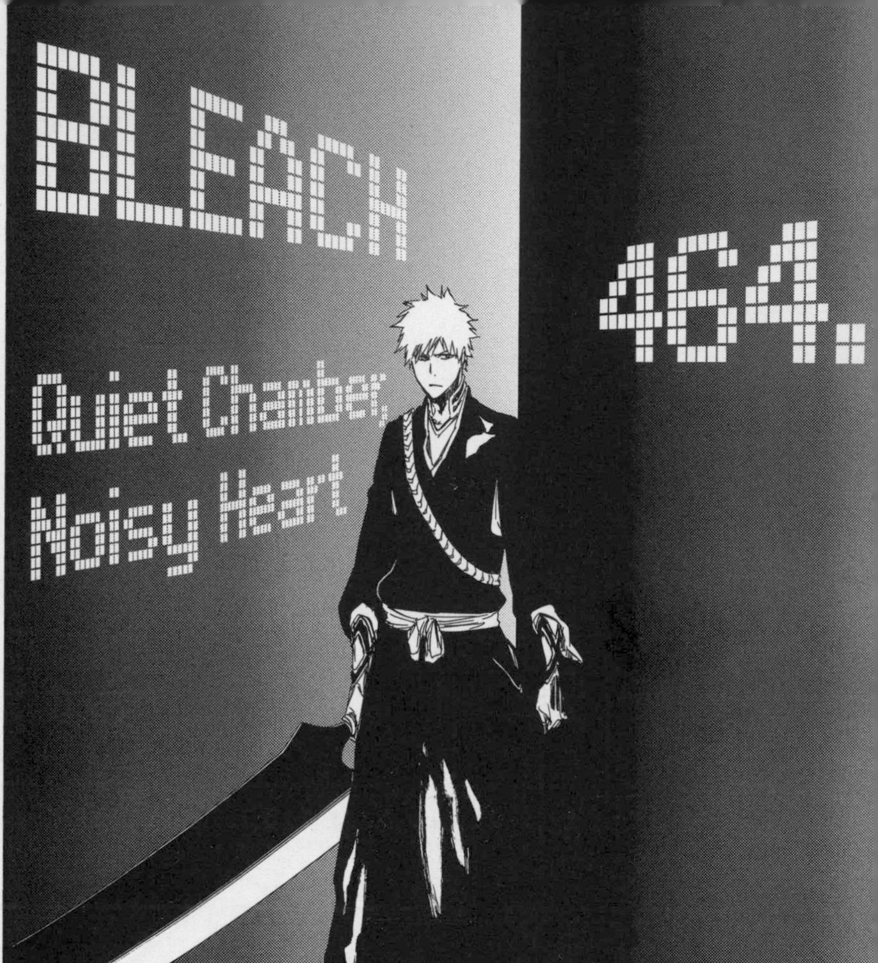
BLEACH
464.
Quiet Chamber,
Noisy Heart

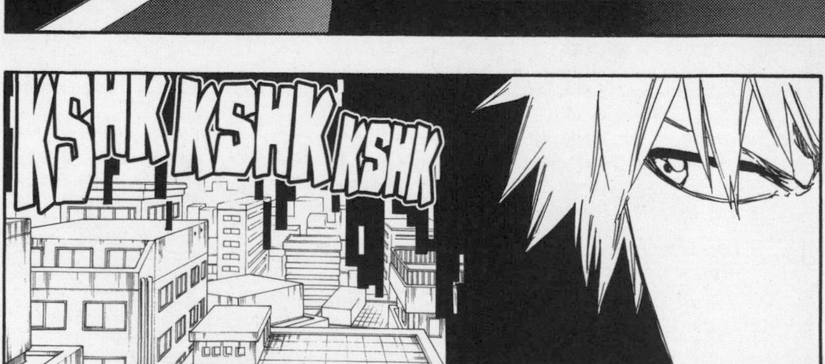
KSHK KSHK KSHK

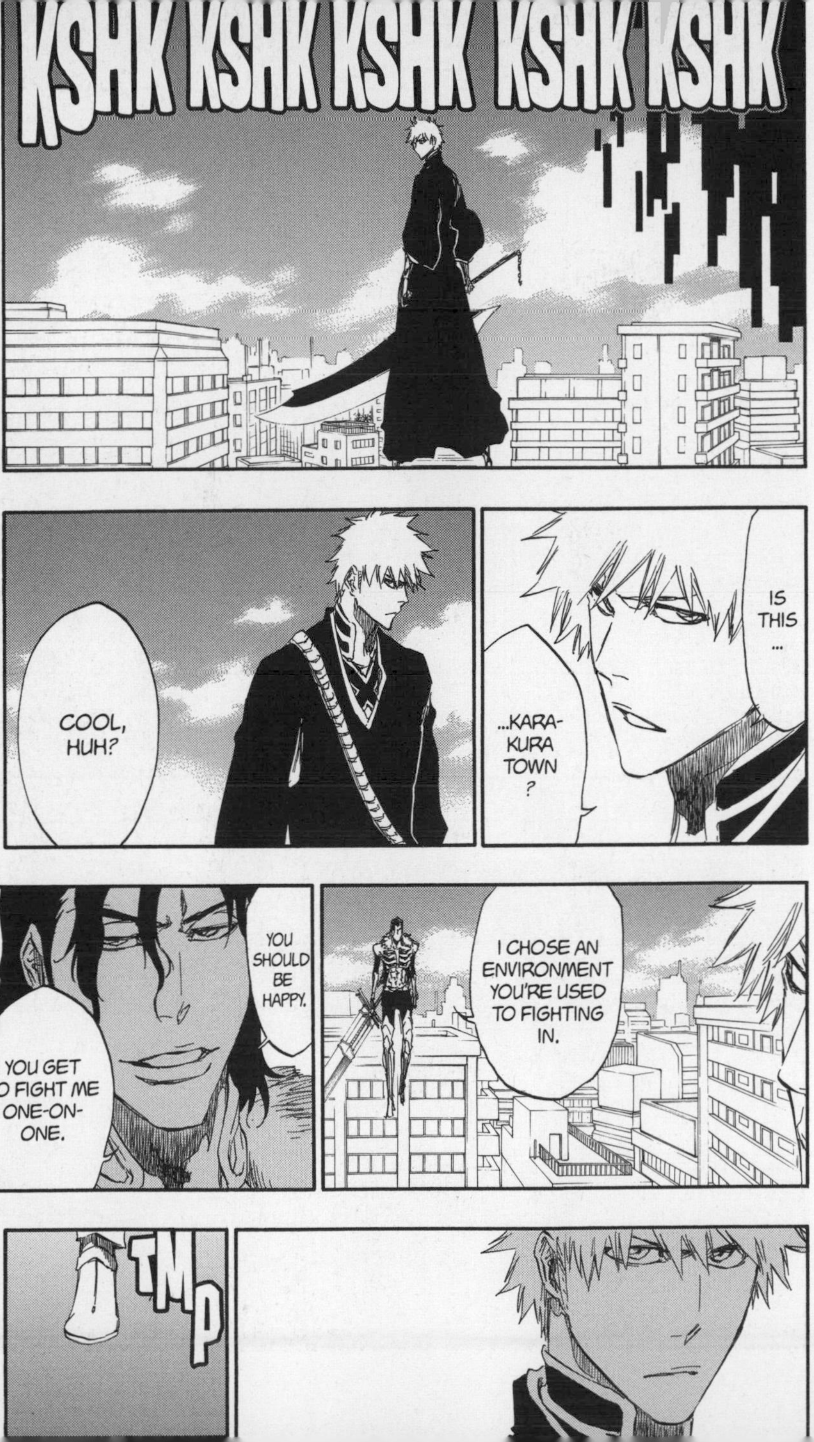
KSHK KSHK KSHK KSHK KSHK
IS THIS ...
...KARA-KURA TOWN?
COOL, HUH?
I CHOSE AN ENVIRONMENT YOU'RE USED TO FIGHTING IN.
YOU SHOULD BE HAPPY.
YOU GET TO FIGHT ME ONE-ON-ONE.
TMP

SORRY, BUT IT'S TWO-ON-ONE...

I HAVE TO APOLOGIZE TO YOU...

KURO-SAKI...

RUKIA HEALED ME.

IT WAS JUST FIRST-AID THOUGH.

I THOUGHT YOU WERE HURT...

URYU.

AFTER WE RETURNED FROM THE SOUL SOCIETY AFTER SAVING RUKIA...

WHEN YOU TOLD ME ABOUT THE DEPUTY BADGE...

...I IMAGINED THAT A DEPUTY SOUL REAPER MUST HAVE EXISTED BEFORE YOU.

AND THAT HE PROBABLY DISAPPEARED.

READ THIS WAY

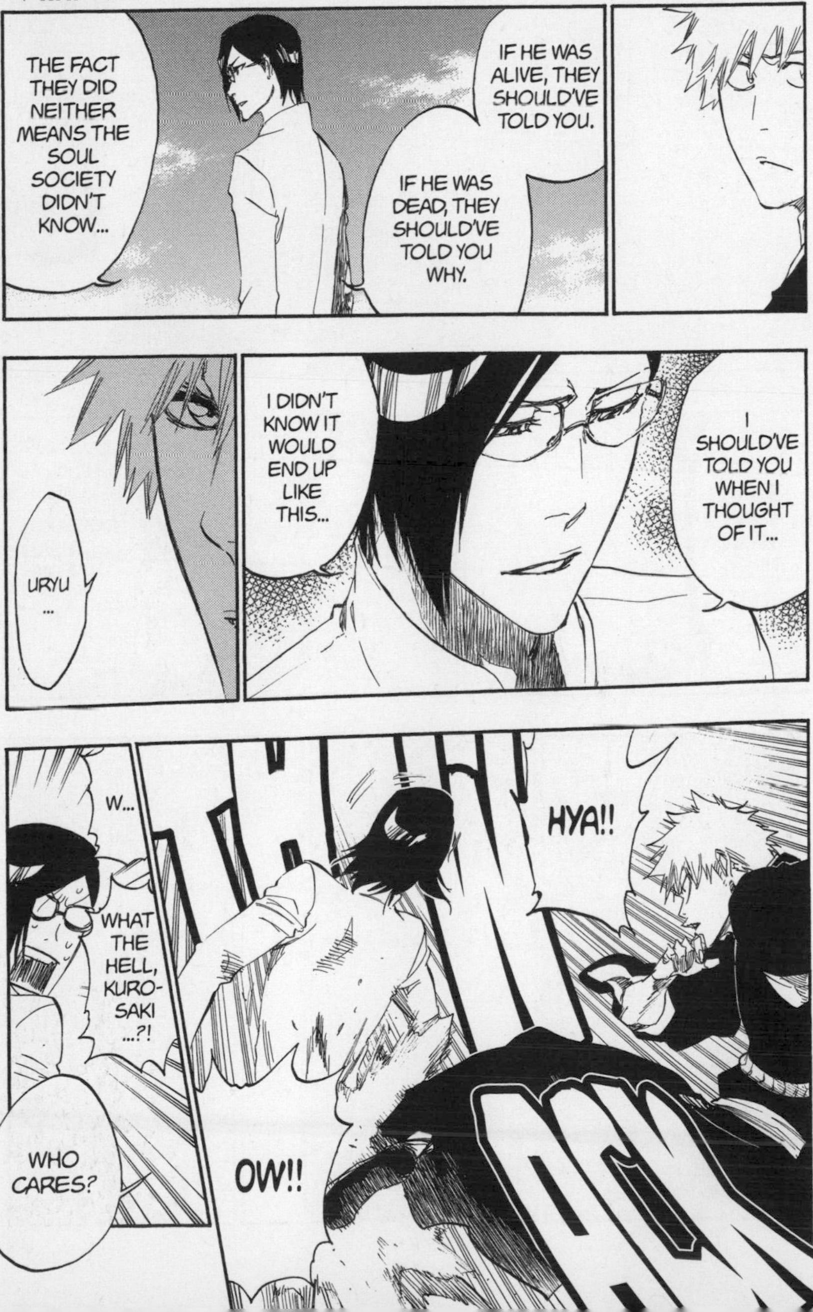
IF HE WAS ALIVE, THEY SHOULD'VE TOLD YOU.
IF HE WAS DEAD, THEY SHOULD'VE TOLD YOU WHY.
THE FACT THEY DID NEITHER MEANS THE SOUL SOCIETY DIDN'T KNOW...
I SHOULD'VE TOLD YOU WHEN I THOUGHT OF IT...
I DIDN'T KNOW IT WOULD END UP LIKE THIS...
URYU ...
HYA!!
OW!!
W...
WHAT THE HELL, KUROSAKI ...?!
WHO CARES?

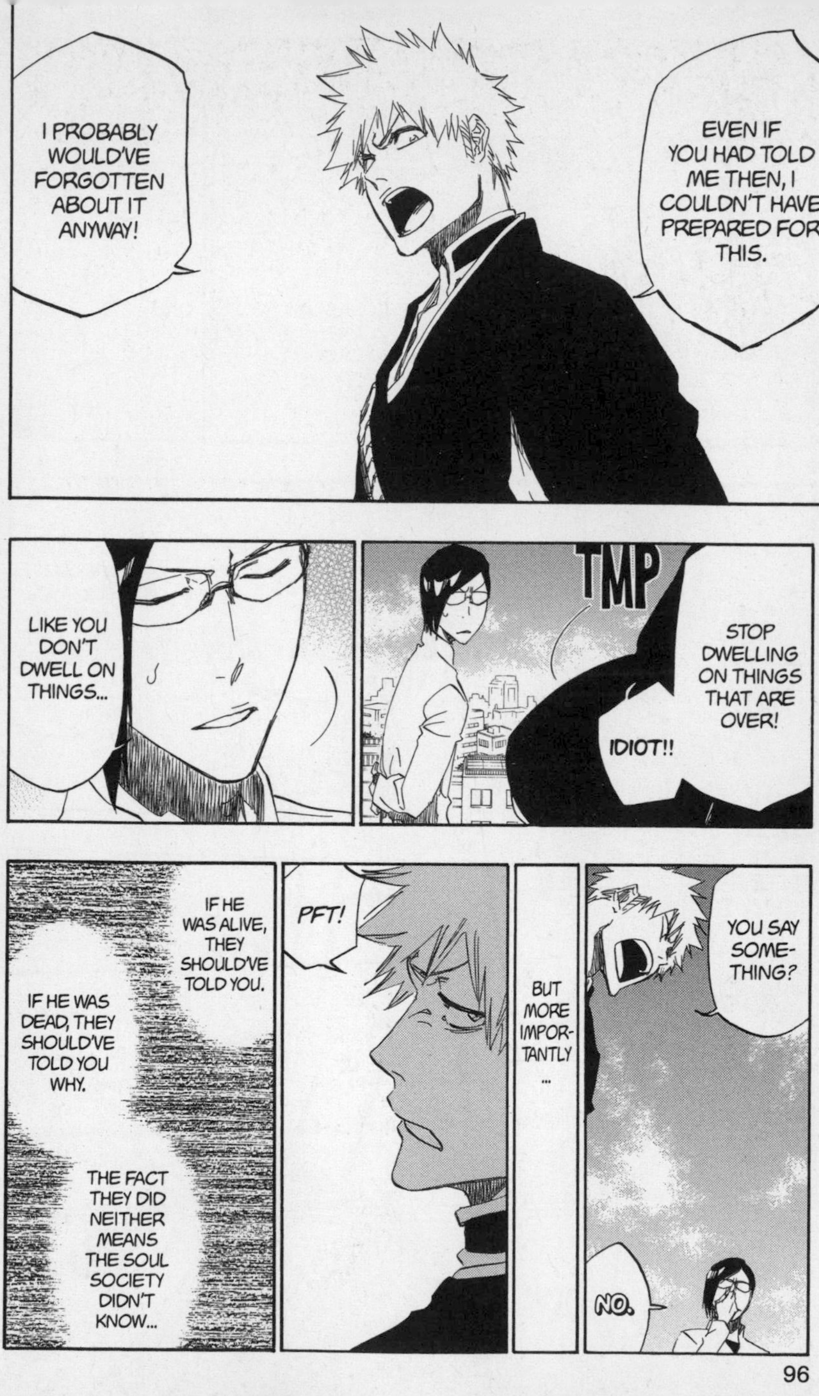
EVEN IF YOU HAD TOLD ME THEN, I COULDN'T HAVE PREPARED FOR THIS.
I PROBABLY WOULD'VE FORGOTTEN ABOUT IT ANYWAY!
TMP
STOP DWELLING ON THINGS THAT ARE OVER!
IDIOT!!
LIKE YOU DON'T DWELL ON THINGS...
YOU SAY SOME-THING?
NO.
BUT MORE IMPOR-TANTLY...
PFT!
IF HE WAS ALIVE, THEY SHOULD'VE TOLD YOU.
IF HE WAS DEAD, THEY SHOULD'VE TOLD YOU WHY.
THE FACT THEY DID NEITHER MEANS THE SOUL SOCIETY DIDN'T KNOW...

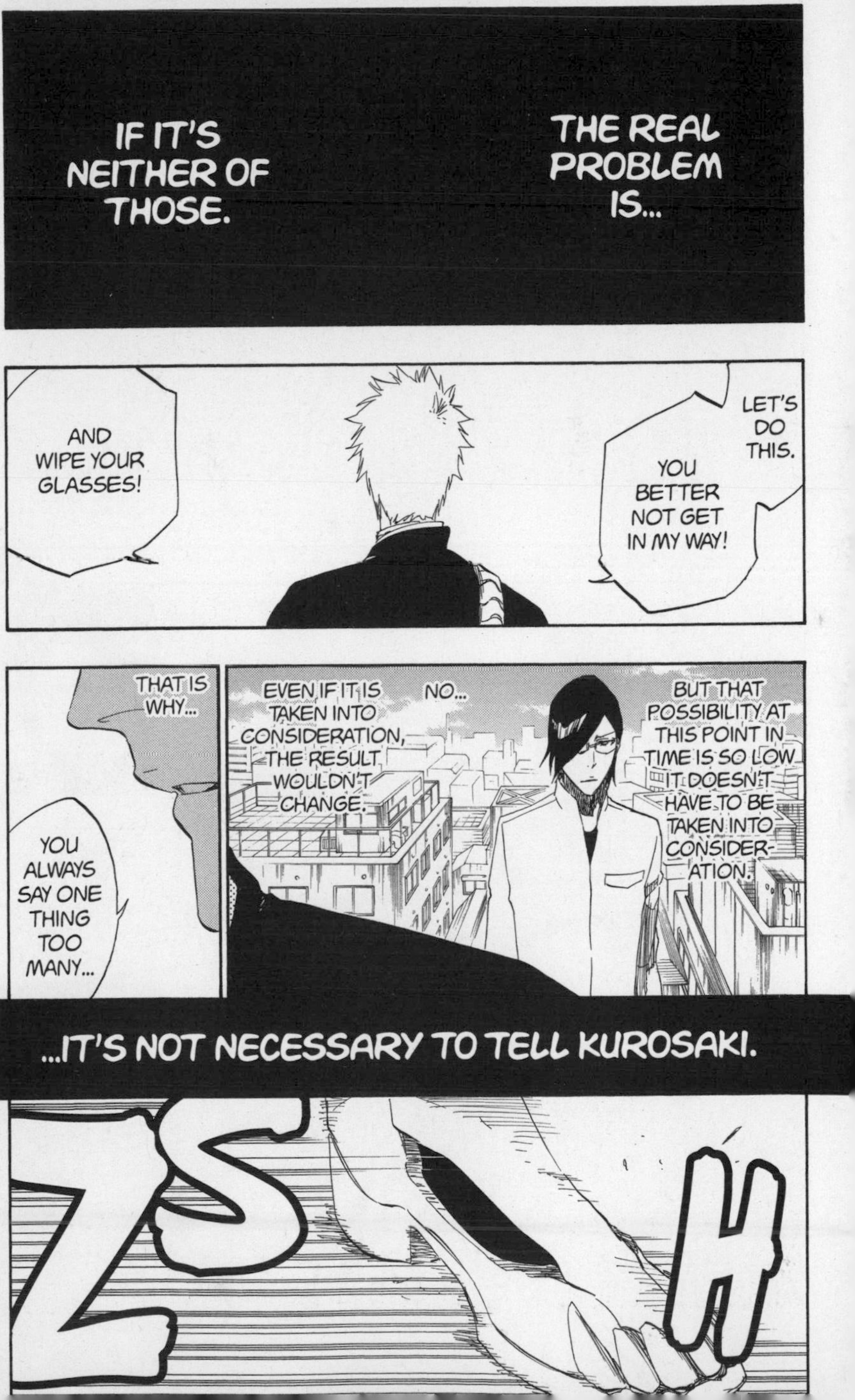
THE REAL PROBLEM IS...
IF IT'S NEITHER OF THOSE.
LET'S DO THIS.
YOU BETTER NOT GET IN MY WAY!
AND WIPE YOUR GLASSES!
BUT THAT POSSIBILITY AT THIS POINT IN TIME IS SO LOW IT DOESN'T HAVE TO BE TAKEN INTO CONSIDER-ATION.
NO...
EVEN IF IT IS TAKEN INTO CONSIDERATION, THE RESULT WOULDN'T CHANGE.
THAT IS WHY...
YOU ALWAYS SAY ONE THING TOO MANY...
...IT'S NOT NECESSARY TO TELL KUROSAKI.
ZSH

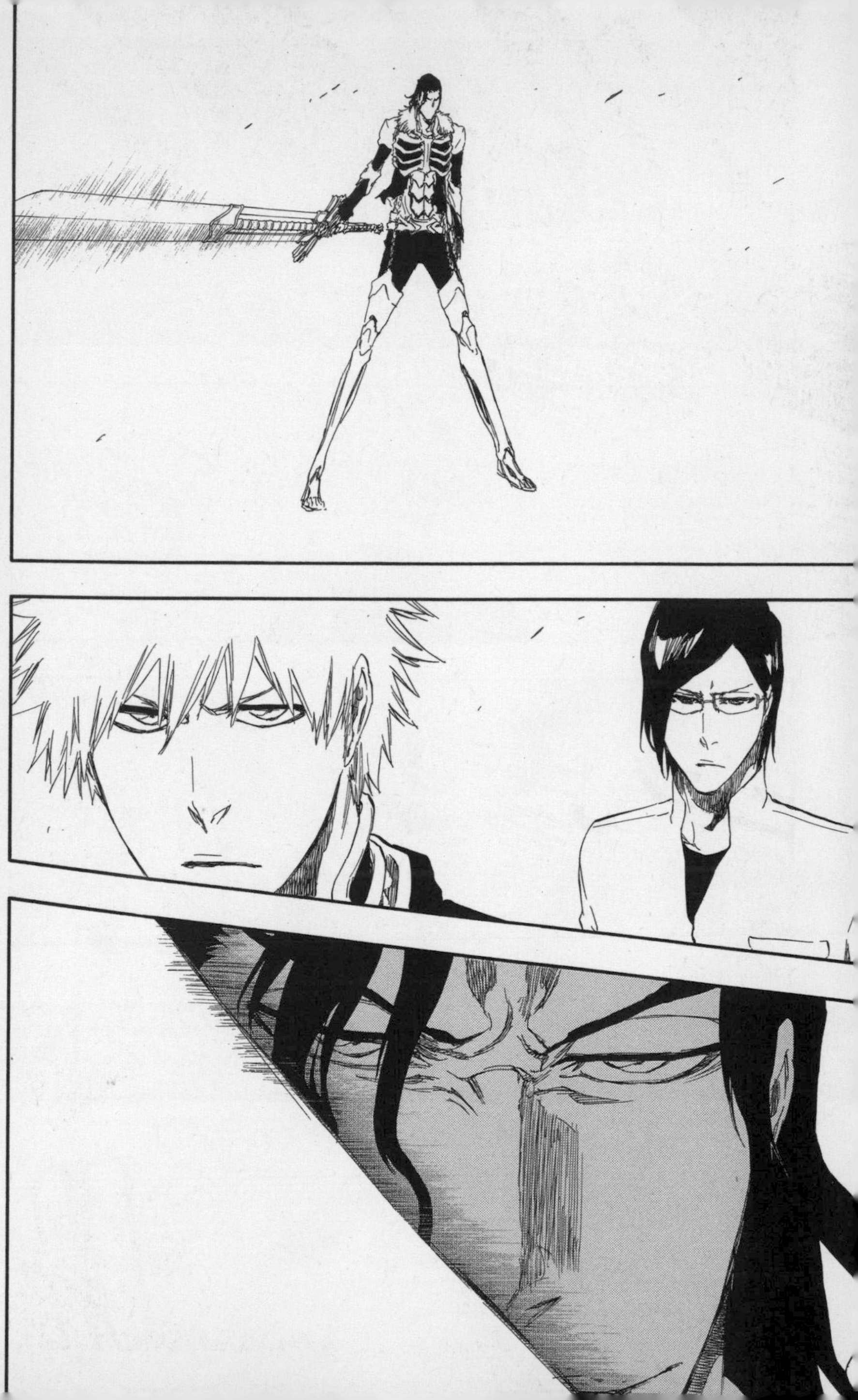

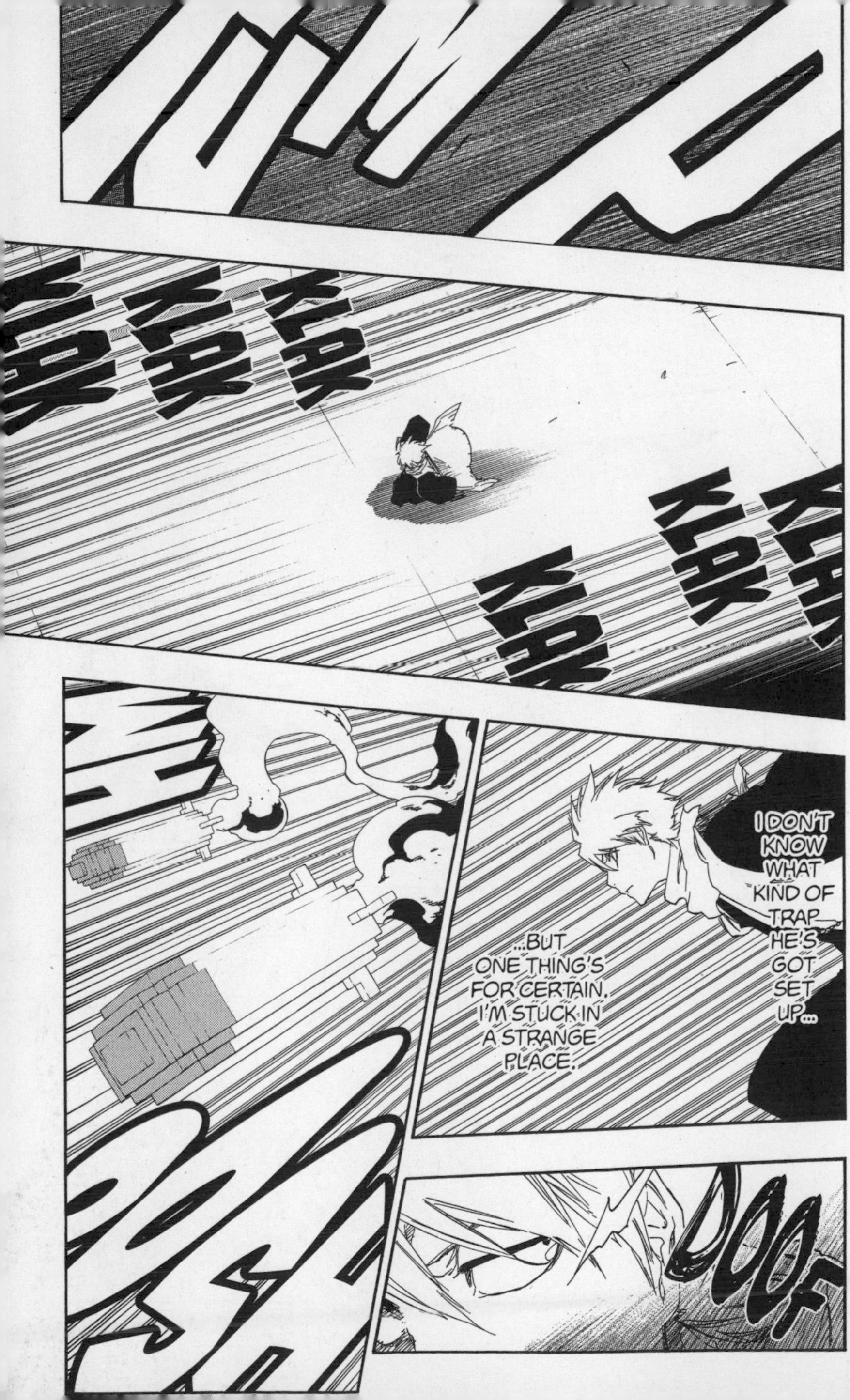
I DON'T KNOW WHAT KIND OF TRAP HE'S GOT SET UP...
...BUT ONE THING'S FOR CERTAIN. I'M STUCK IN A STRANGE PLACE.
DOOF

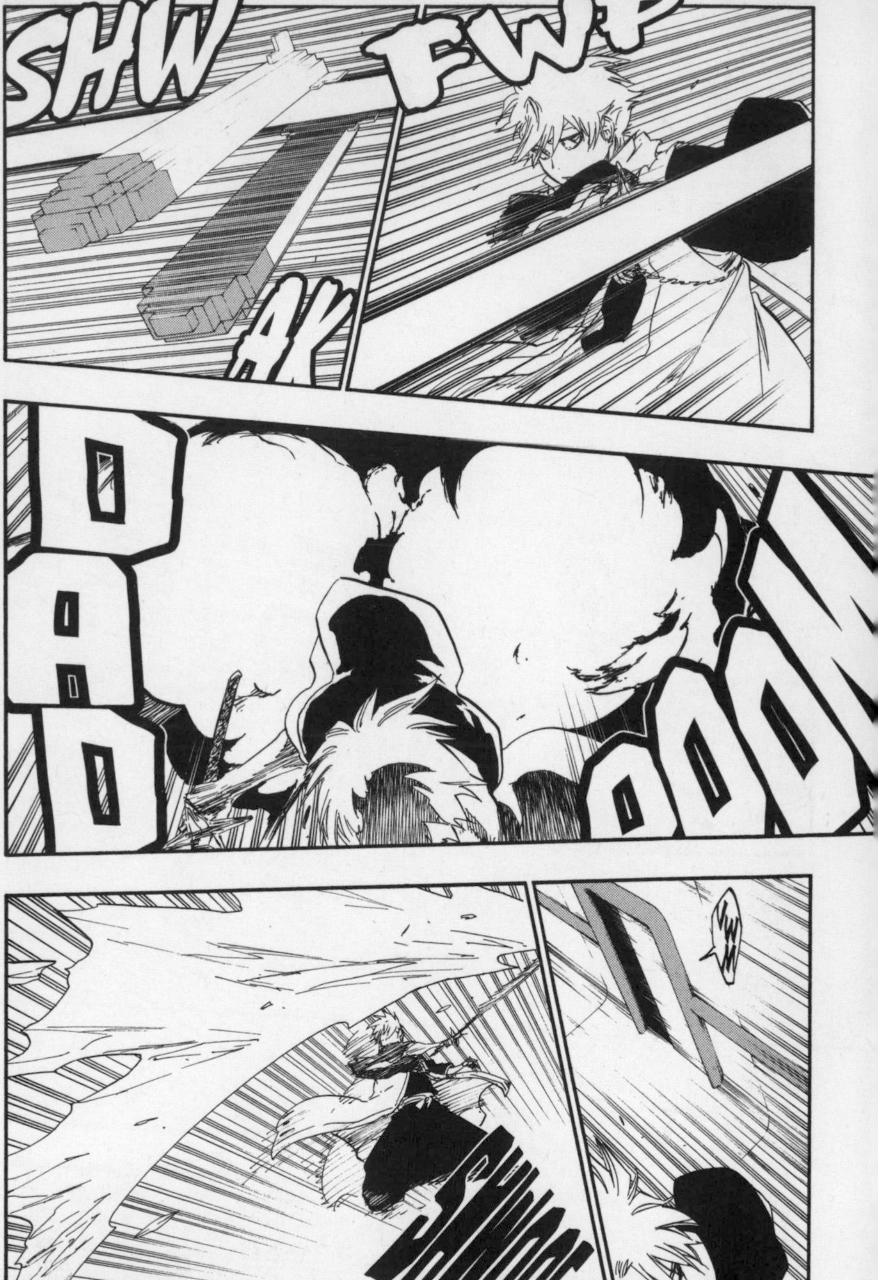
FWP
SHW

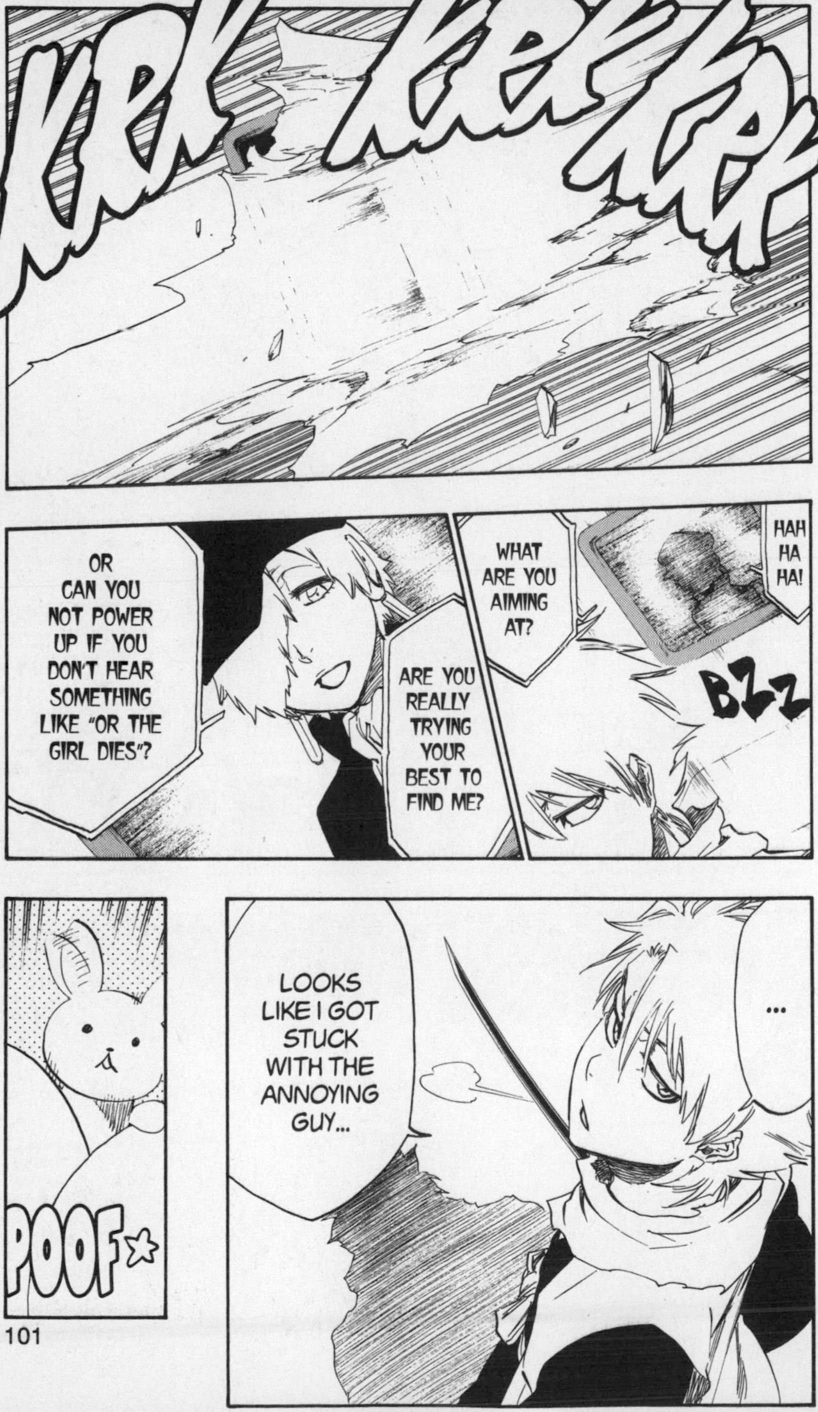
HAH HA HA!
BZZ
WHAT ARE YOU AIMING AT?
ARE YOU REALLY TRYING YOUR BEST TO FIND ME?
OR CAN YOU NOT POWER UP IF YOU DON'T HEAR SOMETHING LIKE "OR THE GIRL DIES"?
...
LOOKS LIKE I GOT STUCK WITH THE ANNOYING GUY...
POOF☆

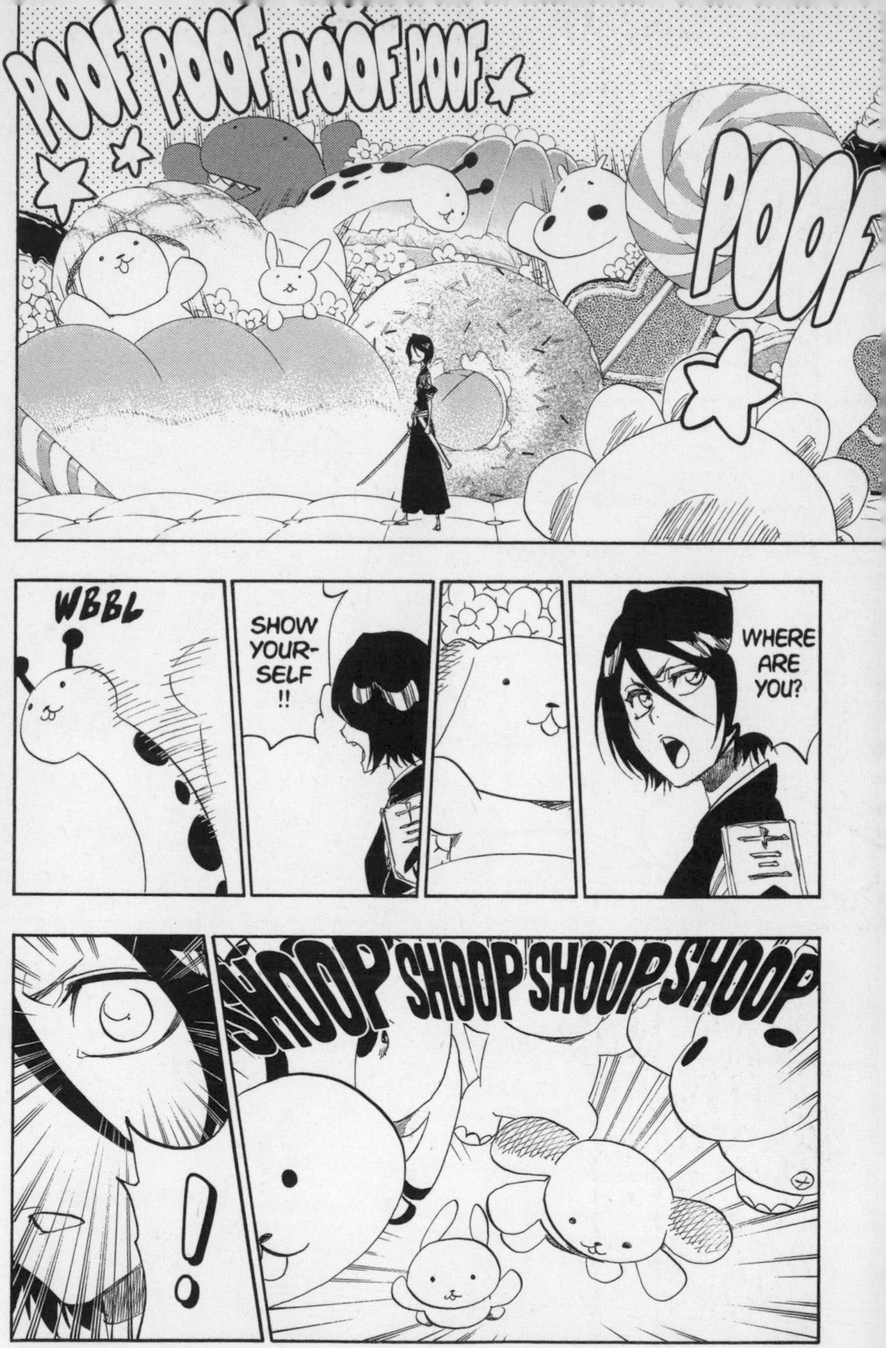
POOF
POOF POOF POOF POOF
WHERE ARE YOU?
SHOW YOUR-SELF !!
WBBL
SHOOP SHOOP SHOOP SHOOP
!

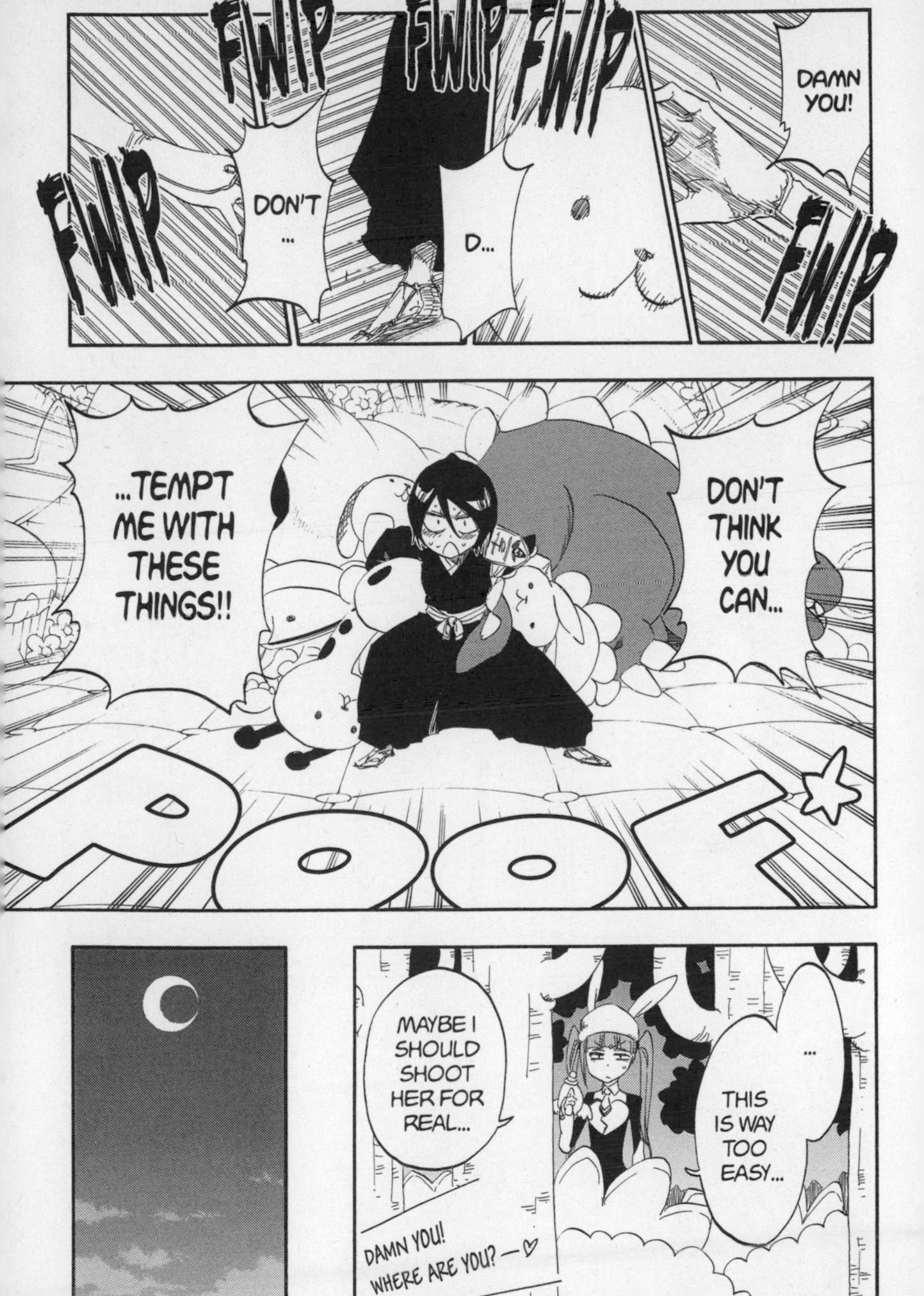
DAMN YOU!
FWIP
FWIP
FWIP
D...
DON'T ...
FWIP
FWIP
DON'T THINK YOU CAN...
...TEMPT ME WITH THESE THINGS!!
POOF
... THIS IS WAY TOO EASY...
MAYBE I SHOULD SHOOT HER FOR REAL...
DAMN YOU! WHERE ARE YOU?—♡

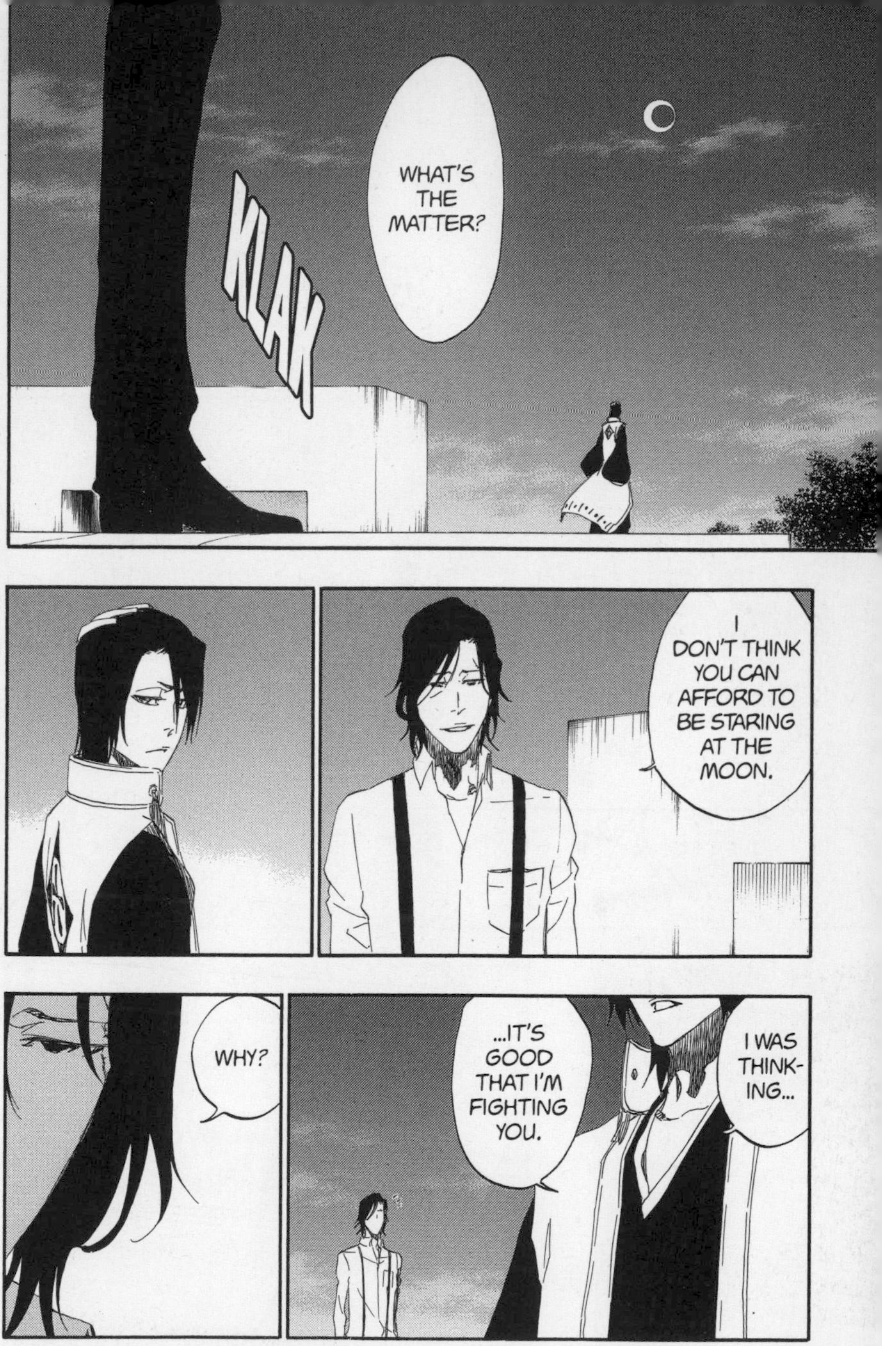
WHAT'S THE MATTER?
KLAK
I DON'T THINK YOU CAN AFFORD TO BE STARING AT THE MOON.
I WAS THINKING...
...IT'S GOOD THAT I'M FIGHTING YOU.
WHY?

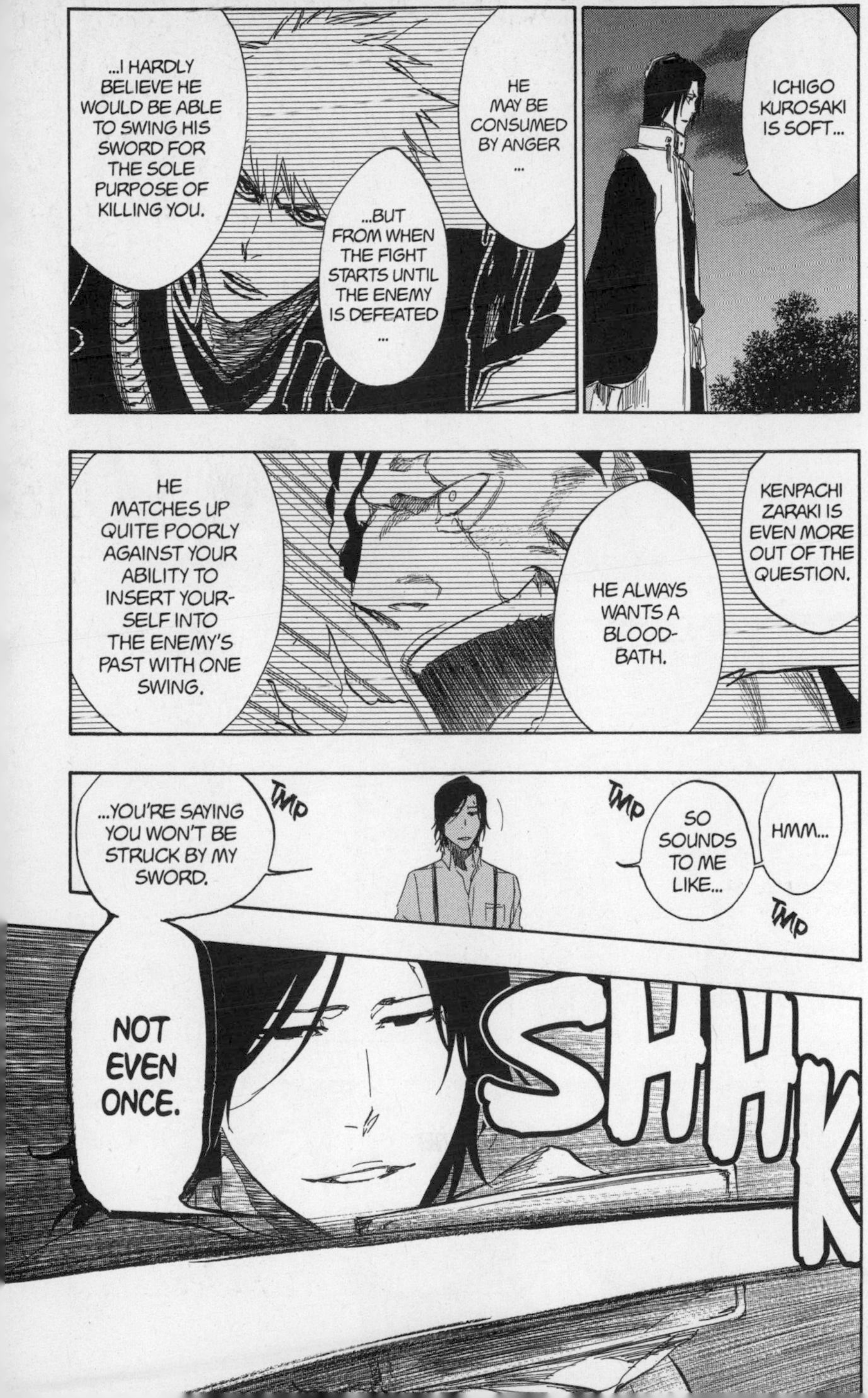
ICHIGO KUROSAKI IS SOFT...
HE MAY BE CONSUMED BY ANGER ...
...BUT FROM WHEN THE FIGHT STARTS UNTIL THE ENEMY IS DEFEATED ...
...I HARDLY BELIEVE HE WOULD BE ABLE TO SWING HIS SWORD FOR THE SOLE PURPOSE OF KILLING YOU.
KENPACHI ZARAKI IS EVEN MORE OUT OF THE QUESTION.
HE ALWAYS WANTS A BLOOD-BATH.
HE MATCHES UP QUITE POORLY AGAINST YOUR ABILITY TO INSERT YOUR-SELF INTO THE ENEMY'S PAST WITH ONE SWING.
HMM...
TMP
SO SOUNDS TO ME LIKE...
TMP
TMP
...YOU'RE SAYING YOU WON'T BE STRUCK BY MY SWORD.
SHHK
NOT EVEN ONCE.

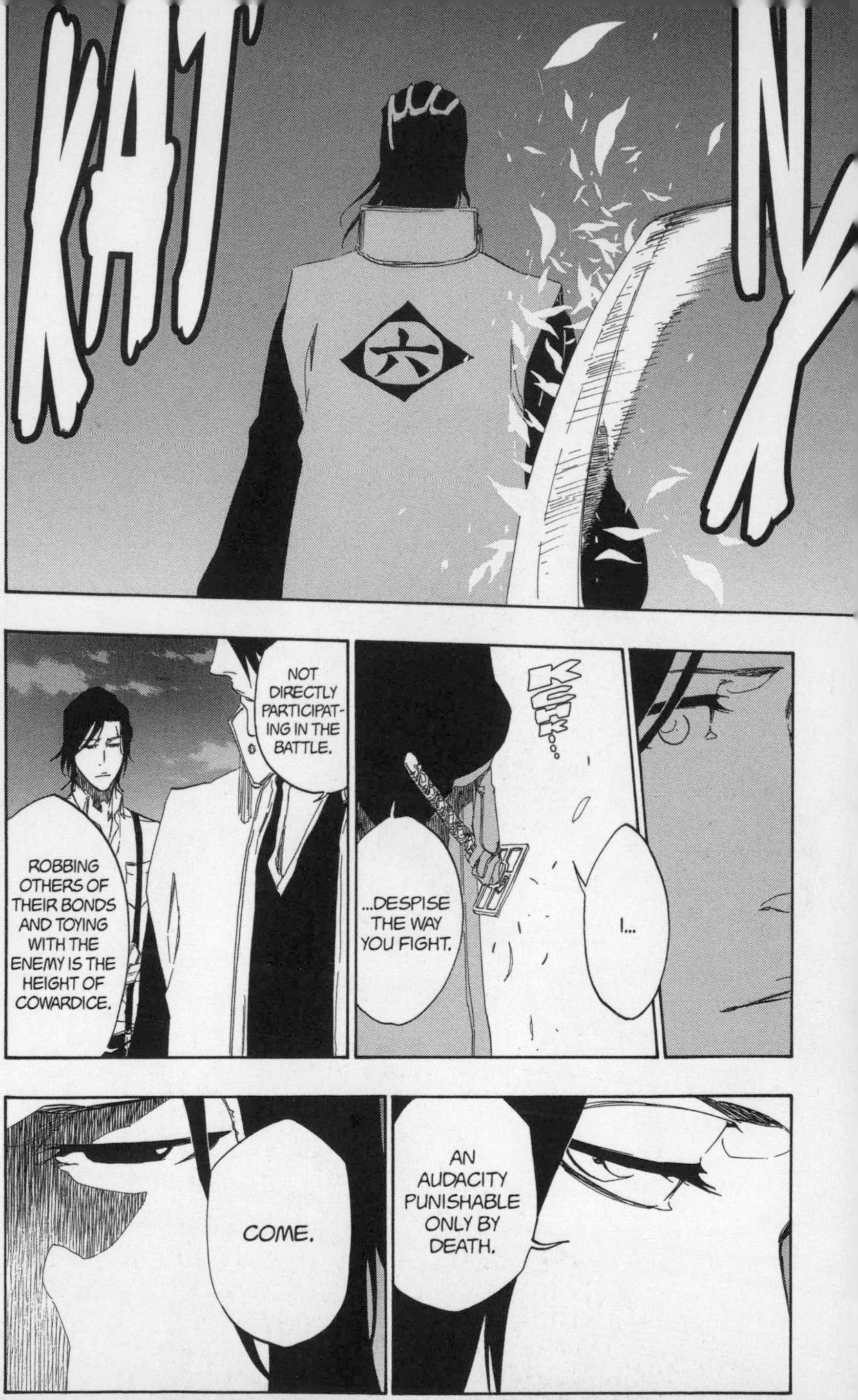
I...
...DESPISE THE WAY YOU FIGHT.
NOT DIRECTLY PARTICIPAT-ING IN THE BATTLE.
ROBBING OTHERS OF THEIR BONDS AND TOYING WITH THE ENEMY IS THE HEIGHT OF COWARDICE.
AN AUDACITY PUNISHABLE ONLY BY DEATH.
COME.

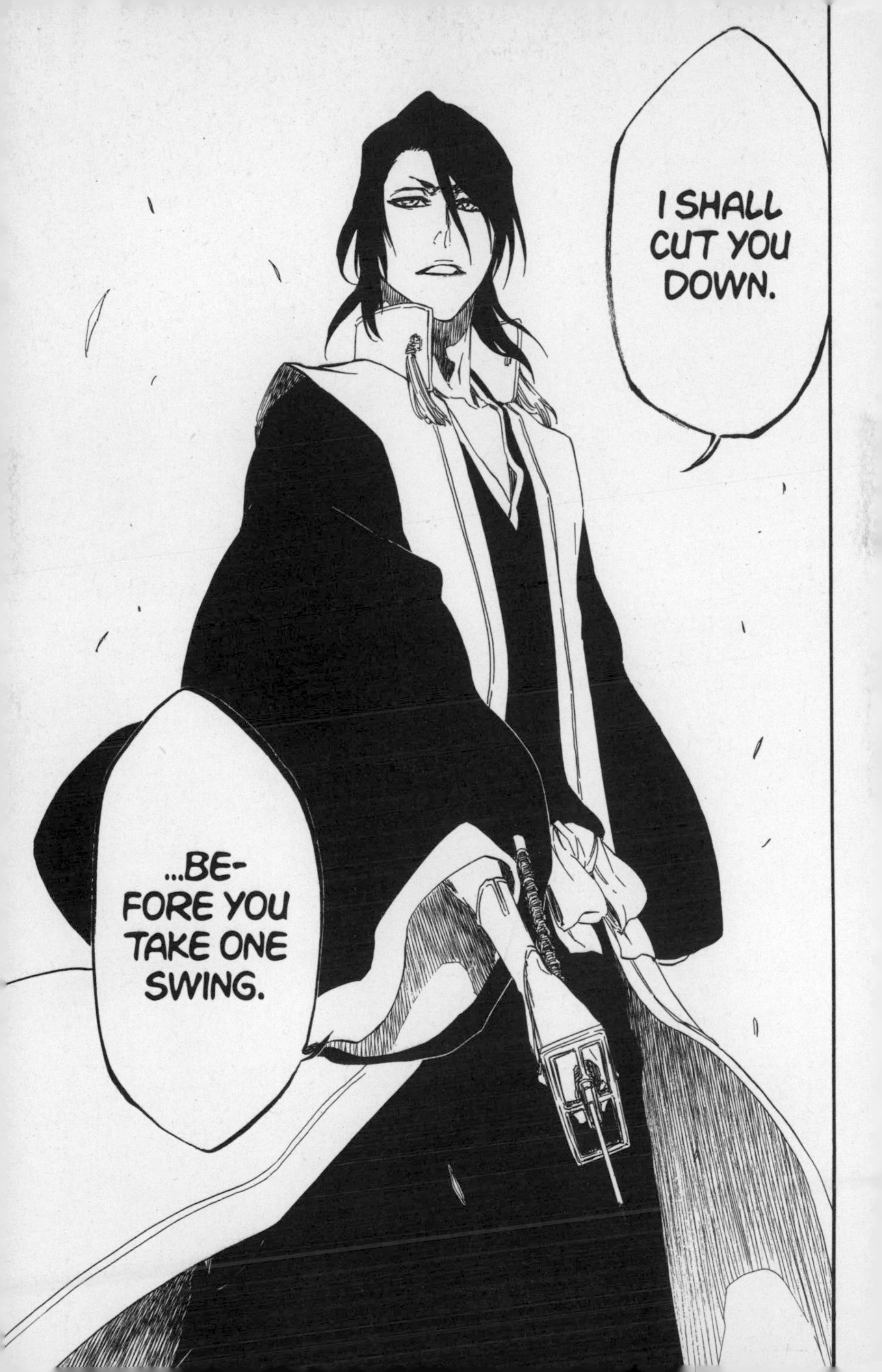
I SHALL CUT YOU DOWN.
...BE-FORE YOU TAKE ONE SWING.

ALTERED THE COLLAR AND FRONT PLACKET OF A STANDARD-ISSUE CAPTAIN'S HAORI. COST HIM THE SAME AMOUNT AS THREE SHEETS OF EXPENSIVE SILK CLOTH.

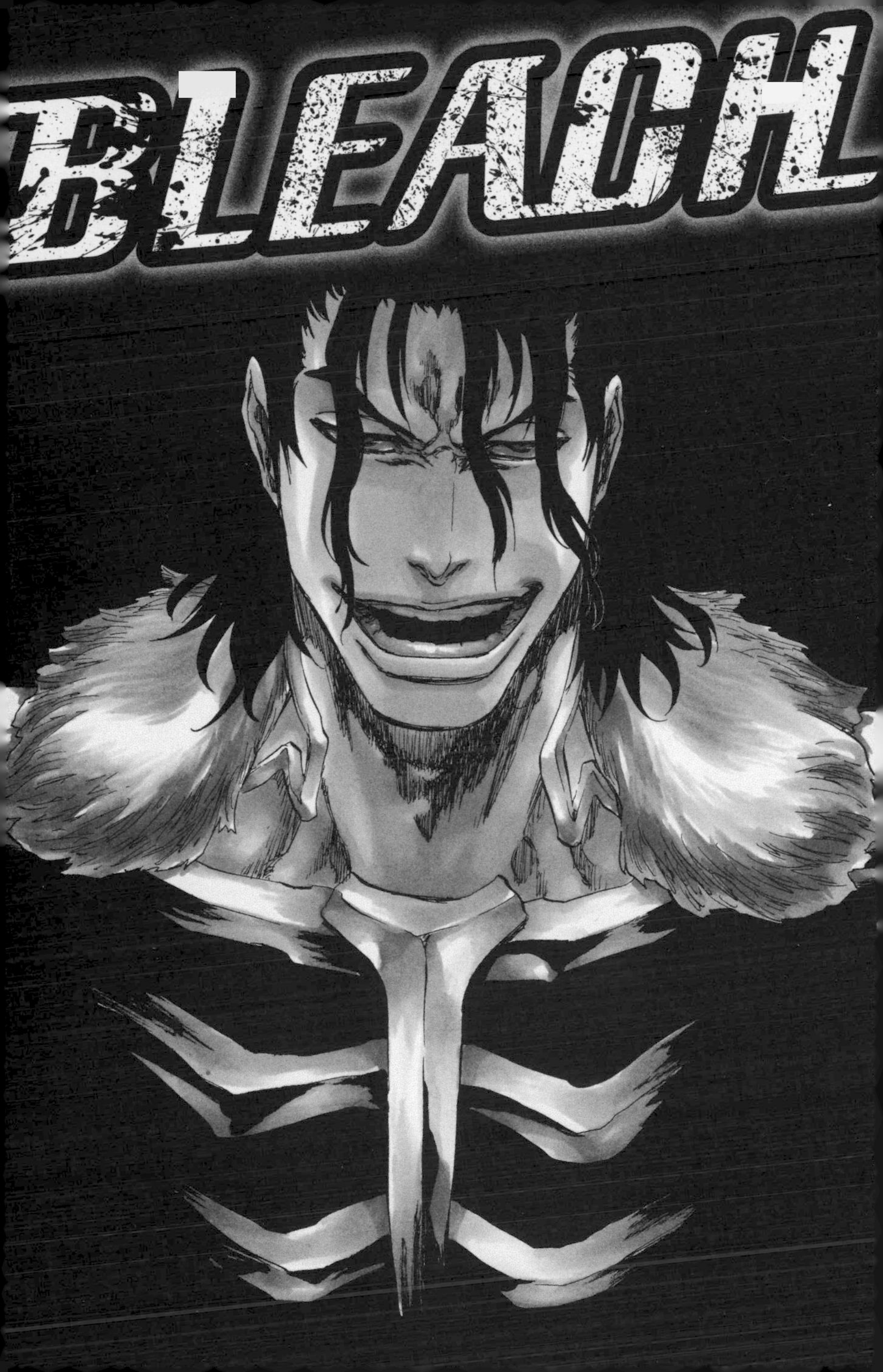
BLEACH

BLEACH
ブリーチ

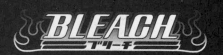

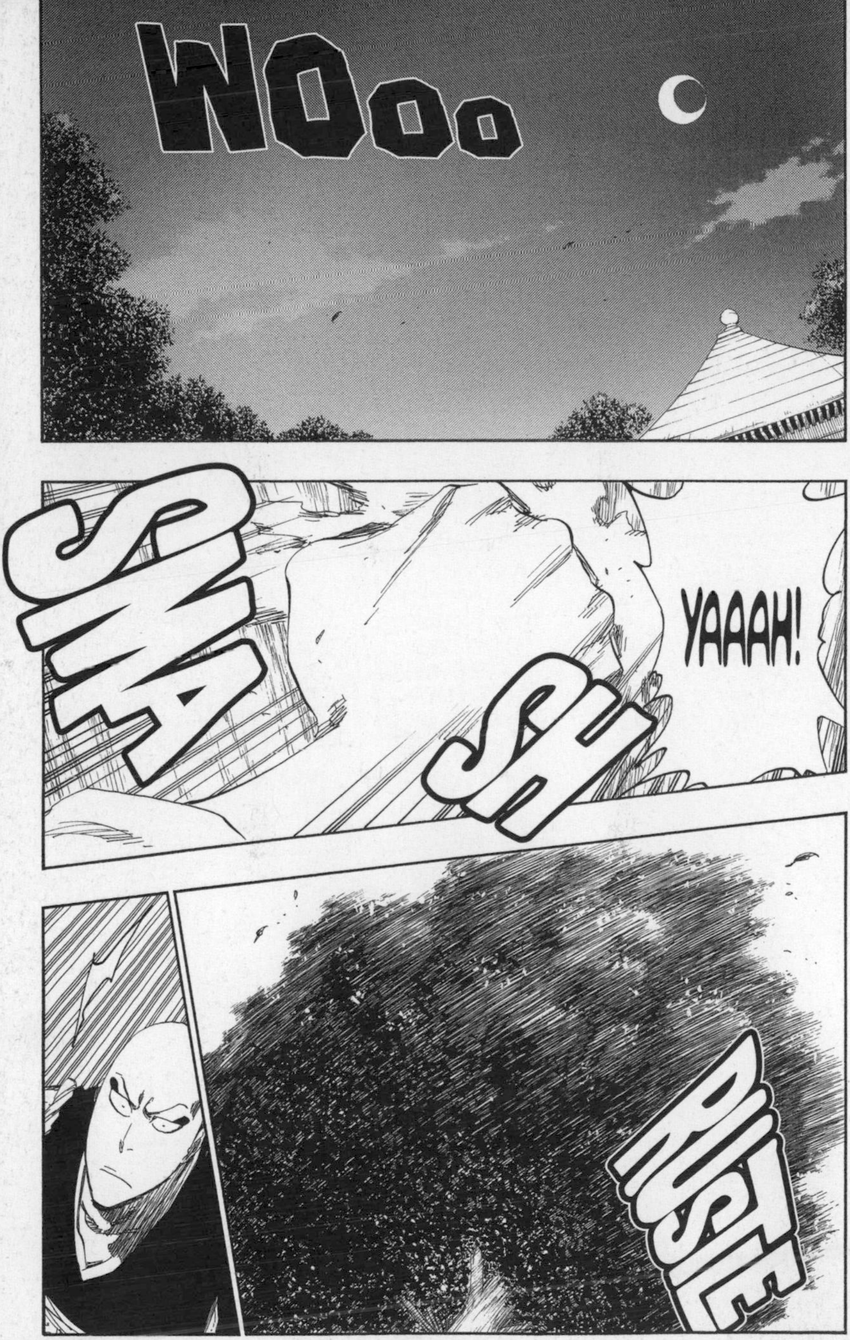
WOooo
YAAAH!
SWA
SH
DUSTE

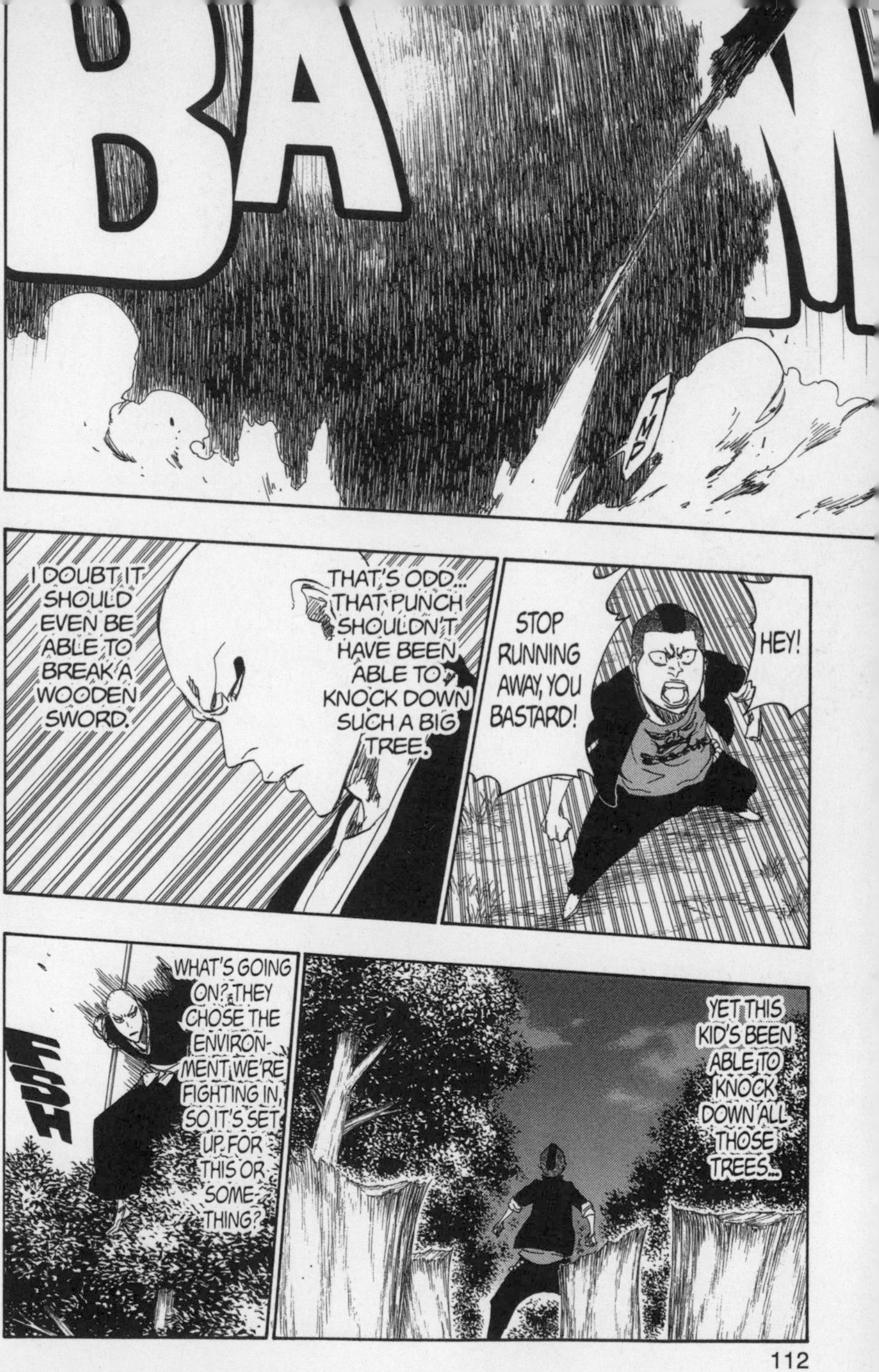
BAM
TMP
HEY!
STOP RUNNING AWAY, YOU BASTARD!
THAT'S ODD... THAT PUNCH SHOULDN'T HAVE BEEN ABLE TO KNOCK DOWN SUCH A BIG TREE.
I DOUBT IT SHOULD EVEN BE ABLE TO BREAK A WOODEN SWORD.
YET THIS KID'S BEEN ABLE TO KNOCK DOWN ALL THOSE TREES...
WHAT'S GOING ON? THEY CHOSE THE ENVIRONMENT WE'RE FIGHTING IN, SO IT'S SET UP FOR THIS OR SOMETHING?

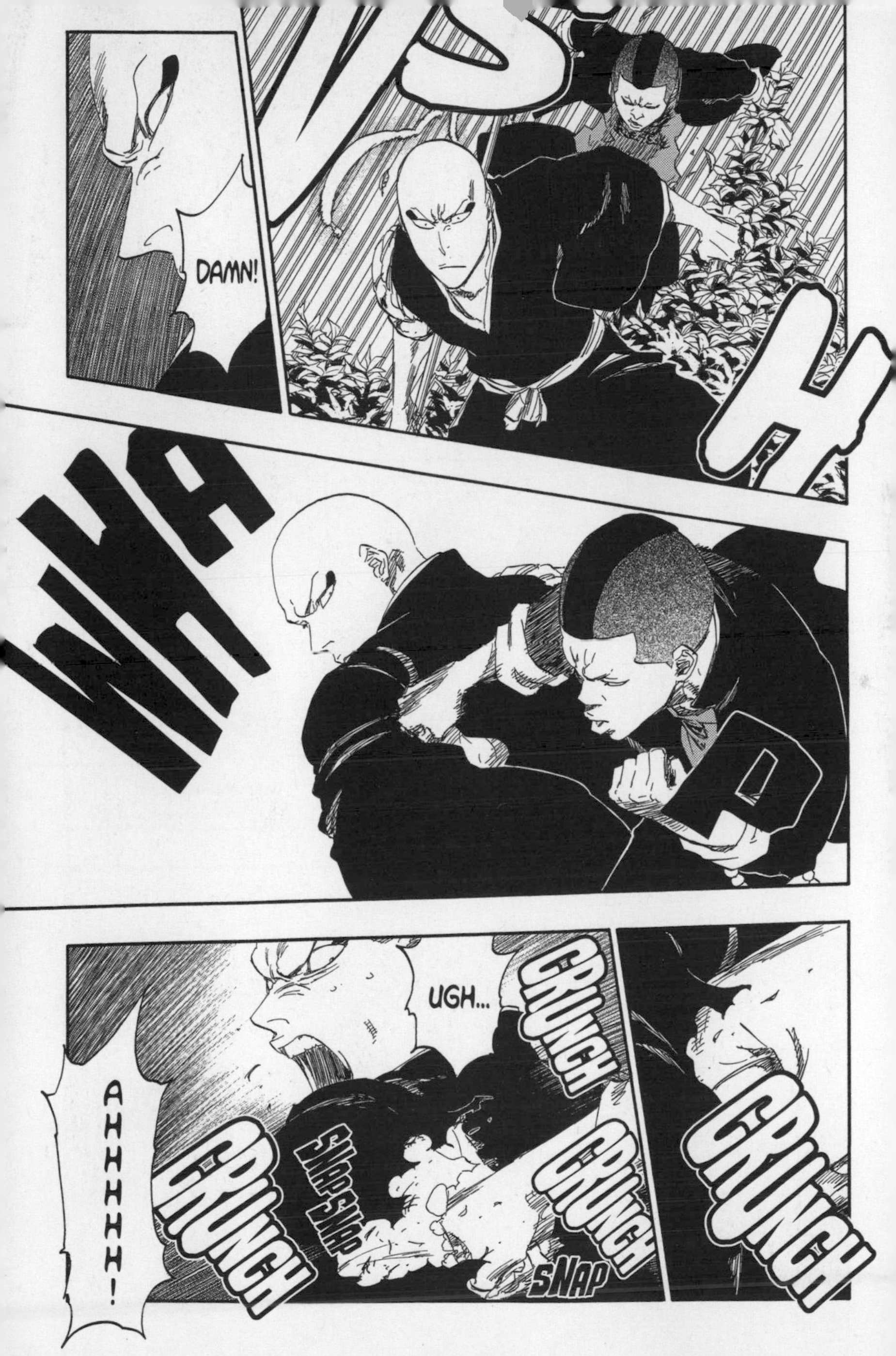
DAMN!
CRUNCH
UGH...
CRUNCH
CRUNCH
SNAP
SNAP SNAP
CRUNCH
AHHHHHH!

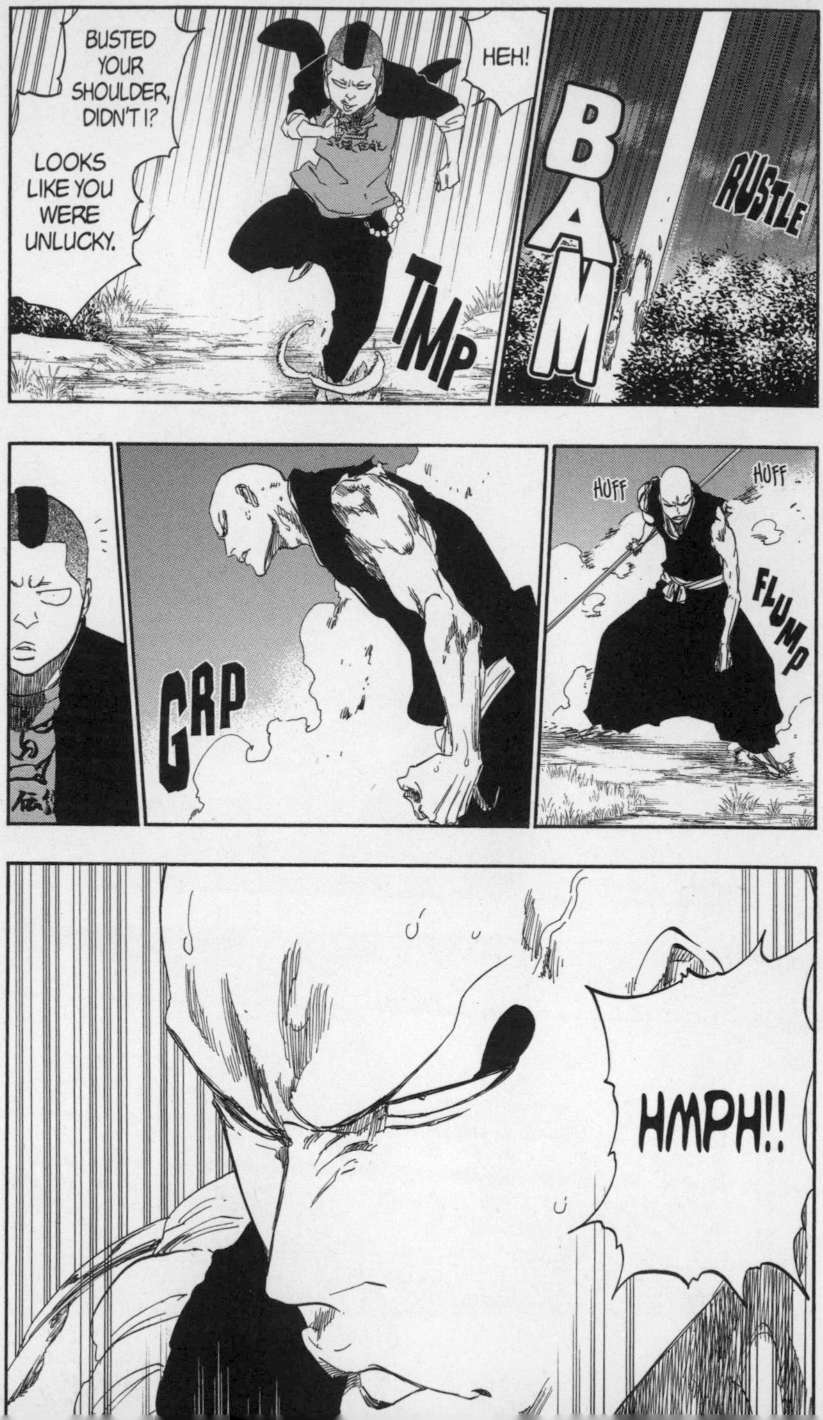
BAM
RUSTLE
HEH!
BUSTED YOUR SHOULDER, DIDN'T I?
LOOKS LIKE YOU WERE UNLUCKY.
TMP
HUFF
HUFF
FLUMP
GRP
HMPH!!

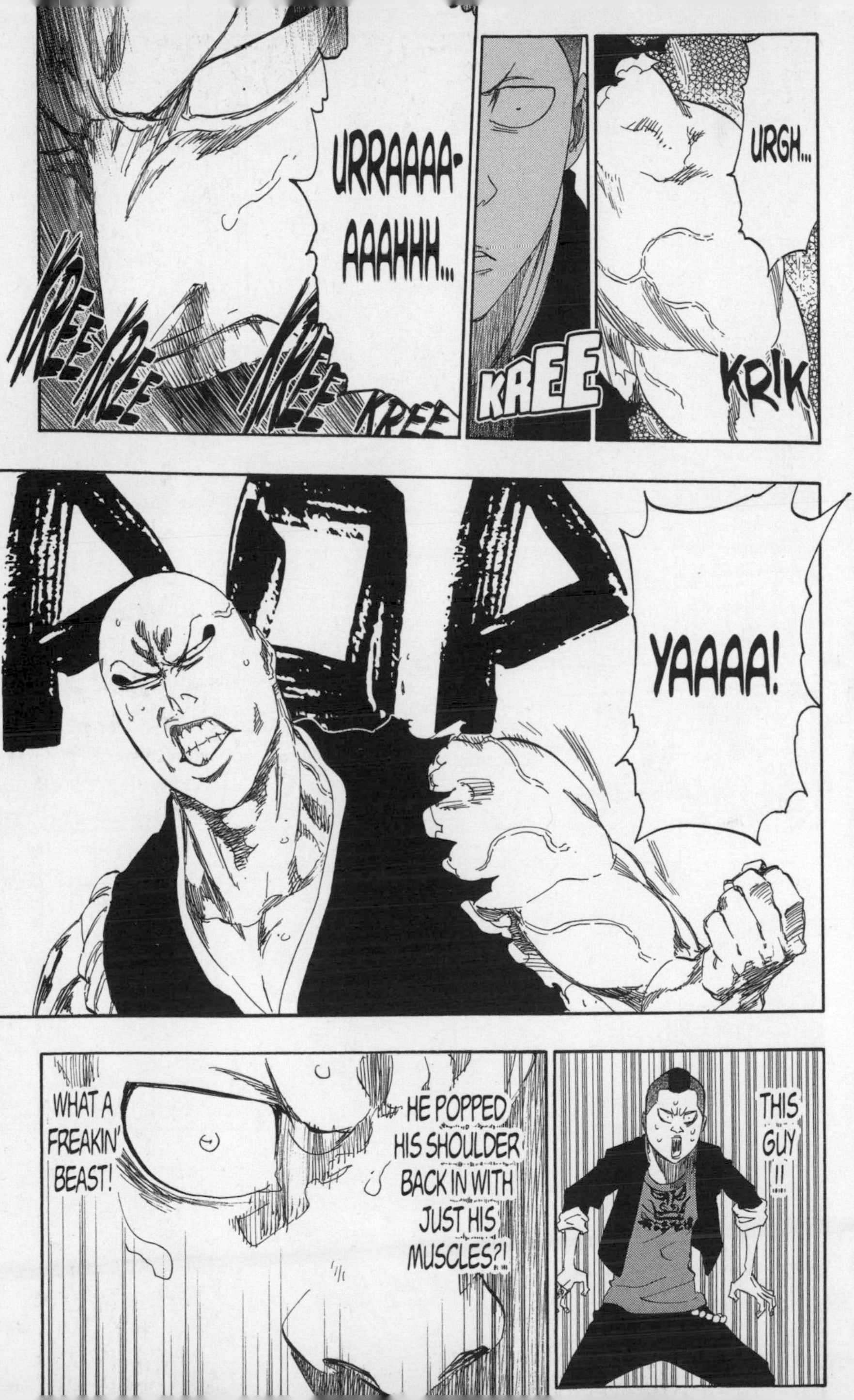
URGH...
KRIK
KREE
URRAAAA-AAAHHH...
KREE KREE
KREE KREE KREE
YAAAA!
THIS GUY!!
HE POPPED HIS SHOULDER BACK IN WITH JUST HIS MUSCLES?!
WHAT A FREAKIN' BEAST!

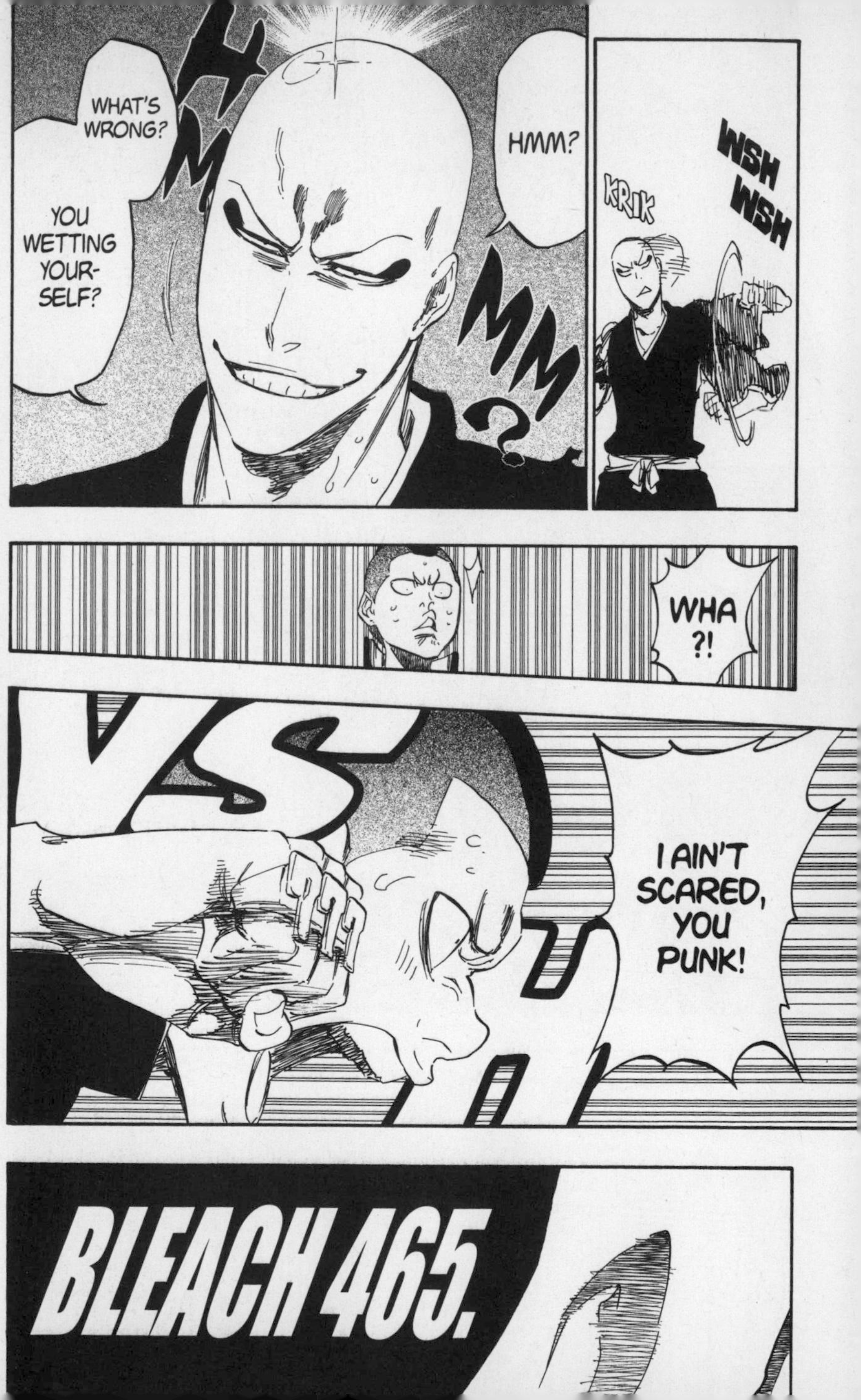
WSH WSH
KRIK
HMM?
HMMM?
WHAT'S WRONG?
YOU WETTING YOURSELF?
WHA ?!
I AIN'T SCARED, YOU PUNK!
BLEACH 465.

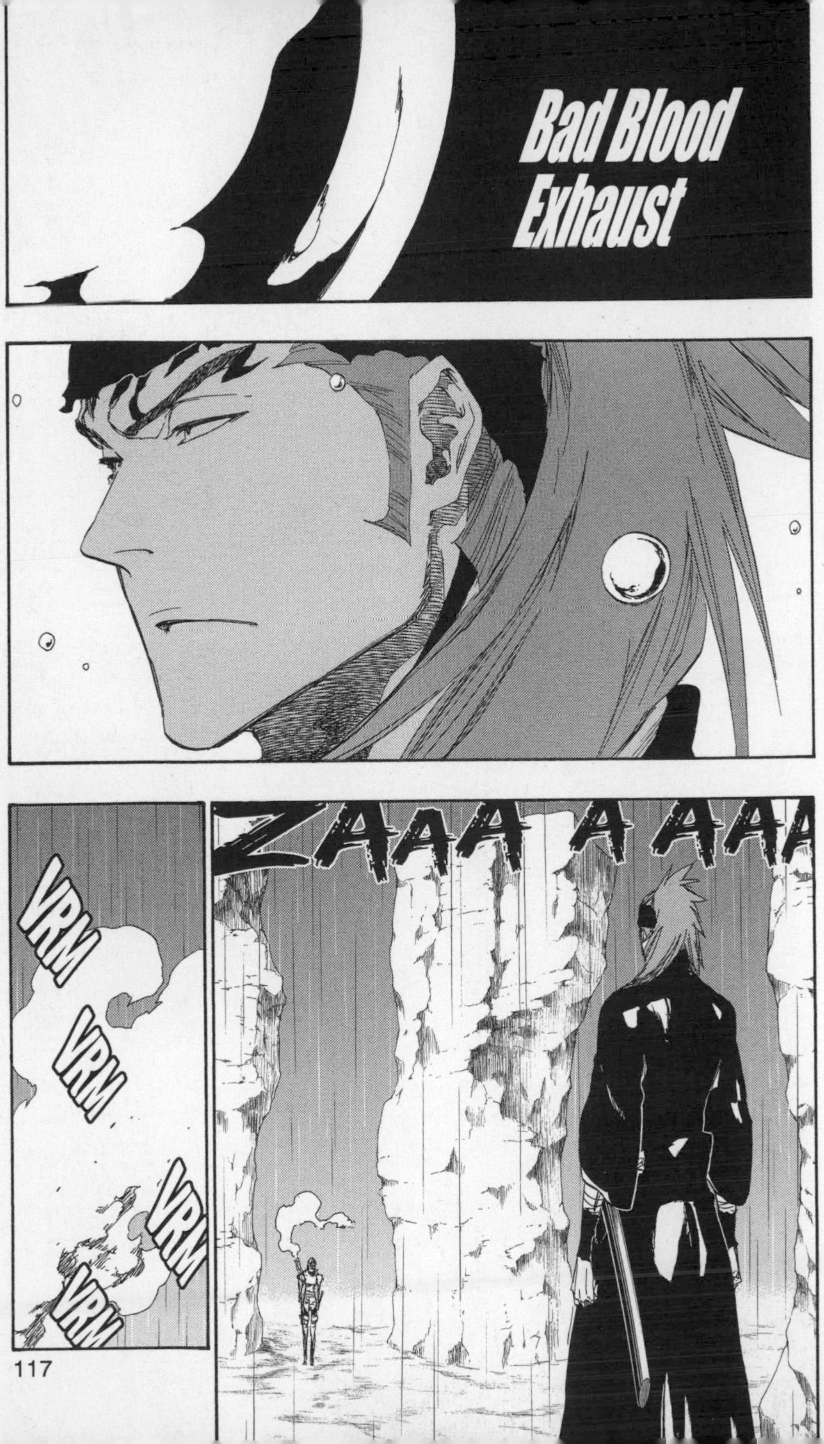
Bad Blood Exhaust
ZAAA A AAA
VRM VRM VRM VRM

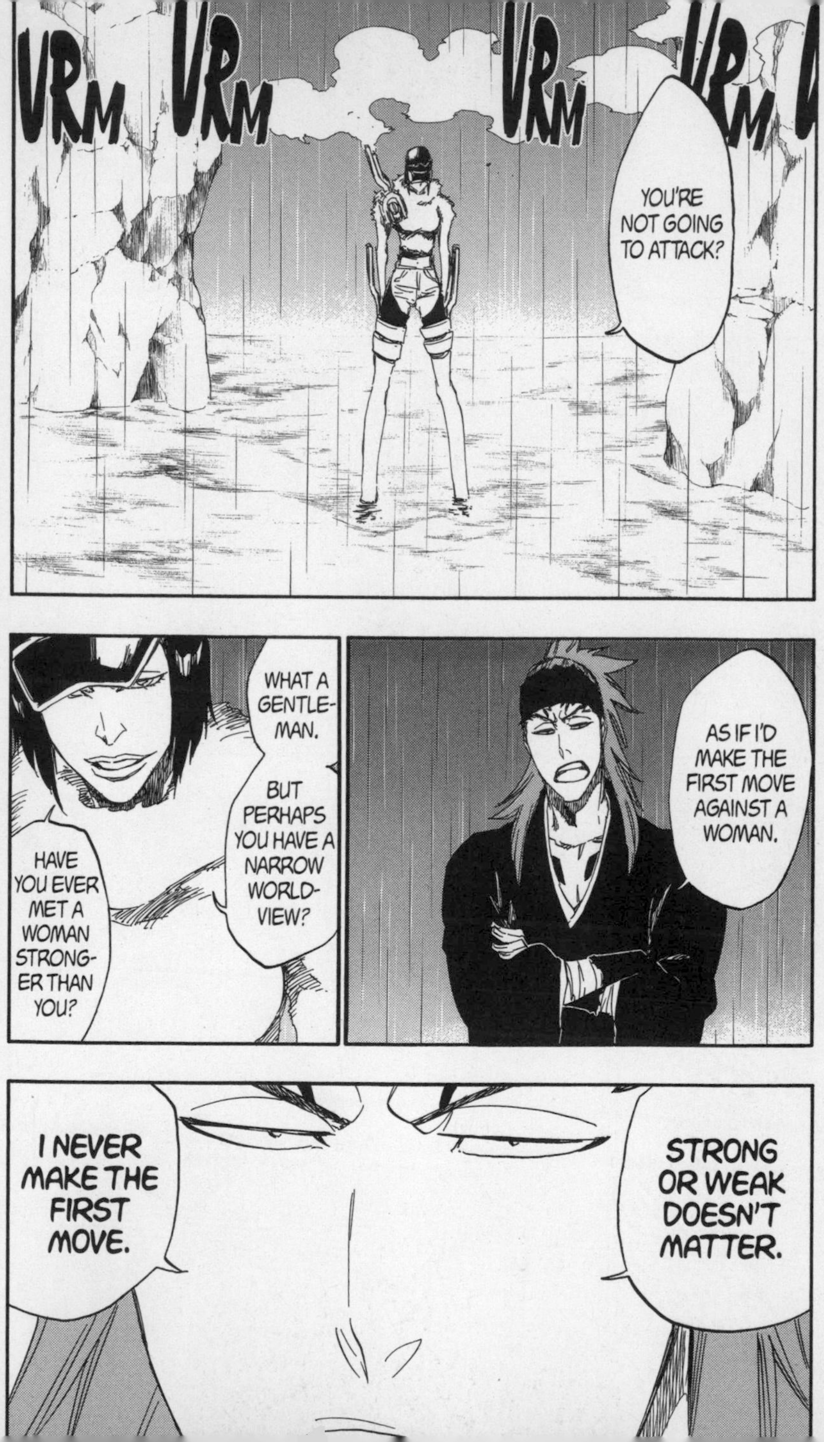
VRM VRM VRM VRM
YOU'RE NOT GOING TO ATTACK?
AS IF I'D MAKE THE FIRST MOVE AGAINST A WOMAN.
WHAT A GENTLEMAN.
BUT PERHAPS YOU HAVE A NARROW WORLDVIEW?
HAVE YOU EVER MET A WOMAN STRONGER THAN YOU?
STRONG OR WEAK DOESN'T MATTER.
I NEVER MAKE THE FIRST MOVE.

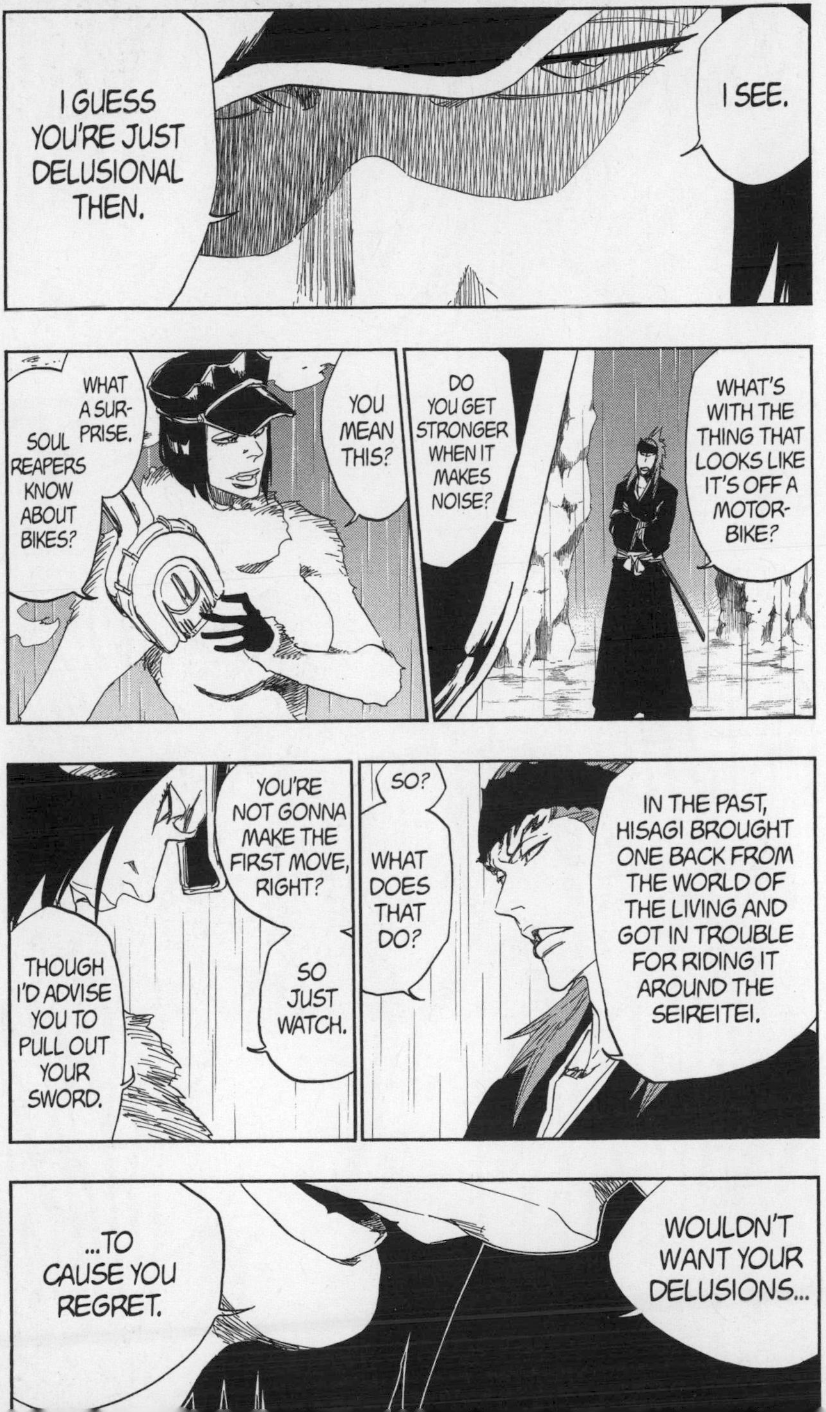
I SEE.
I GUESS YOU'RE JUST DELUSIONAL THEN.
WHAT'S WITH THE THING THAT LOOKS LIKE IT'S OFF A MOTOR-BIKE?
DO YOU GET STRONGER WHEN IT MAKES NOISE?
YOU MEAN THIS?
WHAT A SUR-PRISE.
SOUL REAPERS KNOW ABOUT BIKES?
IN THE PAST, HISAGI BROUGHT ONE BACK FROM THE WORLD OF THE LIVING AND GOT IN TROUBLE FOR RIDING IT AROUND THE SEIREITEI.
SO?
WHAT DOES THAT DO?
YOU'RE NOT GONNA MAKE THE FIRST MOVE, RIGHT?
SO JUST WATCH.
THOUGH I'D ADVISE YOU TO PULL OUT YOUR SWORD.
WOULDN'T WANT YOUR DELUSIONS...
...TO CAUSE YOU REGRET.

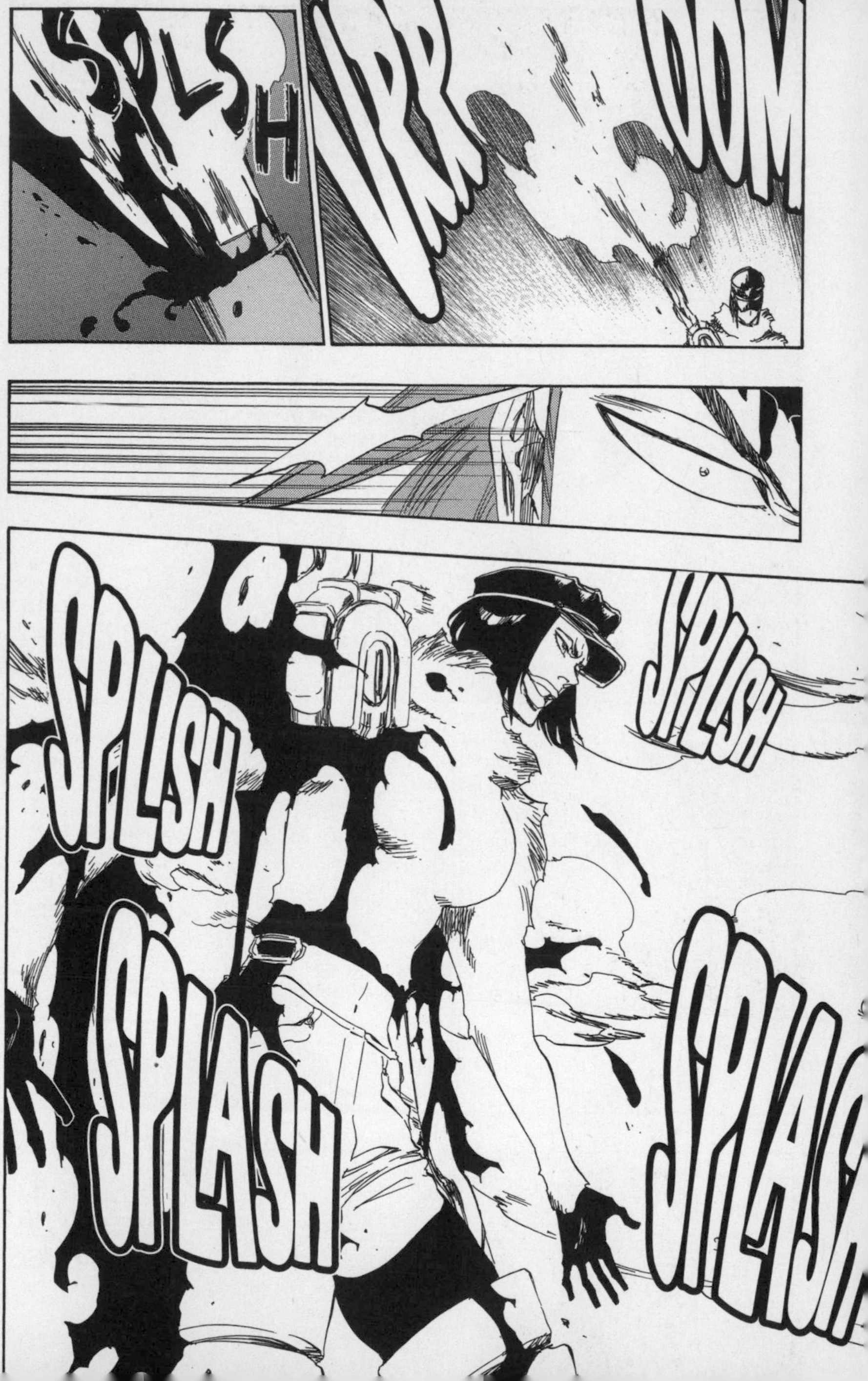
VRR...OOM
SPLSH
SPLSH
SPLSH
SPLASH
SPLASH

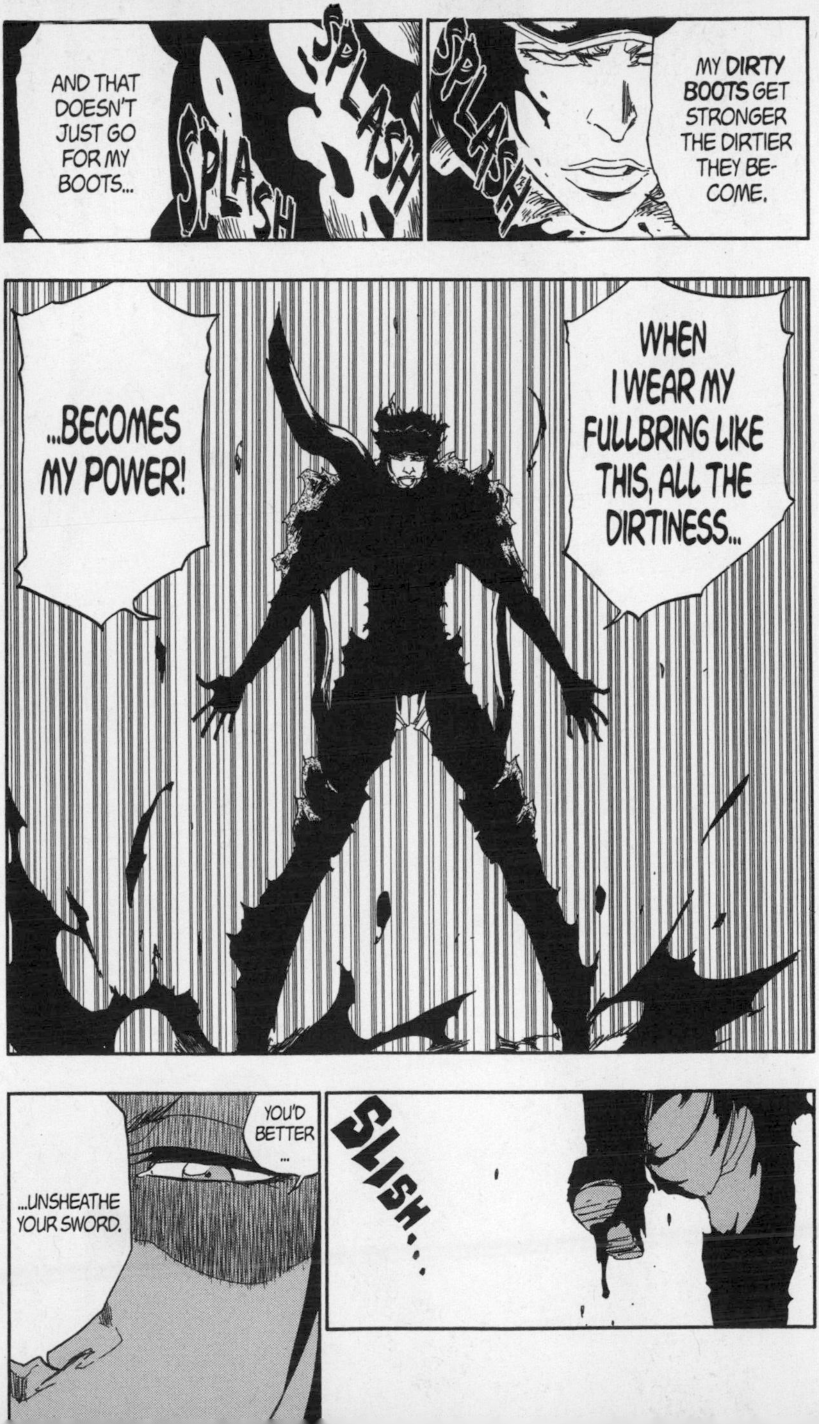
SPLASH
MY DIRTY BOOTS GET STRONGER THE DIRTIER THEY BE-COME.
SPLASH
SPLASH
AND THAT DOESN'T JUST GO FOR MY BOOTS...
WHEN I WEAR MY FULLBRING LIKE THIS, ALL THE DIRTINESS...
...BECOMES MY POWER!
SLISH...
YOU'D BETTER...
...UNSHEATHE YOUR SWORD.

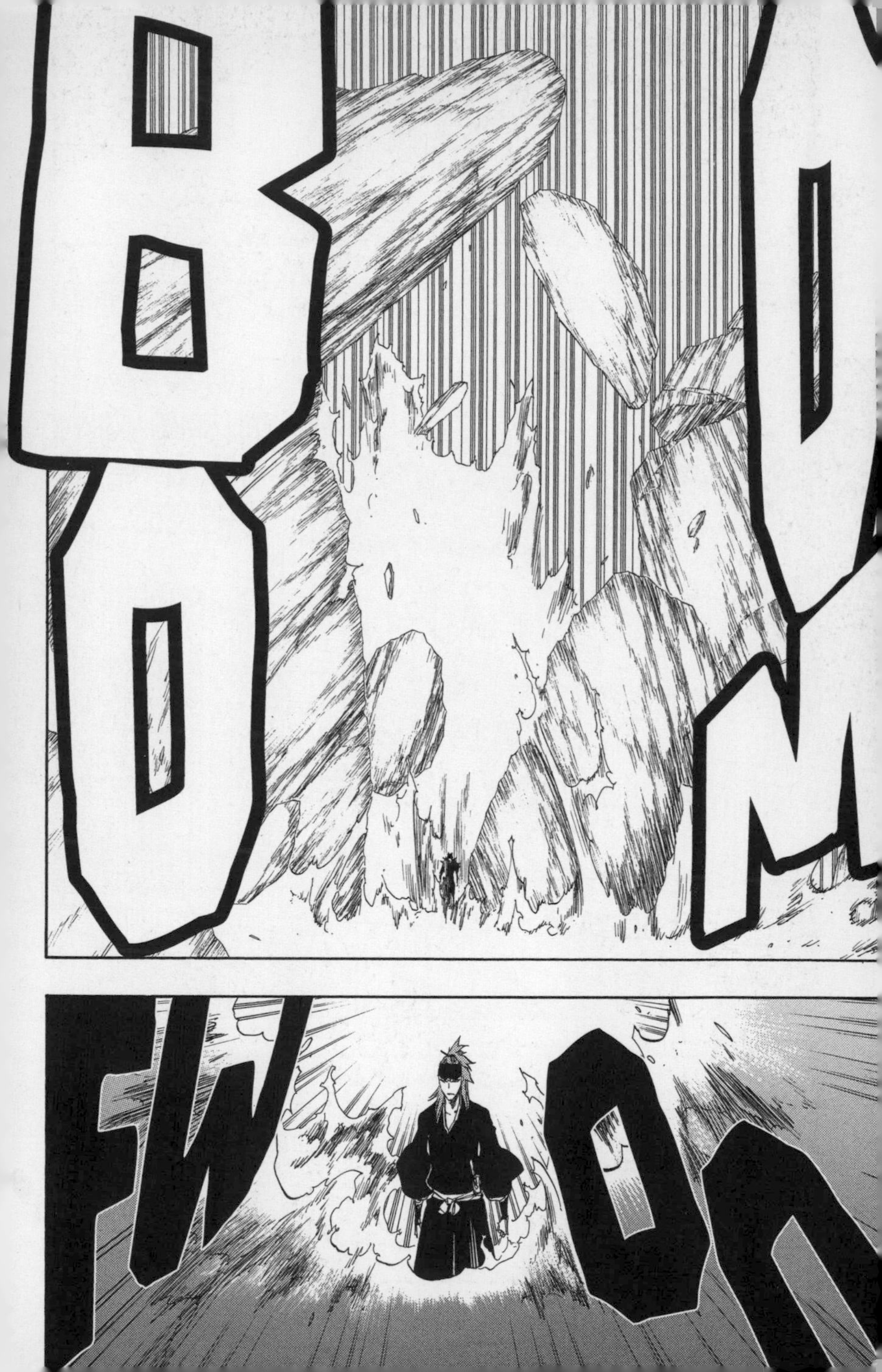
BOOM
FWOO

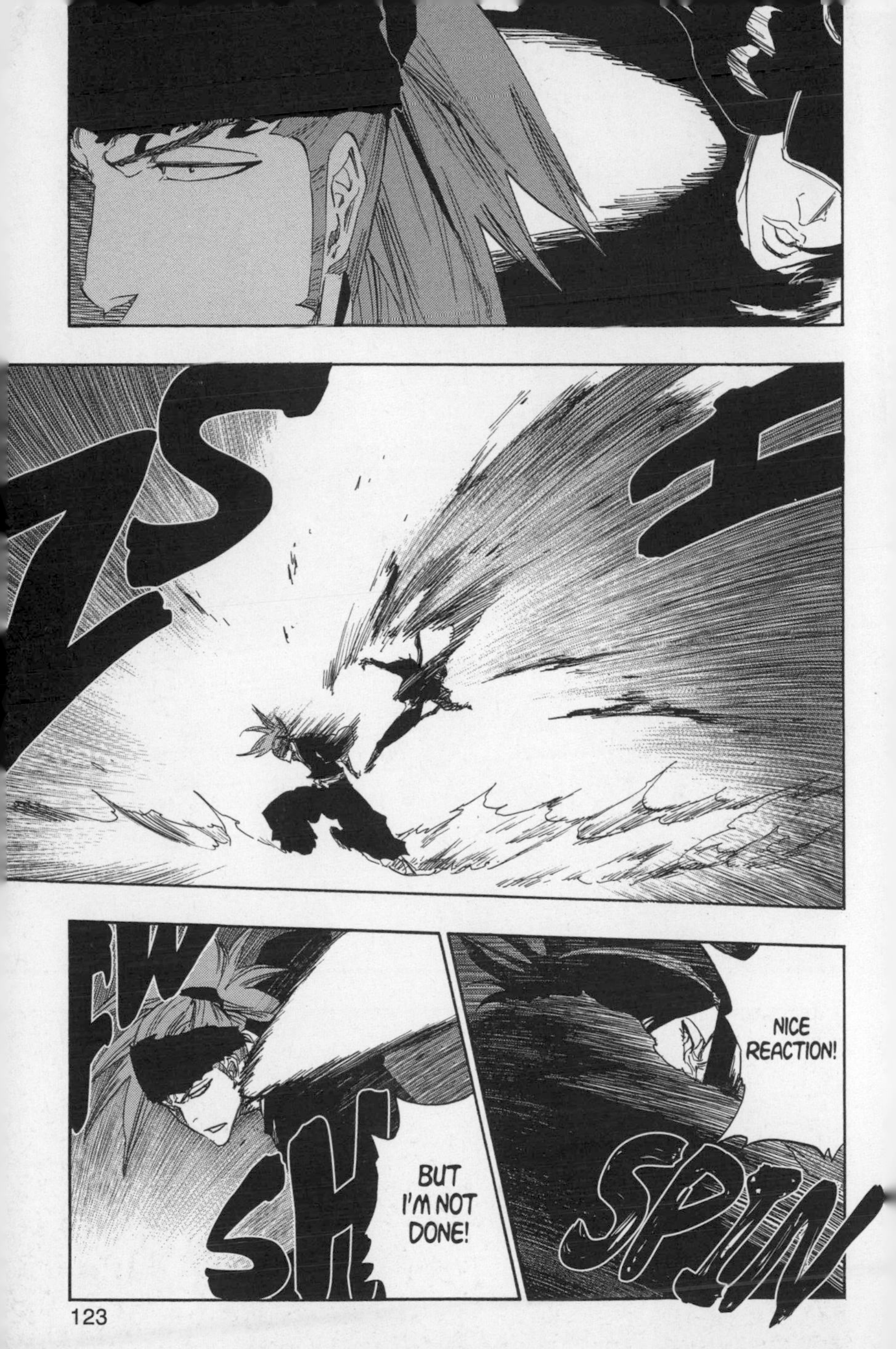
NICE REACTION!
SPIN
BUT I'M NOT DONE!

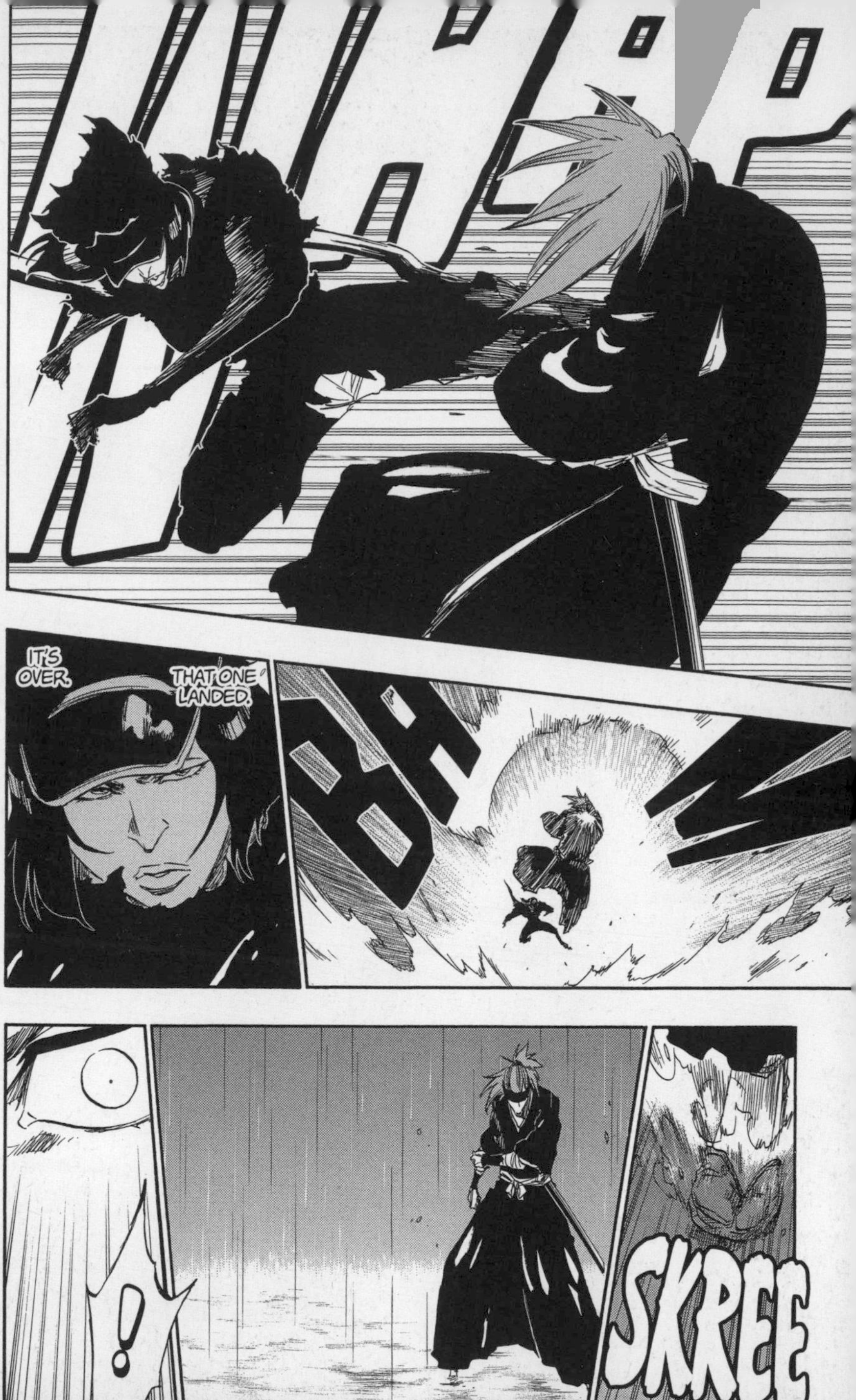
THAT ONE LANDED.
IT'S OVER.
SKREE
!

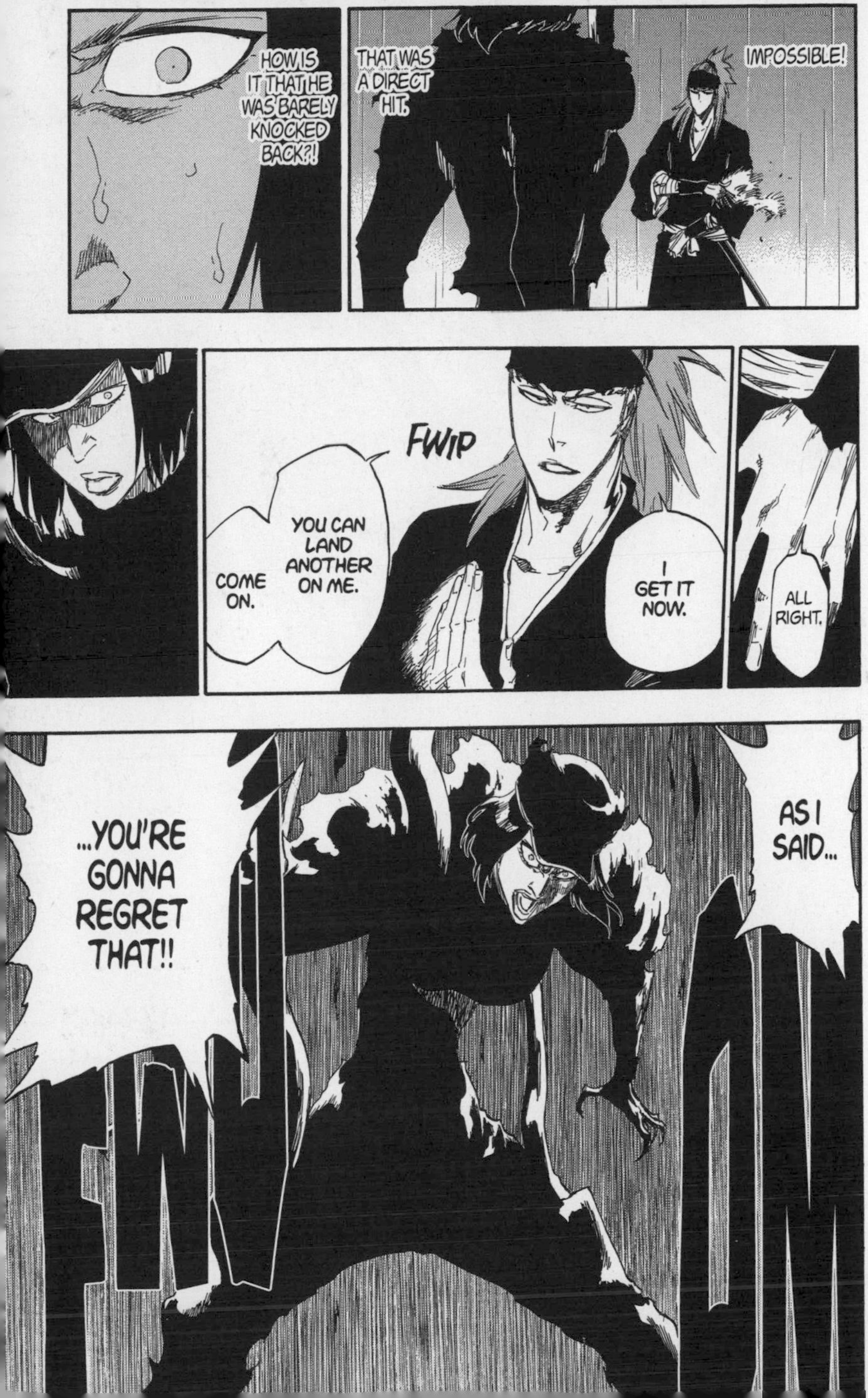
IMPOSSIBLE!
THAT WAS A DIRECT HIT.
HOW IS IT THAT HE WAS BARELY KNOCKED BACK?!
ALL RIGHT.
I GET IT NOW.
FWIP
YOU CAN LAND ANOTHER ON ME.
COME ON.
AS I SAID...
...YOU'RE GONNA REGRET THAT!!

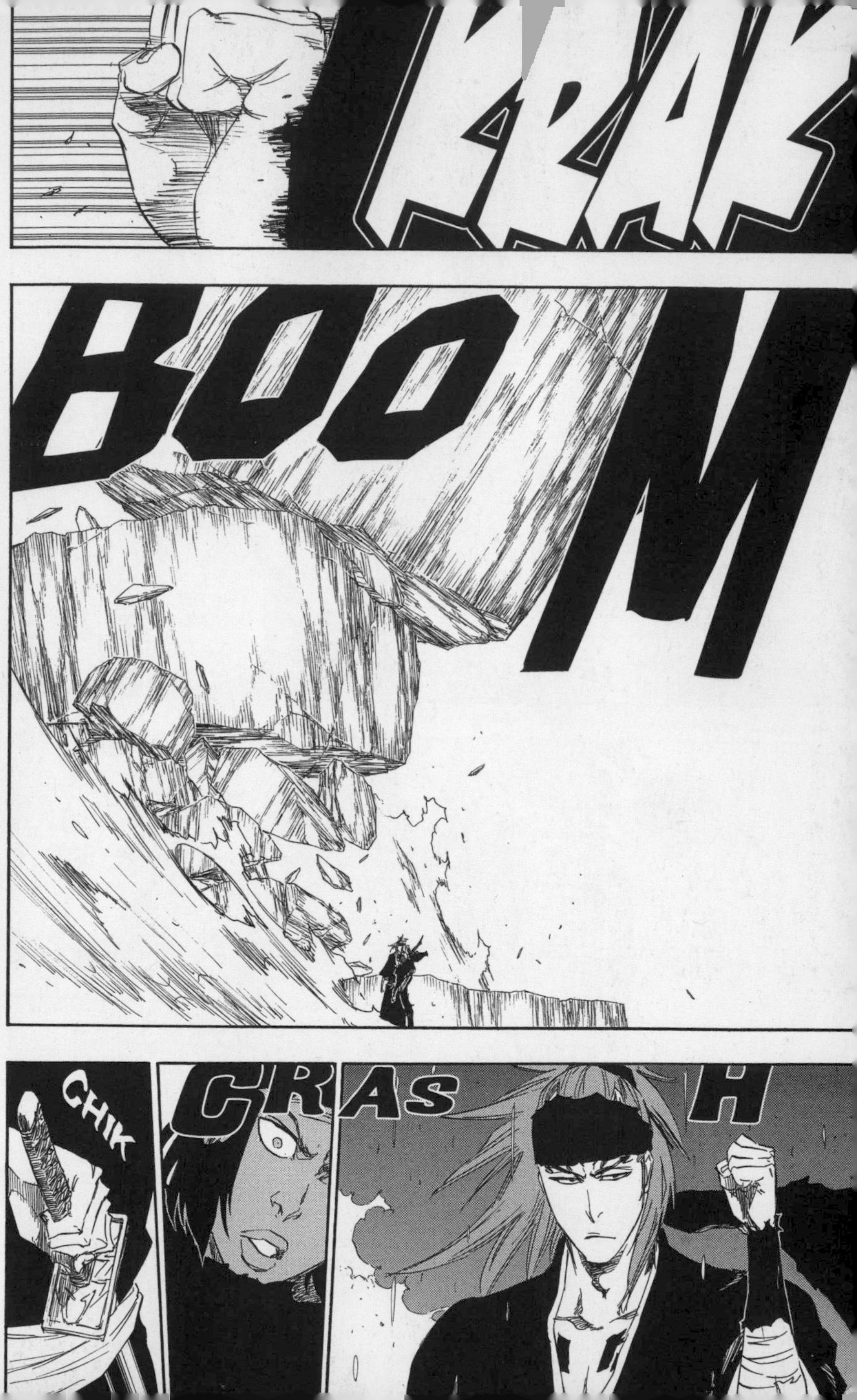
KRAK
BOOM
CRASH
CHIK

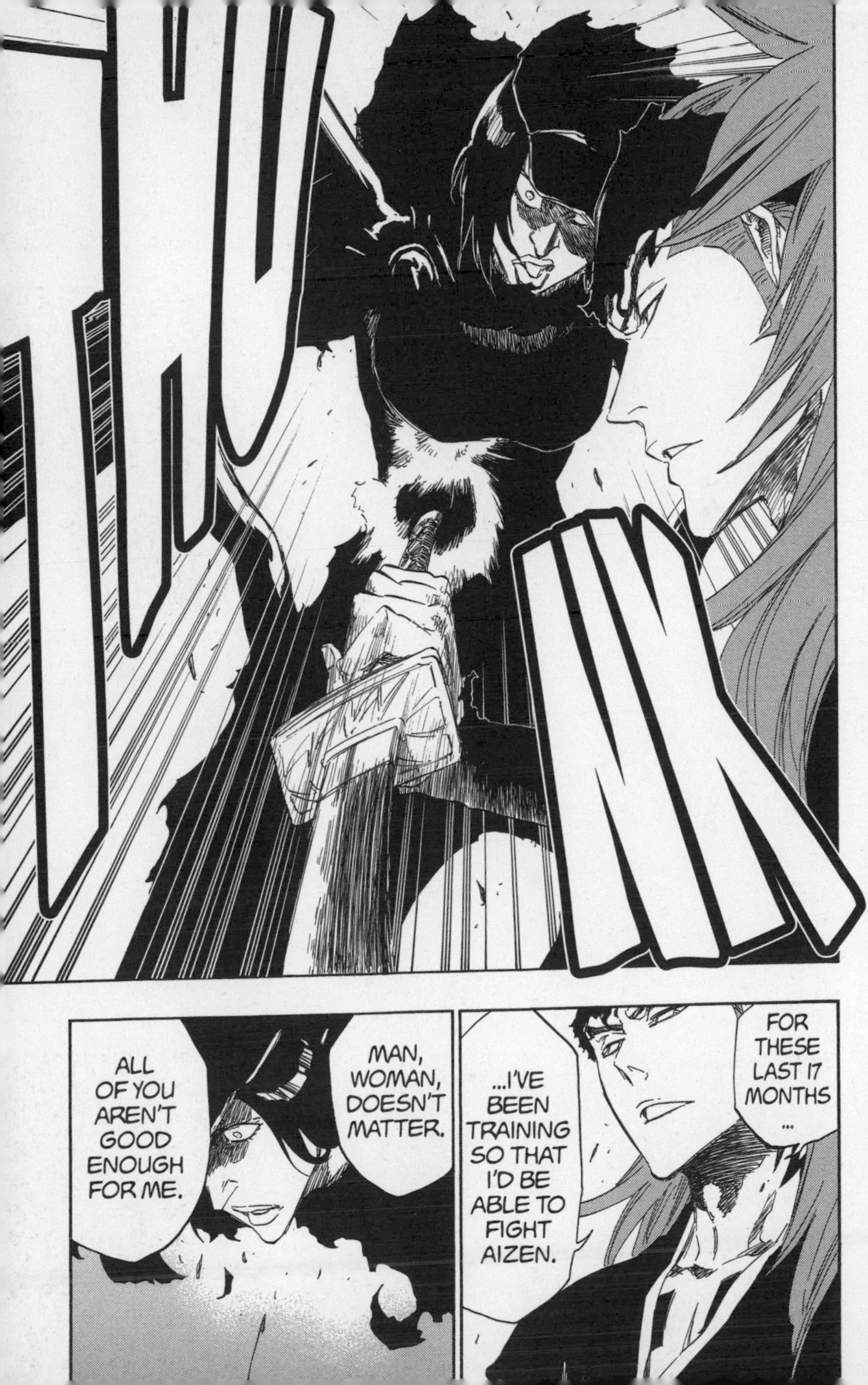
FOR THESE LAST 17 MONTHS ...
...I'VE BEEN TRAINING SO THAT I'D BE ABLE TO FIGHT AIZEN.
MAN, WOMAN, DOESN'T MATTER.
ALL OF YOU AREN'T GOOD ENOUGH FOR ME.

BEGGED A
BLACKSMITH FRIEND
TO MAKE THIS STEEL
HAIRPIN FOR CHEAP
BECAUSE HE'S POOR.
IT COST HIM
1/1000000th
THE COST OF
EXPENSIVE
SILK.

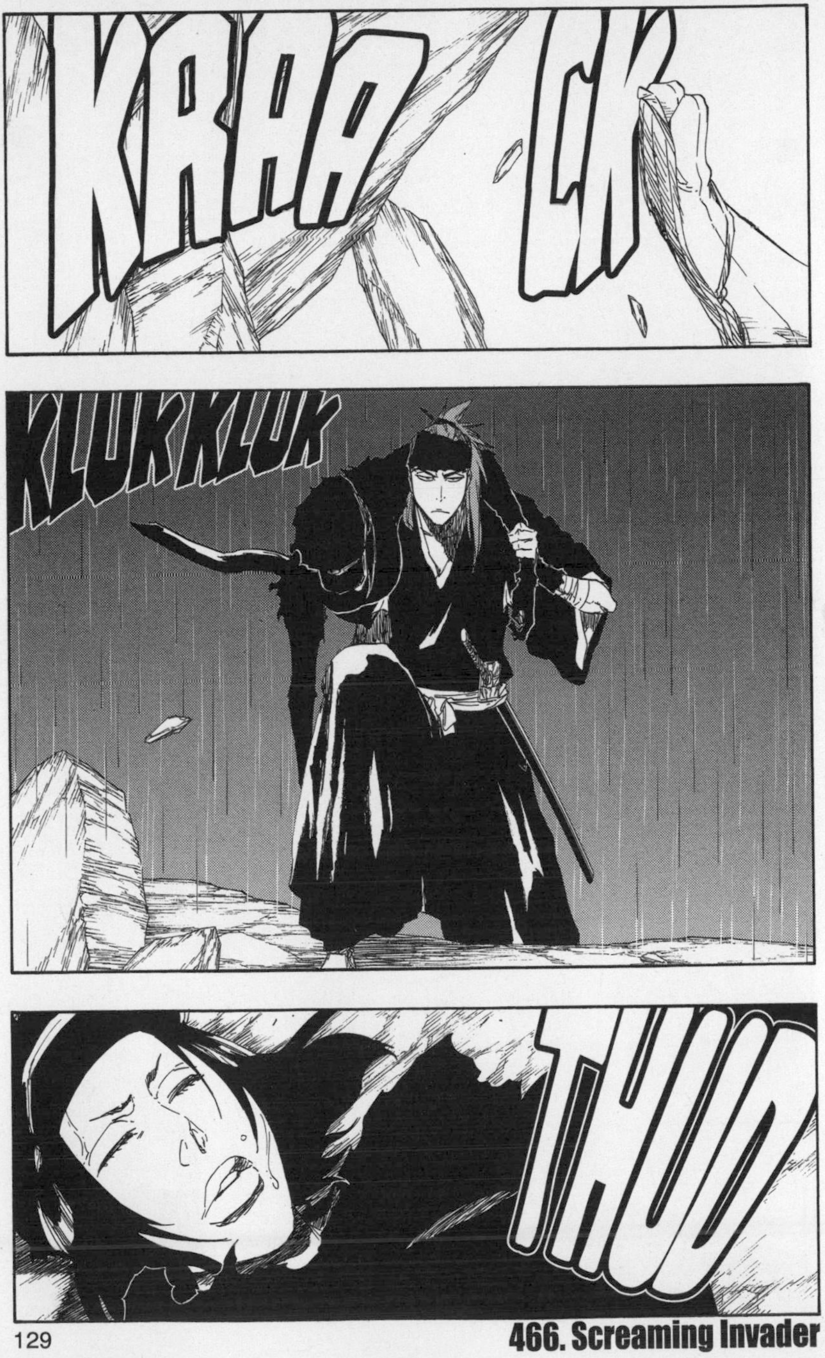
KRAA-CK
KLUK KLUK
THUD

466. Screaming Invader

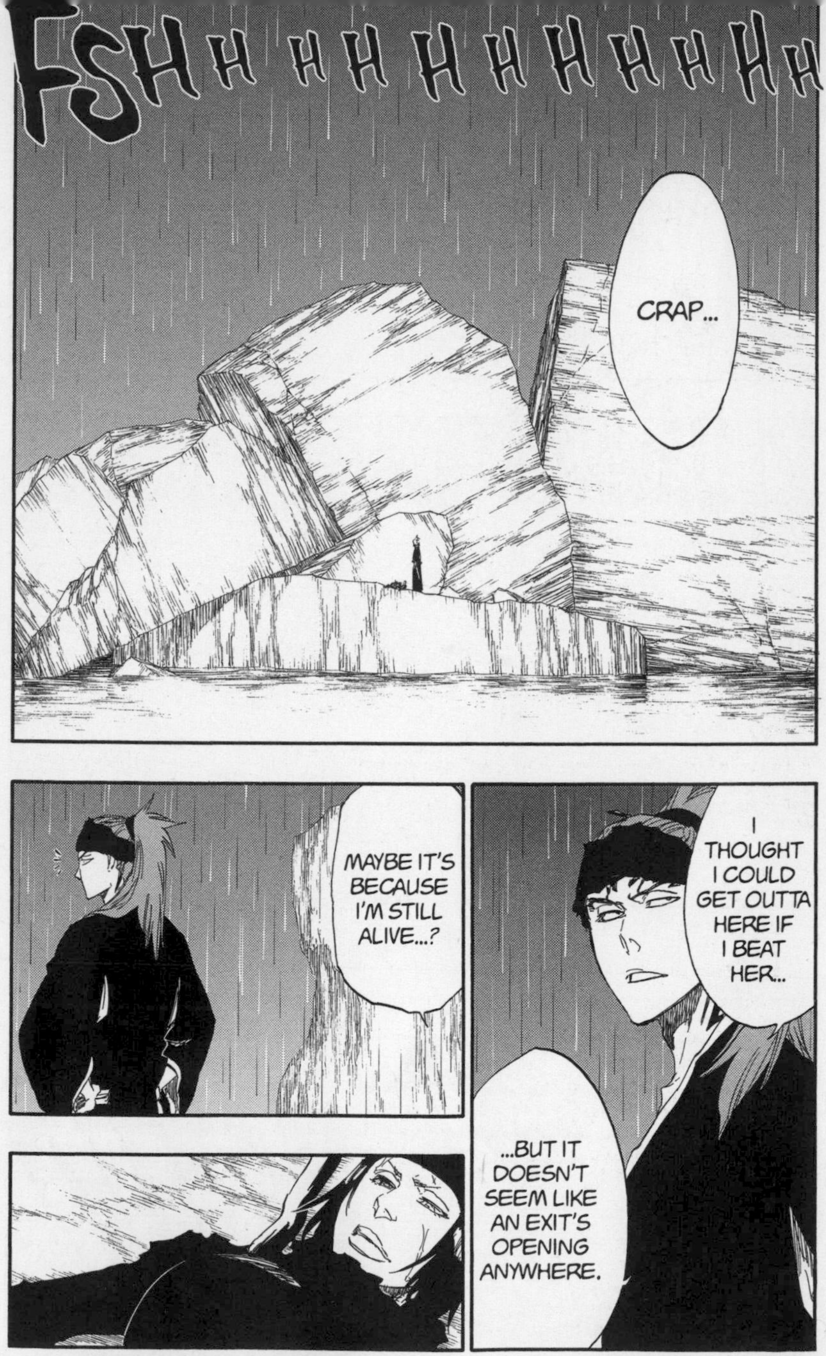
FSHHHHHHHHHHHH
CRAP...
I THOUGHT I COULD GET OUTTA HERE IF I BEAT HER...
...BUT IT DOESN'T SEEM LIKE AN EXIT'S OPENING ANYWHERE.
MAYBE IT'S BECAUSE I'M STILL ALIVE...?

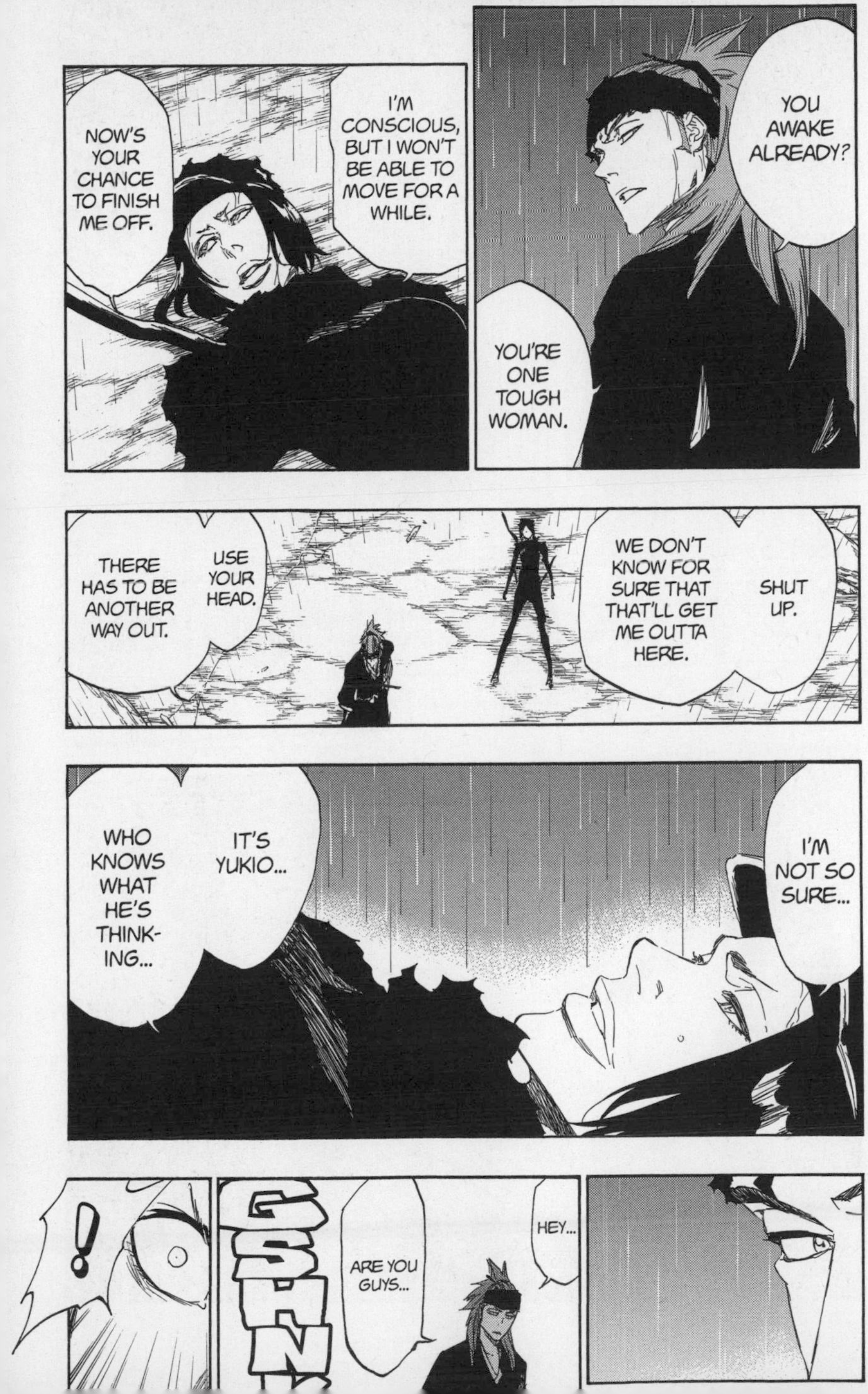
YOU AWAKE ALREADY?
YOU'RE ONE TOUGH WOMAN.
I'M CONSCIOUS, BUT I WON'T BE ABLE TO MOVE FOR A WHILE.
NOW'S YOUR CHANCE TO FINISH ME OFF.
SHUT UP.
WE DON'T KNOW FOR SURE THAT THAT'LL GET ME OUTTA HERE.
USE YOUR HEAD.
THERE HAS TO BE ANOTHER WAY OUT.
I'M NOT SO SURE...
IT'S YUKIO...
WHO KNOWS WHAT HE'S THINKING...
HEY...
ARE YOU GUYS...
GSHN
!

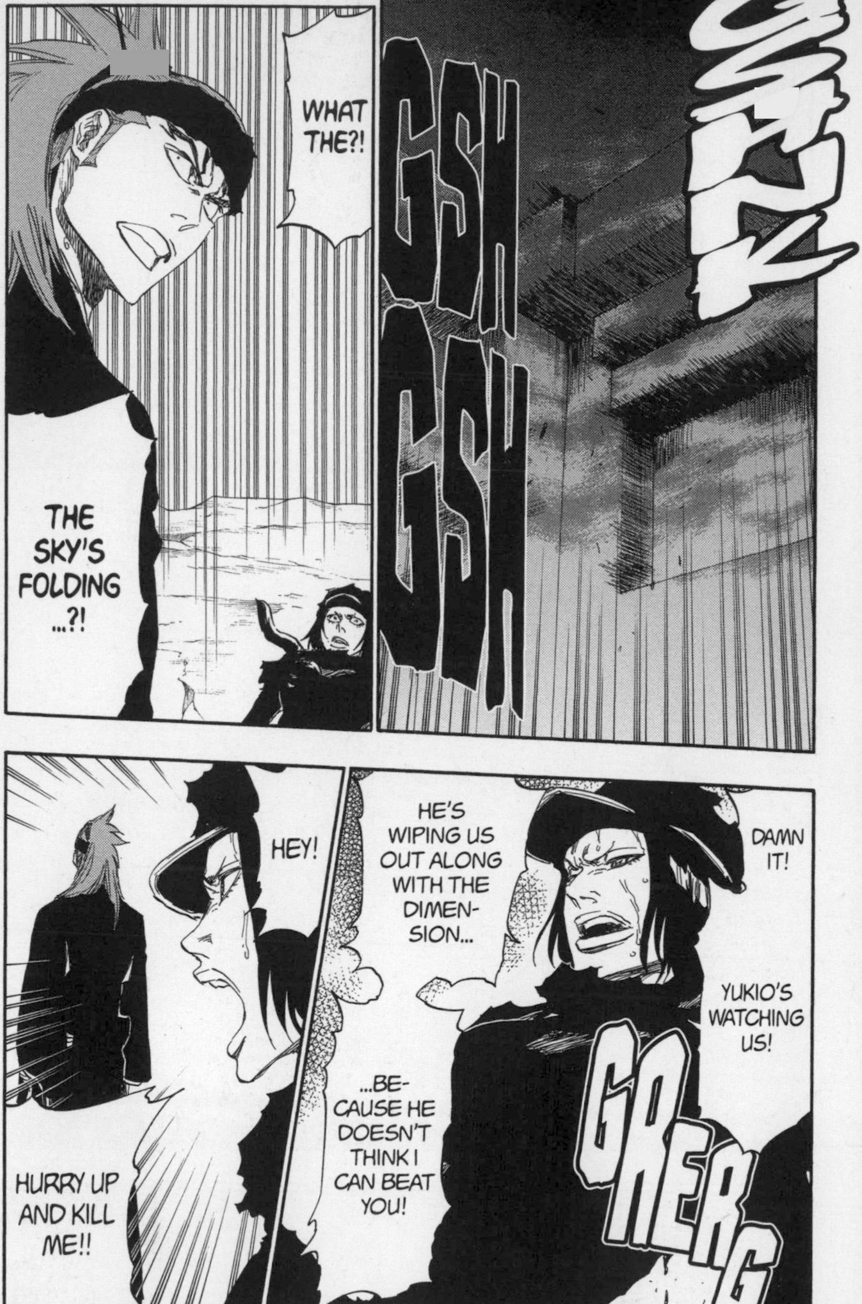
GSH
GSH
WHAT THE?!
THE SKY'S FOLDING ...?!
DAMN IT!
HE'S WIPING US OUT ALONG WITH THE DIMENSION...
YUKIO'S WATCHING US!
GRERG
...BECAUSE HE DOESN'T THINK I CAN BEAT YOU!
HEY!
HURRY UP AND KILL ME!!

YUKIO'S GOT A LOT OF PRIDE!

ONCE ONE OF OUR SPIRITUAL PRESSURES IS OUT, THIS DIMENSION SHOULD AUTOMATICALLY OPEN UP!!

KILL ME!!!

WHY?!!

CAN'T DO THAT.

A MAN WHO LAYS A HAND ON A WOMAN IS TRASH.

LIVING AS TRASH...

...IS THE SAME AS BEING DEAD.

GAK

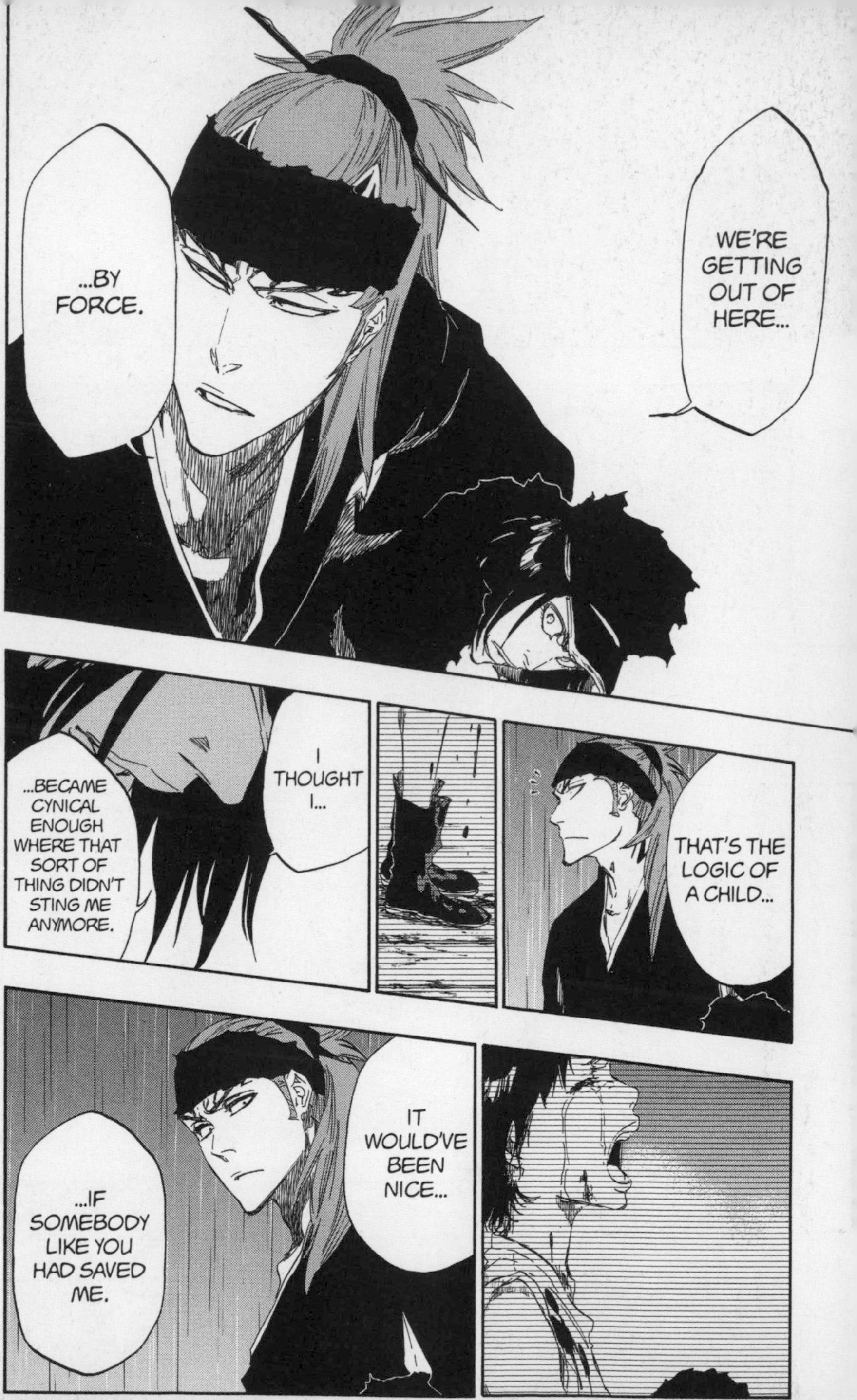
WE'RE GETTING OUT OF HERE...
...BY FORCE.
THAT'S THE LOGIC OF A CHILD...
I THOUGHT I...
...BECAME CYNICAL ENOUGH WHERE THAT SORT OF THING DIDN'T STING ME ANYMORE.
IT WOULD'VE BEEN NICE...
...IF SOMEBODY LIKE YOU HAD SAVED ME.

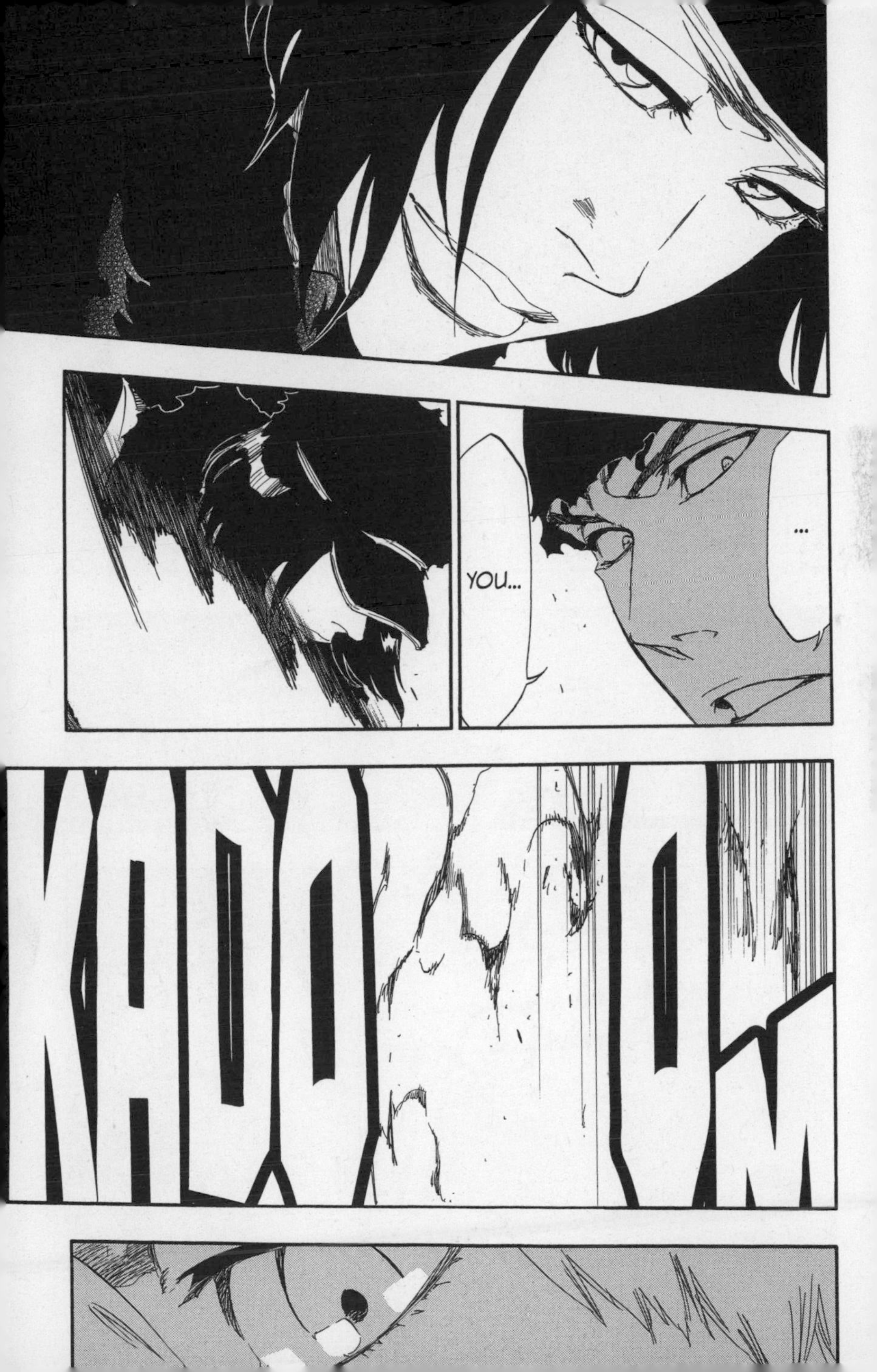
...
YOU...
KADOOOM

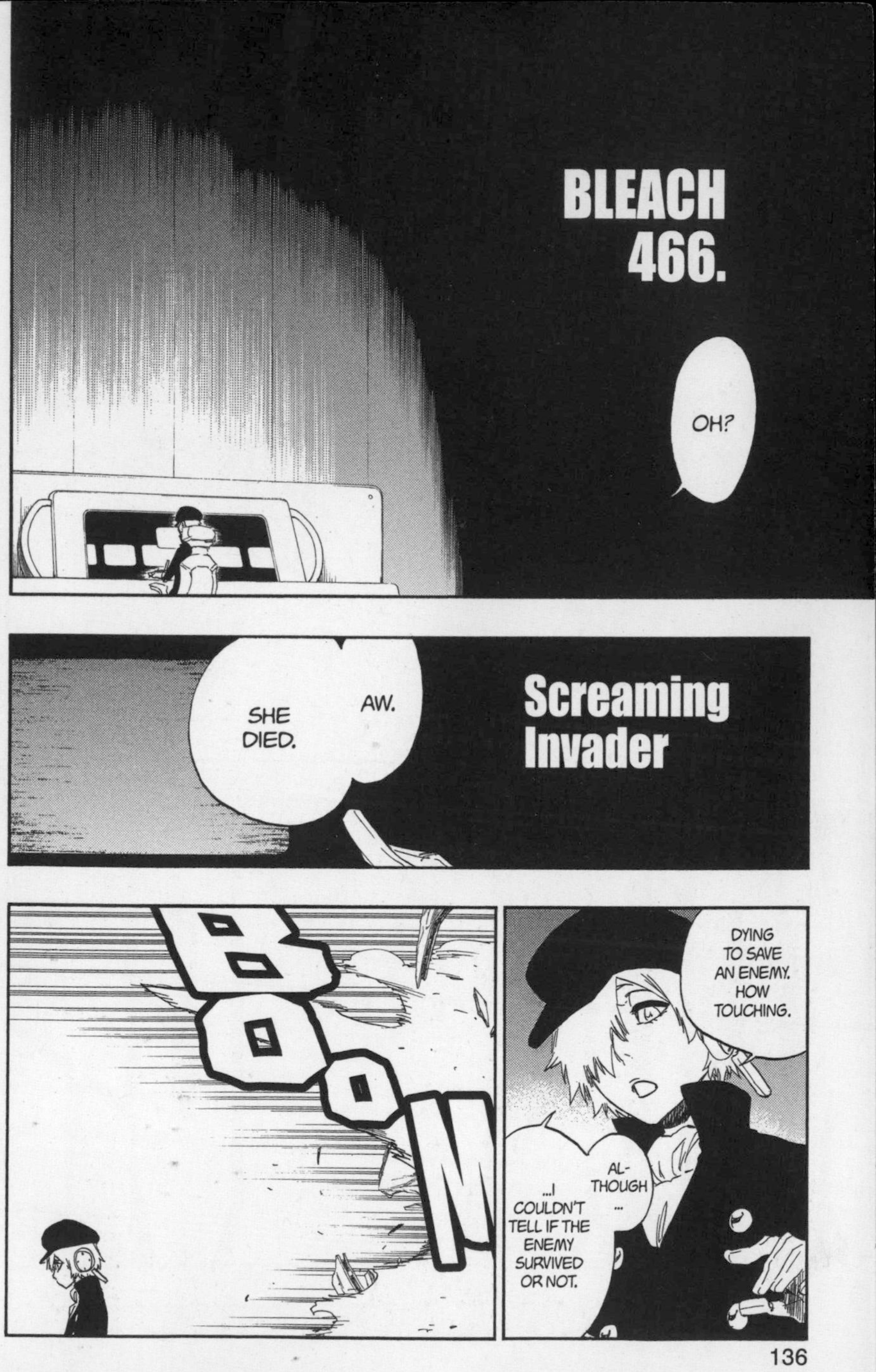
BLEACH
466.
OH?
Screaming Invader
AW.
SHE DIED.
DYING TO SAVE AN ENEMY. HOW TOUCHING.
AL-THOUGH...
...I COULDN'T TELL IF THE ENEMY SURVIVED OR NOT.
BOOM

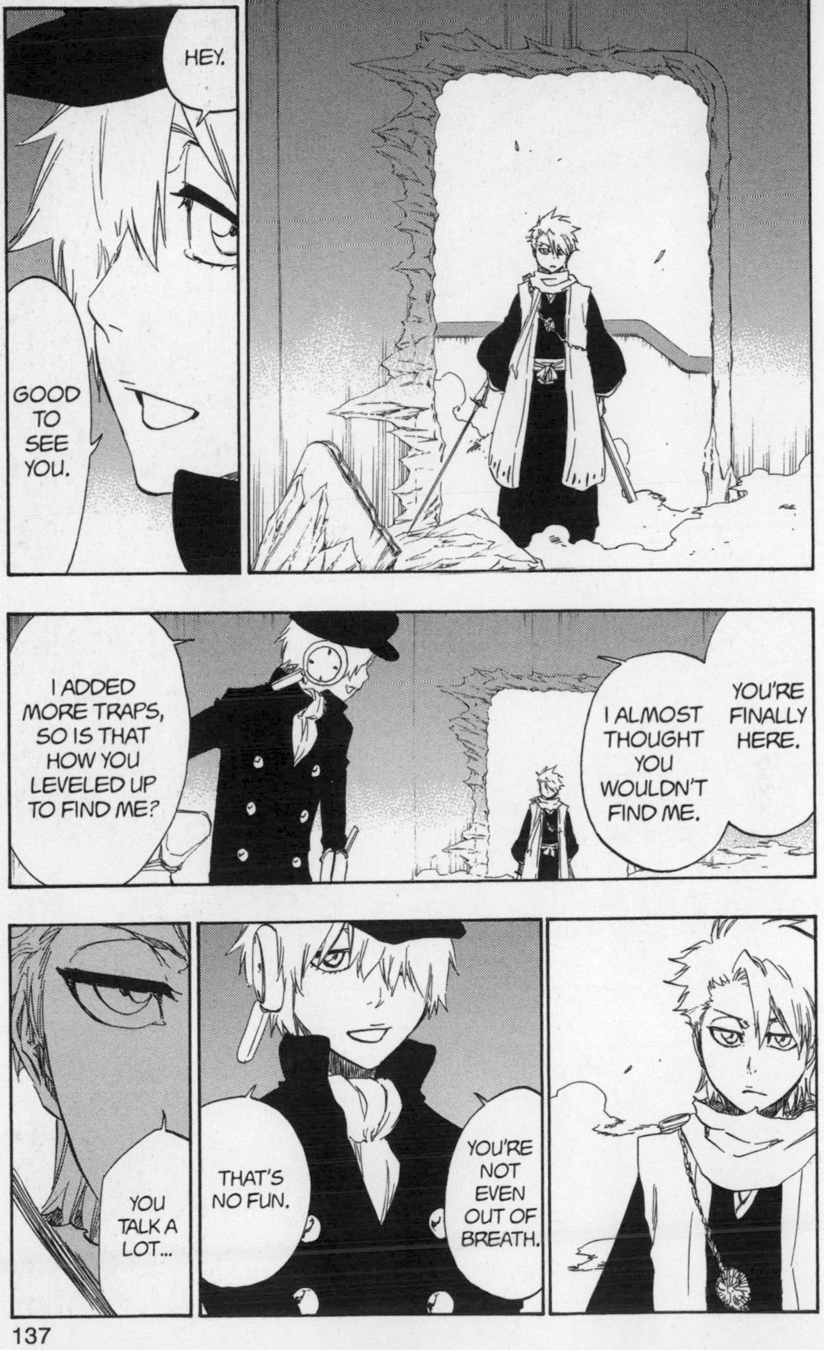
HEY.
GOOD TO SEE YOU.
YOU'RE FINALLY HERE.
I ALMOST THOUGHT YOU WOULDN'T FIND ME.
I ADDED MORE TRAPS, SO IS THAT HOW YOU LEVELED UP TO FIND ME?
YOU'RE NOT EVEN OUT OF BREATH.
THAT'S NO FUN.
YOU TALK A LOT...

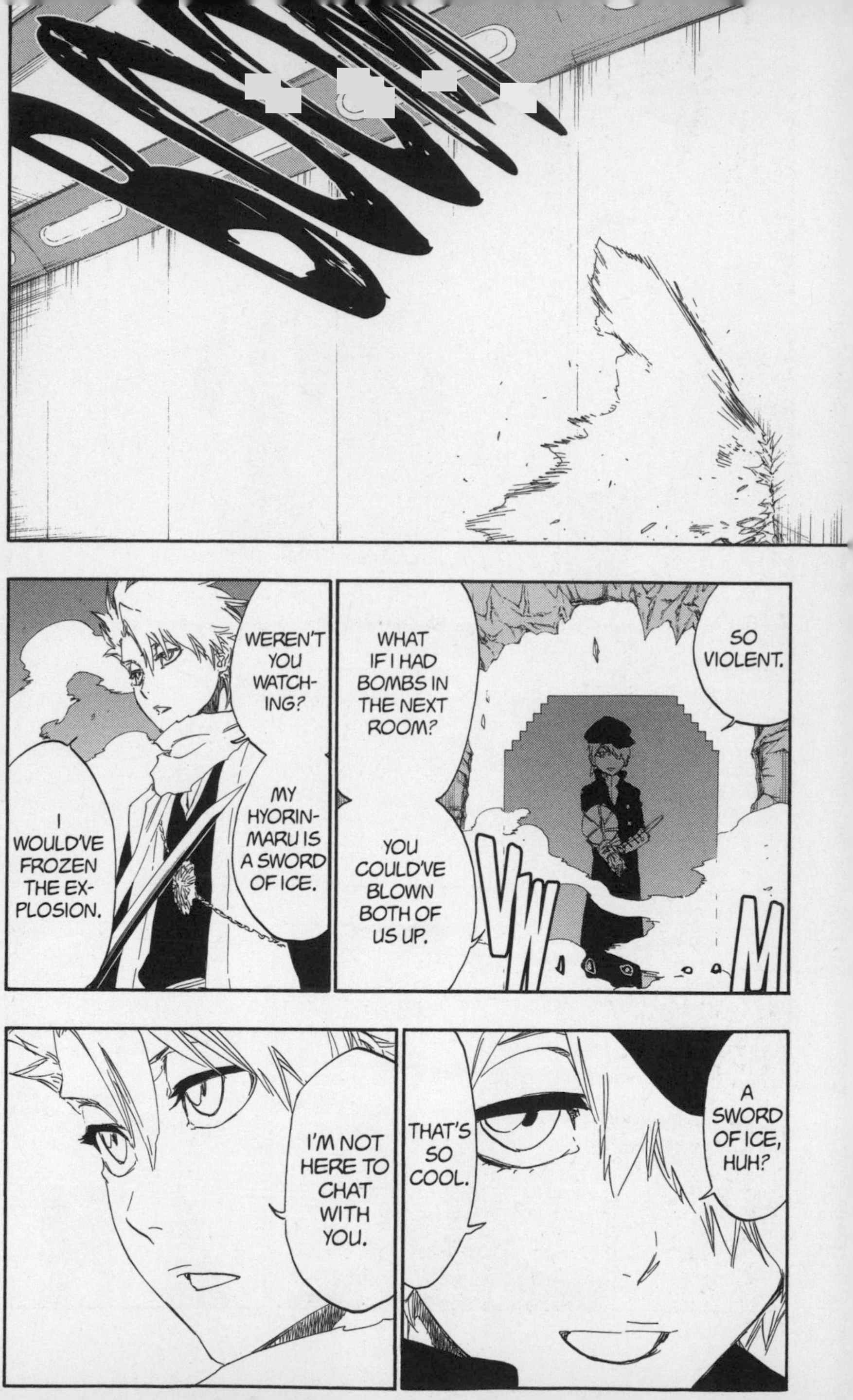
SO VIOLENT.
WHAT IF I HAD BOMBS IN THE NEXT ROOM?
YOU COULD'VE BLOWN BOTH OF US UP.
VW...M
WEREN'T YOU WATCHING?
MY HYORINMARU IS A SWORD OF ICE.
I WOULD'VE FROZEN THE EXPLOSION.
A SWORD OF ICE, HUH?
THAT'S SO COOL.
I'M NOT HERE TO CHAT WITH YOU.

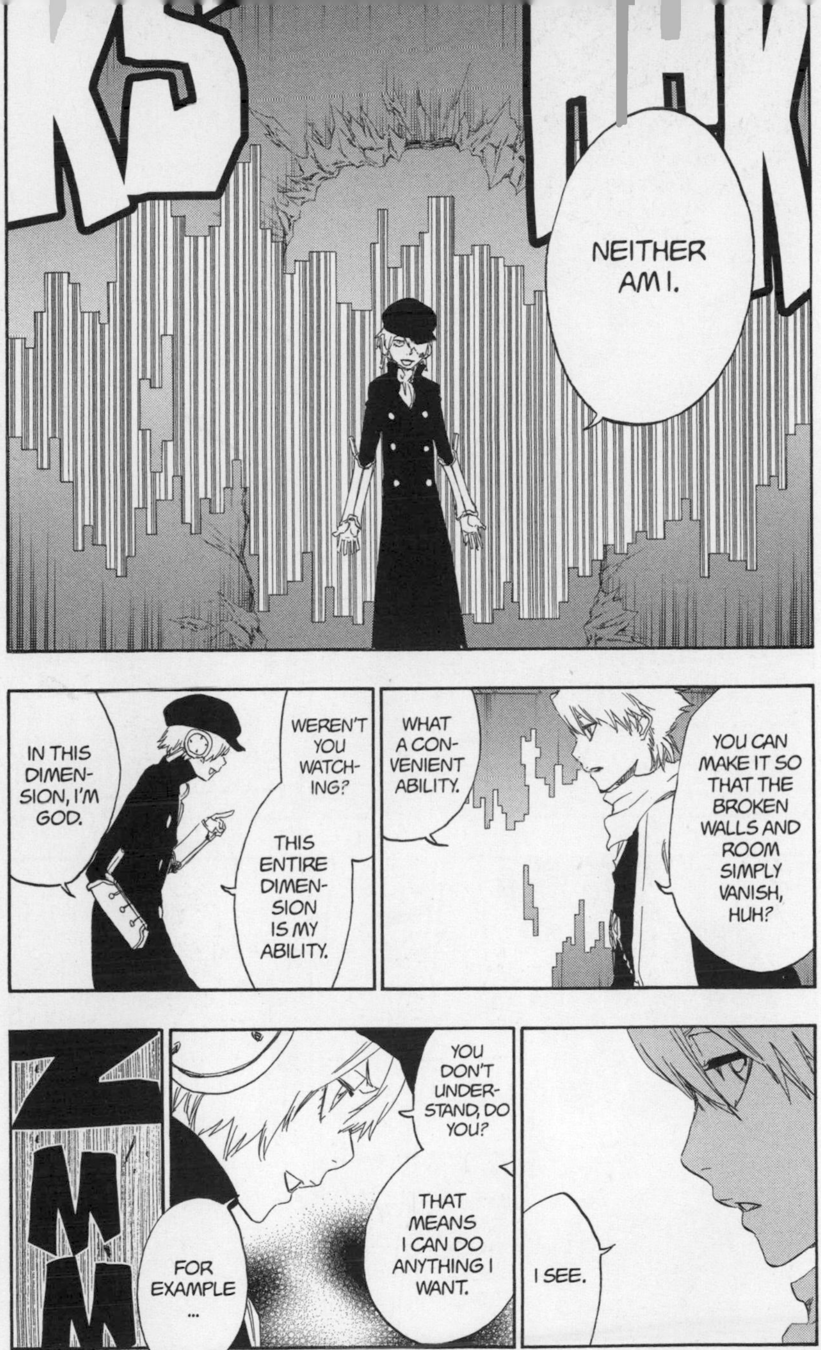
NEITHER AM I.
YOU CAN MAKE IT SO THAT THE BROKEN WALLS AND ROOM SIMPLY VANISH, HUH?
WHAT A CONVENIENT ABILITY.
WEREN'T YOU WATCHING?
THIS ENTIRE DIMENSION IS MY ABILITY.
IN THIS DIMENSION, I'M GOD.
I SEE.
YOU DON'T UNDERSTAND, DO YOU?
THAT MEANS I CAN DO ANYTHING I WANT.
FOR EXAMPLE ...
ZMM

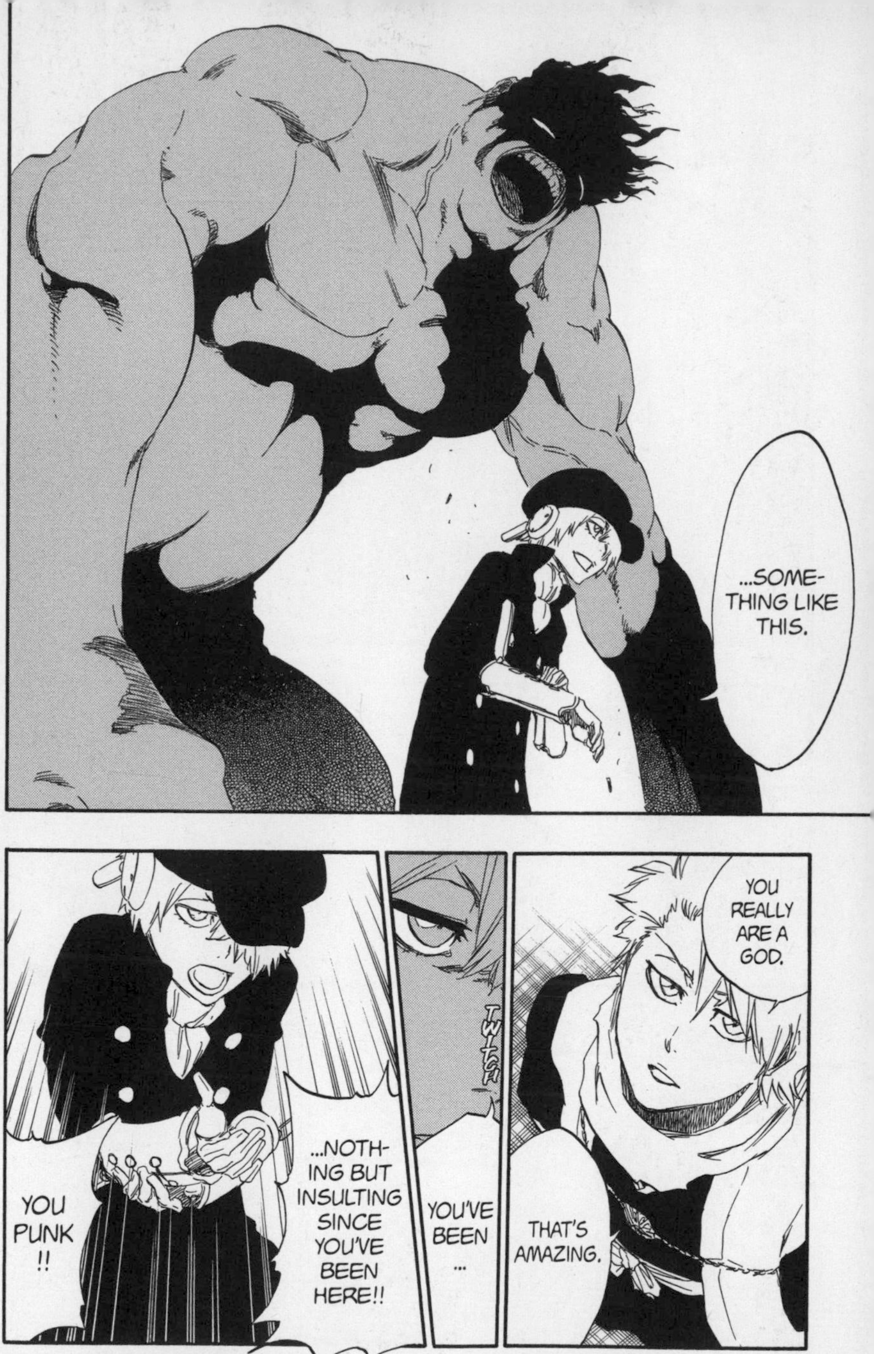
...SOMETHING LIKE THIS.
YOU REALLY ARE A GOD.
THAT'S AMAZING.
TWITCH
YOU'VE BEEN ...
...NOTHING BUT INSULTING SINCE YOU'VE BEEN HERE!!
YOU PUNK!!

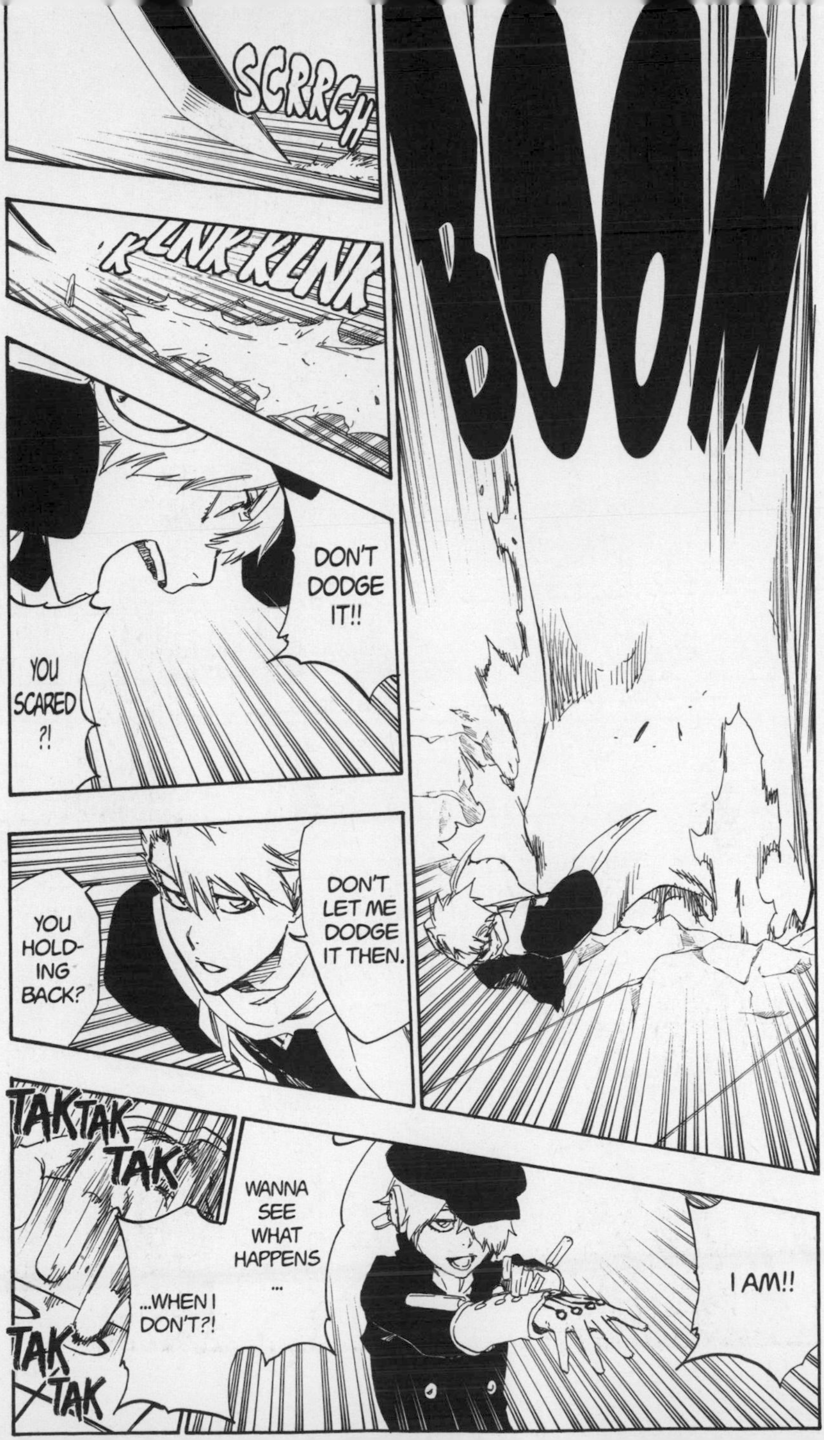
BOOM
SCRRCH
KLNK KLNK
DON'T DODGE IT!!
YOU SCARED ?!
DON'T LET ME DODGE IT THEN.
YOU HOLD-ING BACK?
I AM!!
WANNA SEE WHAT HAPPENS ...
...WHEN I DON'T?!
TAKTAK TAK
TAK TAK

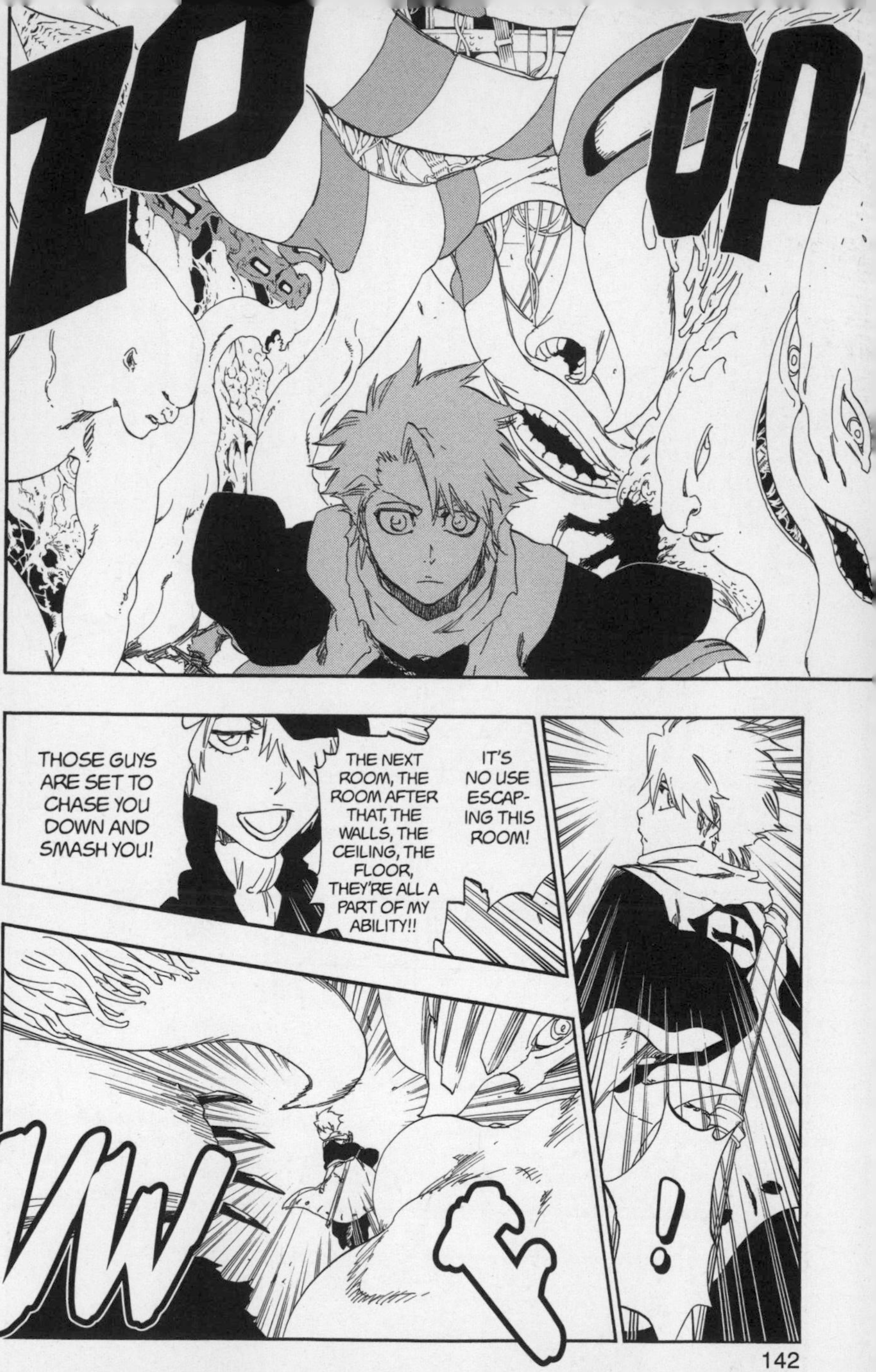
ZO
COP
IT'S NO USE ESCAPING THIS ROOM!
THE NEXT ROOM, THE ROOM AFTER THAT, THE WALLS, THE CEILING, THE FLOOR, THEY'RE ALL A PART OF MY ABILITY!!
THOSE GUYS ARE SET TO CHASE YOU DOWN AND SMASH YOU!
!

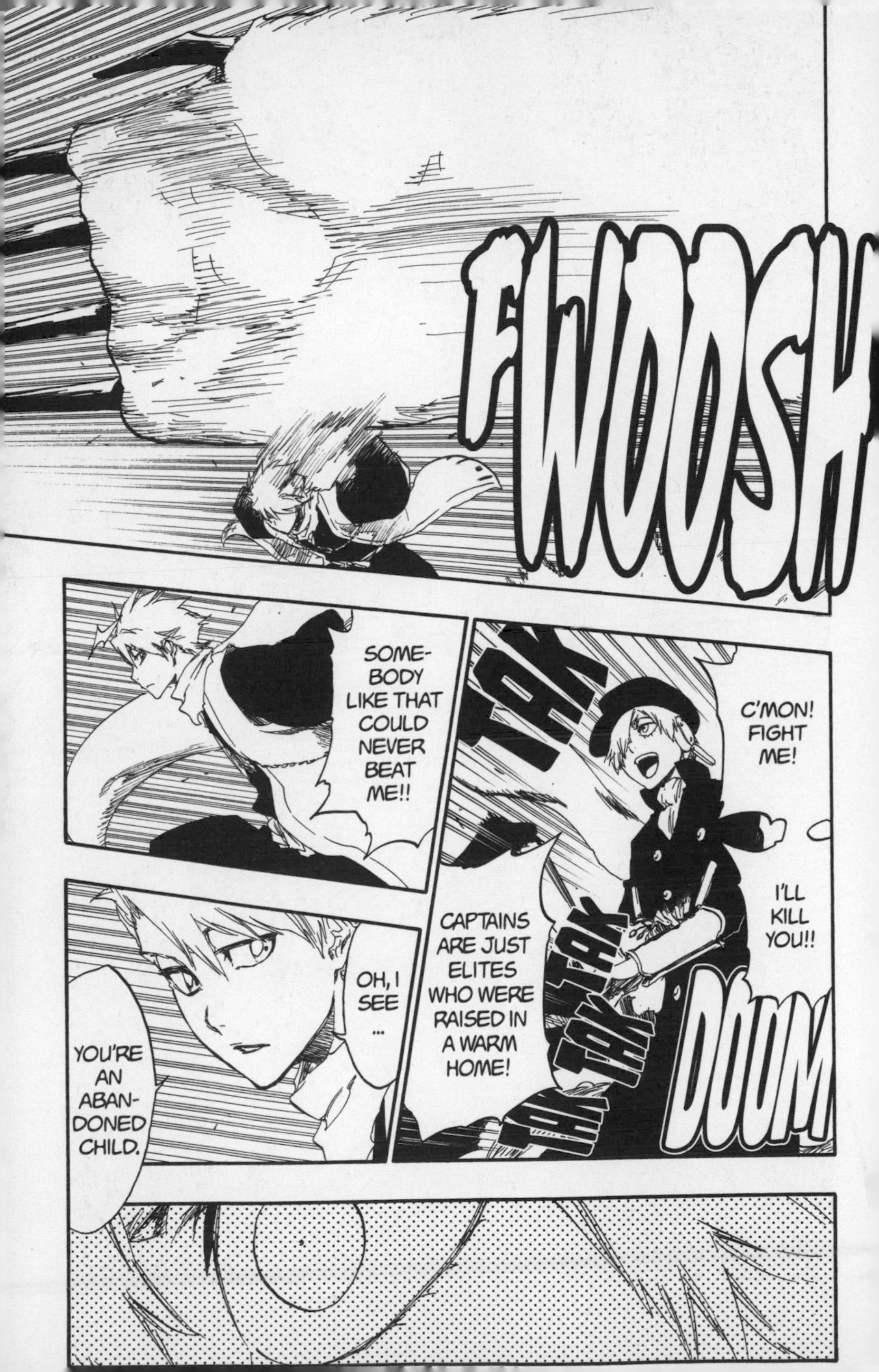
FWOOSH
TAK
C'MON! FIGHT ME!
I'LL KILL YOU!!
CAPTAINS ARE JUST ELITES WHO WERE RAISED IN A WARM HOME!
TAK TAK
DOOM
SOME-BODY LIKE THAT COULD NEVER BEAT ME!!
OH, I SEE ...
YOU'RE AN ABAN-DONED CHILD.

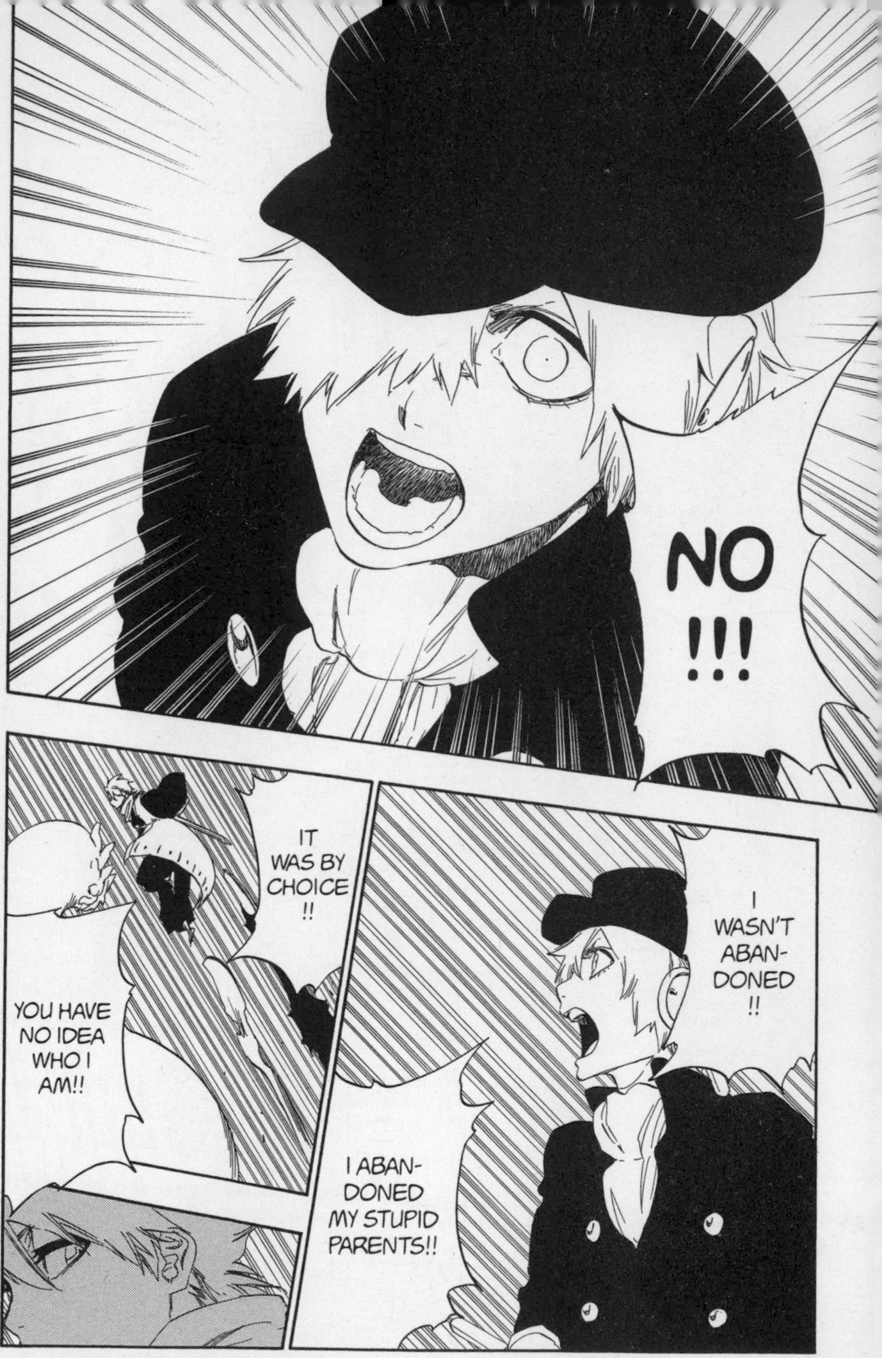
NO !!!
I WASN'T ABAN-DONED !!
I ABAN-DONED MY STUPID PARENTS!!
IT WAS BY CHOICE !!
YOU HAVE NO IDEA WHO I AM!!

READ THIS WAY

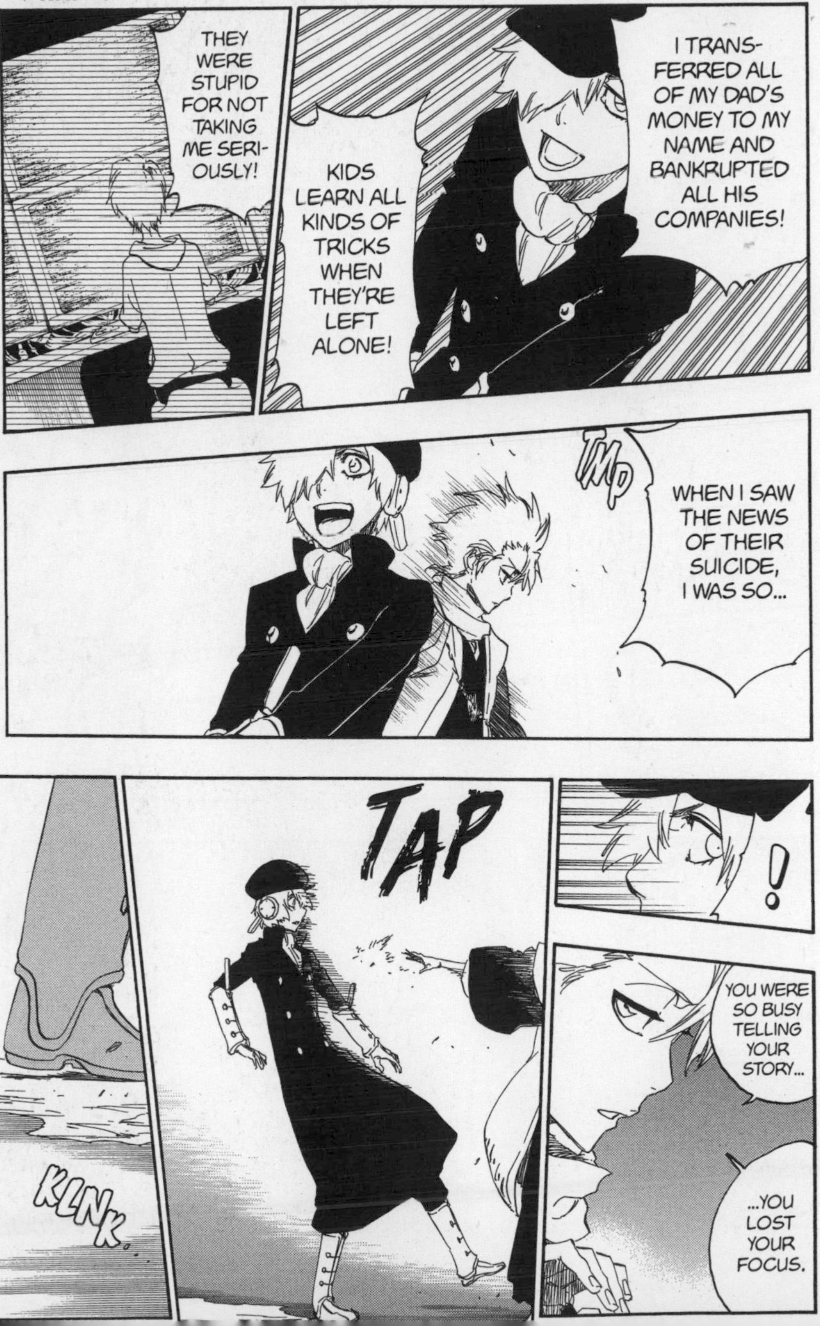

I TRANS-FERRED ALL OF MY DAD'S MONEY TO MY NAME AND BANKRUPTED ALL HIS COMPANIES!
KIDS LEARN ALL KINDS OF TRICKS WHEN THEY'RE LEFT ALONE!
THEY WERE STUPID FOR NOT TAKING ME SERI-OUSLY!
TMP
WHEN I SAW THE NEWS OF THEIR SUICIDE, I WAS SO...
!
YOU WERE SO BUSY TELLING YOUR STORY...
...YOU LOST YOUR FOCUS.
TAP
KLNK

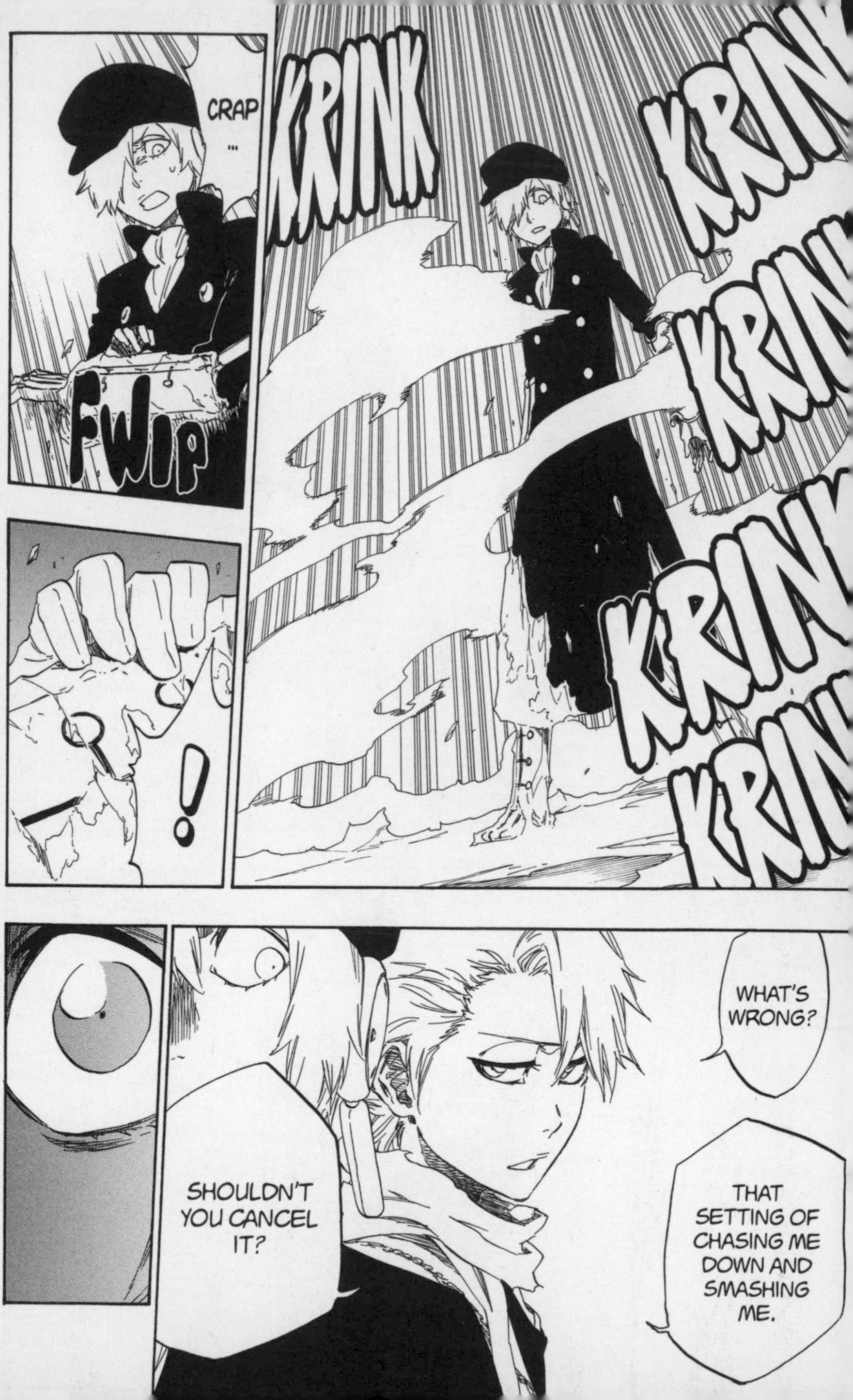

KRINK
KRIN
KRIN
KRIN
KRIN
CRAP ...
FWIP
!
WHAT'S WRONG?
THAT SETTING OF CHASING ME DOWN AND SMASHING ME.
SHOULDN'T YOU CANCEL IT?

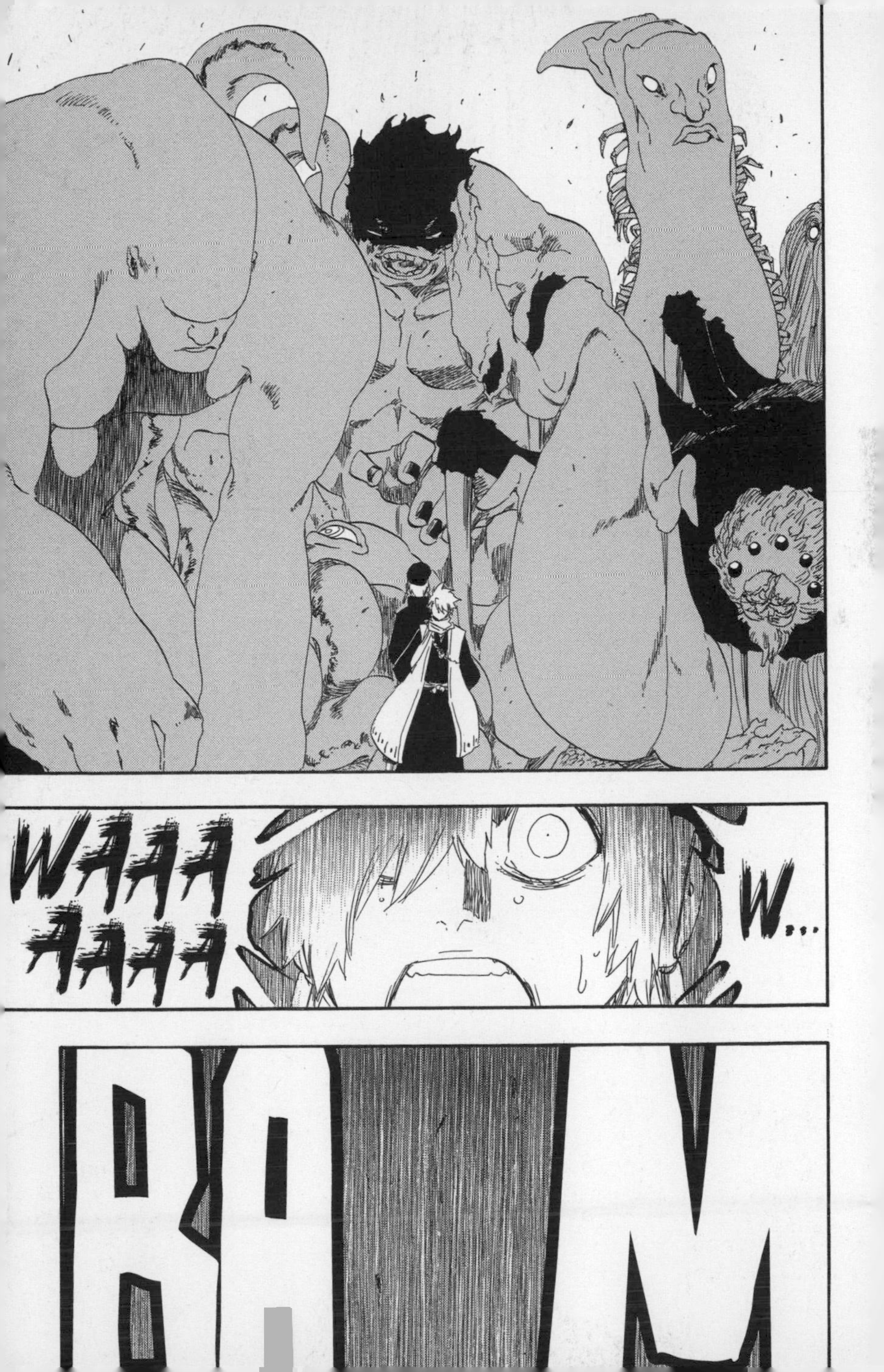
W...
WAAAA
AAAA

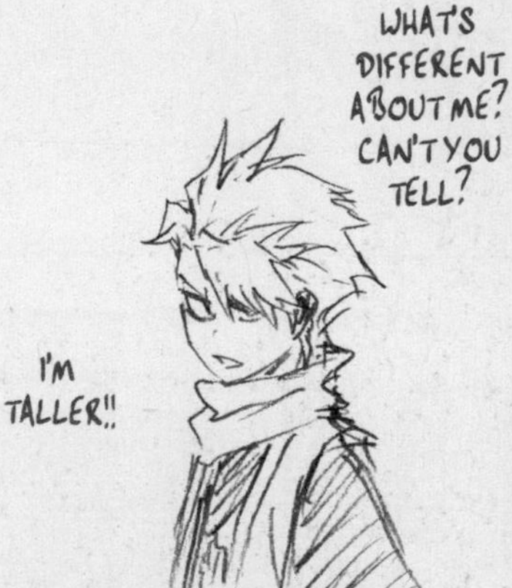
WHAT'S DIFFERENT ABOUT ME? CAN'T YOU TELL?
I'M TALLER!!

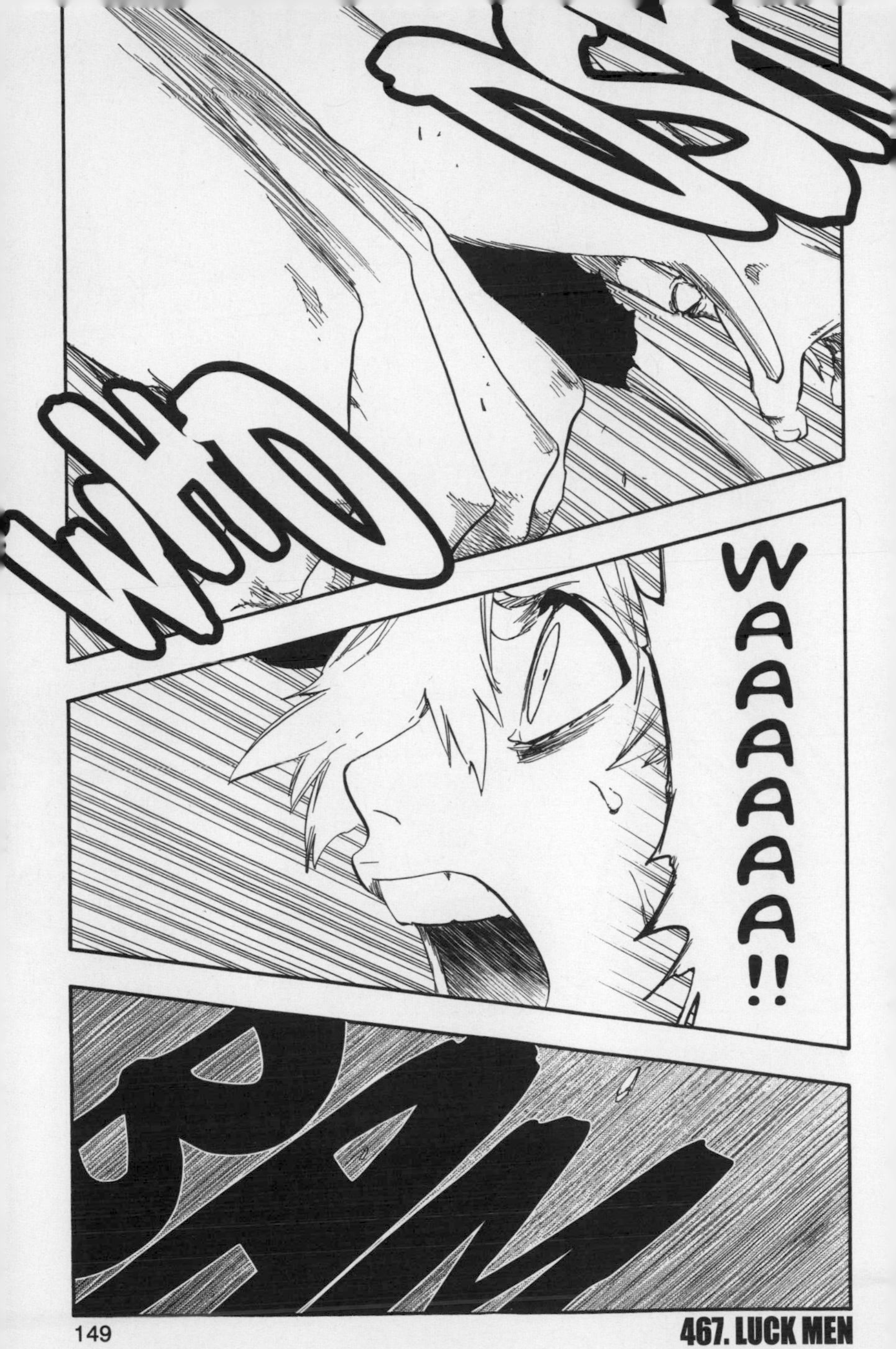
WAAAAAA!!

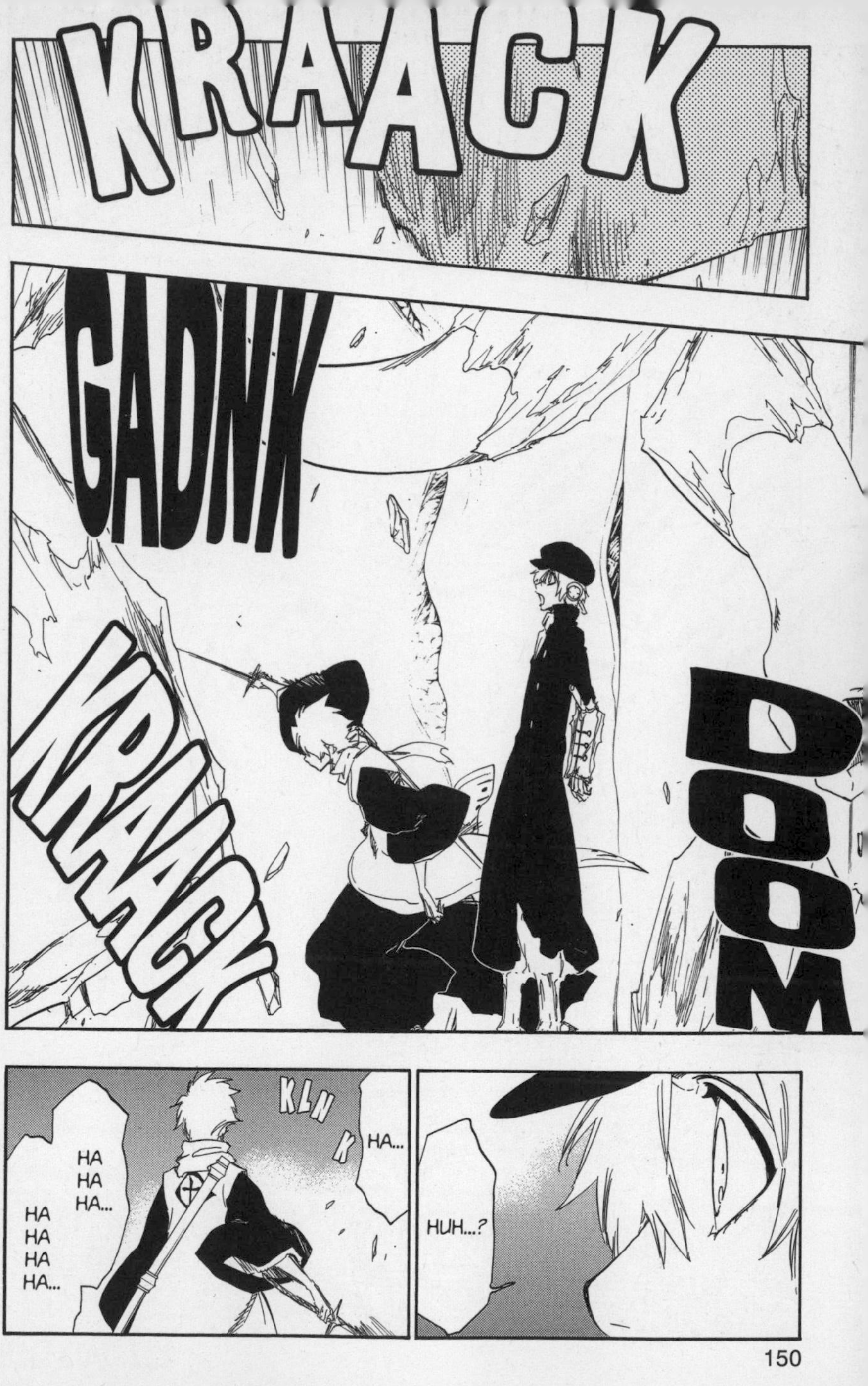
KRAACK
GADNK
DOOM
KRAACK
HUH...?
KLN
K
HA...
HA HA HA...
HA HA HA HA...

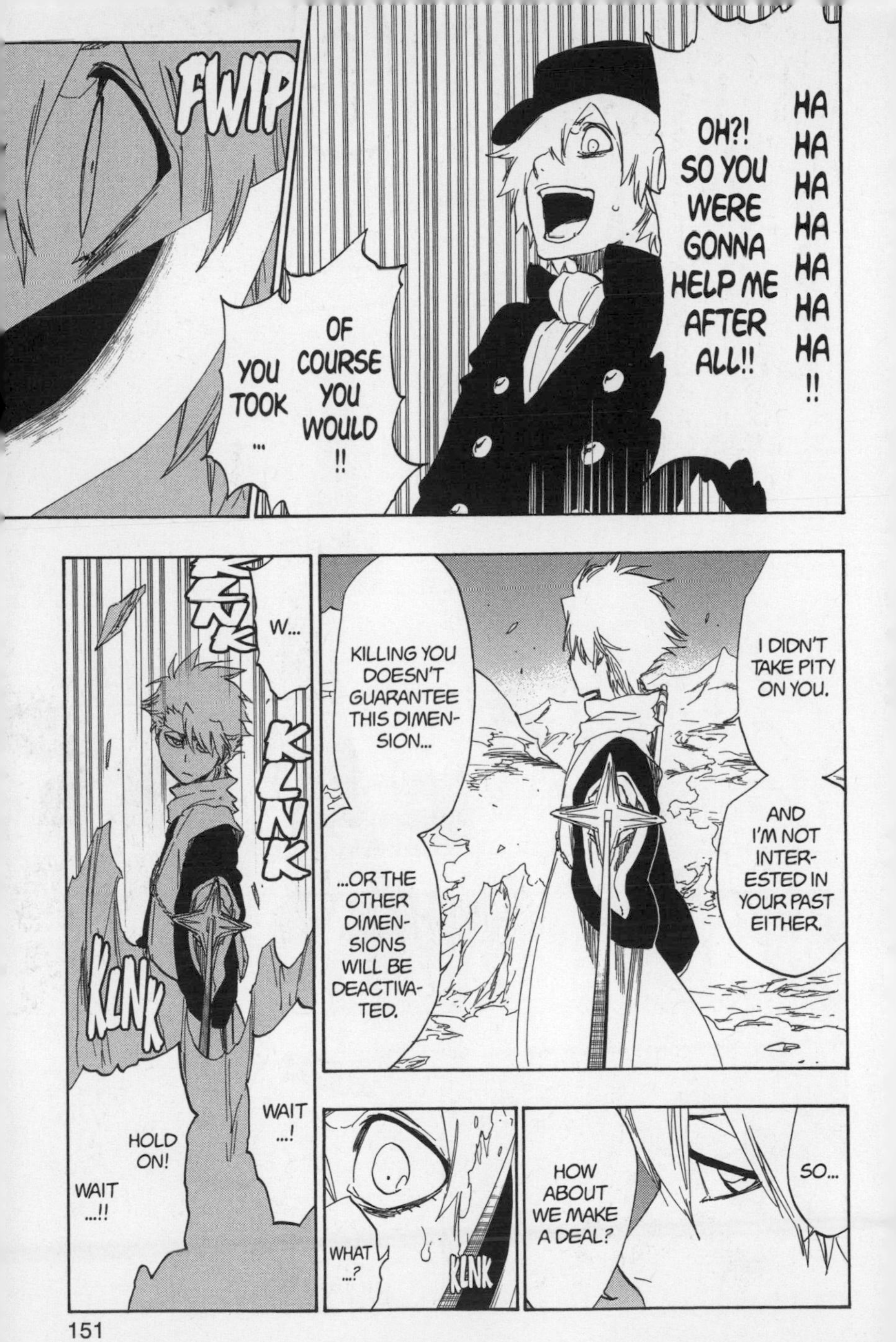
HA HA HA HA HA HA HA !!
OH?! SO YOU WERE GONNA HELP ME AFTER ALL!!
OF COURSE YOU WOULD !!
YOU TOOK ...
FWIP
I DIDN'T TAKE PITY ON YOU.
AND I'M NOT INTER-ESTED IN YOUR PAST EITHER.
KILLING YOU DOESN'T GUARANTEE THIS DIMEN-SION...
...OR THE OTHER DIMEN-SIONS WILL BE DEACTIVA-TED.
SO...
HOW ABOUT WE MAKE A DEAL?
WHAT ...?
KLNK
KLNK
W...
KLNK
KLNK
WAIT ...!
HOLD ON!
WAIT ...!!

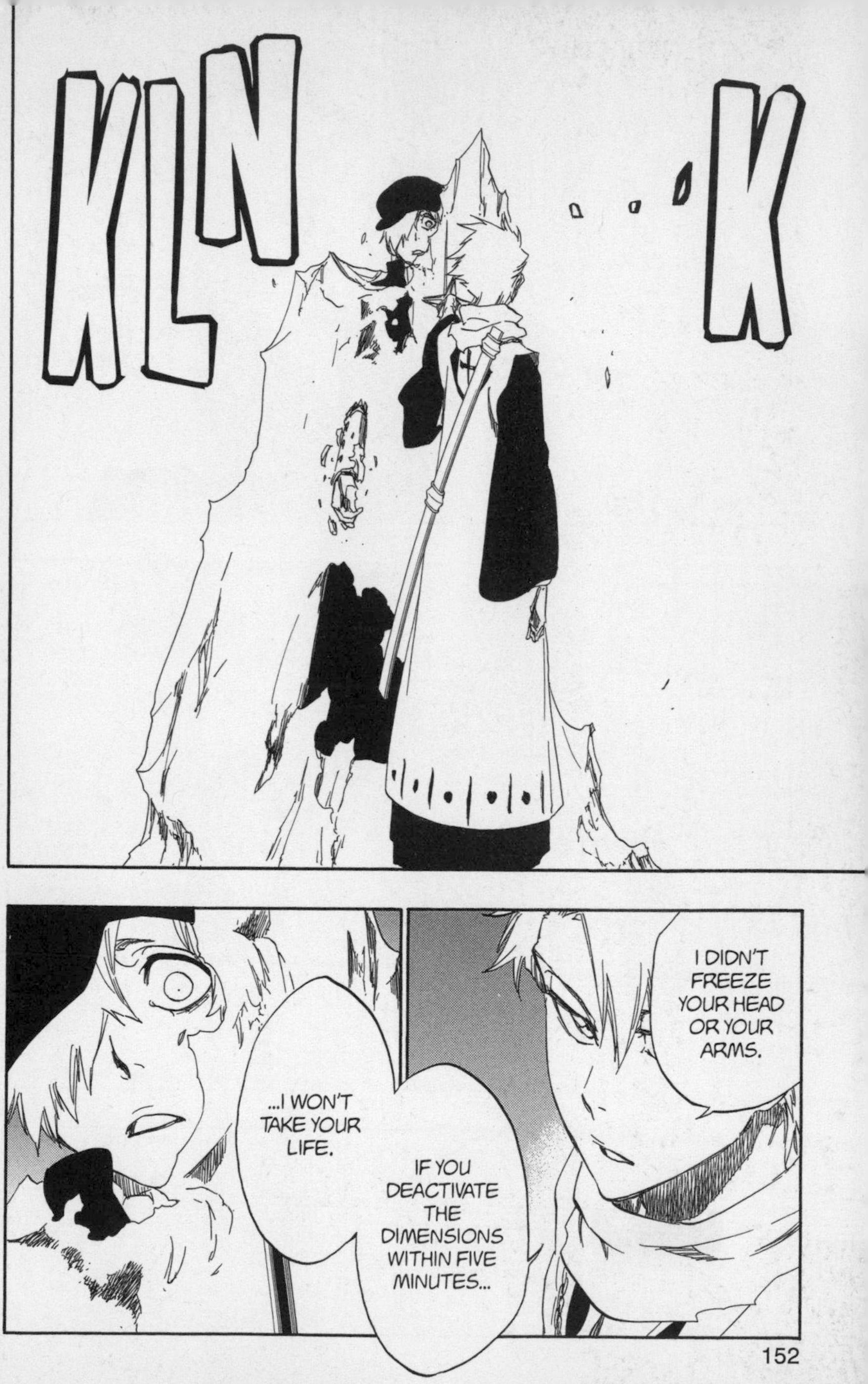
KLN . . K
I DIDN'T FREEZE YOUR HEAD OR YOUR ARMS.
IF YOU DEACTIVATE THE DIMENSIONS WITHIN FIVE MINUTES...
...I WON'T TAKE YOUR LIFE.

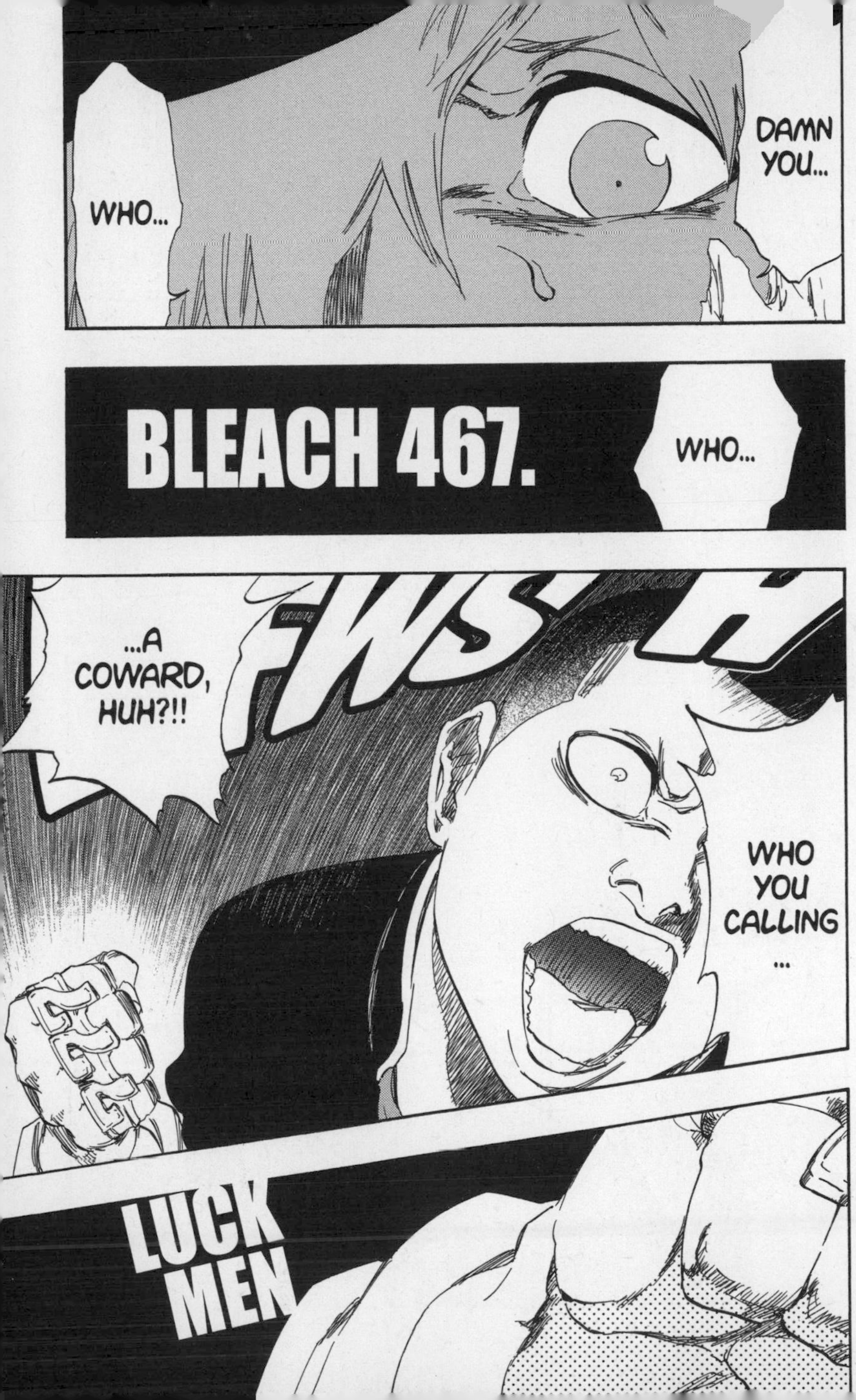
DAMN YOU...
WHO...
WHO...
BLEACH 467.
WHO YOU CALLING ...
...A COWARD, HUH?!!
LUCK MEN

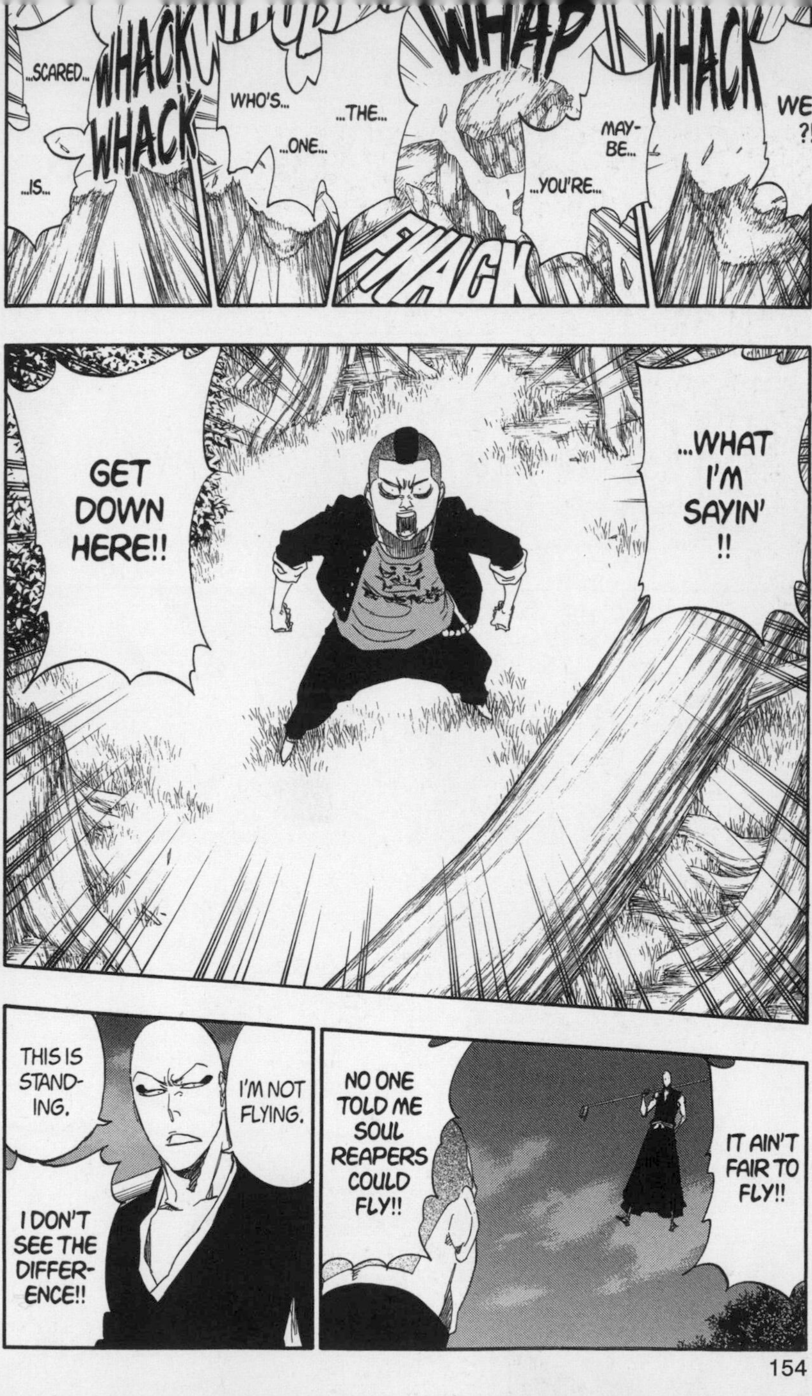
WHACK
WELL ?!
WHAP
MAY-BE...
...YOU'RE...
WHACK
...THE...
...ONE...
WHO'S...
WHACK
WHACK
...SCARED...
...IS...
...WHAT I'M SAYIN' !!
GET DOWN HERE!!
NO ONE TOLD ME SOUL REAPERS COULD FLY!!
IT AIN'T FAIR TO FLY!!
I'M NOT FLYING.
THIS IS STAND-ING.
I DON'T SEE THE DIFFER-ENCE!!

READ THIS WAY

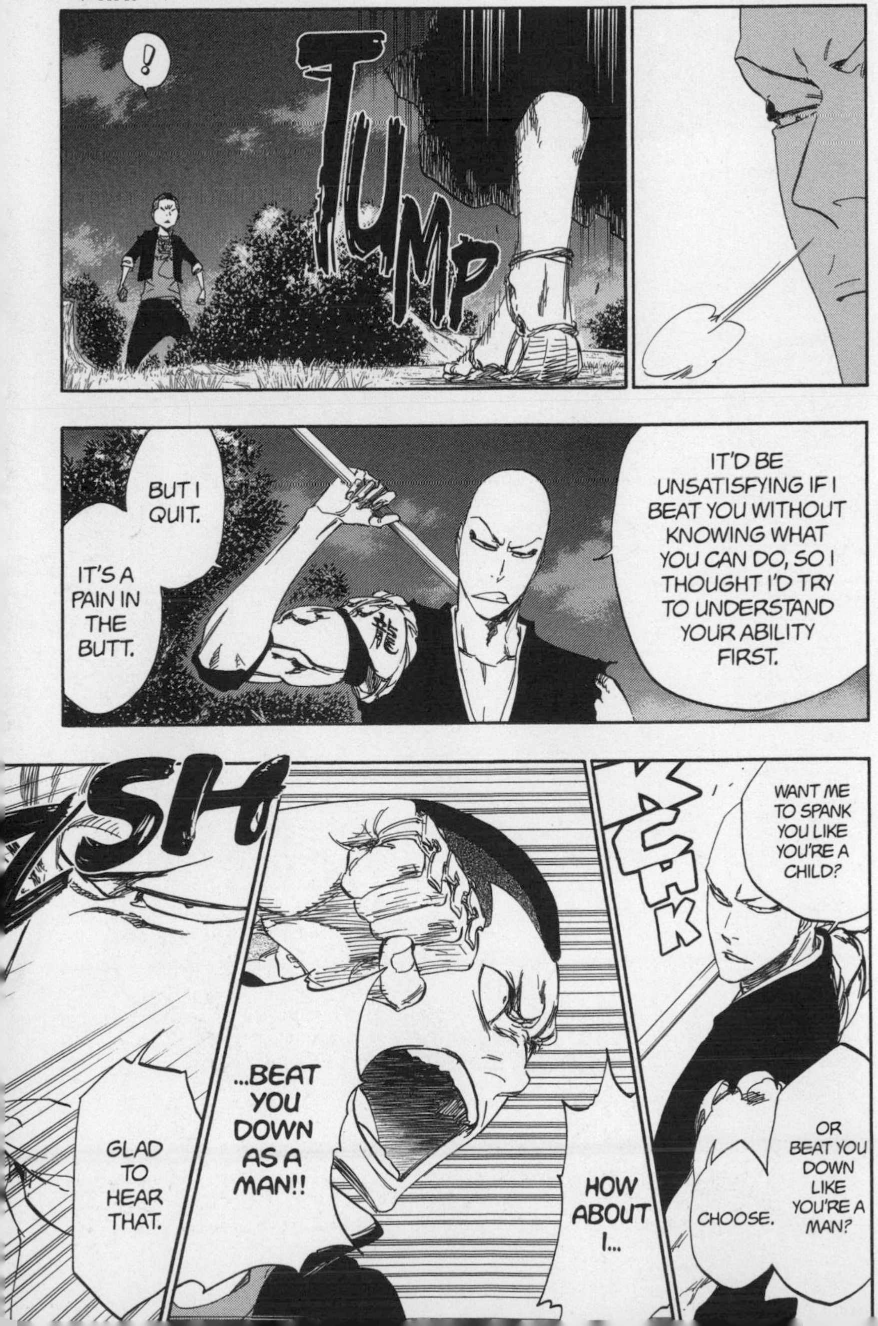
!
TUMP
IT'D BE UNSATISFYING IF I BEAT YOU WITHOUT KNOWING WHAT YOU CAN DO, SO I THOUGHT I'D TRY TO UNDERSTAND YOUR ABILITY FIRST.
BUT I QUIT.
IT'S A PAIN IN THE BUTT.
KCHAK
WANT ME TO SPANK YOU LIKE YOU'RE A CHILD?
OR BEAT YOU DOWN LIKE YOU'RE A MAN?
CHOOSE.
HOW ABOUT I...
...BEAT YOU DOWN AS A MAN!!
ZSH
GLAD TO HEAR THAT.

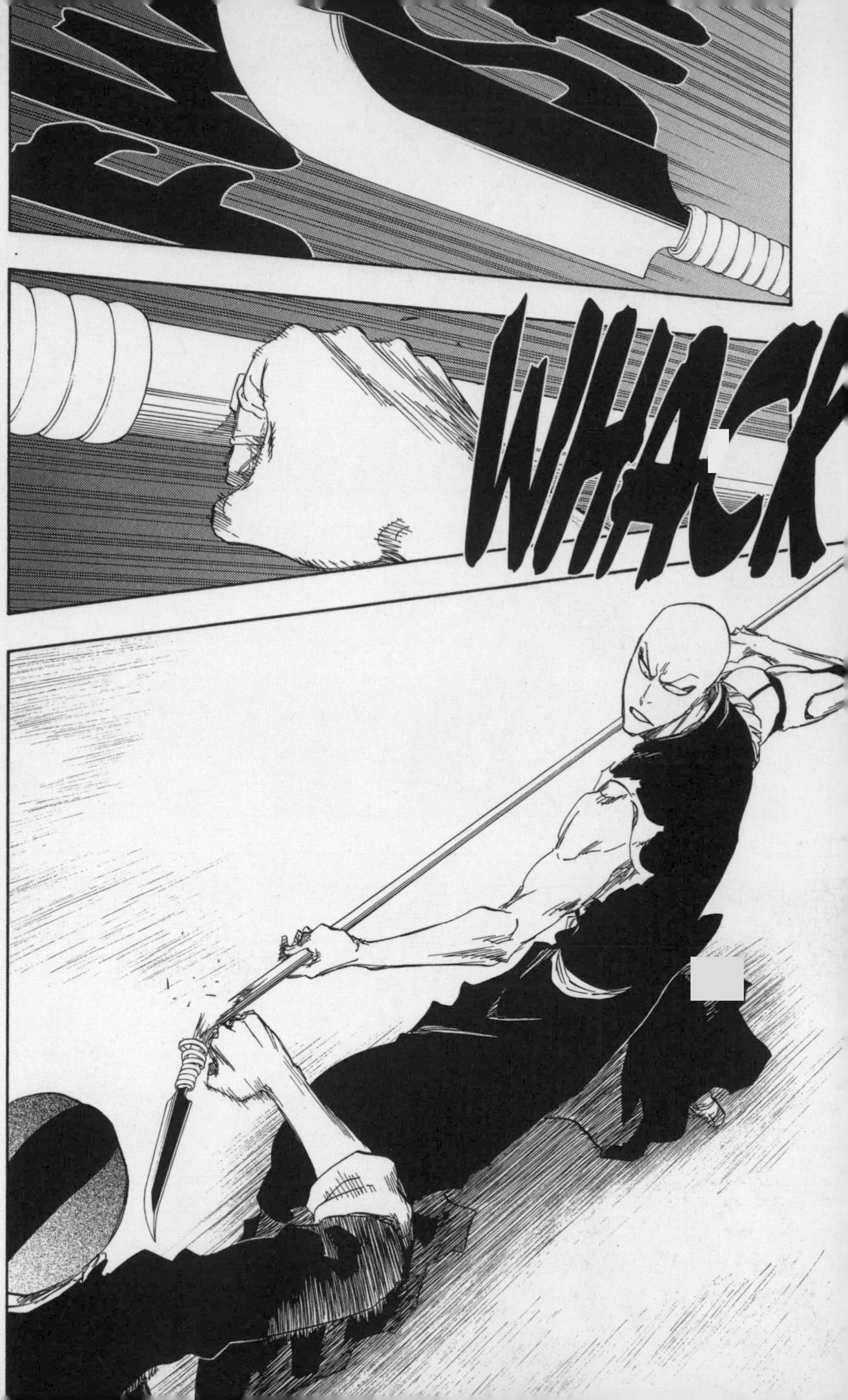
WHACK

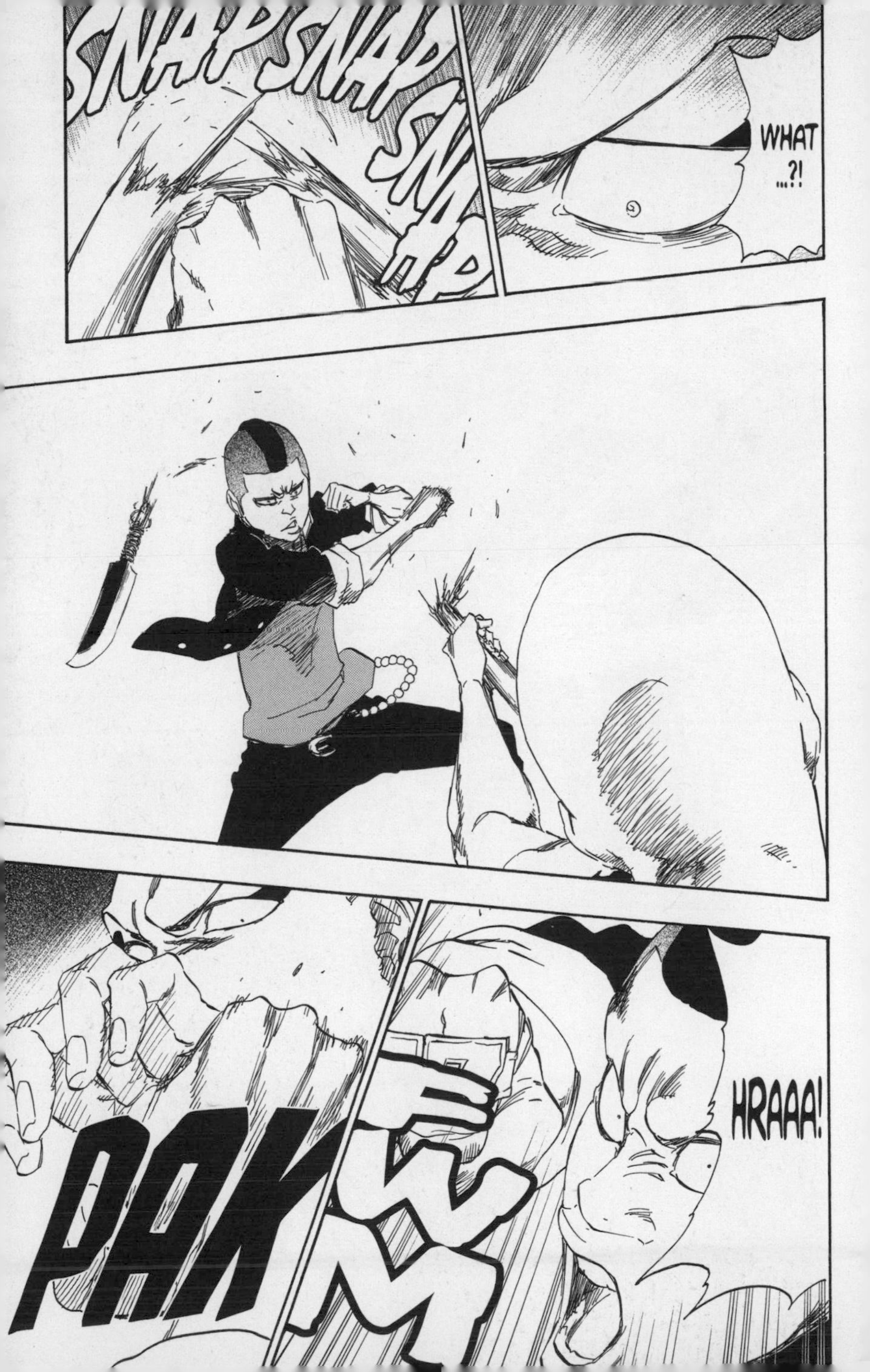
WHAT ...?!
SNAP SNAP SNAP
HRAAA!
PAK

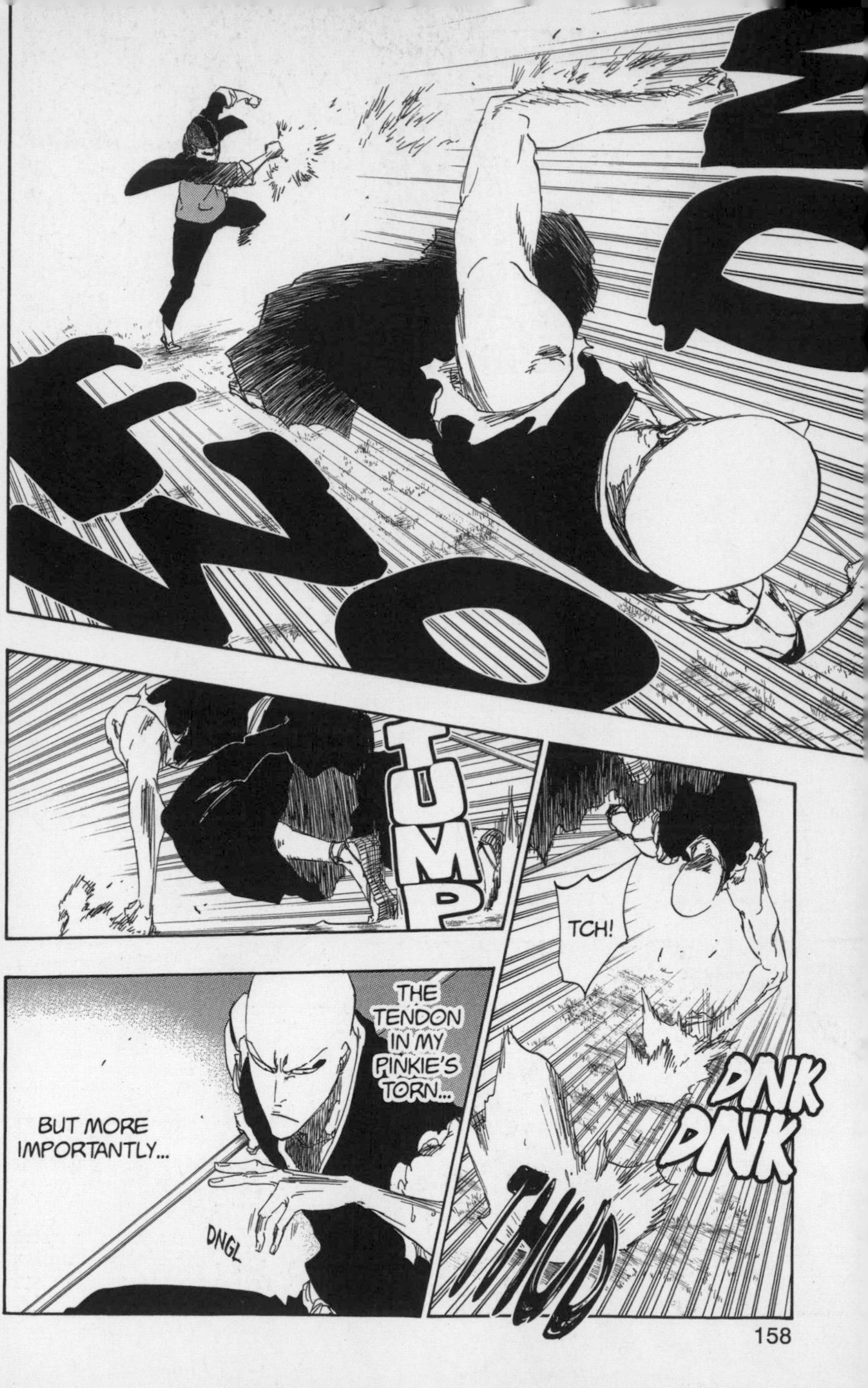
TCH!
DNK DNK
THUD
TUMP
THE TENDON IN MY PINKIE'S TORN...
BUT MORE IMPORTANTLY...
DNGL

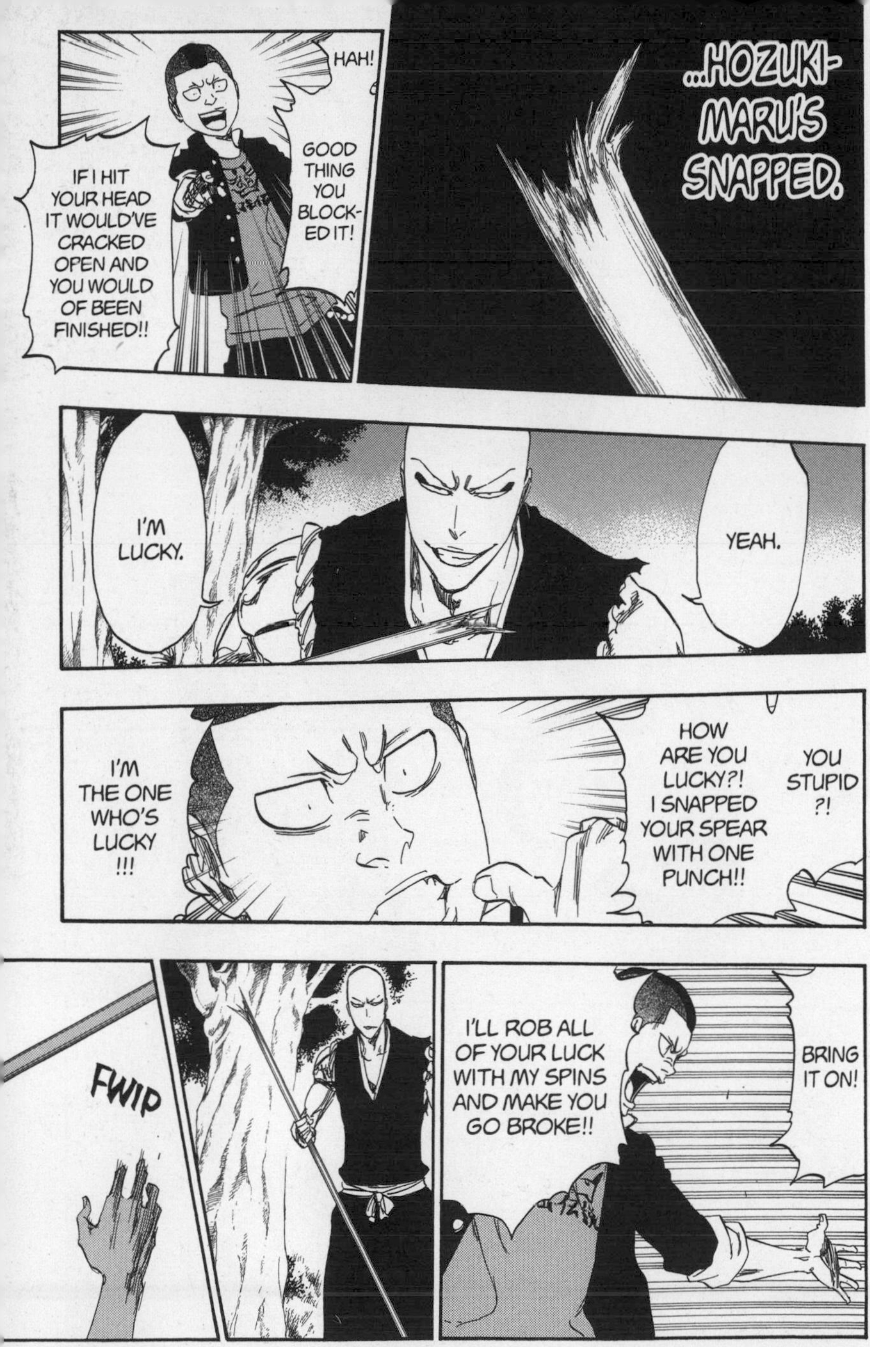
...HOZUKI-MARU'S SNAPPED.
HAH!
GOOD THING YOU BLOCK-ED IT!
IF I HIT YOUR HEAD IT WOULD'VE CRACKED OPEN AND YOU WOULD OF BEEN FINISHED!!
YEAH.
I'M LUCKY.
YOU STUPID?!
HOW ARE YOU LUCKY?! I SNAPPED YOUR SPEAR WITH ONE PUNCH!!
I'M THE ONE WHO'S LUCKY!!!
BRING IT ON!
I'LL ROB ALL OF YOUR LUCK WITH MY SPINS AND MAKE YOU GO BROKE!!
FWIP

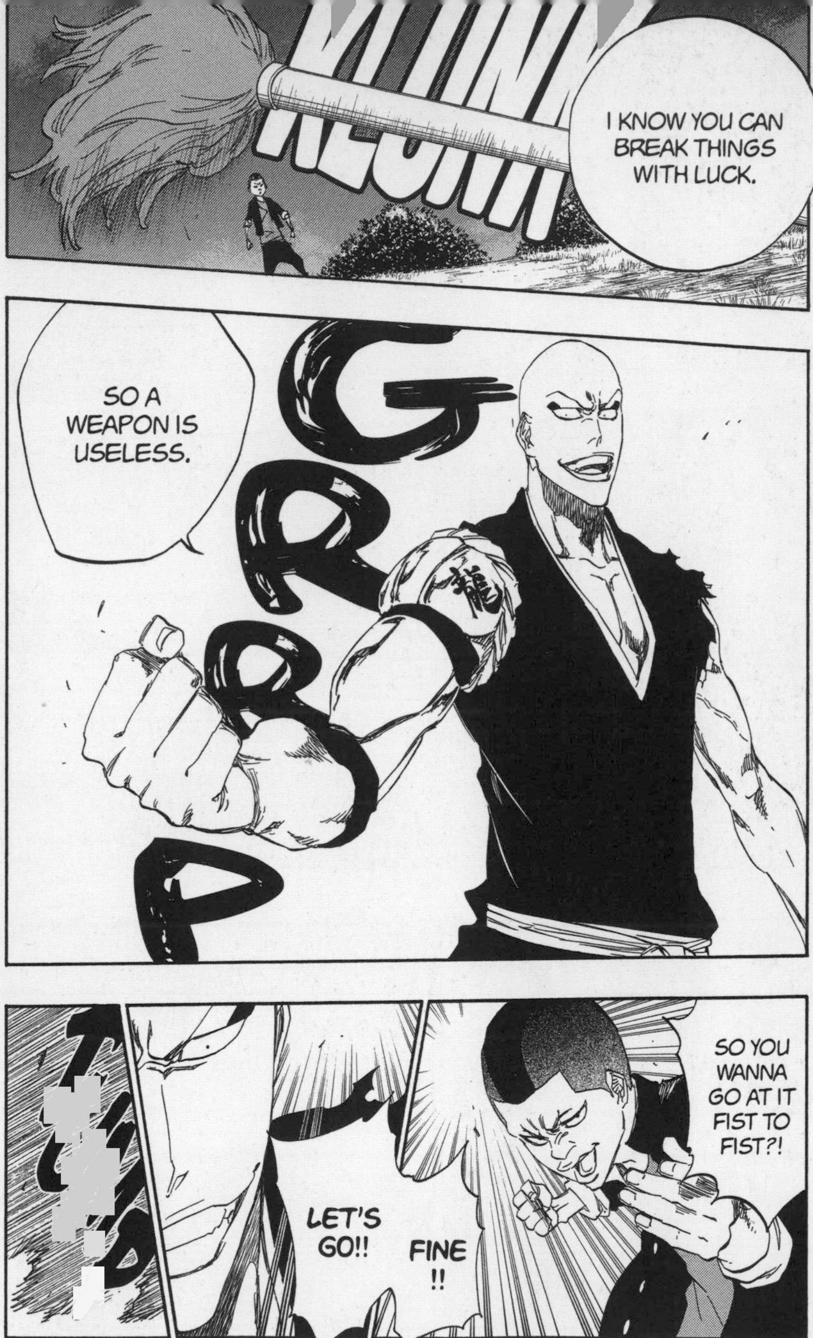
I KNOW YOU CAN BREAK THINGS WITH LUCK.
SO A WEAPON IS USELESS.
SO YOU WANNA GO AT IT FIST TO FIST?!
FINE !!
LET'S GO!!

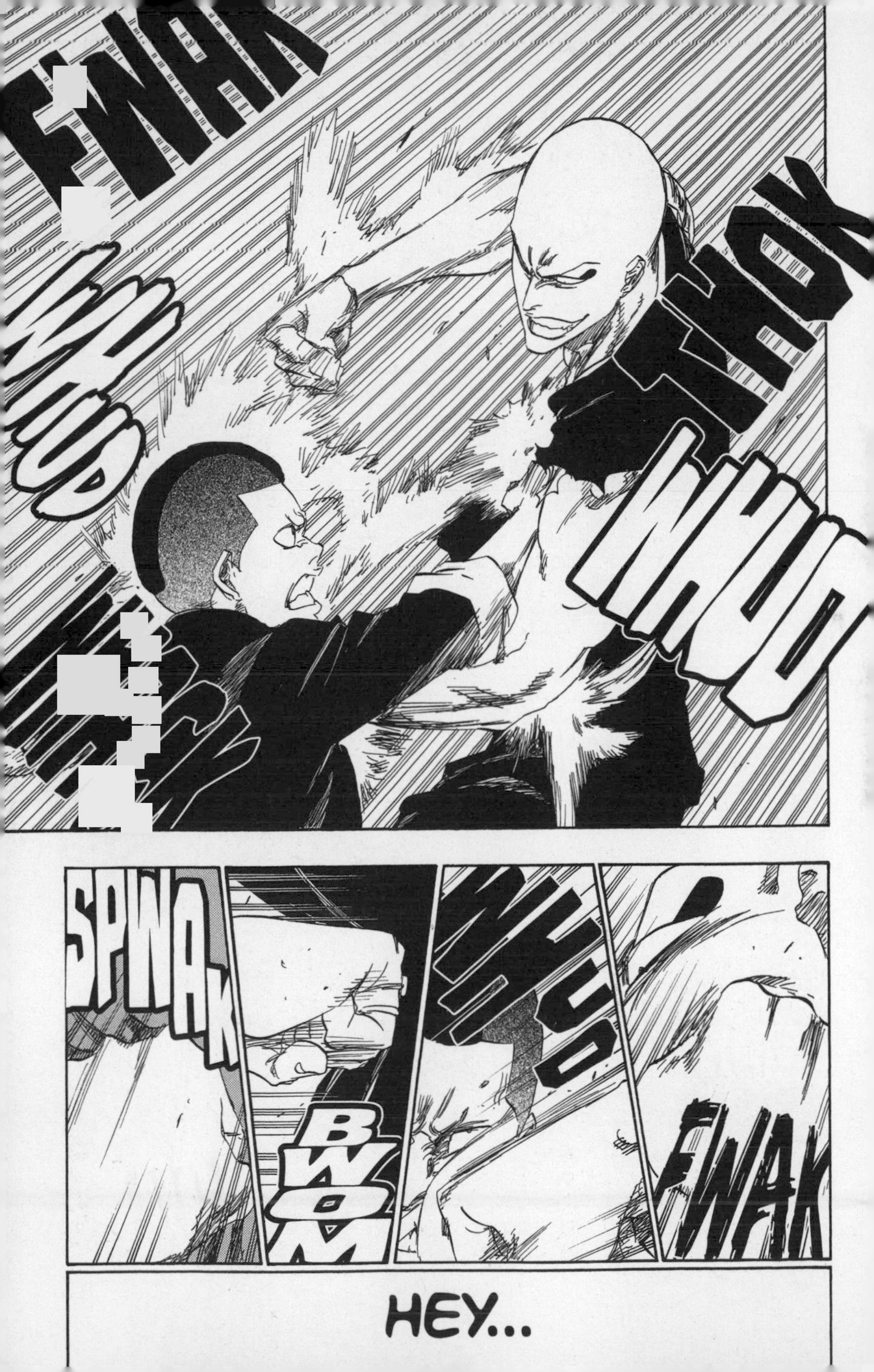
THOK
WHUD
FWAM
FWAK
WHUD
BWOM
SPWAK
HEY...

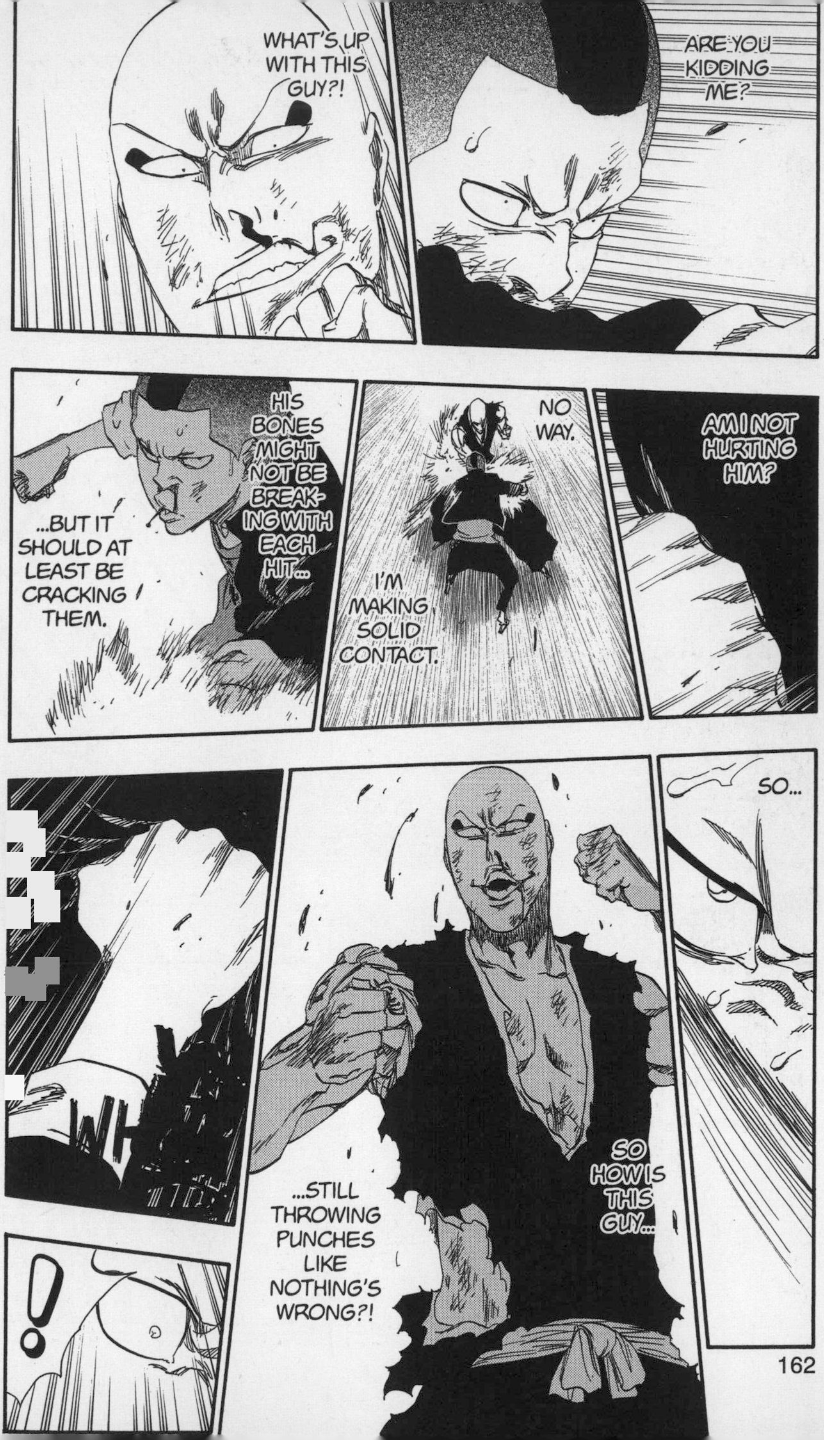
ARE YOU KIDDING ME?
WHAT'S UP WITH THIS GUY?!
AM I NOT HURTING HIM?
NO WAY.
I'M MAKING SOLID CONTACT.
HIS BONES MIGHT NOT BE BREAKING WITH EACH HIT...
...BUT IT SHOULD AT LEAST BE CRACKING THEM.
SO...
SO HOW IS THIS GUY...
...STILL THROWING PUNCHES LIKE NOTHING'S WRONG?!
!

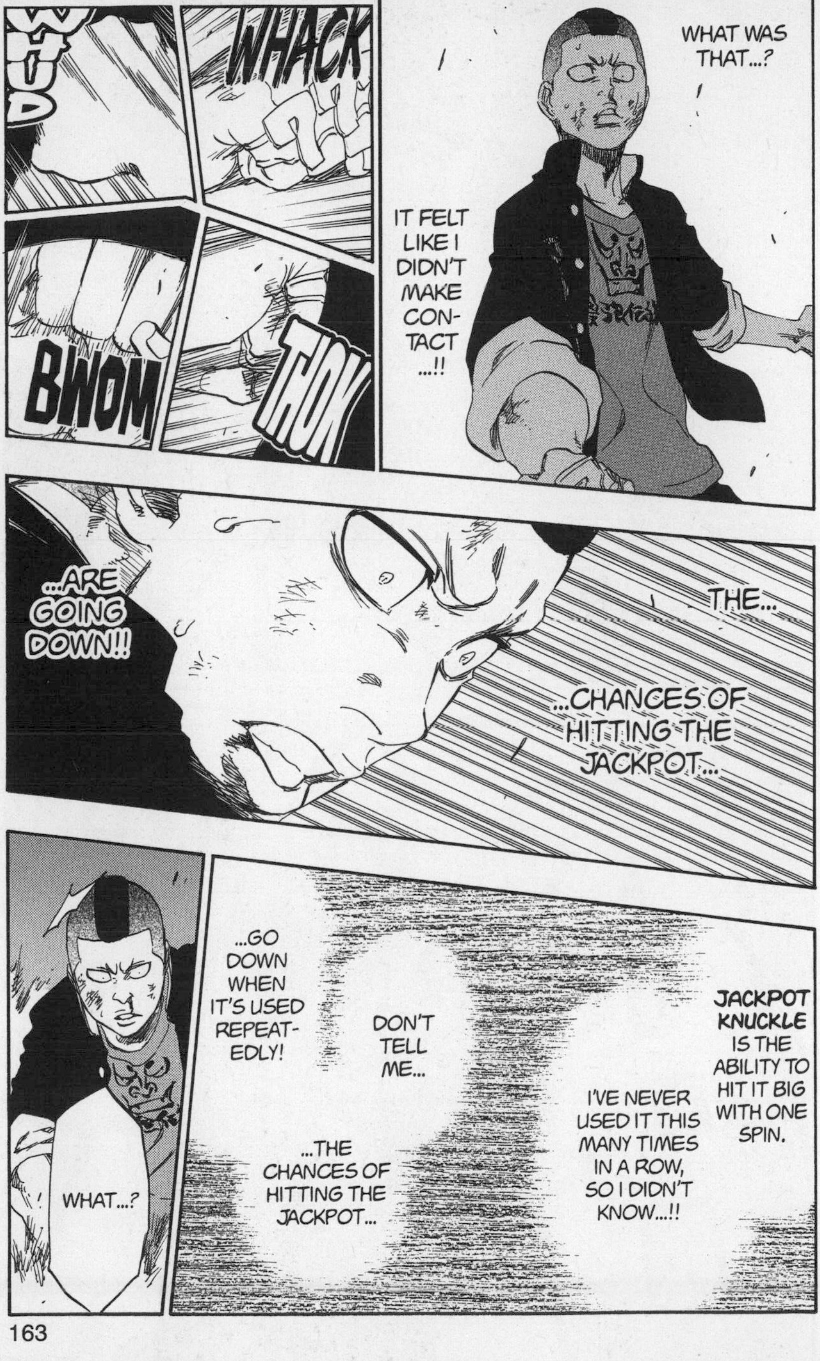
WHAT WAS THAT...?
IT FELT LIKE I DIDN'T MAKE CONTACT...!!
WHACK
WHUD
THUNK
BWOM
THE...
...CHANCES OF HITTING THE JACKPOT...
...ARE GOING DOWN!!
JACKPOT KNUCKLE IS THE ABILITY TO HIT IT BIG WITH ONE SPIN.
I'VE NEVER USED IT THIS MANY TIMES IN A ROW, SO I DIDN'T KNOW...!!
DON'T TELL ME...
...THE CHANCES OF HITTING THE JACKPOT...
...GO DOWN WHEN IT'S USED REPEATEDLY!
WHAT...?

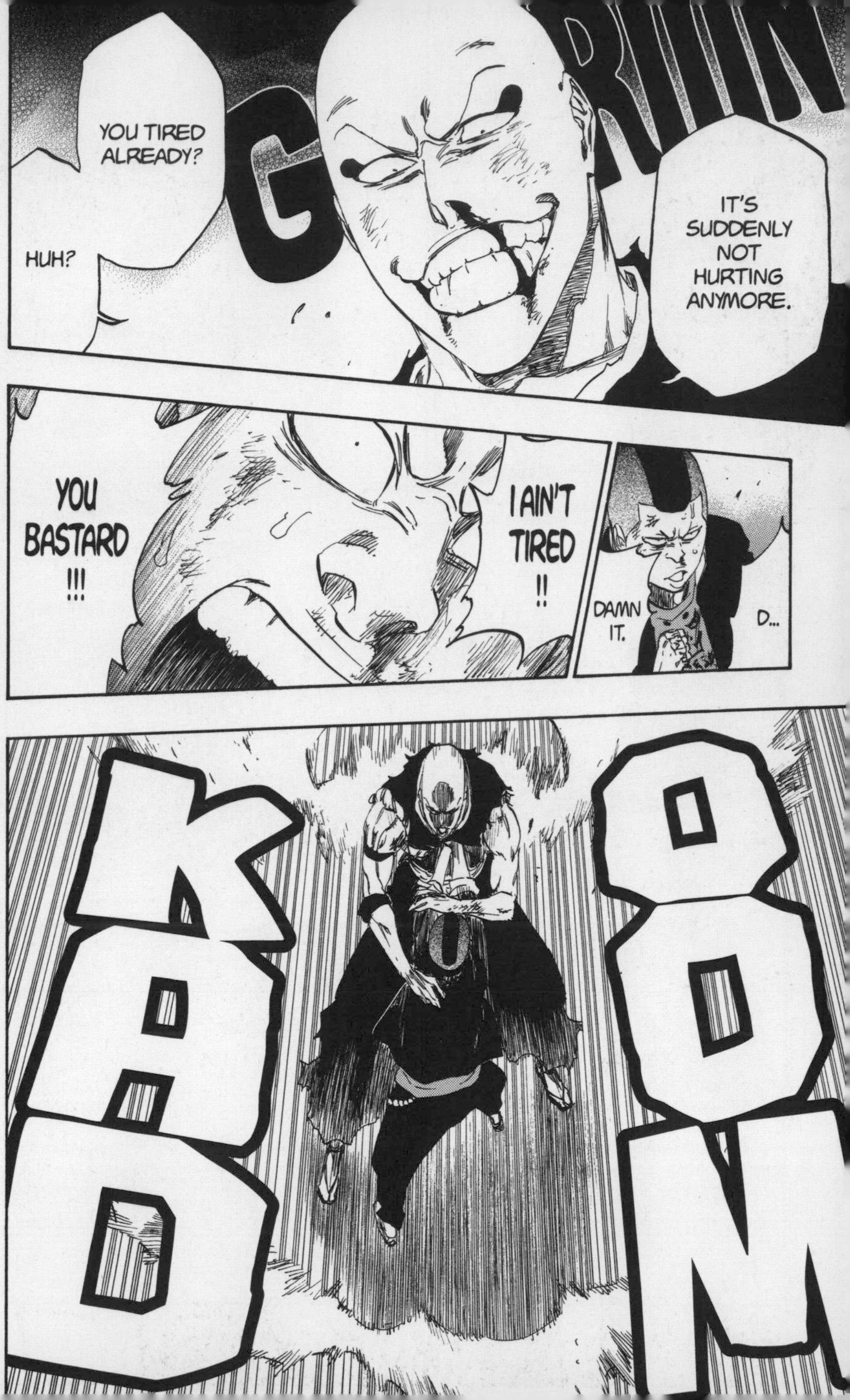
IT'S SUDDENLY NOT HURTING ANYMORE.
YOU TIRED ALREADY?
HUH?
D...
DAMN IT.
I AIN'T TIRED !!
YOU BASTARD !!!
KABOOM

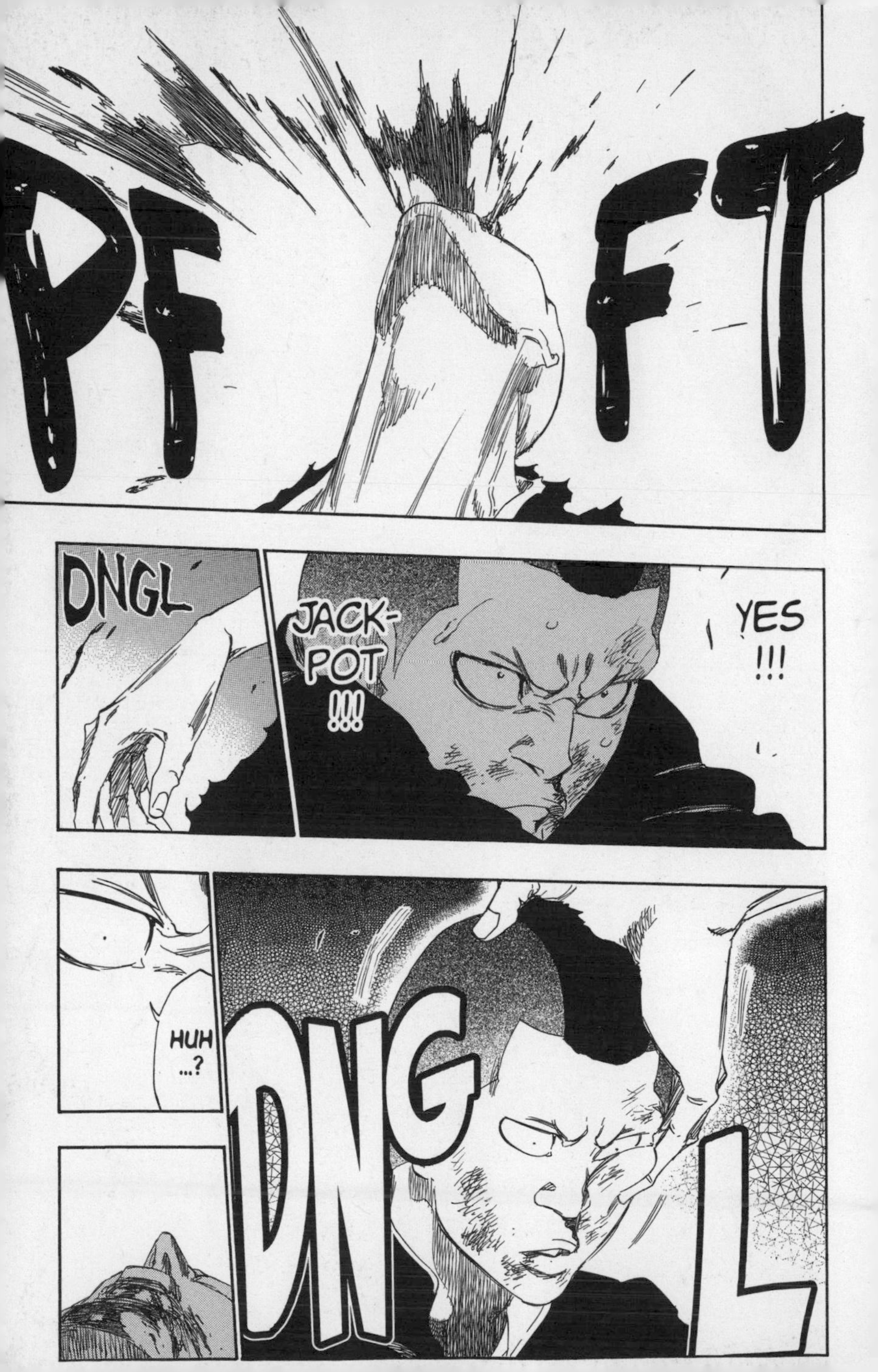
PFFT
YES!!!
JACK-POT!!!
DNGL
DNGL
HUH...?

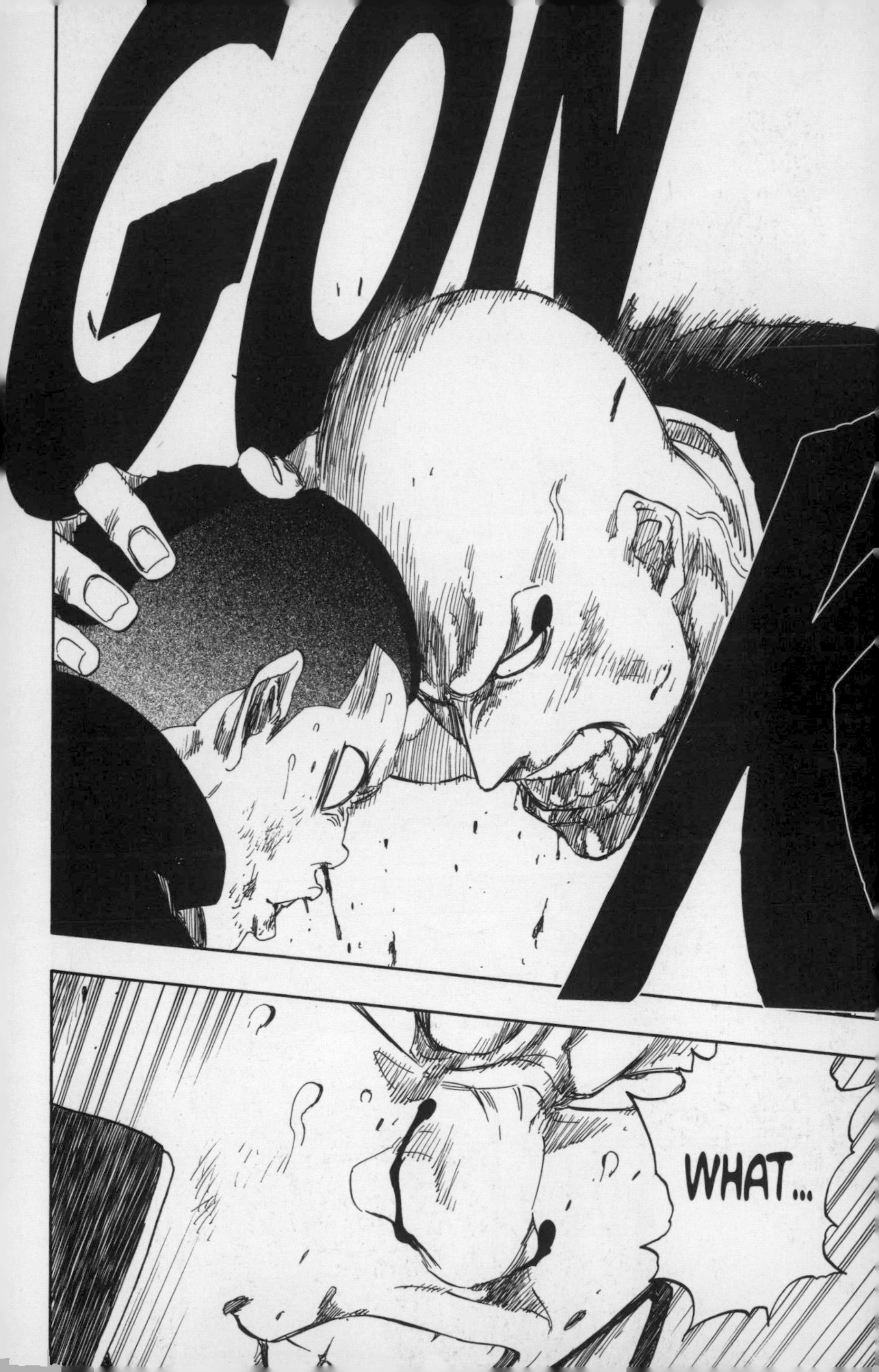
GOIN
WHAT...

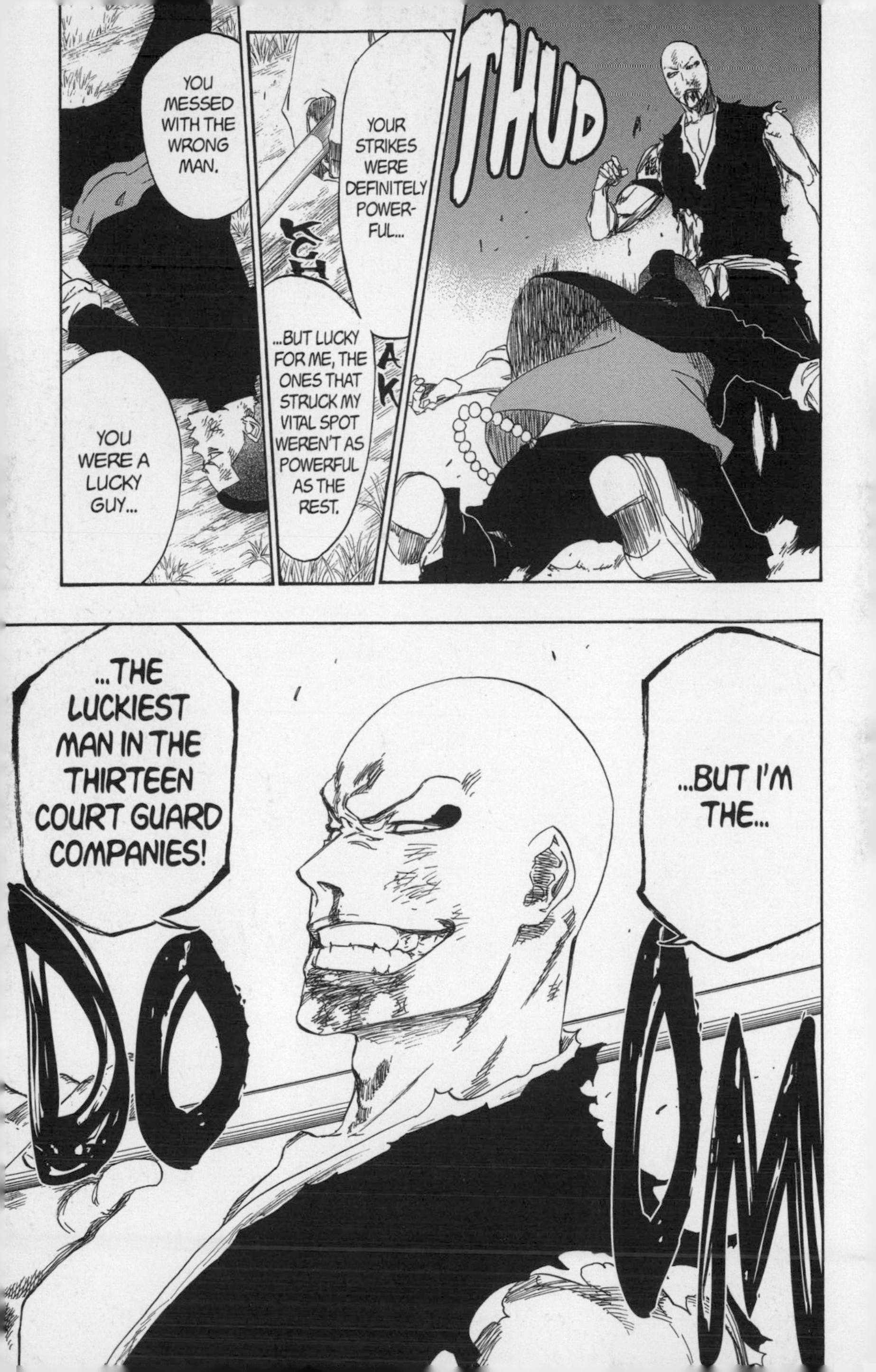
THUD
YOUR STRIKES WERE DEFINITELY POWER-FUL...
KCH
...BUT LUCKY FOR ME, THE ONES THAT STRUCK MY VITAL SPOT WEREN'T AS POWERFUL AS THE REST.
AK
YOU MESSED WITH THE WRONG MAN.
YOU WERE A LUCKY GUY...
...BUT I'M THE...
...THE LUCKIEST MAN IN THE THIRTEEN COURT GUARD COMPANIES!
DOOM

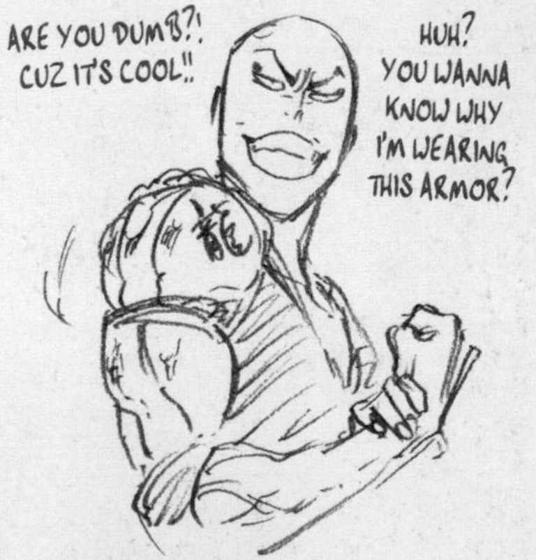
HUH? YOU WANNA KNOW WHY I'M WEARING THIS ARMOR?
ARE YOU DUMB?! CUZ IT'S COOL!!

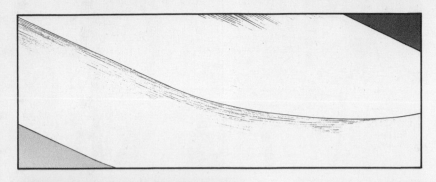

WHAT'S THE MATTER?

169

468. Raid as a Blade

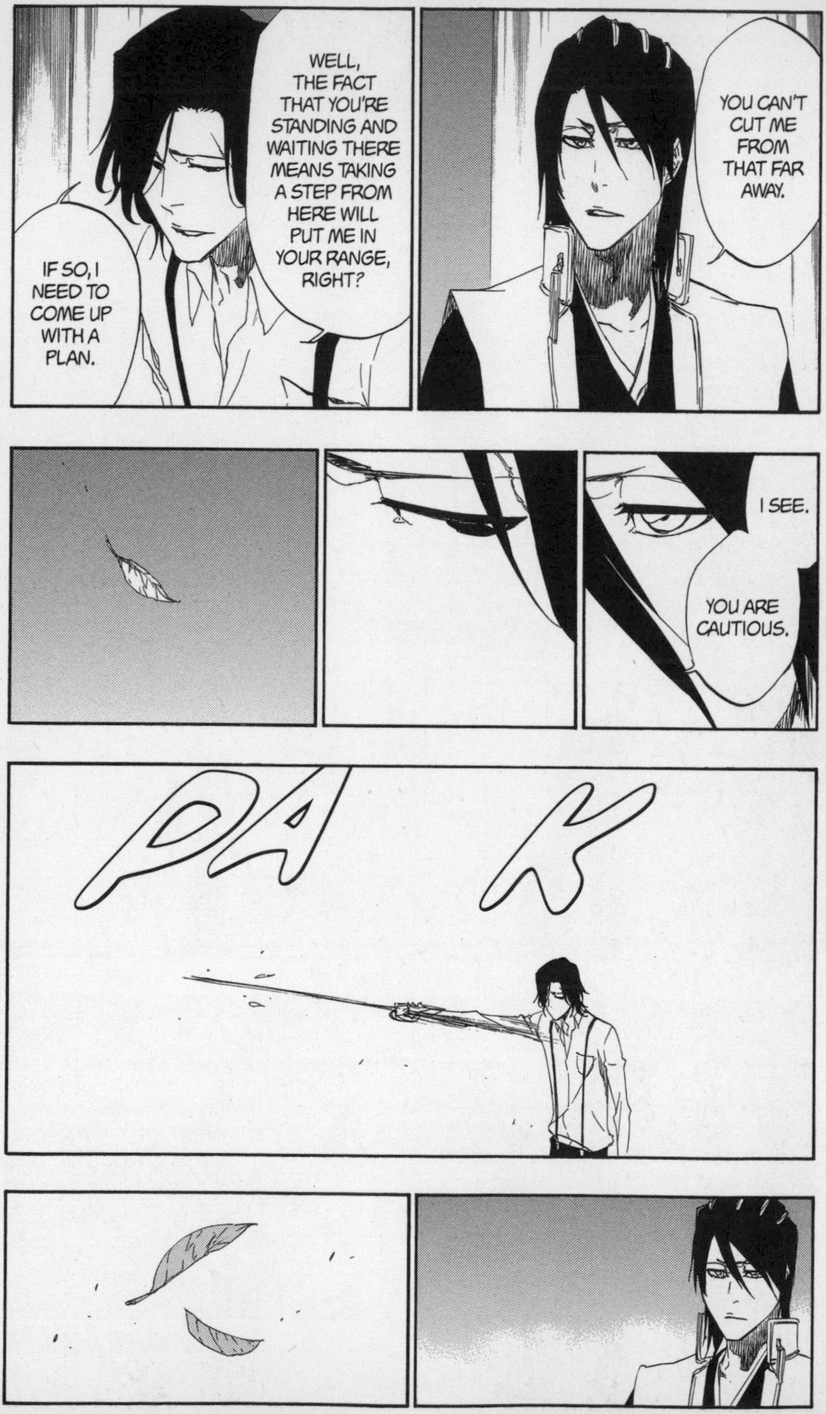
YOU CAN'T CUT ME FROM THAT FAR AWAY.
WELL, THE FACT THAT YOU'RE STANDING AND WAITING THERE MEANS TAKING A STEP FROM HERE WILL PUT ME IN YOUR RANGE, RIGHT?
IF SO, I NEED TO COME UP WITH A PLAN.
I SEE.
YOU ARE CAUTIOUS.
PA K

DID THAT APPEAR LIKE IT HAD MEANING?

SKREEE

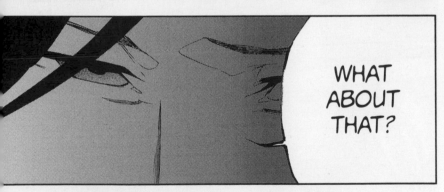

WHAT ABOUT THAT?

OH.

I BELIEVE I SHOULDN'T VIEW THEM AS MEANINGLESS ACTS.

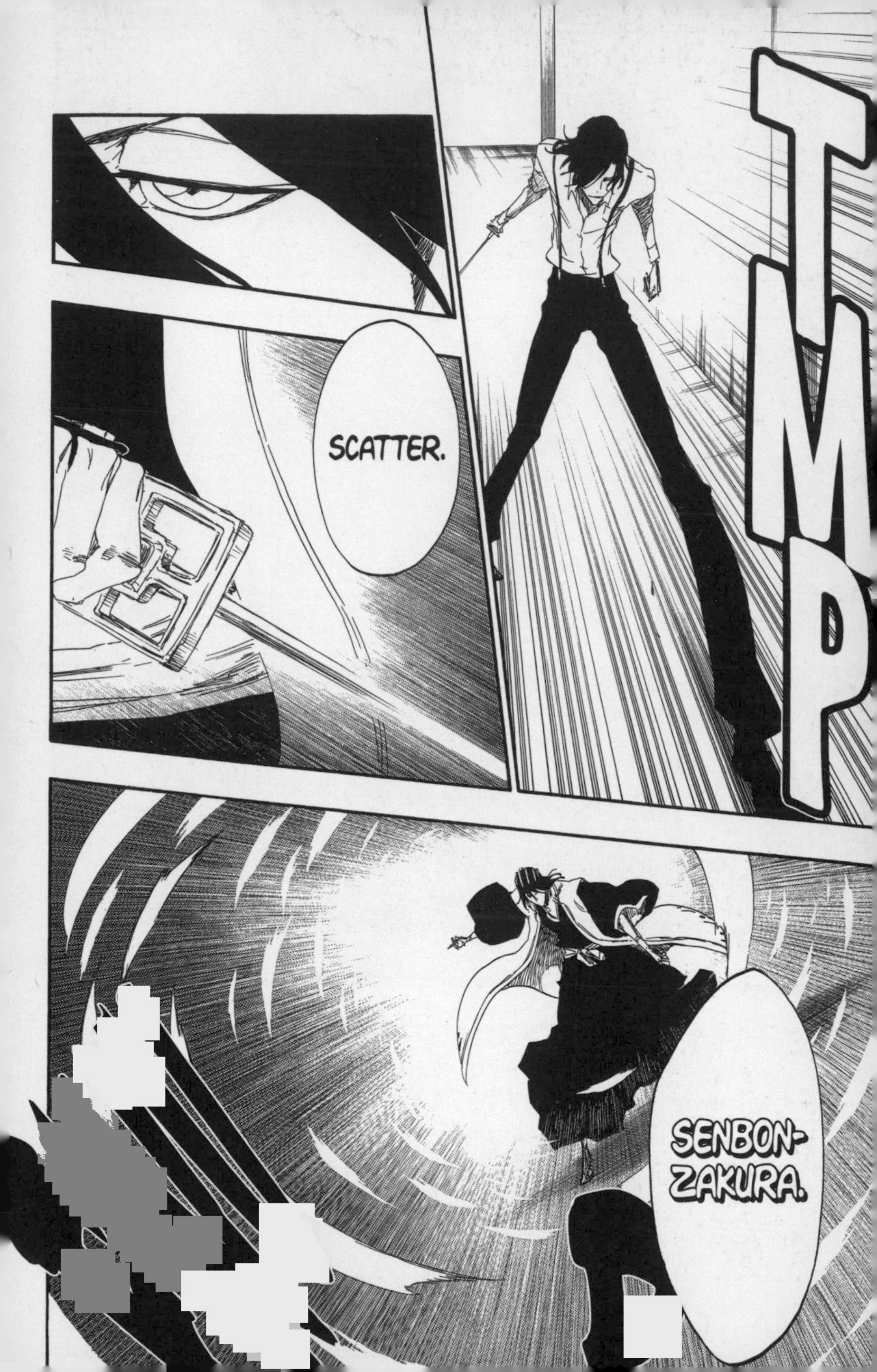
TMP
SCATTER.
SENBON-ZAKURA.

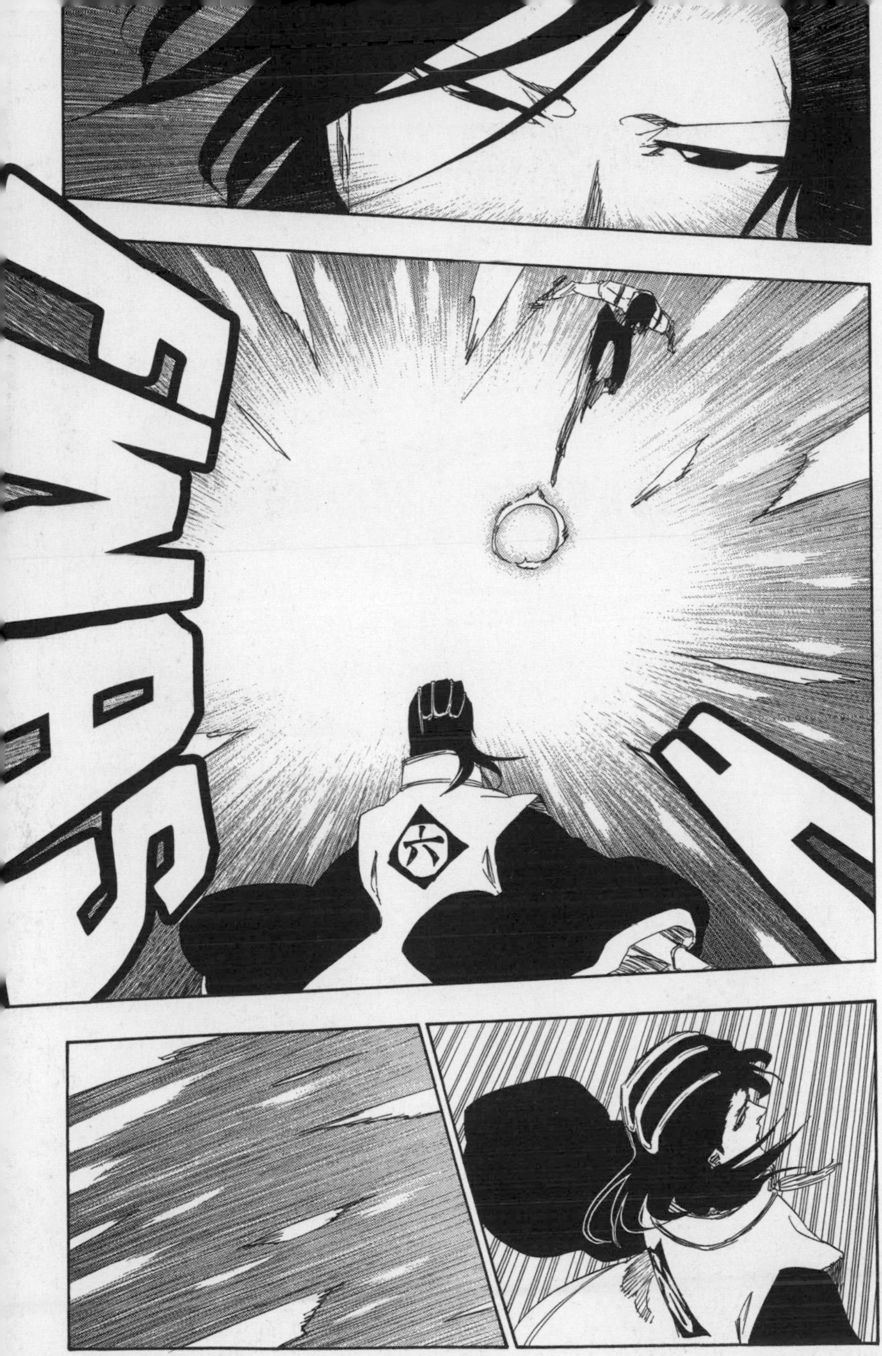

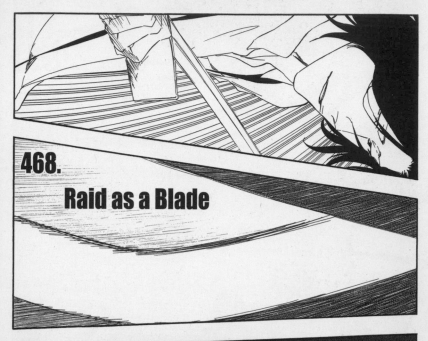

468.

Raid as a Blade

BLEACH

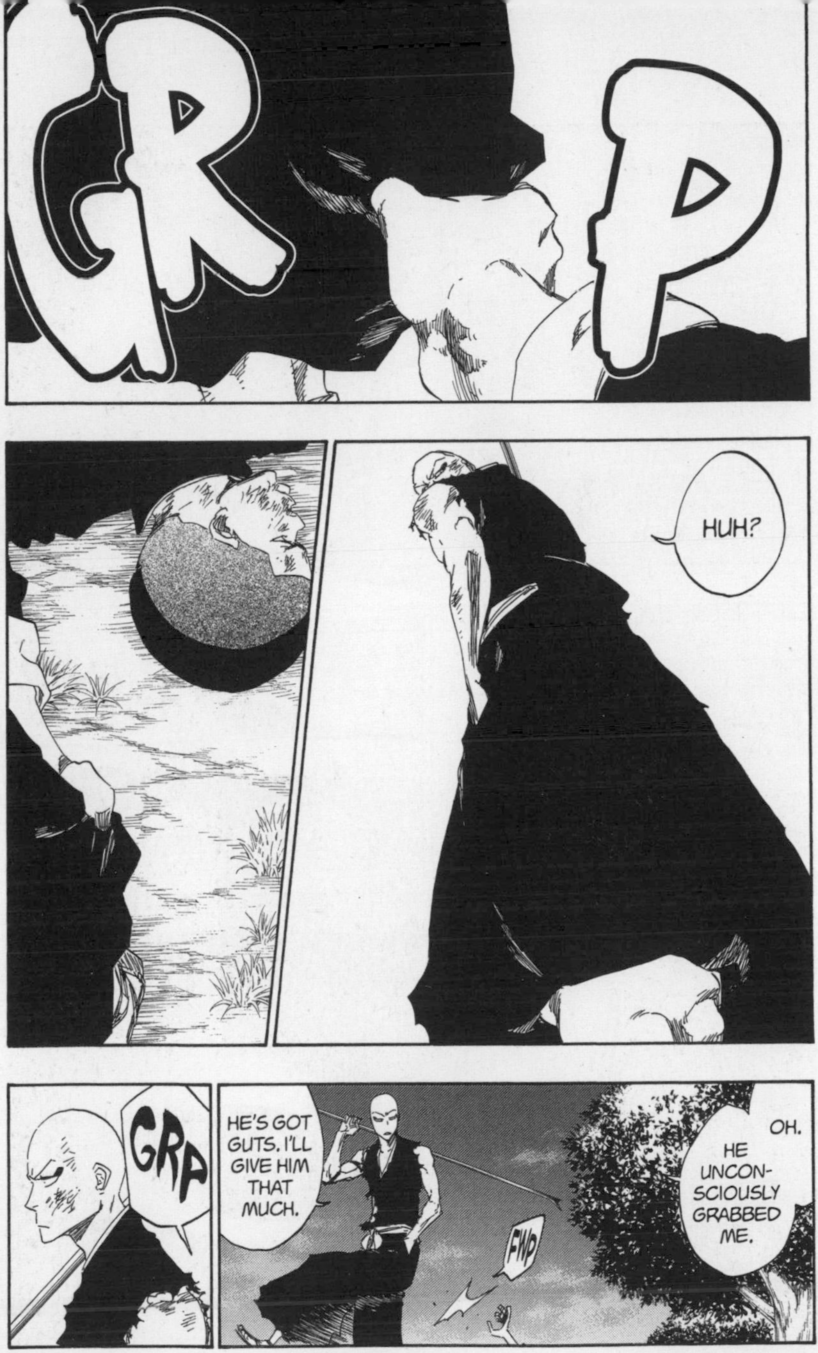
GRP
HUH?
OH.
HE UNCONSCIOUSLY GRABBED ME.
HE'S GOT GUTS. I'LL GIVE HIM THAT MUCH.
FWP
GRP

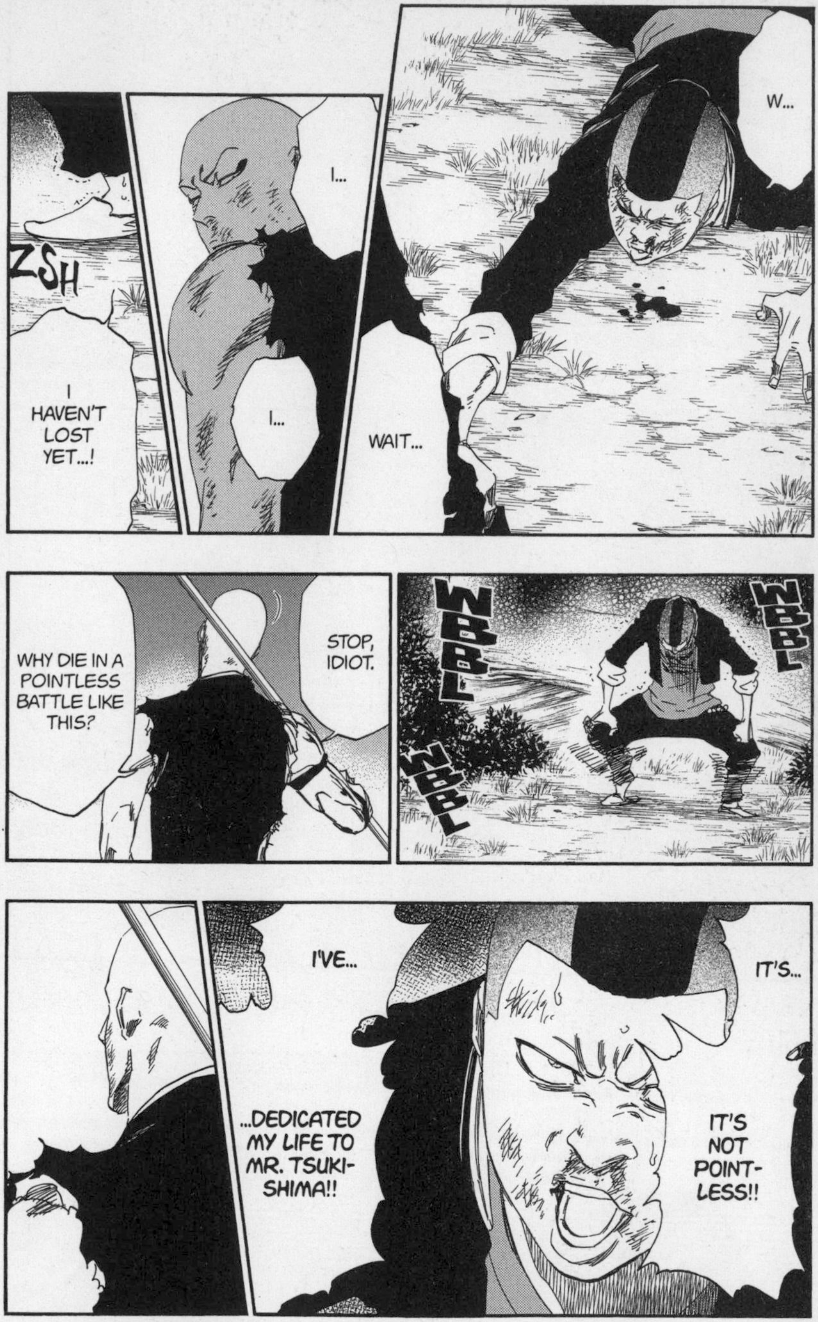
W...
WAIT...
I...
I...
ZSH
I HAVEN'T LOST YET...!
WBBL
WBBL
WBBL
STOP, IDIOT.
WHY DIE IN A POINTLESS BATTLE LIKE THIS?
IT'S...
IT'S NOT POINT-LESS!!
I'VE...
...DEDICATED MY LIFE TO MR. TSUKI-SHIMA!!

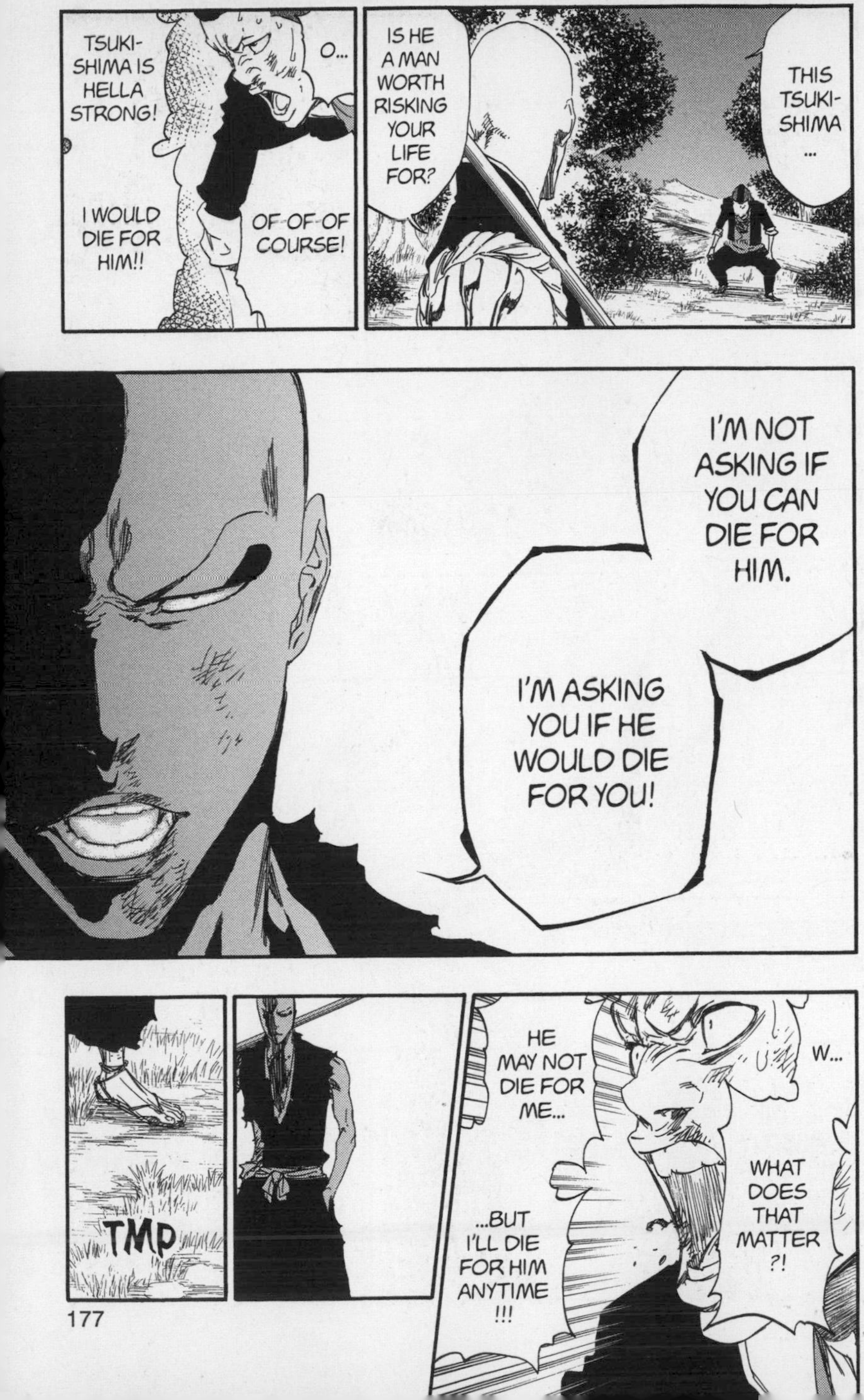
THIS TSUKI-SHIMA ...
IS HE A MAN WORTH RISKING YOUR LIFE FOR?
O...
TSUKI-SHIMA IS HELLA STRONG!
OF-OF-OF COURSE!
I WOULD DIE FOR HIM!!
I'M NOT ASKING IF YOU CAN DIE FOR HIM.
I'M ASKING YOU IF HE WOULD DIE FOR YOU!
W...
WHAT DOES THAT MATTER ?!
HE MAY NOT DIE FOR ME...
...BUT I'LL DIE FOR HIM ANYTIME !!!
TMP

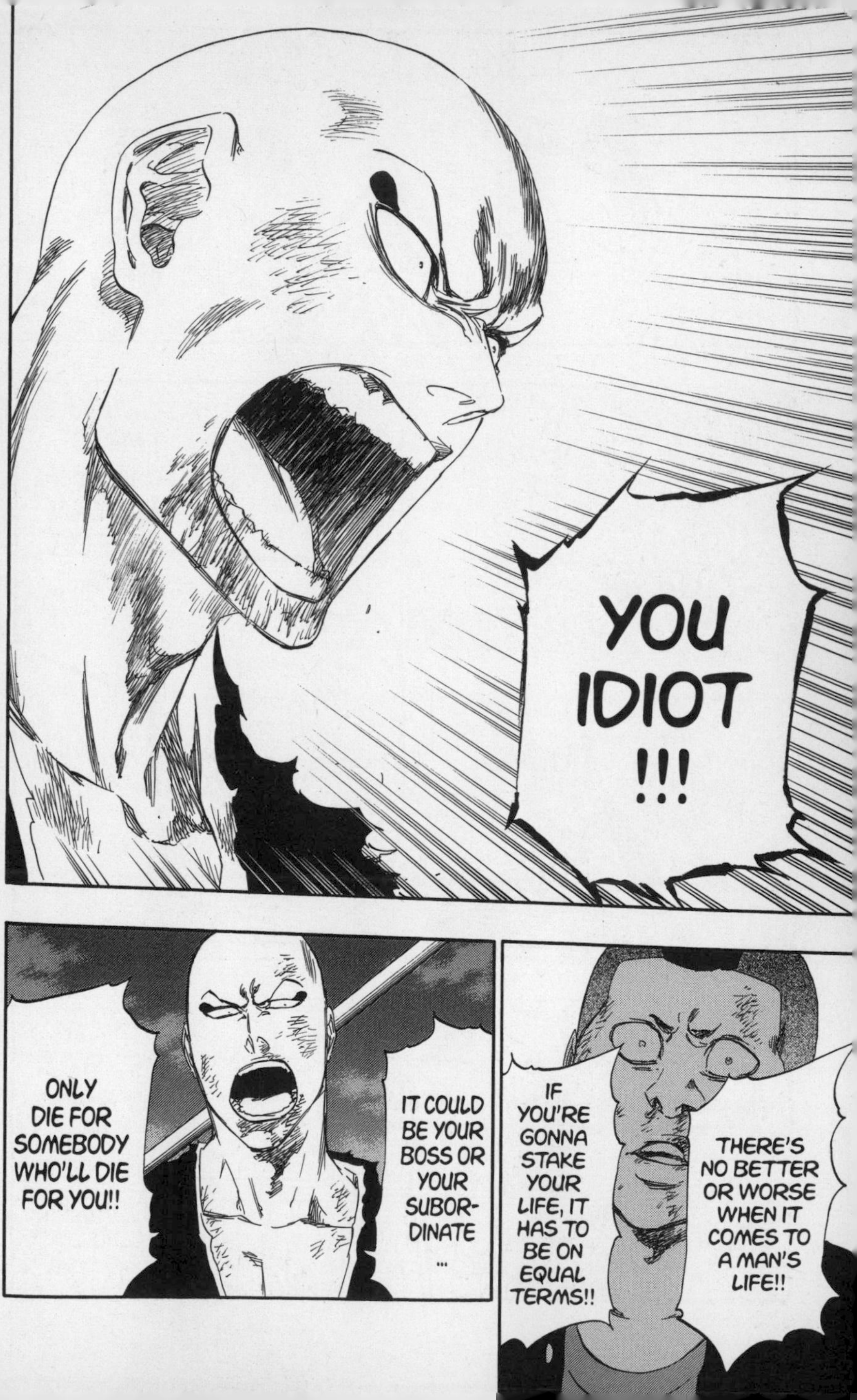
YOU IDIOT !!!
THERE'S NO BETTER OR WORSE WHEN IT COMES TO A MAN'S LIFE!!
IF YOU'RE GONNA STAKE YOUR LIFE, IT HAS TO BE ON EQUAL TERMS!!
IT COULD BE YOUR BOSS OR YOUR SUBOR-DINATE ...
ONLY DIE FOR SOMEBODY WHO'LL DIE FOR YOU!!

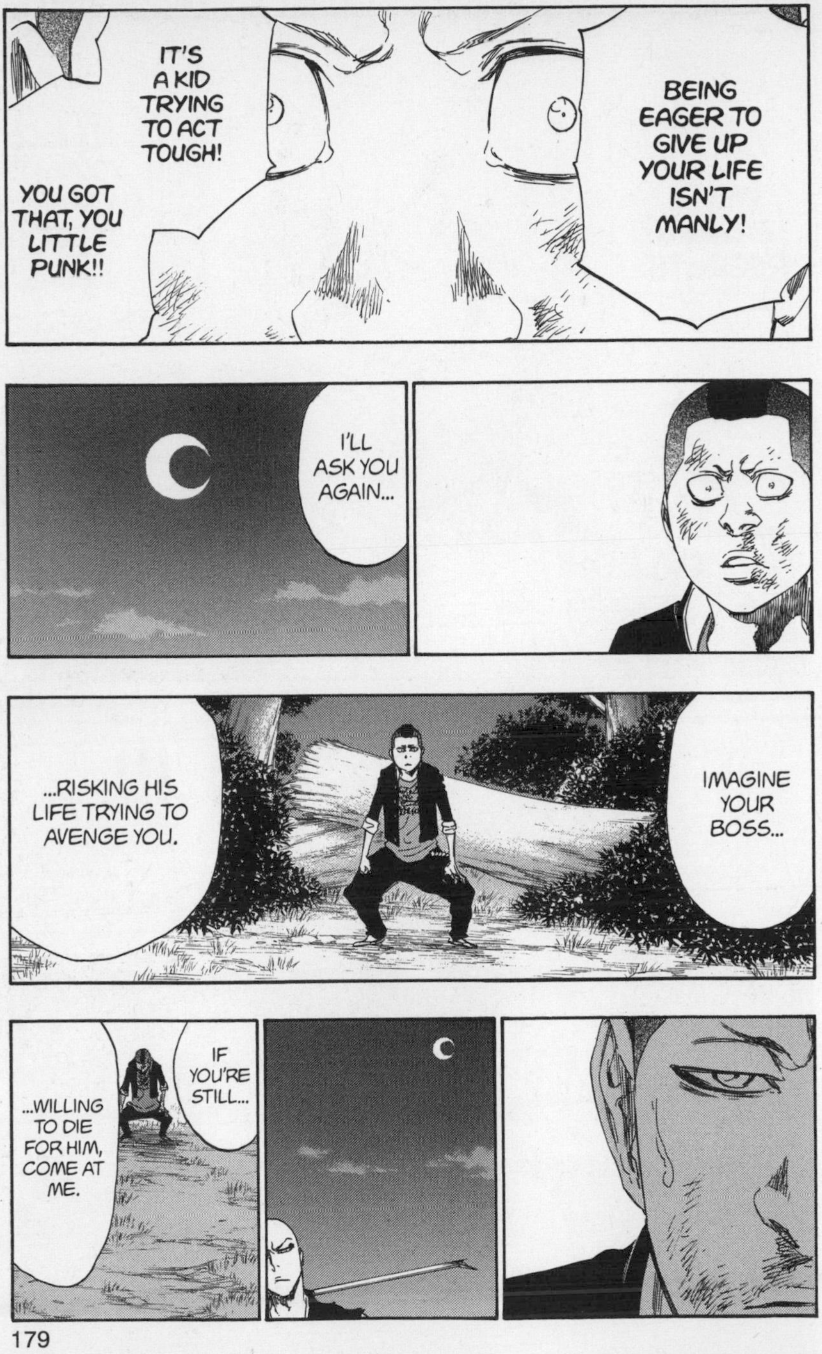
BEING EAGER TO GIVE UP YOUR LIFE ISN'T MANLY!
IT'S A KID TRYING TO ACT TOUGH!
YOU GOT THAT, YOU LITTLE PUNK!!
I'LL ASK YOU AGAIN...
IMAGINE YOUR BOSS...
...RISKING HIS LIFE TRYING TO AVENGE YOU.
IF YOU'RE STILL...
...WILLING TO DIE FOR HIM, COME AT ME.

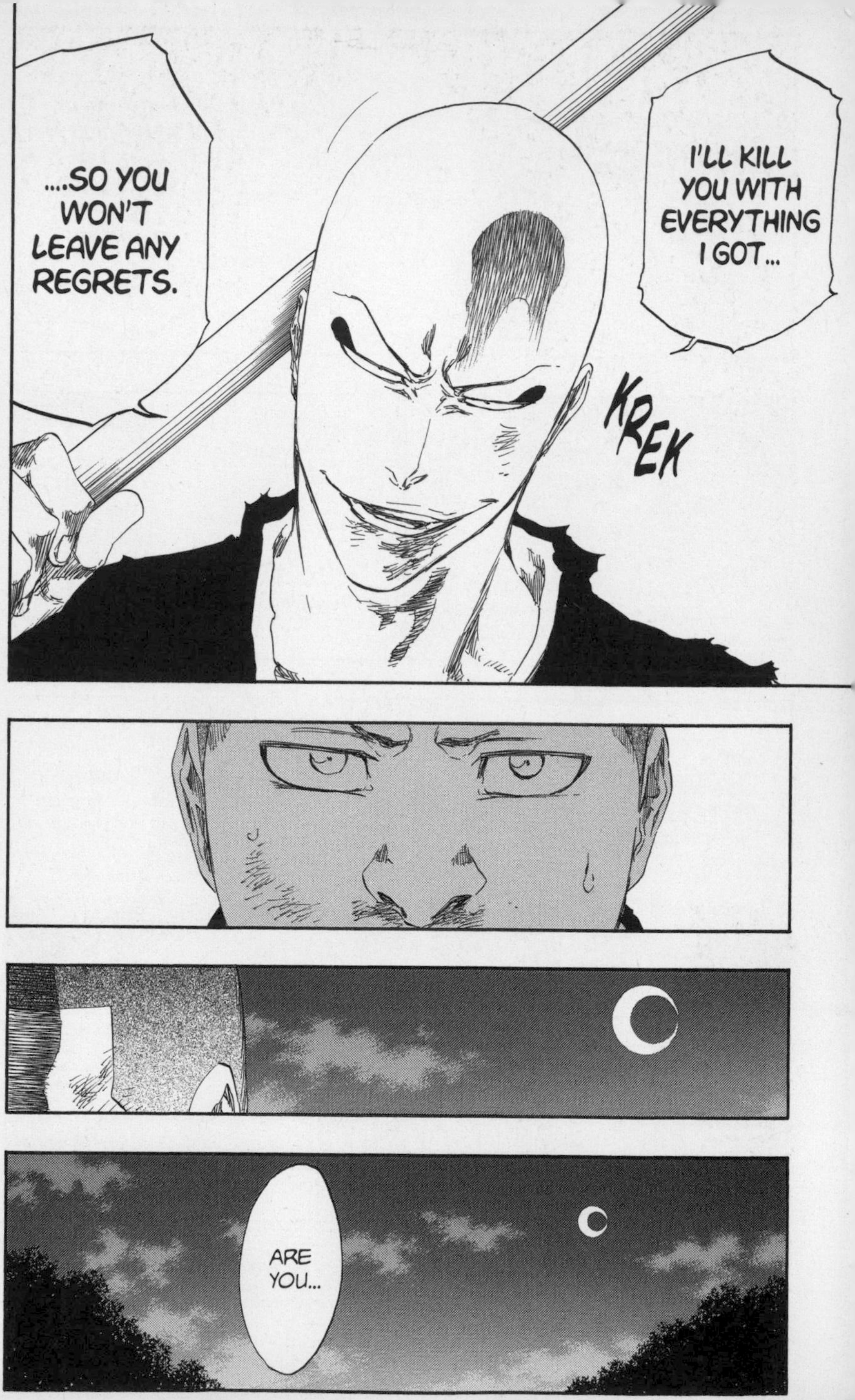
I'LL KILL YOU WITH EVERYTHING I GOT...
KREK
....SO YOU WON'T LEAVE ANY REGRETS.
ARE YOU...

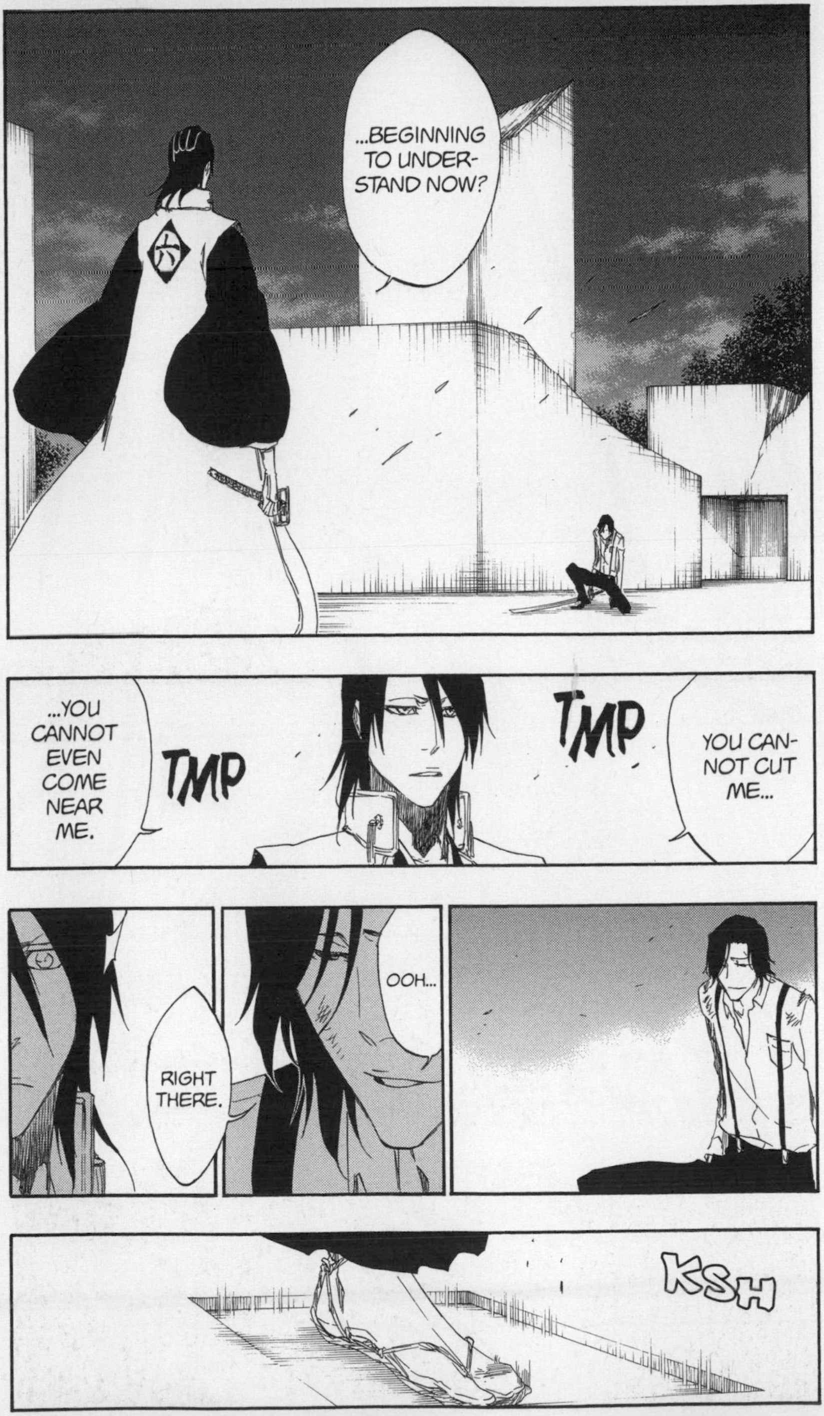
...BEGINNING TO UNDER-STAND NOW?
YOU CAN-NOT CUT ME...
TMP
TMP
...YOU CANNOT EVEN COME NEAR ME.
OOH...
RIGHT THERE.
KSH

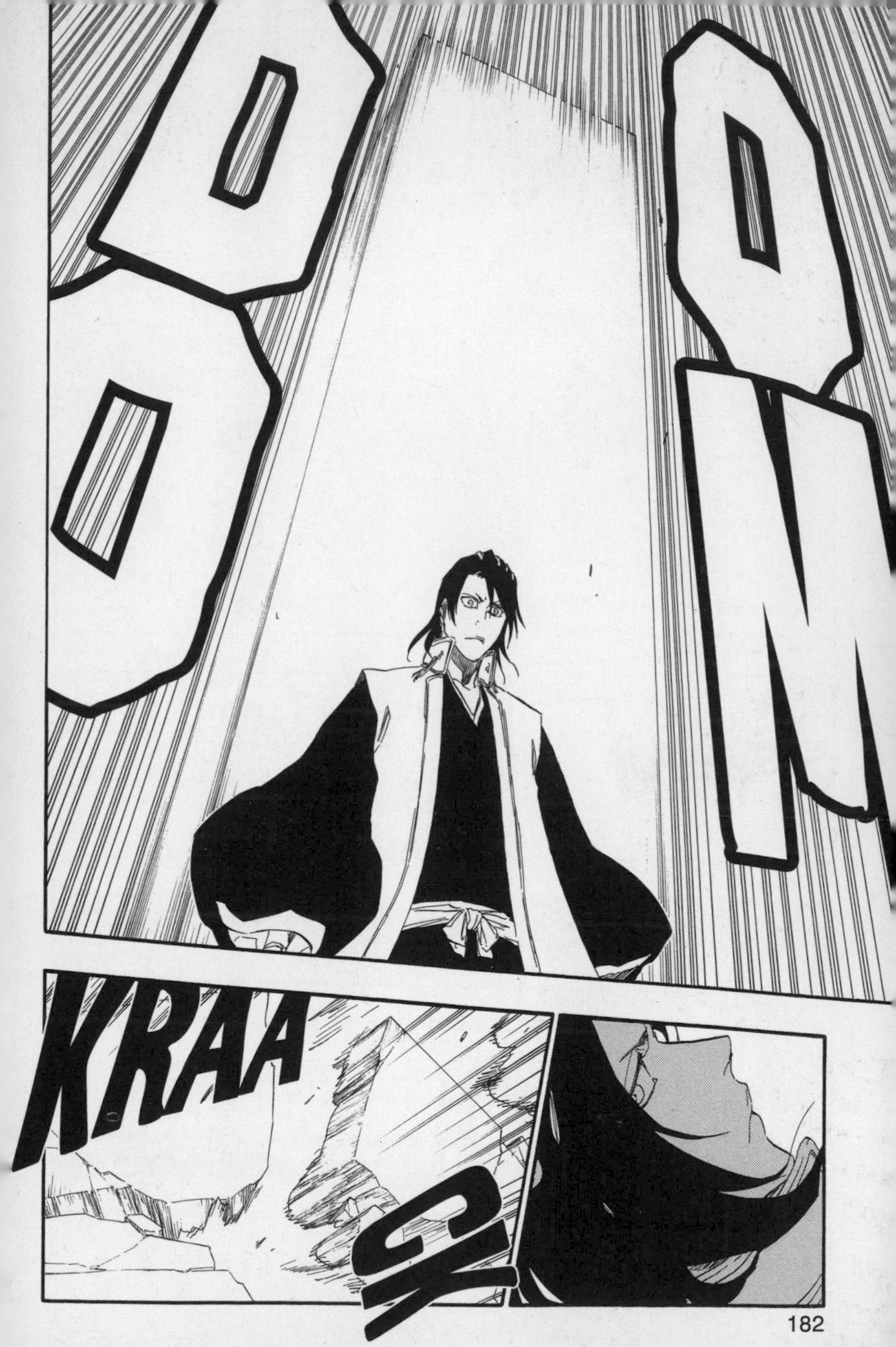
KRAACK

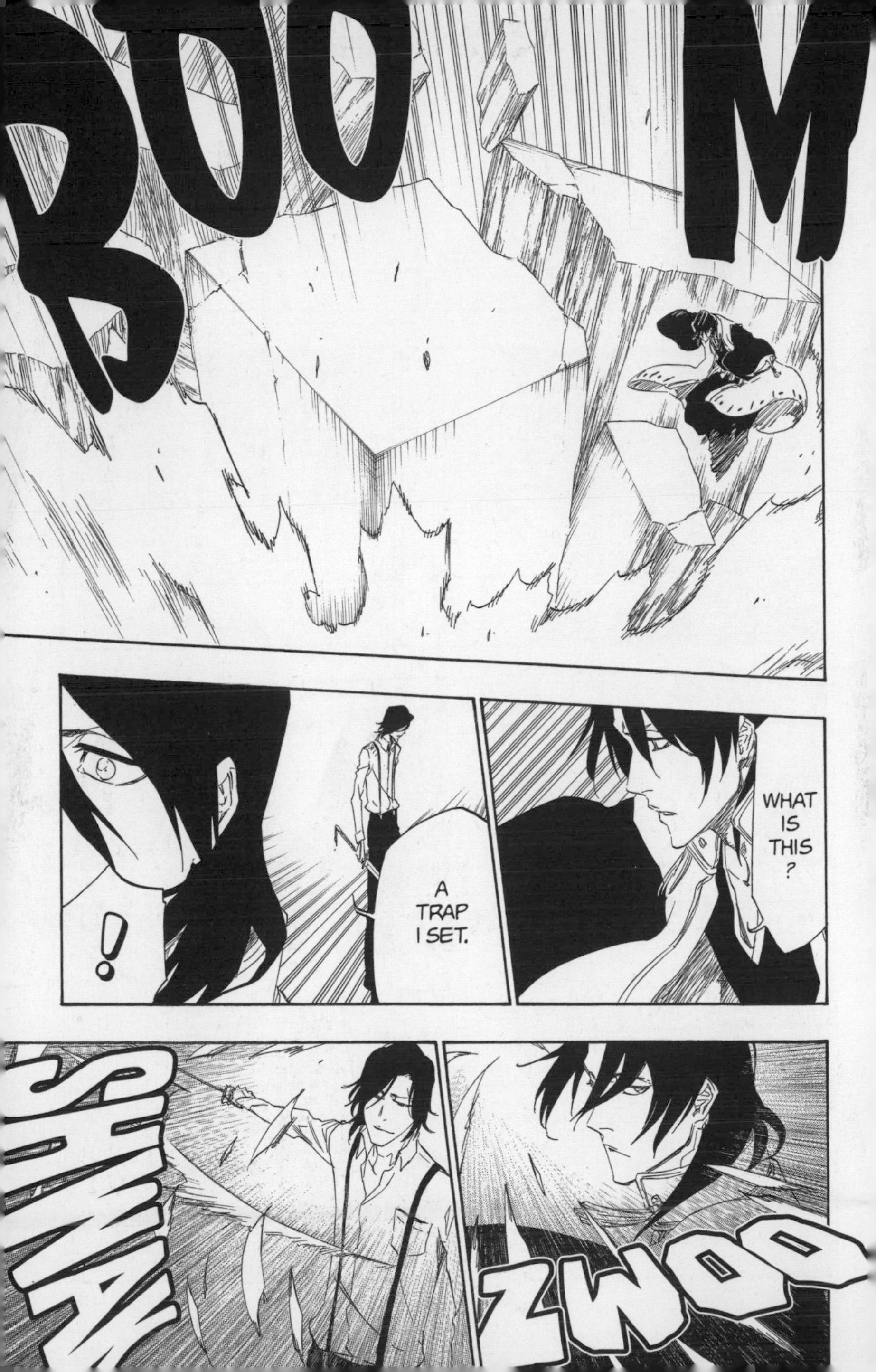
BOOM
WHAT IS THIS?
A TRAP I SET.
!
ZWOO
SHWAK

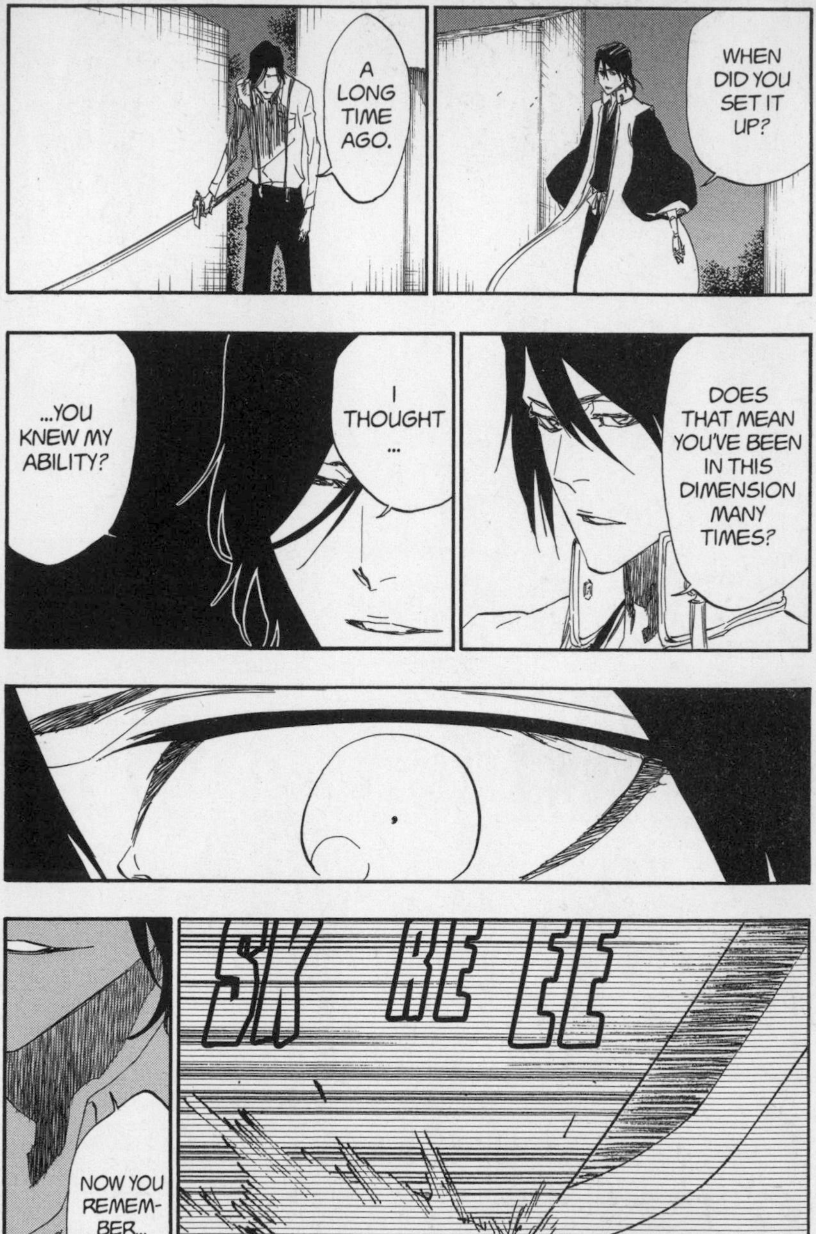
WHEN DID YOU SET IT UP?
A LONG TIME AGO.
DOES THAT MEAN YOU'VE BEEN IN THIS DIMENSION MANY TIMES?
I THOUGHT ...
...YOU KNEW MY ABILITY?
SKREEE
NOW YOU REMEMBER...

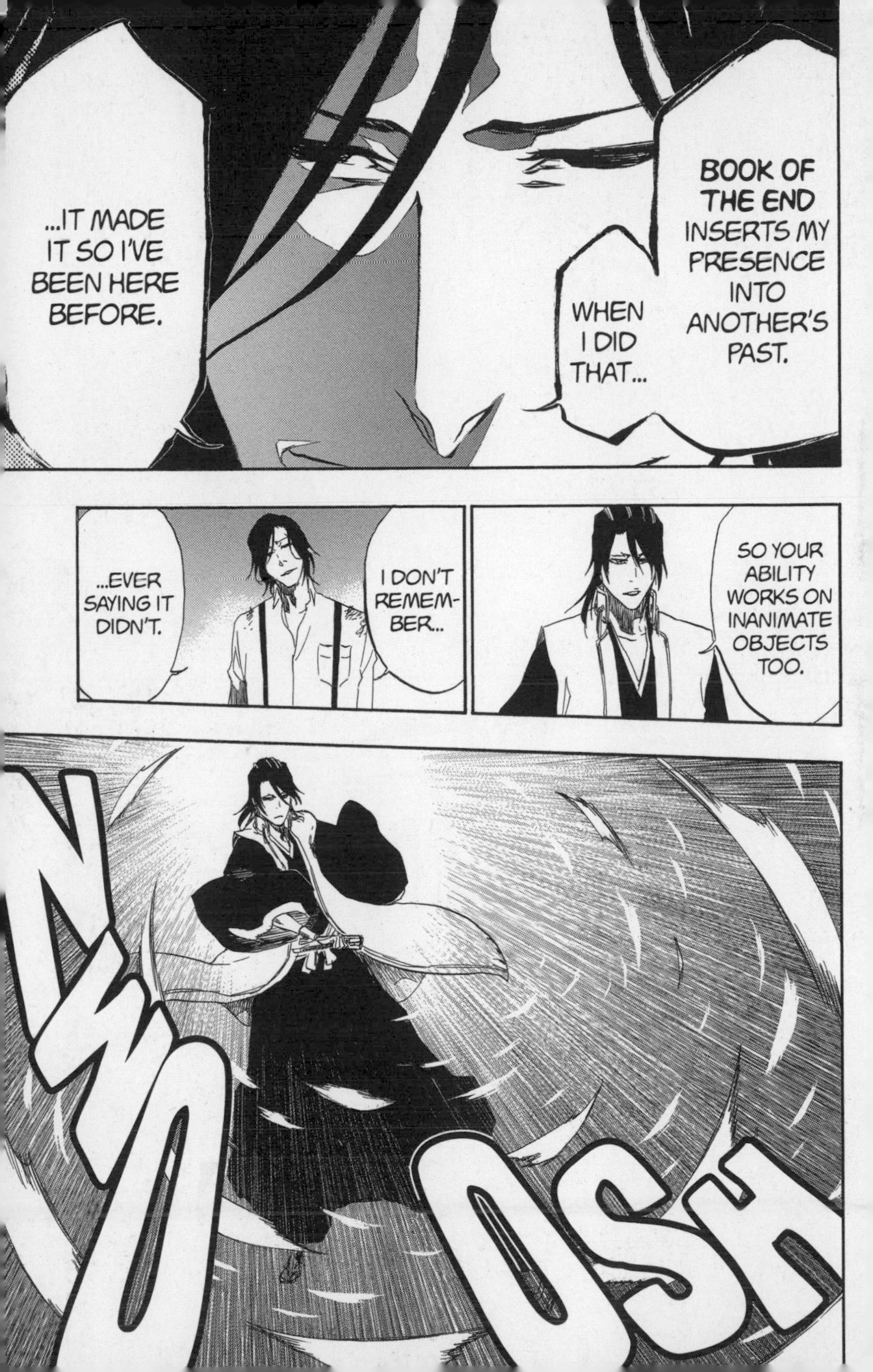
BOOK OF THE END INSERTS MY PRESENCE INTO ANOTHER'S PAST.
WHEN I DID THAT...
...IT MADE IT SO I'VE BEEN HERE BEFORE.
SO YOUR ABILITY WORKS ON INANIMATE OBJECTS TOO.
I DON'T REMEMBER...
...EVER SAYING IT DIDN'T.

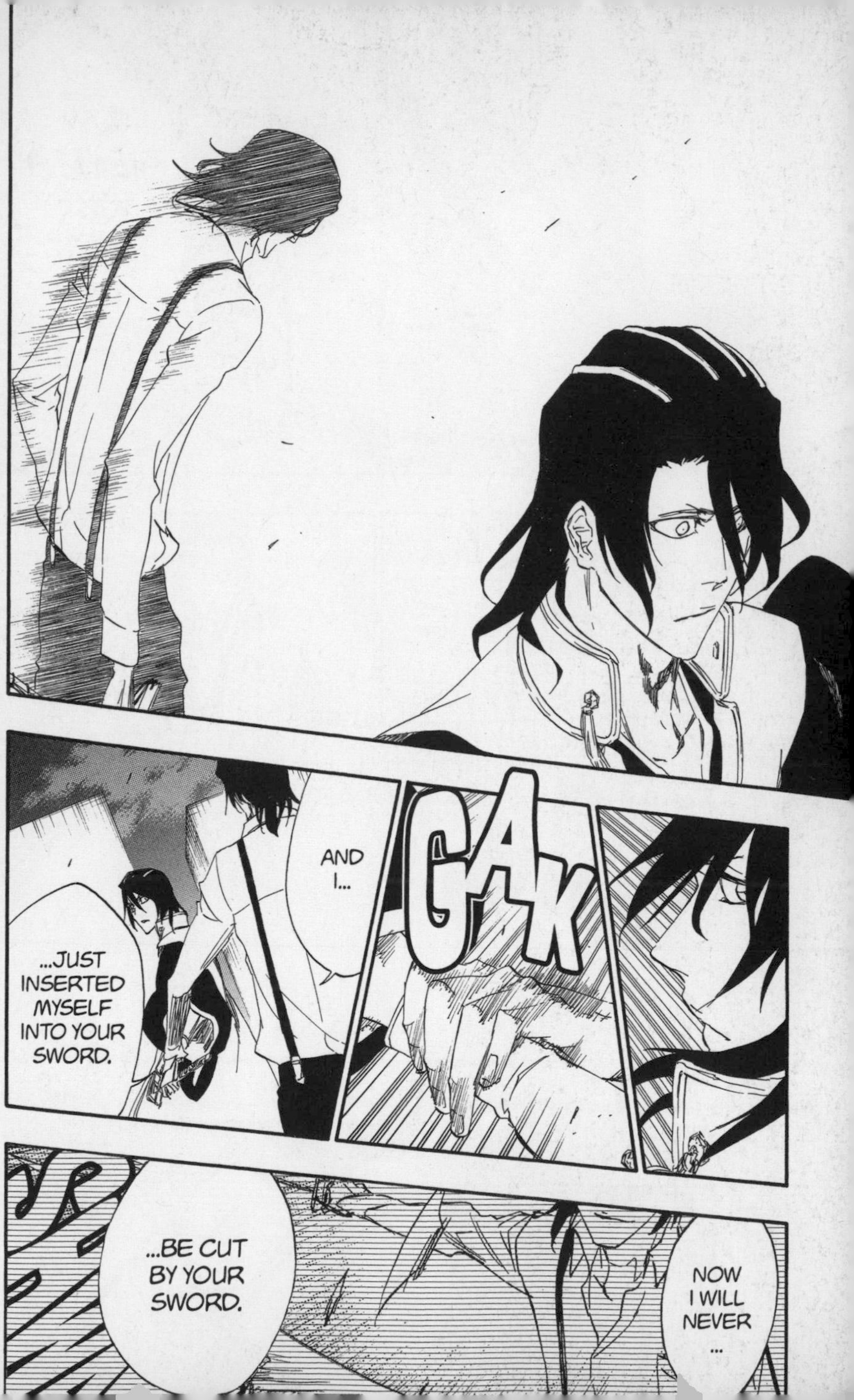
GAK
AND I...
...JUST INSERTED MYSELF INTO YOUR SWORD.
NOW I WILL NEVER ...
...BE CUT BY YOUR SWORD.

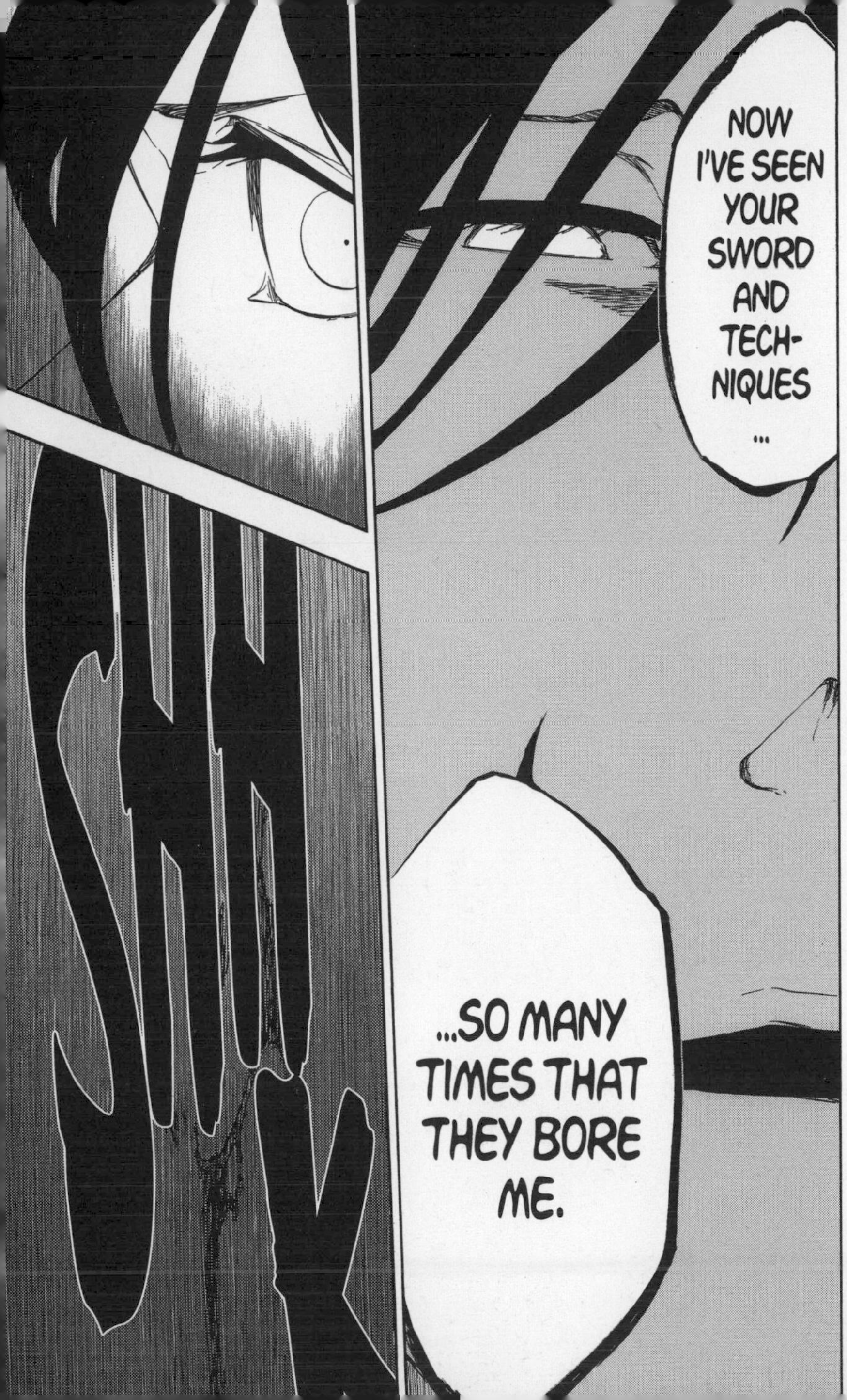
NOW I'VE SEEN YOUR SWORD AND TECH-NIQUES ...
...SO MANY TIMES THAT THEY BORE ME.

raid on you deep

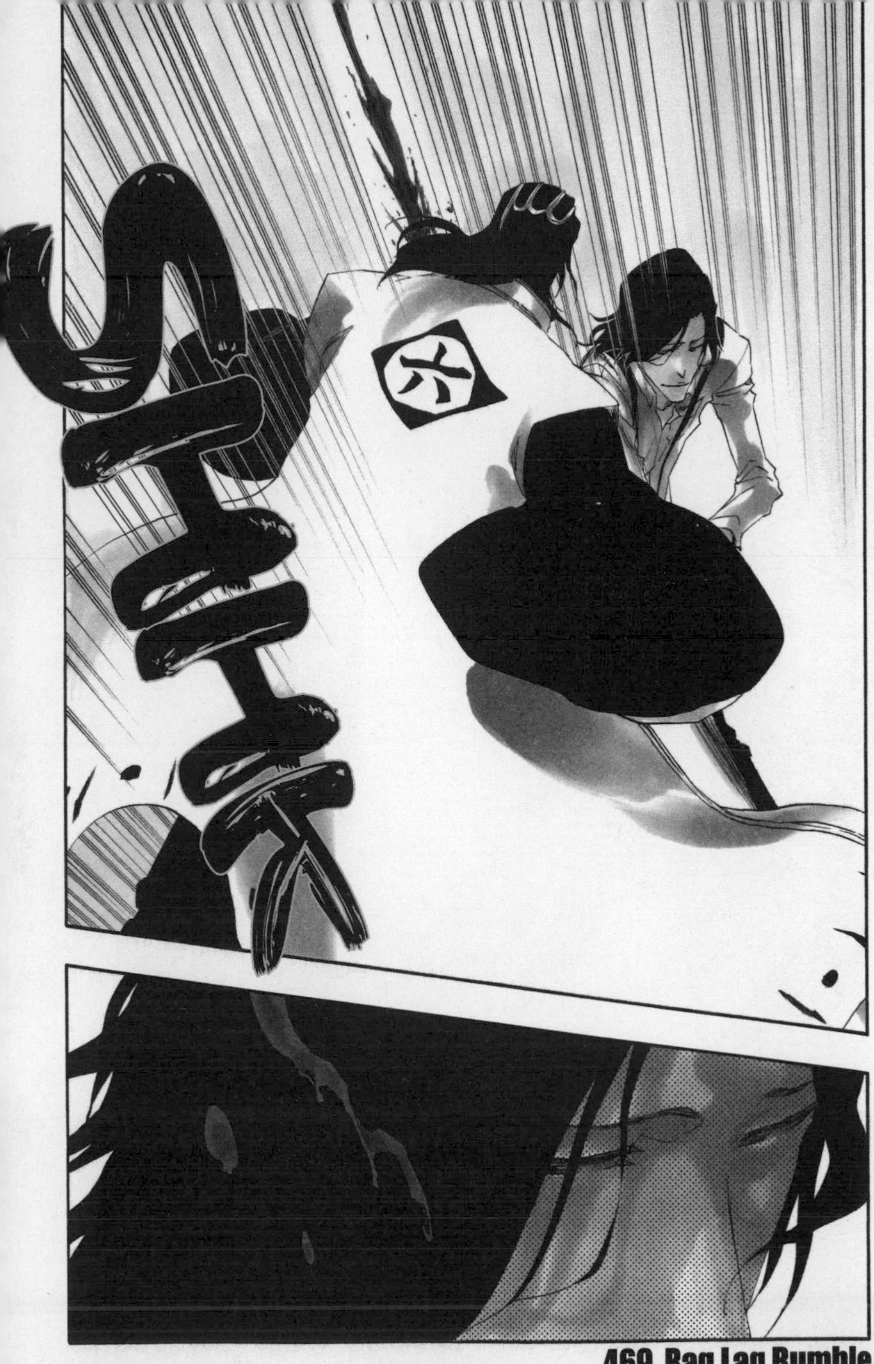

469. Rag Lag Rumble

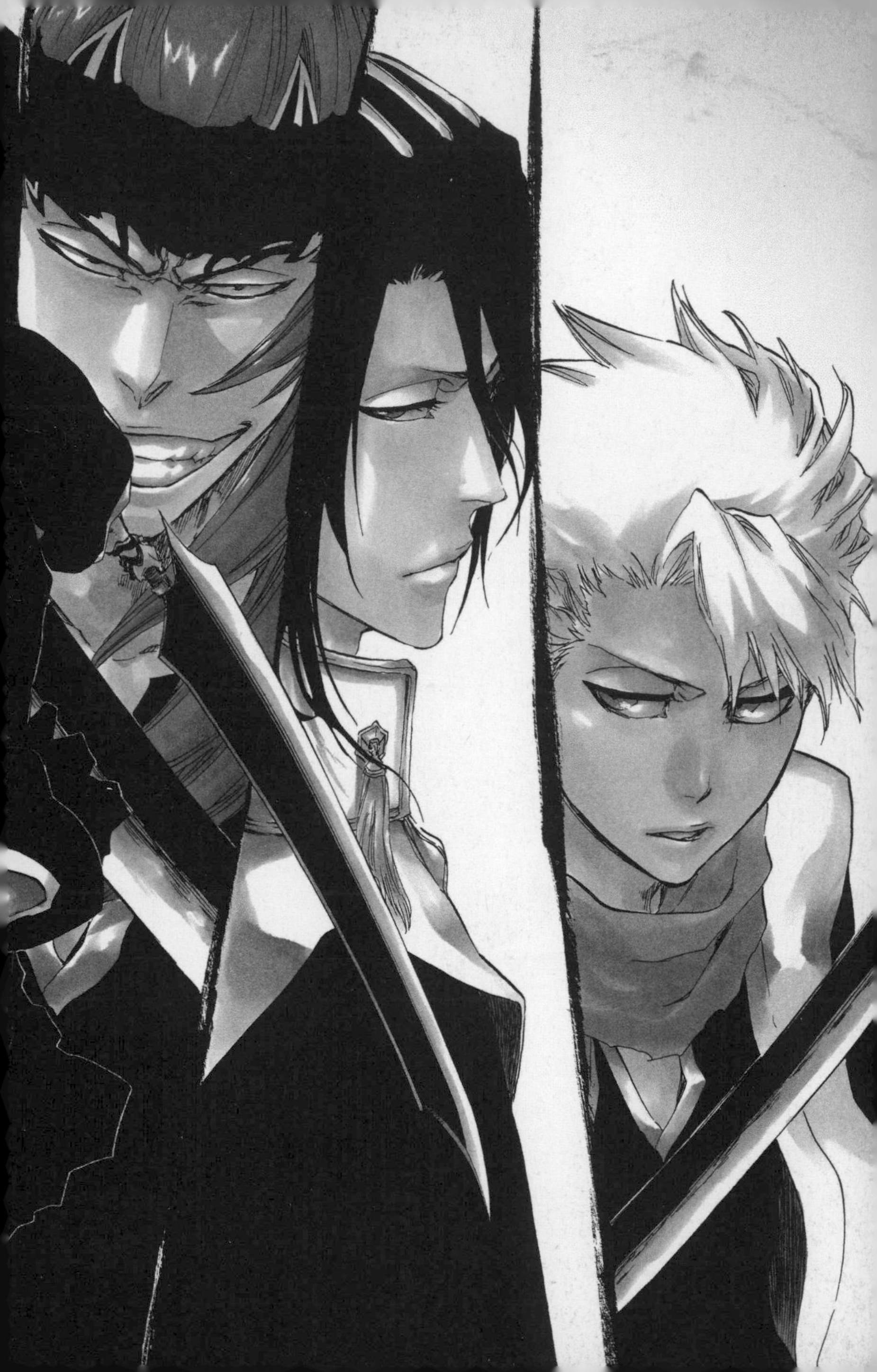

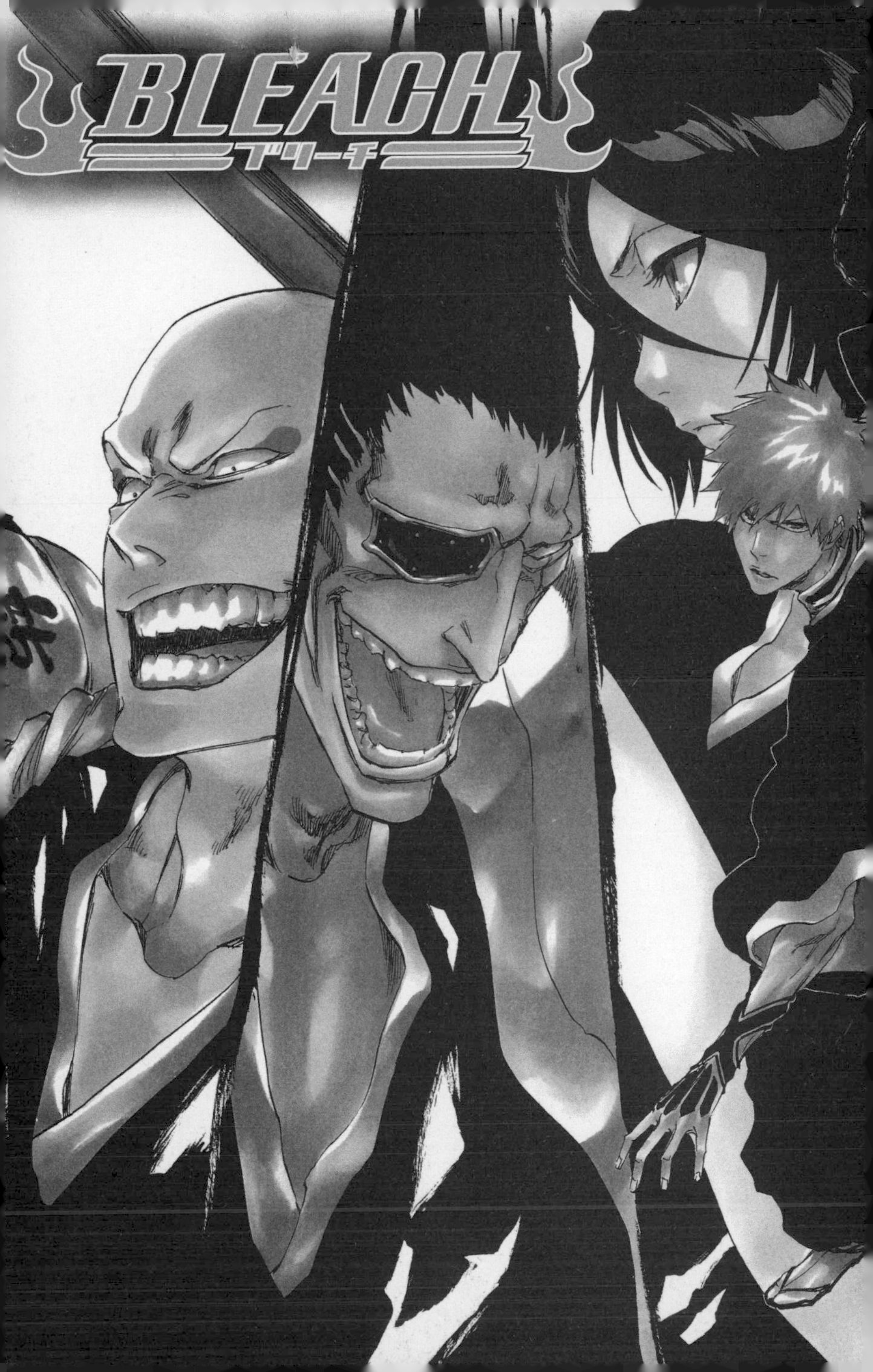
BLEACH
ブリーチ

BLEACH
ブリーチ

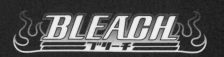

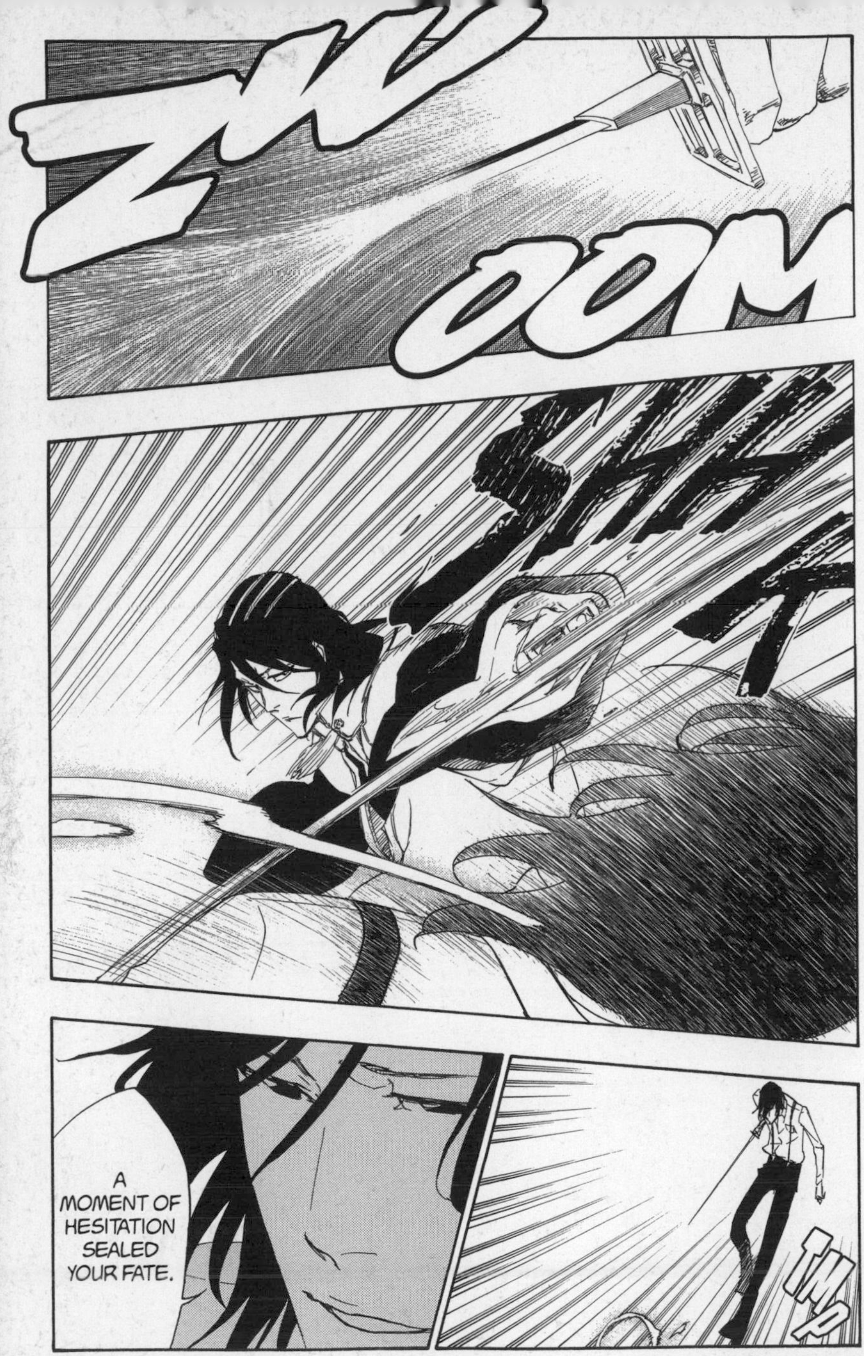
ZWOOM
TMP
A MOMENT OF HESITATION SEALED YOUR FATE.

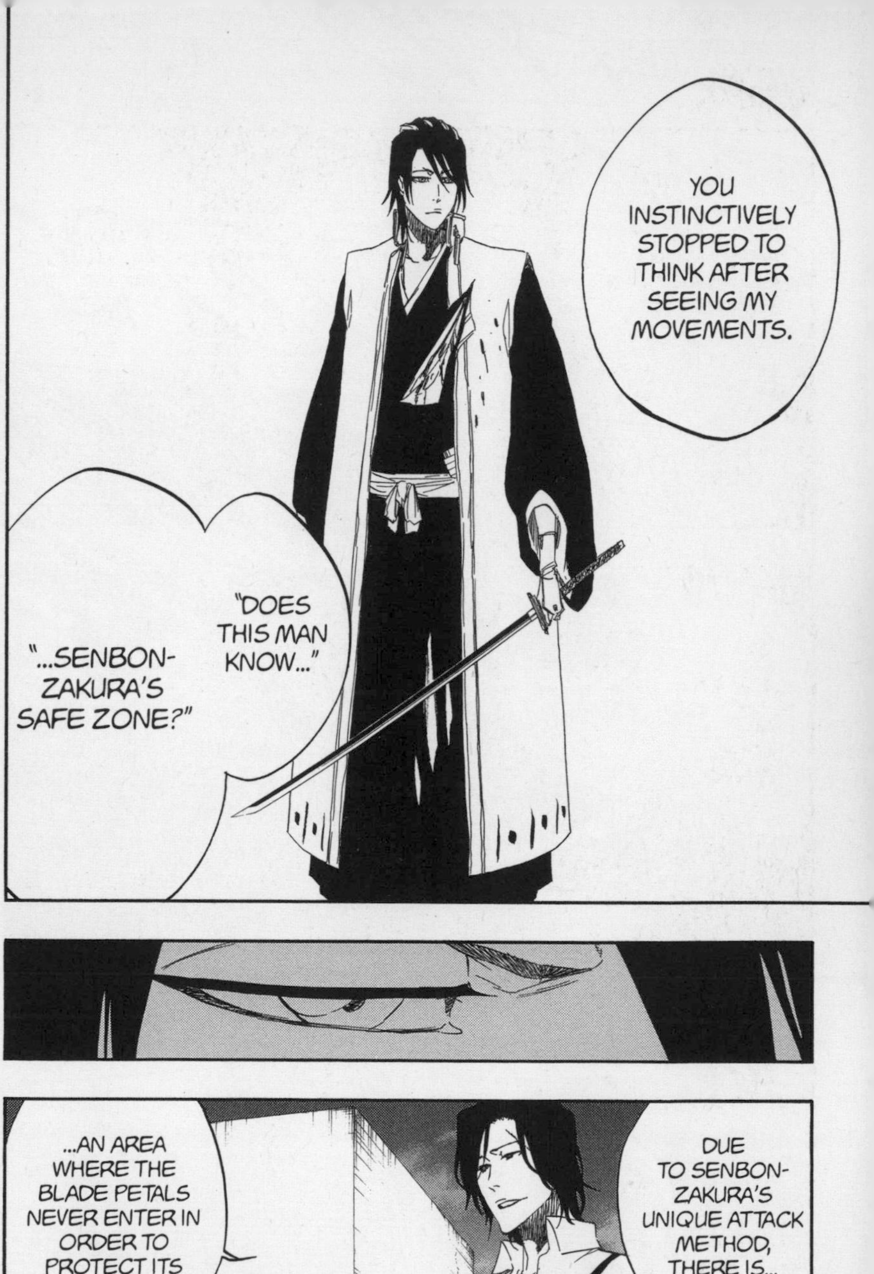
YOU INSTINCTIVELY STOPPED TO THINK AFTER SEEING MY MOVEMENTS.
"DOES THIS MAN KNOW..."
"...SENBON-ZAKURA'S SAFE ZONE?"
DUE TO SENBON-ZAKURA'S UNIQUE ATTACK METHOD, THERE IS...
...AN AREA WHERE THE BLADE PETALS NEVER ENTER IN ORDER TO PROTECT ITS USER.

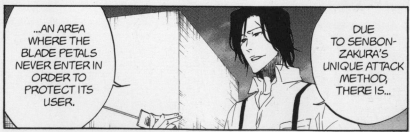

READ THIS WAY

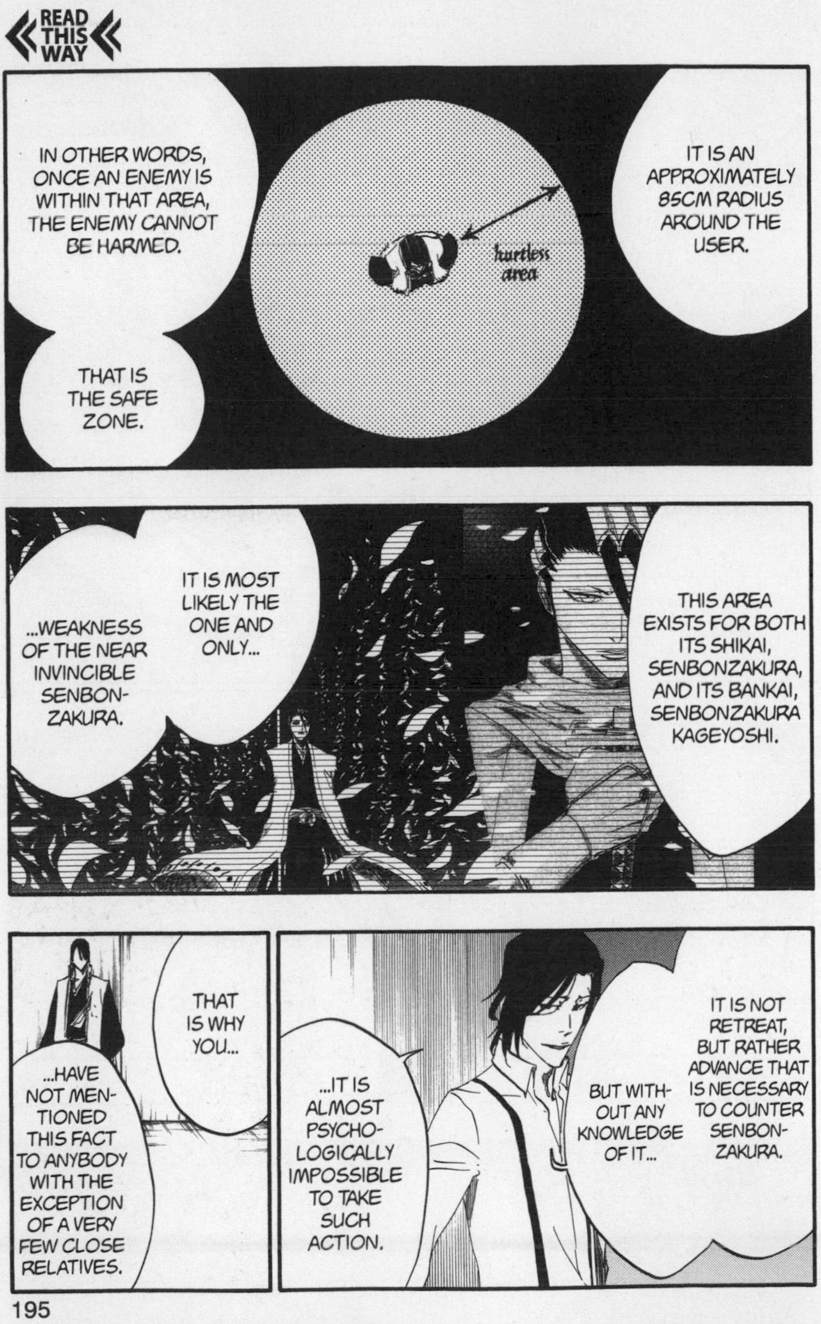
IT IS AN APPROXIMATELY 85CM RADIUS AROUND THE USER.
hurtless area
IN OTHER WORDS, ONCE AN ENEMY IS WITHIN THAT AREA, THE ENEMY CANNOT BE HARMED.
THAT IS THE SAFE ZONE.
THIS AREA EXISTS FOR BOTH ITS SHIKAI, SENBONZAKURA, AND ITS BANKAI, SENBONZAKURA KAGEYOSHI.
IT IS MOST LIKELY THE ONE AND ONLY...
...WEAKNESS OF THE NEAR INVINCIBLE SENBON-ZAKURA.
IT IS NOT RETREAT, BUT RATHER ADVANCE THAT IS NECESSARY TO COUNTER SENBON-ZAKURA.
BUT WITH-OUT ANY KNOWLEDGE OF IT...
...IT IS ALMOST PSYCHO-LOGICALLY IMPOSSIBLE TO TAKE SUCH ACTION.
THAT IS WHY YOU...
...HAVE NOT MEN-TIONED THIS FACT TO ANYBODY WITH THE EXCEPTION OF A VERY FEW CLOSE RELATIVES.

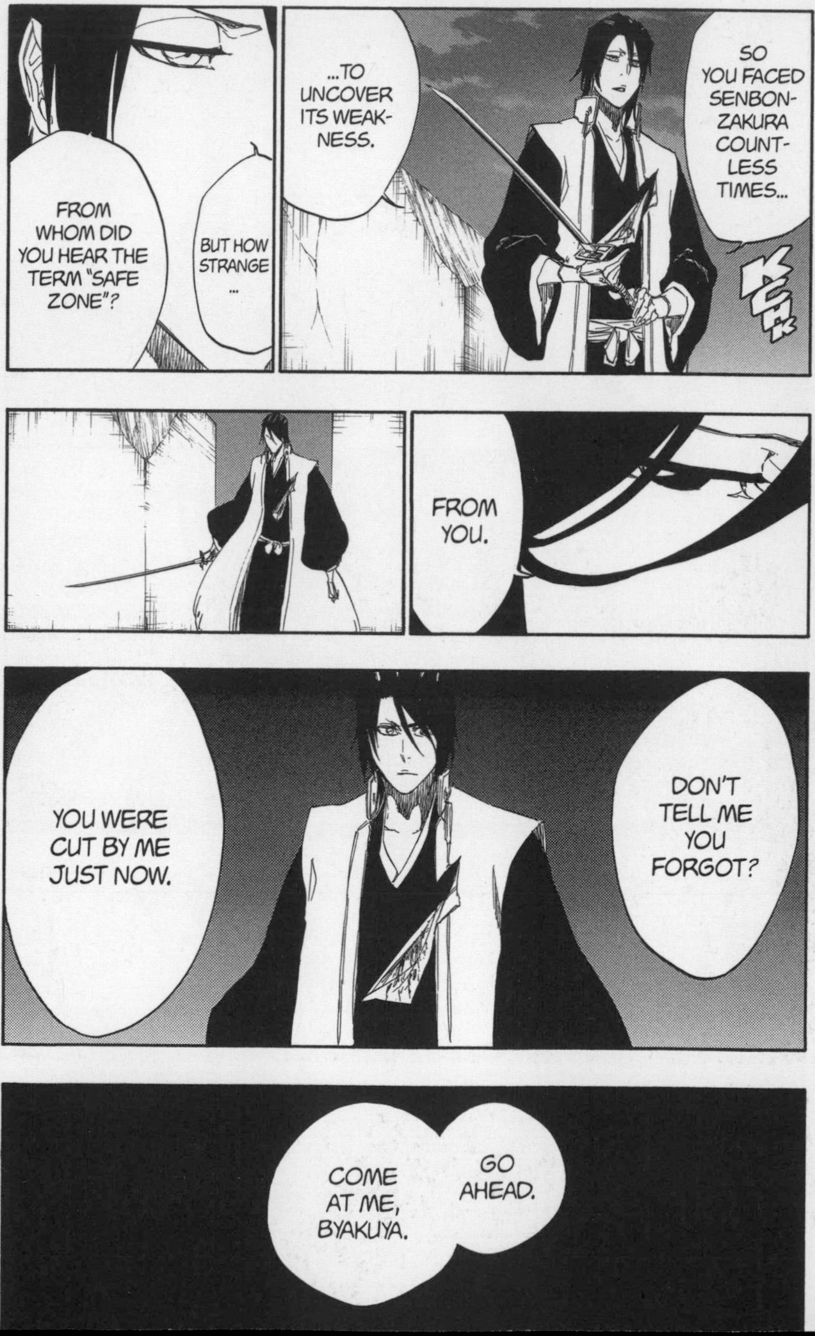
SO YOU FACED SENBON-ZAKURA COUNTLESS TIMES...
KCHK
...TO UNCOVER ITS WEAKNESS.
BUT HOW STRANGE...
FROM WHOM DID YOU HEAR THE TERM "SAFE ZONE"?
FROM YOU.
DON'T TELL ME YOU FORGOT?
YOU WERE CUT BY ME JUST NOW.
GO AHEAD.
COME AT ME, BYAKUYA.

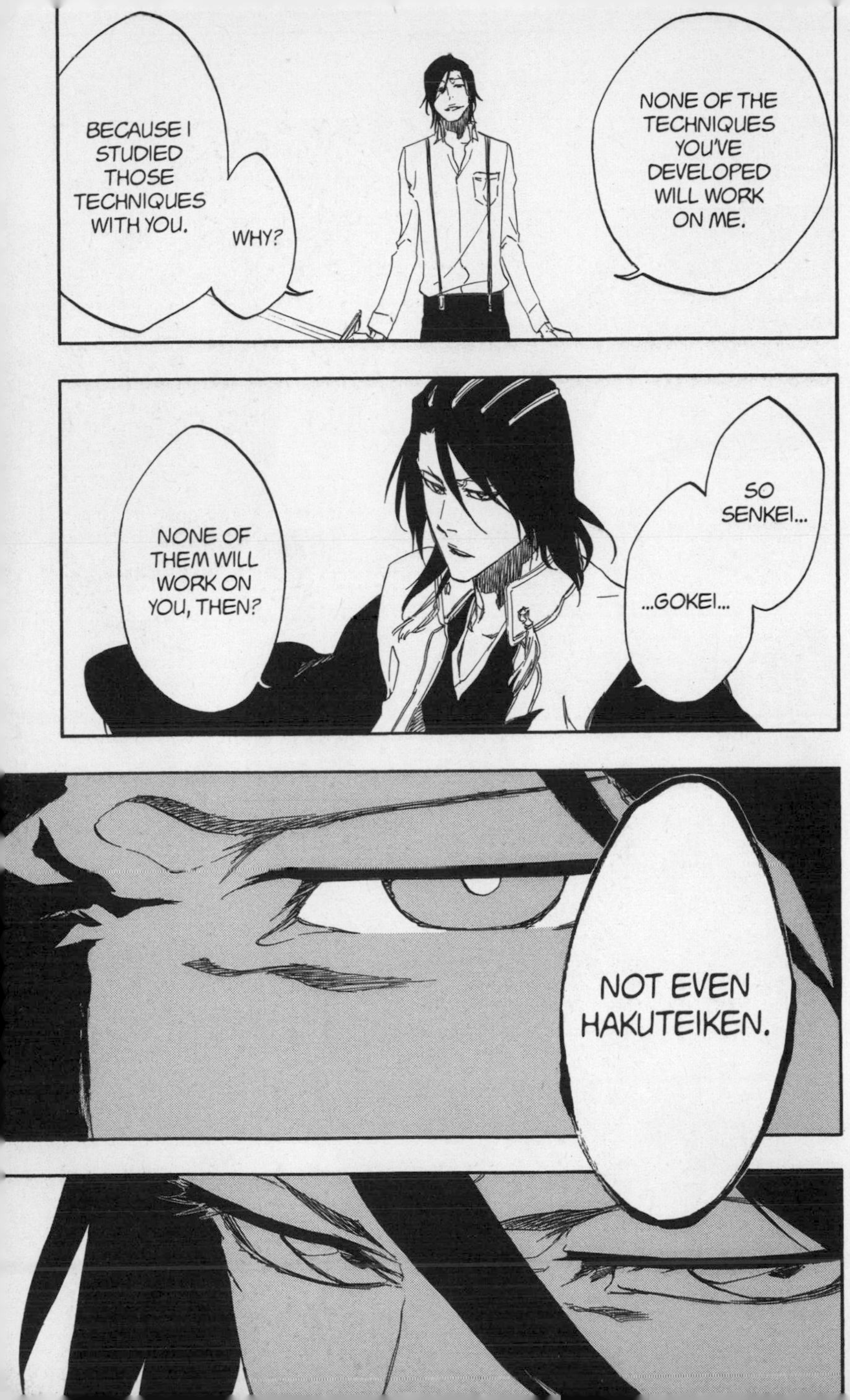
NONE OF THE TECHNIQUES YOU'VE DEVELOPED WILL WORK ON ME.
WHY?
BECAUSE I STUDIED THOSE TECHNIQUES WITH YOU.
SO SENKEI...
...GOKEI...
NONE OF THEM WILL WORK ON YOU, THEN?
NOT EVEN HAKUTEIKEN.

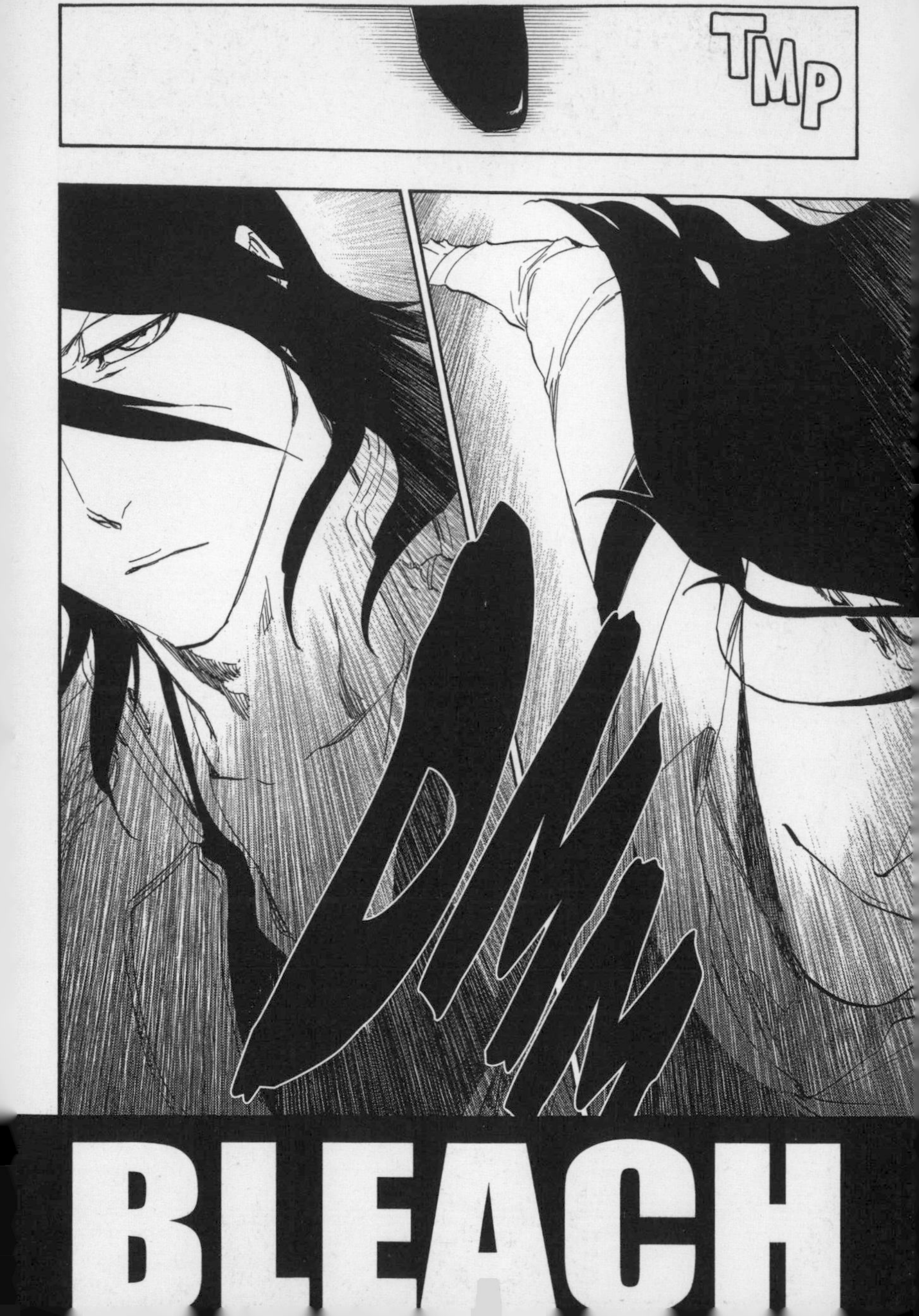
TMP
DMM
BLEACH

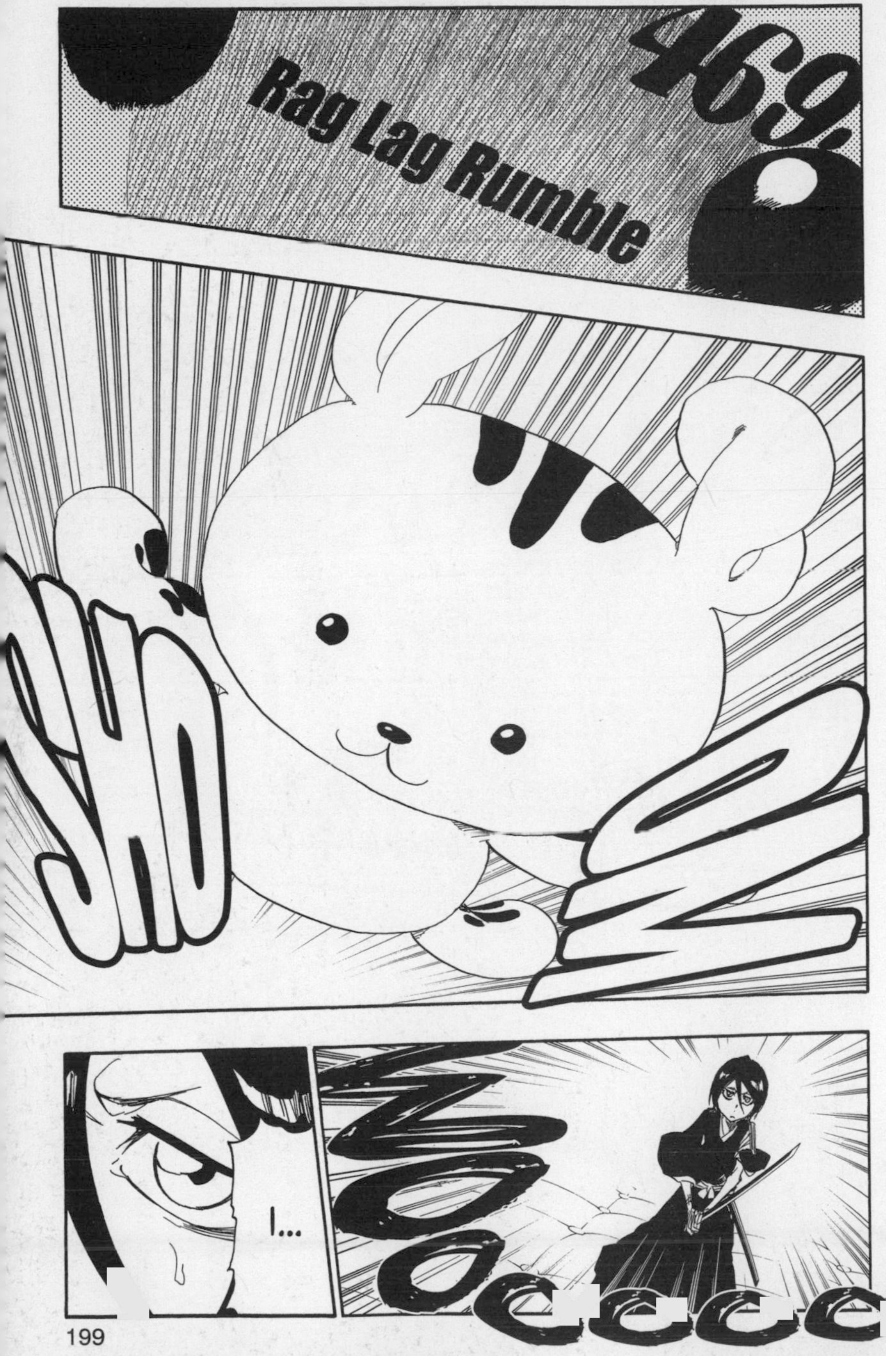
469.
Rag Lag Rumble
I...

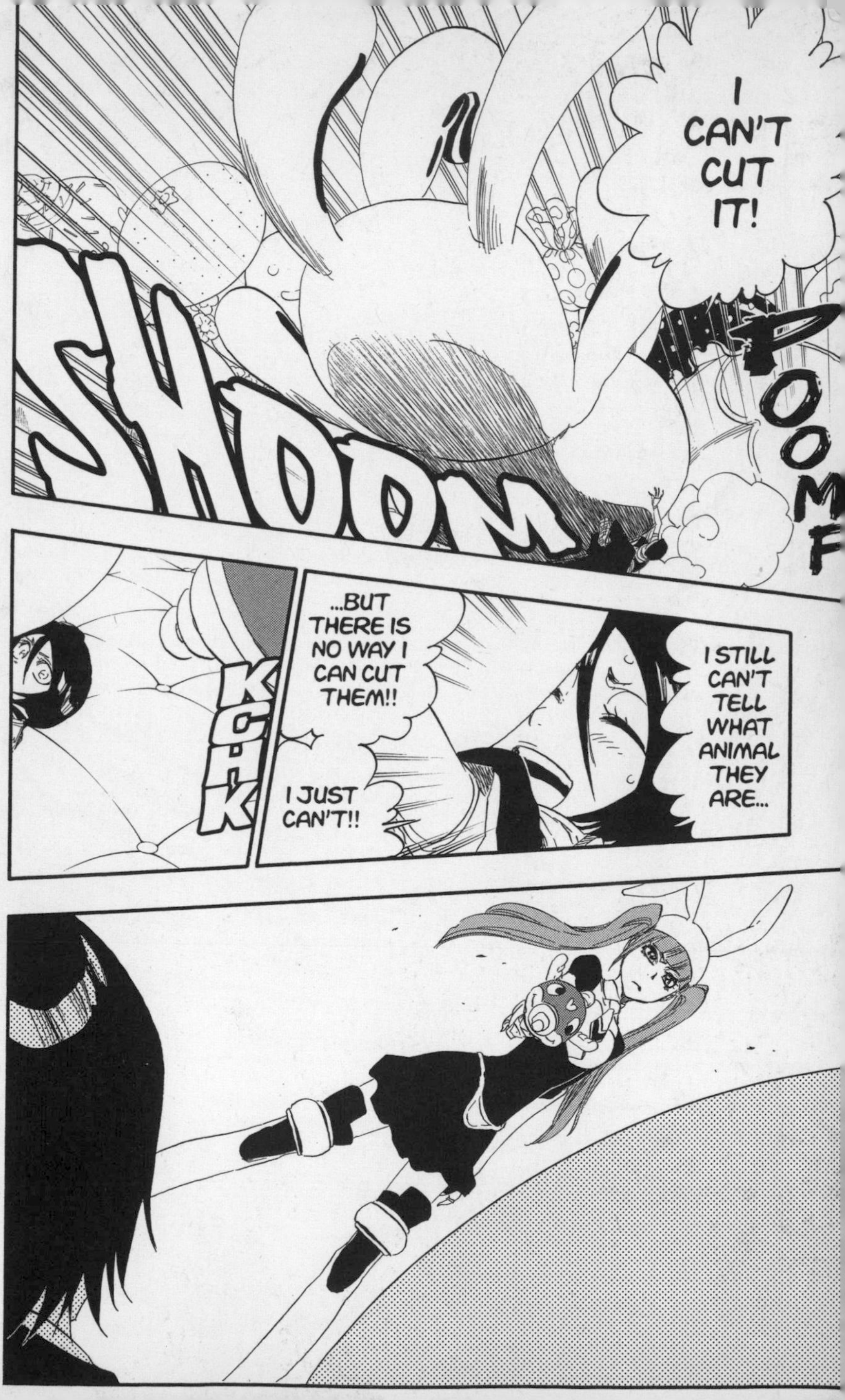
I CAN'T CUT IT!
POOMF
SHOOM
I STILL CAN'T TELL WHAT ANIMAL THEY ARE...
...BUT THERE IS NO WAY I CAN CUT THEM!!
I JUST CAN'T!!
KCHK

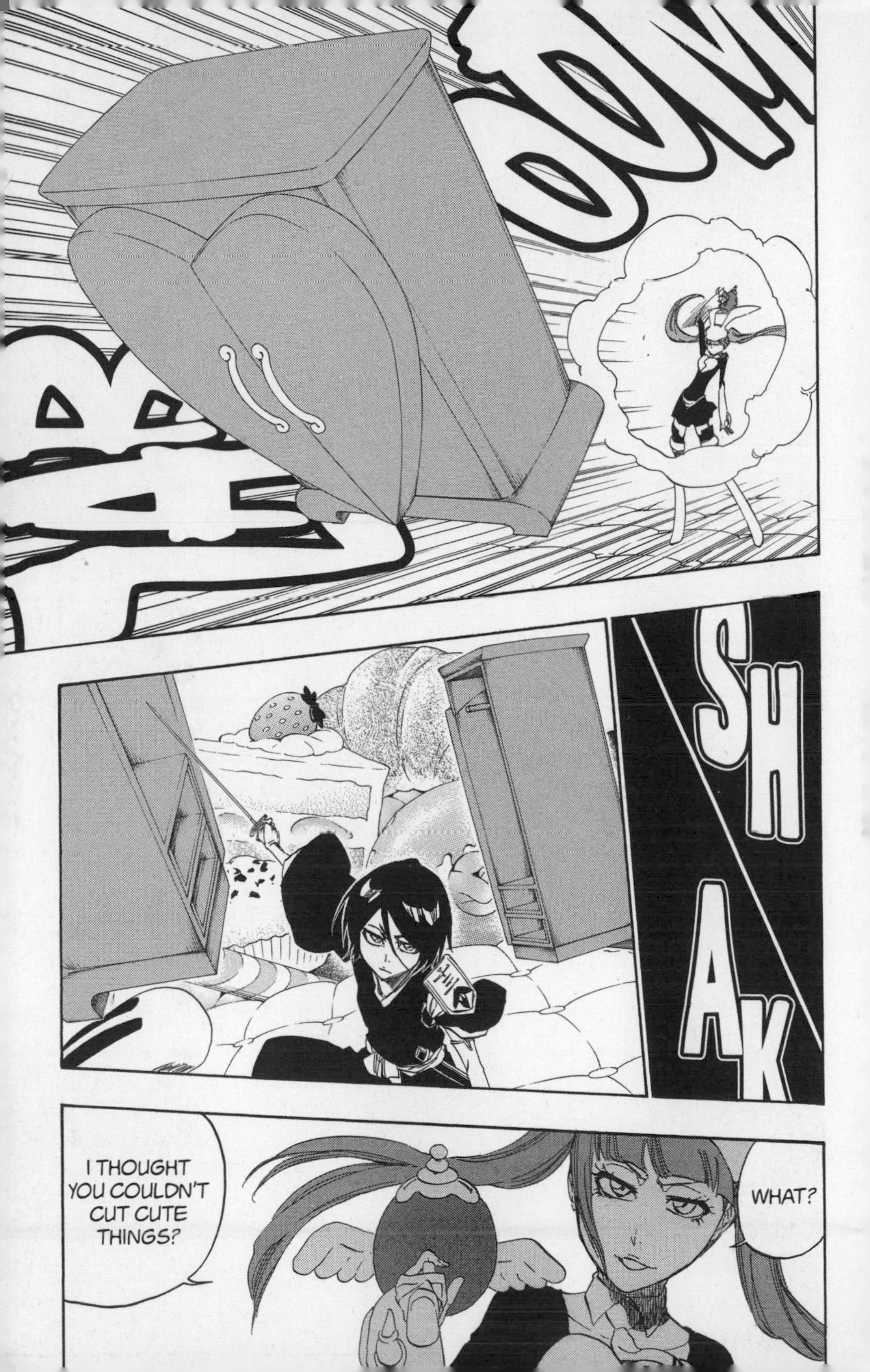
SHAAK
WHAT?
I THOUGHT YOU COULDN'T CUT CUTE THINGS?

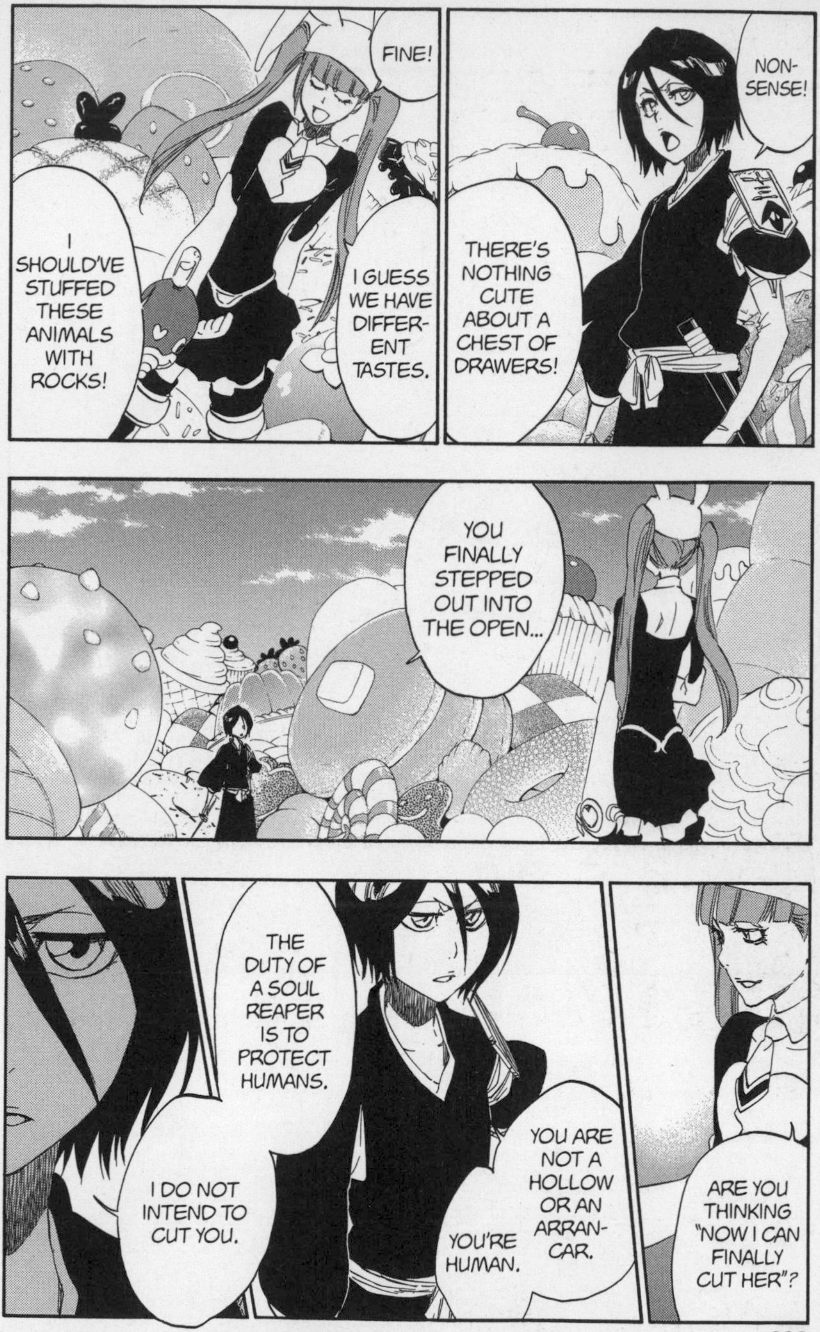
NON-SENSE!
THERE'S NOTHING CUTE ABOUT A CHEST OF DRAWERS!
FINE!
I GUESS WE HAVE DIFFER-ENT TASTES.
I SHOULD'VE STUFFED THESE ANIMALS WITH ROCKS!
YOU FINALLY STEPPED OUT INTO THE OPEN...
ARE YOU THINKING "NOW I CAN FINALLY CUT HER"?
YOU ARE NOT A HOLLOW OR AN ARRAN-CAR.
YOU'RE HUMAN.
THE DUTY OF A SOUL REAPER IS TO PROTECT HUMANS.
I DO NOT INTEND TO CUT YOU.

READ THIS WAY

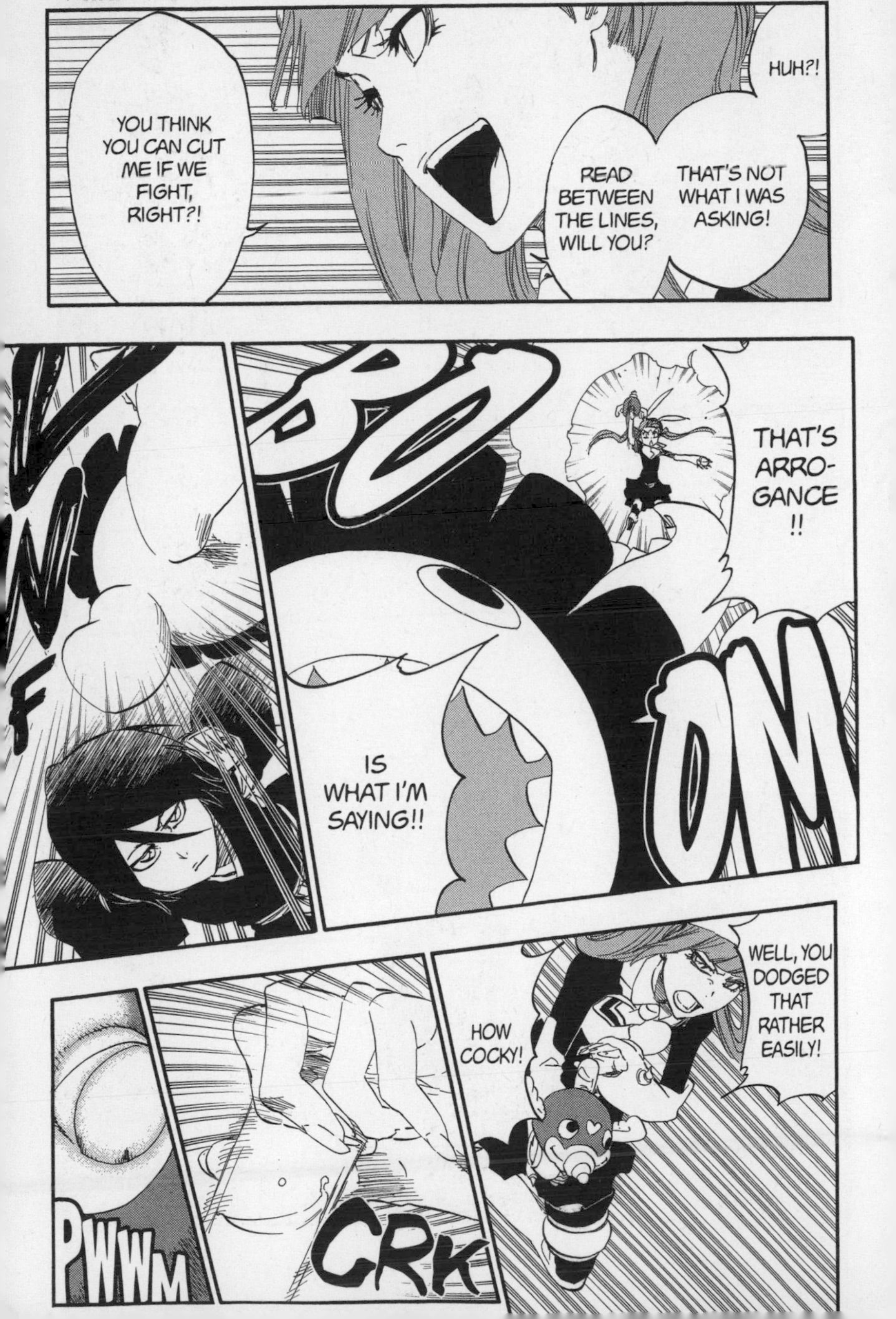

HUH?!
THAT'S NOT WHAT I WAS ASKING!
READ BETWEEN THE LINES, WILL YOU?
YOU THINK YOU CAN CUT ME IF WE FIGHT, RIGHT?!
THAT'S ARRO- GANCE !!
IS WHAT I'M SAYING!!
WELL, YOU DODGED THAT RATHER EASILY!
HOW COCKY!
CRK
PWWM

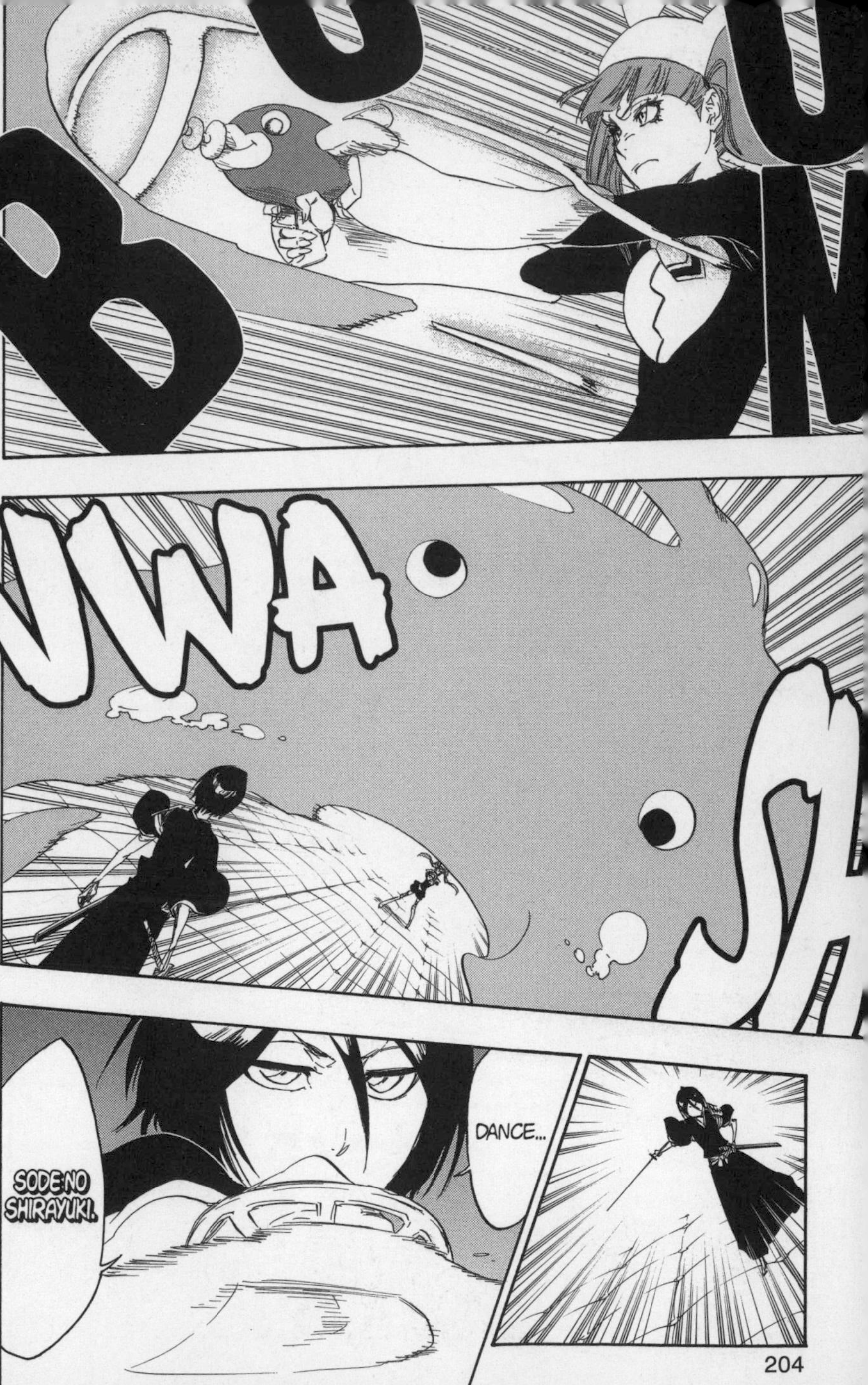
DANCE...
SODE NO SHIRAYUKI.

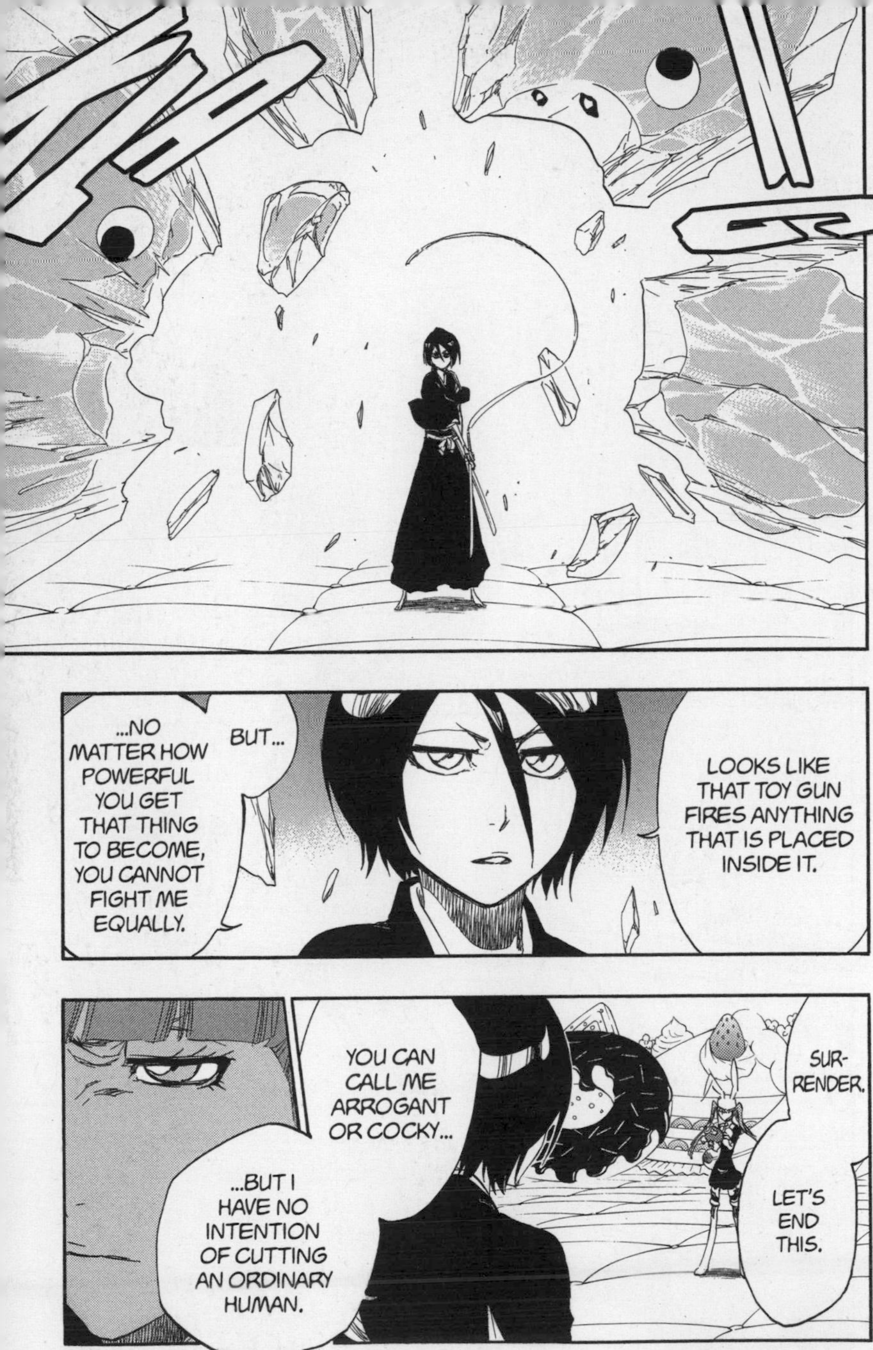
LOOKS LIKE THAT TOY GUN FIRES ANYTHING THAT IS PLACED INSIDE IT.
BUT...
...NO MATTER HOW POWERFUL YOU GET THAT THING TO BECOME, YOU CANNOT FIGHT ME EQUALLY.
SUR-RENDER.
LET'S END THIS.
YOU CAN CALL ME ARROGANT OR COCKY...
...BUT I HAVE NO INTENTION OF CUTTING AN ORDINARY HUMAN.

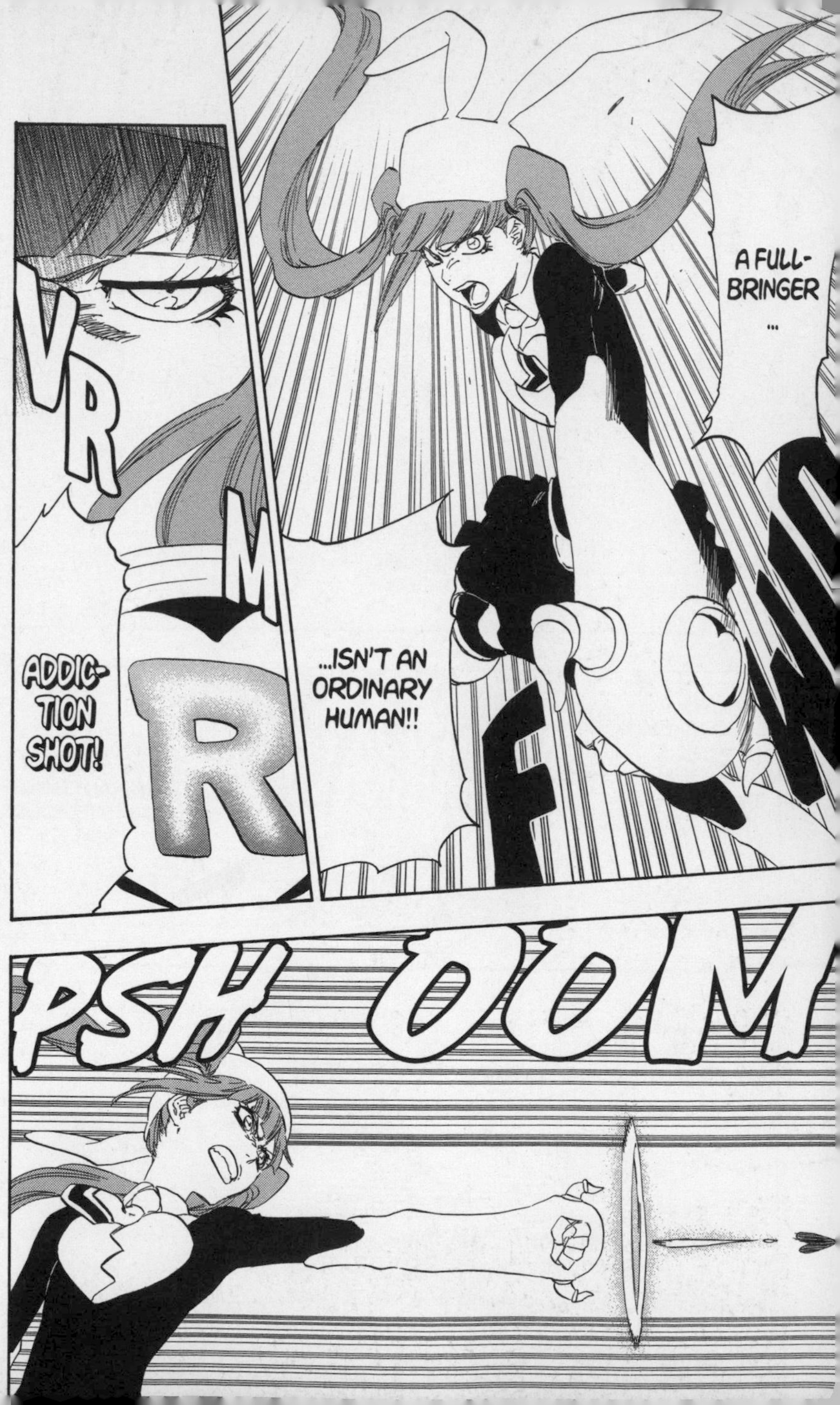
A FULL-BRINGER ...
...ISN'T AN ORDINARY HUMAN!!
VR
M
ADDICTION SHOT!
PSH OOM

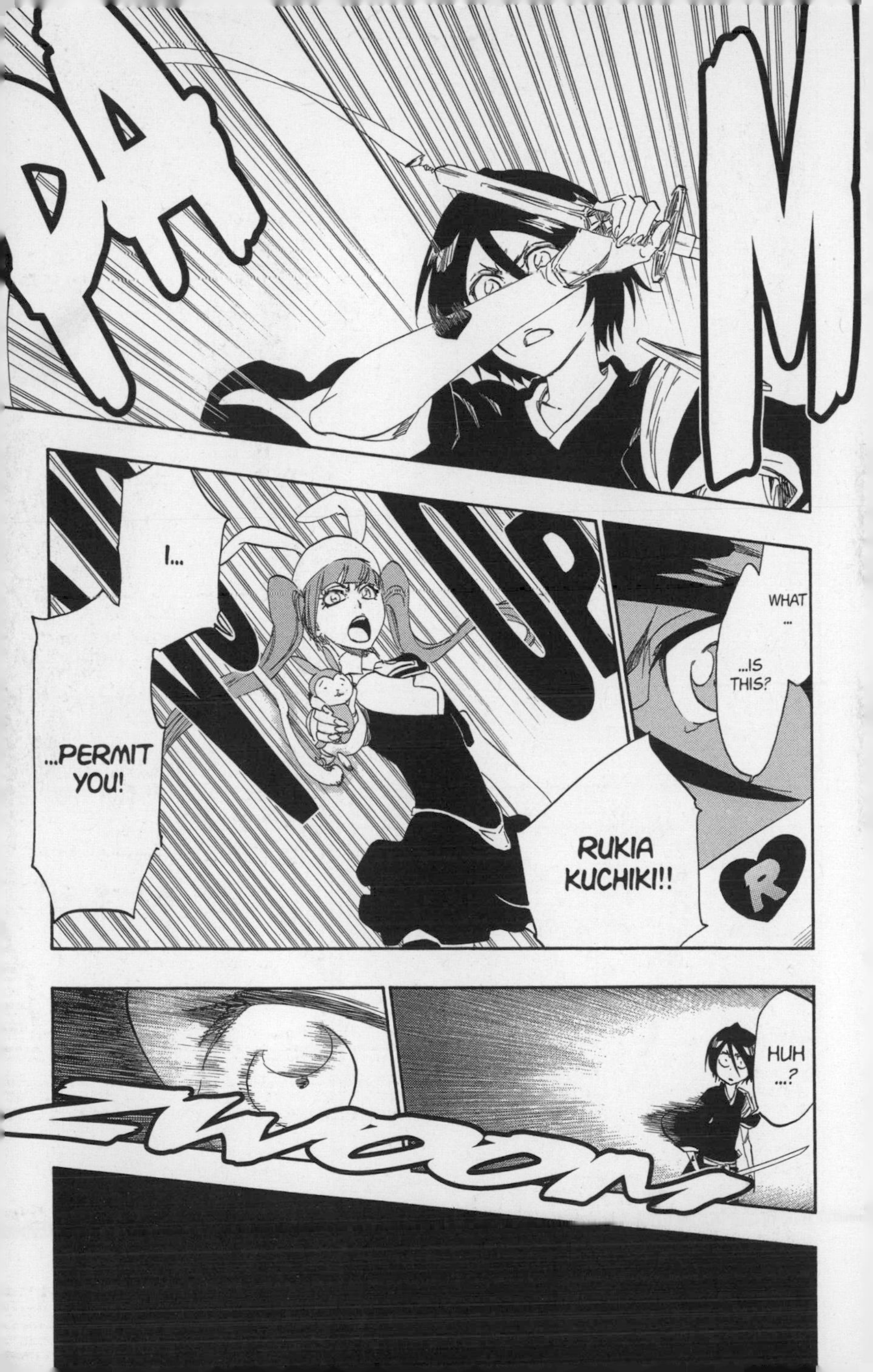
WHAT ... ...IS THIS?
I...
...PERMIT YOU!
RUKIA KUCHIKI!!
R
HUH ...?

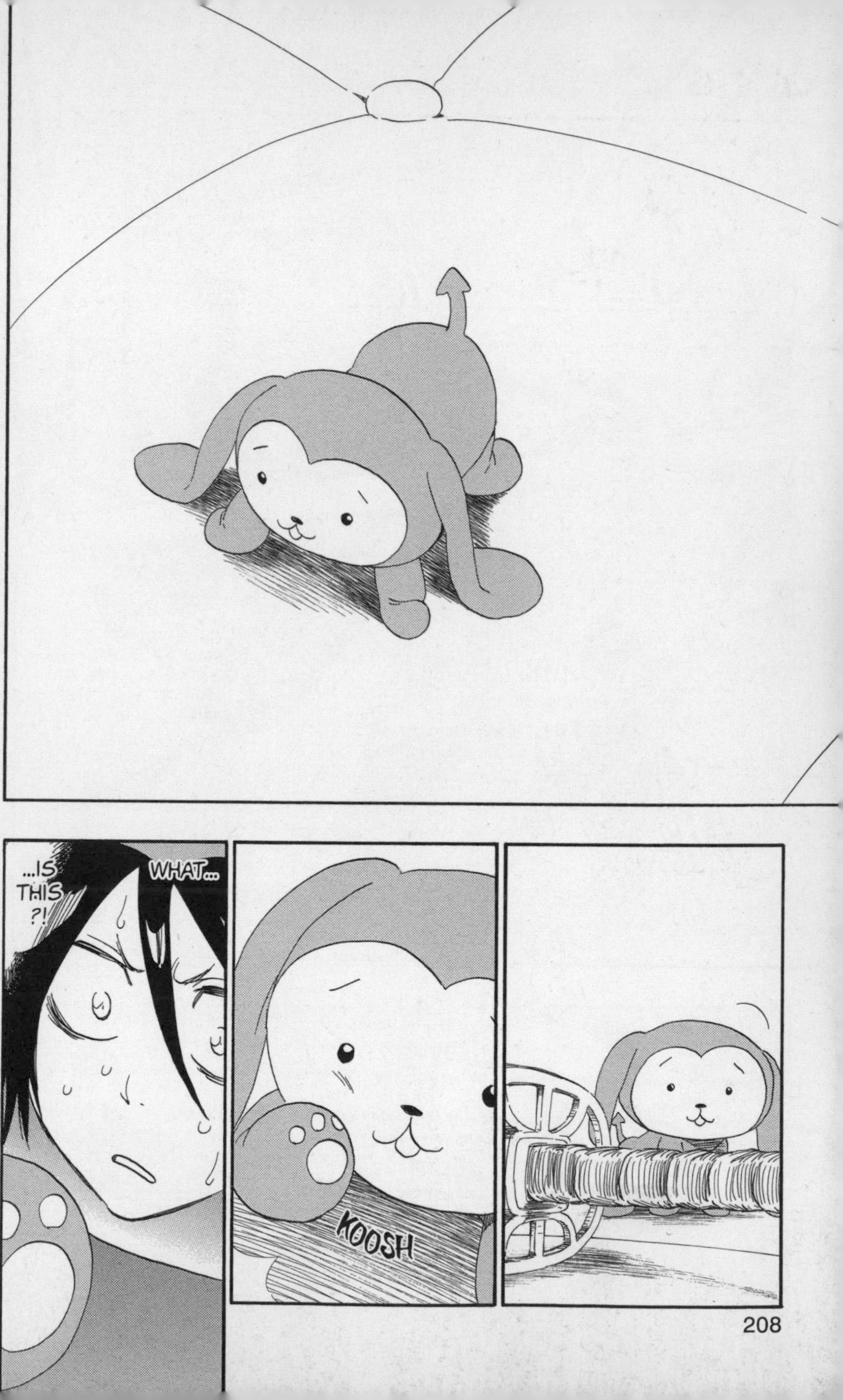
KOOSH
WHAT...
...IS THIS ?!

READ THIS WAY

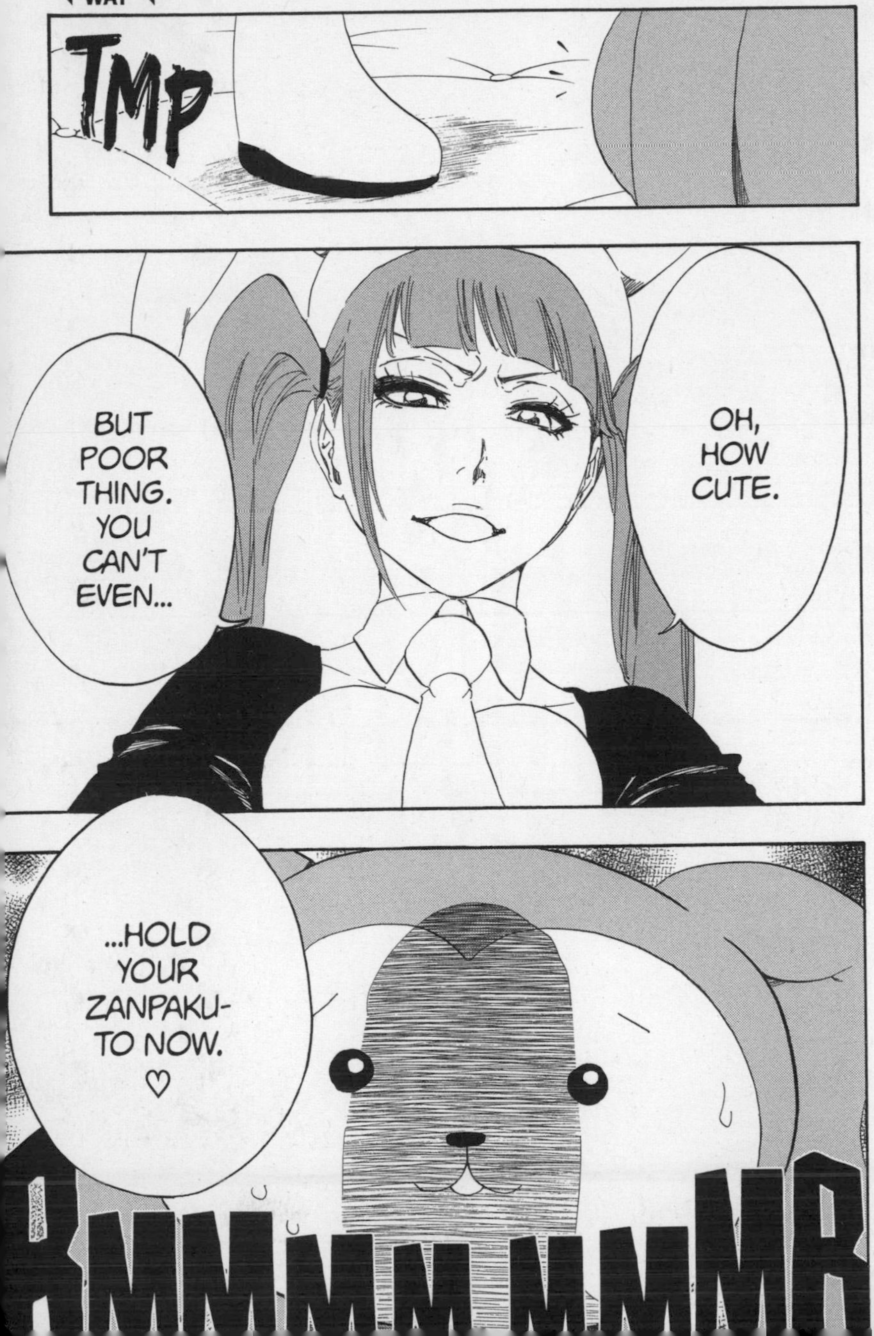
TMP
OH, HOW CUTE.
BUT POOR THING. YOU CAN'T EVEN...
...HOLD YOUR ZANPAKU-TO NOW. ♡
RMMMMMMMR

CONTINUED IN BLEACH 54

Bleach
[The Agent Lost]
Volume
Personal files
2

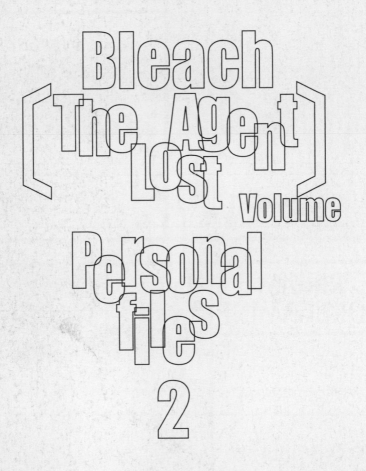

ORIHIME
INOUE

Height/157cm
Weight/49kg

AB Cookies clerk

RIRUKA
DOKUGAMINE

Height/156cm
Weight/43kg

D.O.B/April 14
Blood Type/BO

XCUTION Member
Membership No. 003

YASUTORA SADO

Height/197cm
Weight/118kg

Gonzales Gym Member

YUKIO HANS VORARLBERNA

Height/154cm
Weight/40kg

D.O.B/December 23
Blood Type/AB
XCUTION Member
Membership No. 005

Next Volume Preview

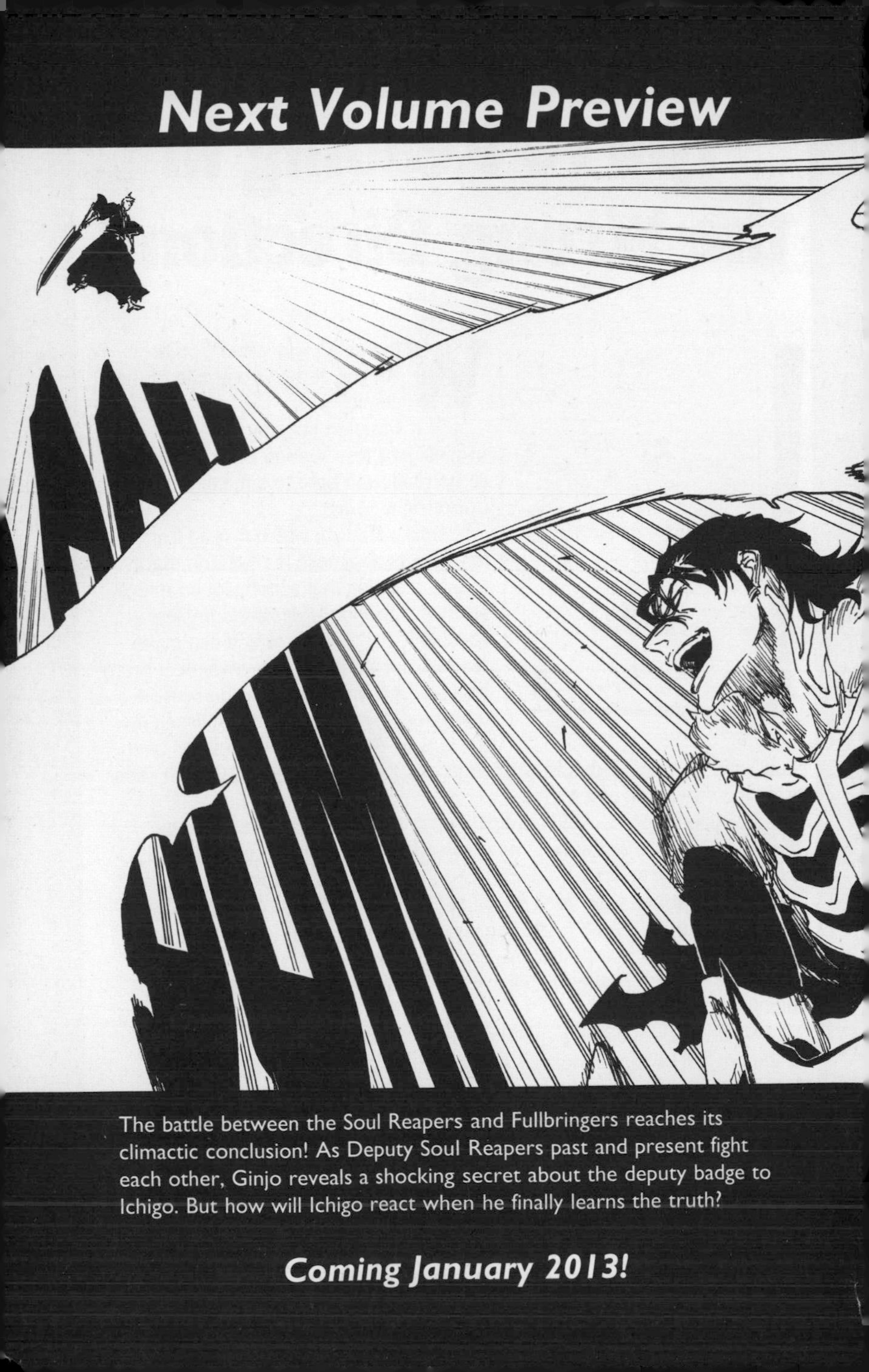

The battle between the Soul Reapers and Fullbringers reaches its climactic conclusion! As Deputy Soul Reapers past and present fight each other, Ginjo reveals a shocking secret about the deputy badge to Ichigo. But how will Ichigo react when he finally learns the truth?

Coming January 2013!

You're Reading in the Wrong Direction!!

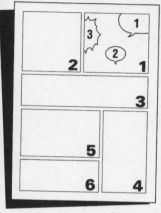

Whoops! Guess what? You're starting at the wrong end of the comic!

…It's true! In keeping with the original Japanese format, **Bleach** is meant to be read from right to left, starting in the upper-right corner.

Unlike English, which is read from left to right, Japanese is read from right to left, meaning that action, sound effects and word-balloon order are completely reversed… something which can make readers unfamiliar with Japanese feel pretty backwards themselves. For this reason, manga or Japanese comics published in the U.S. in English have sometimes been published "flopped"—that is, printed in exact reverse order, as though seen from the other side of a mirror.

By flopping pages, U.S. publishers can avoid confusing readers, but the compromise is not without its downside. For one thing, a character in a flopped manga series who once wore in the original Japanese version a T-shirt emblazoned with "M A Y" (as in "the merry month of") now wears one which reads "Y A M"! Additionally, many manga creators in Japan are themselves unhappy with the process, as some feel the mirror-imaging of their art skews their original intentions.

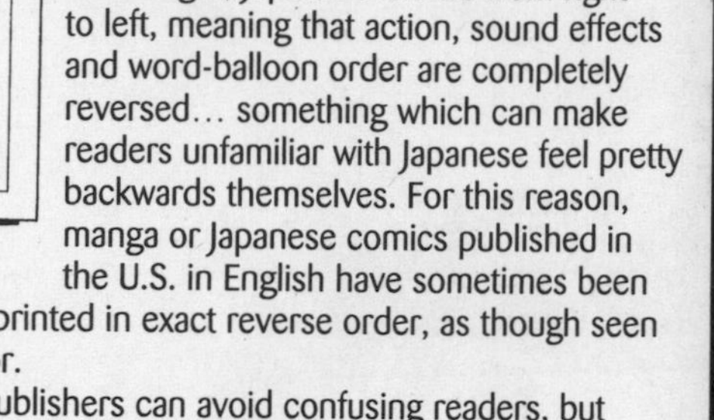

We are proud to bring you Tite Kubo's **Bleach** in the original unflopped format. For now, though, turn to the other side of the book and let the adventure begin…!

—Editor

BLEACH
VOL. 53: THE DEATHBERRY RETURNS 2
SHONEN JUMP Manga Edition

STORY AND ART BY
TITE KUBO

Translation/Joe Yamazaki
Touch-up Art & Lettering/Mark McMurray
Design/Kam Li
Editor/Alexis Kirsch

BLEACH © 2001 by Tite Kubo. All rights reserved. First published
in Japan in 2001 by SHUEISHA Inc., Tokyo. English translation rights
arranged by SHUEISHA Inc.

Printed in the U.S.A.

Published by VIZ Media, LLC
P.O. Box 77010
San Francisco, CA 94107

10 9 8 7 6 5 4 3 2 1
First printing, December 2012

I've been getting into foreign board games recently. I started after friends recommended some to me. Those friends finally left their board games at my place the other day. Did they get me into them just so they'd have a place to play...?

-Tite Kubo

BLEACH is author Tite Kubo's second title. Kubo made his debut with ZOMBIEPOWDER., a four-volume series for WEEKLY SHONEN JUMP. To date, BLEACH has been translated into numerous languages and has also inspired an animated TV series that began airing in the U.S. in 2006. Beginning its serialization in 2001, BLEACH is still a mainstay in the pages of WEEKLY SHONEN JUMP. In 2005, BLEACH was awarded the prestigious Shogakukan Manga Award in the shonen (boys) category.

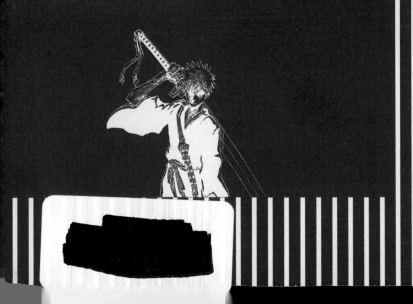